Popular Music and Society

SECOND EDITION

Brian Longhurst

polity

First published in 2007 by Polity Press
Reprinted 2008

Polity Press
65 Bridge Street
Cambridge CB2 1UR, UK

Polity Press
350 Main Street
Malden, MA 02148, USA

ISBN-13: 978-07456-3162-2
ISBN-13: 978-07456-3163-9 (pb)

A catalogue record for this book is available from the British Library.

Typeset in 10.5 on 13 pt Quadraat
by Servis Filmsetting, Manchester
Printed and bound in Great Britain by MPG Books Ltd, Bodmin, Cornwall

The publisher has used its best endeavours to ensure that the URLs for external websites referred to in this book are correct and active at the time of going to press. However, the publisher has no responsibility for the websites and can make no guarantee that a site will remain live or that the content is or will remain appropriate.

Every effort has been made to trace all copyright holders, but if any have been inadvertently overlooked the publishers will be pleased to include any necessary credits in any subsequent reprint or edition.

For further information on Polity, visit our website: www.polity.co.uk

Contents

Figures

Tables

Boxes

Acknowledgements

I would like to thank Nick Abercrombie, whose idea it first was that I should write a book on this topic, thereby suggesting an opportunity to develop some thoughts on an area of culture which has always been very important to me. Thanks also to Nick Abercrombie and Celia Lury for their extensive and very helpful comments on the drafts of the first edition. Their supportive criticism and encouragement improved the book greatly. Countless discussions with Nick, especially most recently on media audiences and media studies, have also influenced other areas of the book in all sorts of ways.

Most of the first edition of this book was written during my first ever period of four months' academic study leave. I would like to thank those colleagues in the Sociology Department at the University of Salford who took on extra duties during this time and hope that I didn't irritate them too much with my obvious glee at having some time to work on a project in a consistent and undisturbed way.

Some of the ideas in chapter 5 first saw light of day in collaborative work, to which Scott Lash contributed greatly. These ideas were also tried out in seminars in the Sociology Departments of the Universities of Lancaster, Edinburgh and Manchester and at the annual conference of the British Sociological Association. Thanks to everyone who participated and commented.

Some of the material in chapters 7 and 8 benefited from comments passed by colleagues at a seminar in the Department of Sociology at the University of Salford. Discussions in the Lancaster/Salford Audiences Group were also of great help and I would like to thank all the participants for their input. Discussion of the work of Larry Grossberg proved particularly thought-provoking.

Thanks additionally to Sue Smart, who always answered my hopelessly naive questions about word-processing in a helpful way and who sorted out some of the figures in the first edition, when my limited skills were not up to the job. All at Polity Press have been very helpful; special thanks to Pam Thomas on the first edition and Andrea Drugan on the second.

The preparation of the second edition of the book took place during another period of study leave. I would like to thank my colleagues in the Sociology Subject Group, the School of English, Sociology, Politics and Contemporary History and the Faculty of Arts, Media and Social Sciences at the University of Salford for their support in this respect. My thinking since the publication of the first edition has been helped by numerous conversations with colleagues. In this respect I have benefited from the ideas of Eamonn Carrabine and Dan Laughey, as well as the encouragement of Derek Scott and Sheila Whiteley in particular. The comments from the publisher's readers were also very helpful.

At points, this book argues that music is very important to members of society in emotional ways that cannot be put into words. That argument in part stems from my own feelings about music and personal life. Thanks therefore are due to my parents who always had music around and respected my own musical tastes, which can't always have been easy. I would like to thank my father in particular, whose musical creativity I have not appreciated enough, for all the times he played 'The Old Music Master' for me in the back room at Shakespeare Road when I was a child. Also going back to childhood, thanks to my cousin, Terry Boiston, who exposed me to Elvis Presley and Otis Redding, leaving me with continuing attachments.

As always, my biggest debts are to those who live with me, putting up with my current musical tastes. James keeps me up to date and provides excellent radio programmes. Tim inspires with his musical creativity, jazz performances and his thirst for knowledge. Bernadette continues to put on the music that I would not hear otherwise, listened to a significant part of my record collection one night in the very early days and, most importantly, is always there in every respect. All of us seeing Bonnie 'Prince' Billy and Harem Scarem in Ardross in April 2006 was very special.

The author and publishers wish to thank the following for permission to use copyright material:

American Sociological Review and Richard A. Peterson for Table 1.1 from David Berger and Richard A. Peterson, 'Cycles in Symbol Production: the case of popular music', *American Sociological Review* 40 (1975)

Berg Publishers for Figure 9.1 from D. Muggleton, *Inside Subculture* (2000).

British Phonographic Industry Ltd. for material in Tables 7.1 and 7.2 and Figure 7.3.

Cambridge University Press for Box 7.1 from D. Laing, 'World Record Sales 1992-2002', *Popular Music*, 23 (2004); Box 9.1 from Tia DeNora, *Music in Everyday Life* (2000).

Charly records for Box 3.3 from the sleeve notes for Jimmy Reed *Upside Your Head* (1980), by Cliff White, courtesy of Charly Records.

Jonathan Cape and Hill and Wang for Figure 5.4, an excerpt from *Mythologies* by Roland Barthes, translated by Annette Lavers. Translation copyright © 1972 by Jonathan Cape Ltd. Reprinted by permission of Jonathan Cape and of Hill and Wang, a division of Farrar, Straus and Giroux, LLC.

Constable Publishers Limited for Figures 1.6, 1.7, 1.8 and 1.9 from R. Wallis and K. Malm, *Big Musics from Small Peoples* (1984).

The *Economist Newspaper* Limited for Box 1.1, copyright © The Economist 2005.

Faber and Faber Ltd. for Box 2.2 from J. Savage, *England's Dreaming: Sex Pistols and Punk Rock* (1991) and Box 2.6 from J. J. Beadle, *Will Pop Eat Itself? Pop Music in the Soundbite Era* (1993) © 1993 by Jeremy J. Beadle, reprinted by permission of Faber and Faber Inc., an affiliate of Farrar, Straus and Giroux, LLC.

the *Guardian* for material in Box 1.4 by Owen Gibson; Box 2.4 by Pat Kane; Box 4.4 by Caroline Sullivan; Box 8.1 by Steven Wells. Copyright *the Guardian*.

HarperCollins Publishers Ltd and Hill and Wang for Box 5.1, an excerpt from *Image/Music/Text* by Roland Barthes, translated by Stephen Heath. English translation copyright © 1977 by Stephen Heath. Reprinted by permission of HarperCollins and of Hill and Wang, a division of Farrar, Straus and Giroux, LLC.

Hutchinson and Co. for Figure 7.6 from S. Hall and T. Jefferson (eds), *Resistance Through Rituals: Youth Subcultures in Post-War Britain* (1976).

The *Independent on Sunday* for Box 1.2 by Jeremy Warner.

The International Federation of the Phonographic Industry for Figures 1.3 and 1.4 from *World Sales 1989* (1990).

International Music Publications Limited for the lyrics quoted in Figure 5.7 from 'Material Girl' by Peter Brown and Robert Rans as recorded by Madonna.

Lawrence and Wishart for Box 6.2 from E. Carrabine and B. Longhurst, 'Mosaics of Omnivorousness: Middle-Class Youth and Popular Culture', in *New Formations* 38: *Hating Tradition Properly: the Legacy of the Frankfurt School in Cultural Studies* (1999).

Manchester University Press and the authors for Box 4.2 from D. Hatch and S. Millward, *From Blues to Rock: An Analytical History of Pop Music* (1987).

Open University for Figure 7.7 from R. Middleton and J. Muncie, 'Pop Culture, Pop Music and Post-war Youth: Countercultures', Unit 20 of the Open University course of *Popular Culture*.

Open University Press and the authors for Figures 5.5 and 5.6 from R. Middleton, *Studying Popular Music* (1990); Table 5.1 from D. Laing, *One Chord Wonders: Power and Meaning in Punk Rock* (1985); Box 3.2 from D. Bradley, *Understanding Rock 'n' Roll: Popular Music in Britain 1955-1964* (1992).

Oxford University Press for Figure 3.4 and Box 2.3 from M. Bayton, *Frock Rock: Women Performing Popular Music* (1998); Figure 5.1 from R. Middleton, 'Introduction' to *Reading Pop: Approaches to Textual Analysis in Popular Music* (2000), by permission of Oxford University Press.

Penguin Books Limited for Box 7.2 from David Robins and Philip Cohen, *Knuckle Sandwich: Growing up in the Working-Class City* (1978) copyright © David Robins and Philip Cohen, 1978.

Pluto Press for Boxes 2.1 and 2.5 from S. Steward and S. Garratt, *Signed, Sealed and Delivered: True Life Stories of Women in Pop* (1984).

Polity Press for Figures IN.1 and IN.2 from D. Held, *Introduction to Critical Theory: Horkheimer to Habermas* (1980); Box 6.1 from S. Thornton, *Club Cultures: Music, Media and Subcultural Capital* (1996).

Routledge Publishers for Figure 1.1 from J. Bishop, 'Building international empires of sound: concentrations of power and property in the "global" music market', in *Popular Music and Society* 28 (2005); Figure 1.2 from Paul Bagguley, 'Post-Fordism and enterprise culture: flexibility, autonomy and changes in economic organization' in R. Keat and N. Abercrombie (eds), *Enterprise Culture* (1991); Figure 5.7 from Barbara Bradby, 'Like a virgin-mother?: materialism and maternalism in the songs of Madonna', from *Cultural Studies* 6 (1992); Figure 5.8 from E. Ann Kaplan, *Rocking Around the Clock: Music Television, Postmodernism, and Consumer Culture* (1987); Figure 6.1 from P. Bourdieu, *Distinction* (1984); Box 8.2 from H. Jenkins *Textual Poachers: Television Fans and Participatory Culture* (1992).

S. T. Publishing for Box 1.3 from George Marshall, *The Two Tone Story* (1990).

Sage Publications for Figures 9.2, 9.3 and 9.4 from N. Abercrombie and B. Longhurst, *Audiences* (1998) copyright © N. Abercrombie and B. Longhurst, 1998.

Serpent's Tail for Box 4.3 from D. Toop, *Rap Attack 3* (1999).

Souvenir Press for Box 3.1 from C. Gillet, *The Sound of the City: The Rise of Rock and Roll* (1983).

TNS World Panel Entertainment for Tables IN.3, 7.3, 7.4 and 7.5 from *BPI Statistical Handbook 2005*.

University of Massachusetts Press for Figure 2.3 from *On Becoming a Rock Musician* by H. Stith Bennett, copyright © 1980 by University of Massachusetts Press.

University of Minnesota Press for Figures 5.9, 5.10 and 5.11, and Box 5.2 from Andrew Goodwin, *Dancing in the Distraction Factory: Music, Television, and Popular Culture* (1992), copyright © University of Minnesota Press.

Virago Press and Random House, Inc. for Box 4.1 from M. Angelou, *Singin' and Swingin' and Gettin' Merry Like Christmas*, copyright © by Maya Angelou 1976, published by Random House 1976 and Virago Press 1985.

Preface

This book is written for undergraduate students. It aims to provide an introduction to the area of popular music and society that will be useful to those taking courses in the areas of the sociology of culture, cultural studies, communication studies and media studies. It will also be of interest to those more general readers wanting an overview of contemporary developments in the sociological study of popular music. My aim has partly been to locate the analysis of popular music in the context of more general debates about culture, its analysis and effects.

The book includes accounts of the main theories in the area of popular music, as well as reviewing the most important substantive studies which have appeared in this field. It also includes a significant amount of empirical data where relevant. In addition to words on the page, the book uses three main devices to convey information and illustrate the accounts and theories.

Figures, which often summarize whole arguments or the most salient parts of them, are used in a number of places. These summaries are represented in diagrams or lists of points. I have created some of the figures myself and others are drawn from other sources, which are given with the figures. My view is that a clear diagram is often a useful way of conveying the sense of an argument and can help in the understanding of the overall structure or main themes. It is a device which is under-employed in sociology.

There are also a number of tables in the book. In the main, these contain quantitative data and are distinguished from figures on that basis. The data given most often refer to the United Kingdom, though figures are also provided for world record sales and so on. Salient points to be drawn from the tables are discussed in the text of the book. However, the data may also be of use in student project work and essays, where other issues may be important.

The third device is the box. Boxes have been used to set off material which goes beyond the main flow of the text, but which illustrates key points. The boxes also use some of the less sociological writing on popular music, which can be very informative and provoke thought on the nature of contemporary music. My hope is that these boxes might encourage the reader to seek out this literature, which contains some of the most pleasurable writing on pop music. There is also a fair amount of quotation from important sources, which is used in a direct way in the main text of the book.

The book is written in the belief that the pleasures of pop music and its analysis can be combined. It is a common experience for anyone teaching a course on the media to be approached at some point by a student who says that their pleasures in television or film have been ruined by the analysis carried out on them (see Carrabine and Longhurst 1997/8 for discussion and empirical investigation). Those of us who teach such courses can often recall such feelings when we were first introduced to the study of media. My (perhaps inadequate) response is to suggest that the pleasures of analysis can lead to new enjoyments of the media texts themselves. In my view, this is a part of the 'sociological imagination' and something to be welcomed. I hope that the arguments and studies reviewed in this book contribute to such analytic pleasures. Certainly, working through the material did not detract from my pleasure in pop music and often stimulated me to explore new areas in a different frame of mind or dig out (again) old, and almost forgotten, records, CDs and tapes. I hope some of this comes through in the text.

In the book, I use 'popular music' as an overall term. There is much debate about the meanings of terms like pop and rock, which is examined at several places in the book, and I do not want to begin with extensive consideration of this issue. I ask the reader to go along with me in adopting a relatively broad and open categorization of popular music – at least at the beginning of the book.

More detail on the contents of each chapter can be found at the end of chapter 1, where the logic of the arrangement of the chapters should be apparent from the discussions and criticism of general theories contained therein.

In preparing the second edition of this book, I have taken the opportunity to update all the chapters with data and the most important studies that have been carried out since this book was first published. In addition, two new chapters (6 and 9) have been included to capture what I see as particularly significant developments. This has resulted in a substantially longer and more detailed text.

Introduction: Constraints and Creativity – Arguments and Framework

Not long after the publication of the first edition of this book, I was invited to give a talk to a meeting of the Stephen Sondheim Society. The organizer of this group, which consisted of enthusiasts for the musicals of the American composer, had read my book and thought that a presentation of its broad themes would be of interest. I duly gave the talk, in which I outlined some of the main ideas of the book. This seemed to go quite well and we had an interesting exchange of ideas. At one point a particularly lively discussion was generated by a question from the audience, which, as I remember it, went something along the lines of: 'Why study the musicals of Sondheim at all? After all they are simply great works of art.' There were different views expressed in the audience in response. The question is both very significant and in many respects common. Another version would be whether it is possible to write about a form like music at all. Not very surprisingly, I think that a sociological approach (that is significantly informed by cultural and media studies) is useful and that it is therefore possible to write about music in context in interesting and informative ways. The content of the book is, I hope, a demonstration of that value. However, to illuminate why this is so, more needs to be said by way of introduction to locate the approach of this book in the field of studies of popular music in particular and other media in general, and to indicate my general response to the Sondheim Society questioner.

In broad terms, I think that there are two main ways in which popular music has been written about academically, journalistically and by enthusiasts: in a critical mode and a celebratory mode. Each of these modes has a 'political' and an 'aesthetic' dimension, which are sometimes linked together or conflated. The critical mode is against popular music (or indeed popular culture) in two main ways therefore. For example, it can be seen as a form of commercial activity that is about selling forms of music for profit, or it is seen as having regressive ideas about 'race' or 'gender' in it. Moreover, in the 'aesthetic' mode, the music can be seen as 'rubbish', poor art, trite and so on. This sort of critique has been developed in very sophisticated ways by authors like Adorno and I consider this at some length below, but it is also familiar in other forms of writing.

The celebratory mode is, in effect, the mirror image of the critical. The music is valued because it expresses values that criticize dominant political powers, or enables the expression of ideas that seek social and cultural change; it may also be seen as innovative and doing new things in musical terms and is thus to be valued aesthetically. These positions are common and apply to other media as well. However, in my view they are limited, especially as starting positions for searching engagement with a form like popular music. They are limited, as they remain stuck on a terrain of debate that constrains innovation. In a book about audiences, Nick Abercrombie and

I made a similar sort of argument about audience research, maintaining that it was constrained by a research agenda that focused on whether people in the audience were incorporated by or resisted media messages (see Abercrombie and Longhurst 1998 and chapter 9 below). Eamonn Carrabine and I made a similar argument about research on youth subcultures (Carrabine and Longhurst 1999).

For reasons that I hope will become clear as this book progresses, I do not want to inhabit this ground, not least because I do not think that a better understanding of the complexities of music in society can be produced from such bases. I therefore seek neither to criticize popular music nor to celebrate it per se. Rather, I seek to analyse it on the basis of the interrogation of the now extensive research on it. To my mind, this does not mean that I can't develop a critical or indeed celebratory argument about some forms of music, but it is likely that there will be contradictory elements to these arguments. Thus, as another reader of the first edition of this book once said to me, I am as much a 'fan' of some forms of popular music as the next person. However, one thing that my reading has convinced me of is that forms of popular culture such as popular music are full of contradictions. Thus, I may greatly like the music of Miles Davis (the African American trumpeter), and find his social location in the changing nature of American society from the 1920s to 1990s intriguing, while deploring his reported violence to women and attitudes to some of his collaborators. In the end, it makes little sense to me to attempt to resolve those contradictions: we live them as human beings, researchers, students and fans.

On this basis, the aims of this Introduction are to introduce significant sociologically informed, general accounts of the nature and place of popular music in society; and to criticize these accounts in moving towards a framework to be used in the subsequent presentation of the material in this book. Three bodies of literature are considered. First, the work of Adorno on the culture industry and popular music; second, the Weberian examination of rationalization; and third, contemporary approaches based on audience research, which seek to move away from some of the themes central to these earlier accounts. The first two of these approaches can be seen as 'critical' and the third has been argued to be more celebratory. In this Introduction, most space is devoted to the first two approaches, as they will not be treated at length elsewhere, though issues they raise are examined in a number of other places. Key aspects of the third body of literature are considered in more detail in chapters 7, 8 and 9 (and see also for my version of a summary, Abercrombie and Longhurst 1998).

Commodification and standardization: Adorno and popular music

The British sociologist and pop writer, Simon Frith, draws attention to the key importance of Theodor Adorno's work on music in the following way:

> Adorno's is the most systematic and most searing analysis of mass culture and the most challenging for anyone claiming even a scrap of value for the products that come churning out of the music industry. His argument . . . is that modern capital is burdened by the problem of overproduction. Markets

can only be stimulated by creating needs . . . needs which are the result of capital rather than human logic and therefore, inevitably, false. The culture industry is the central agency in contemporary capitalism for the production and satisfaction of false needs. (Frith 1983: 44–5)

This book takes up Frith's argument that Adorno's analysis is a challenge to those who seek to recognize some value in pop music. However, my suggestion is that the generality of Adorno's work also represents a challenge of a rather different kind to those who want to engage in the systematic and specific analysis of the place of pop music in society. I shall explain why Adorno's arguments represent such a challenge to analysis in a short while. However, before this is possible, it is necessary to examine his position in more detail.

Adorno (1903–69) was a member of the Frankfurt School of theorists and writers, founded at the University of Frankfurt in 1923, who developed critical theory as an attempt to further social change from within a broadly Marxist understanding of the structure of society. Along with other figures, such as Max Horkheimer (1895–1971), Herbert Marcuse (1898–1979) and, most recently, Jürgen Habermas (1929–), Adorno criticized capitalism's control over social life and the subsequent inequalities this causes. In his work with Horkheimer, Adorno maintained that the culture industry was central to capitalist domination (Adorno and Horkheimer 1977).

In contemporary capitalist societies, the culture industry produces forms of culture which are commodities. Culture is something that is produced to be bought and sold on a market, to generate more money. It possesses exchange value and the companies that produce culture do so to make a profit from it. According to the Frankfurt School writers, such commodification had become increasingly widespread, penetrating all aspects of cultural production and social life. This led to a standardization of the products of the culture industries, which in turn induced passivity in those who consume the culture industry products. Held explains:

> The main characteristics of the culture industry reflect the difficult problem it faces. It must at once both sustain interest and ensure that the attention it attracts is insufficient to bring its produce into disrepute. Thus, commercial entertainment aims at an attentive but passive, relaxed and uncritical reception, which it induces through the production of 'patterned and pre-digested' cultural entities. (1980: 94)

For Adorno, popular music is a part of the culture industry. An important claim that he makes about popular music is that it is standardized. In his view, the whole product is standardized, including types of songs, songs themselves and parts of songs. Thus, if Adorno had been writing about popular music today, instead of in the 1930s, '40s and '50s, he might argue, first, that popular music is divided into a number of standardized types: heavy metal, country, folk, blues, soul, urban, dance, rock and so on, which are immediately recognizable to the audience. Second, he might maintain that the music and songs within these types are themselves standardized into a small number of different structures. Therefore, a musicological analysis would show that one heavy metal track is very much like another in its essential structure and form (Walser 1993). There are a small number of components to such tracks, which, on Adorno's account, are interchangeable. As he says, 'the beginning of the chorus is replaceable by the beginning of innumerable other choruses' (1990: 303).

In Adorno's account, the parts of a piece of popular music are interchangeable. Gendron explains such 'part interchangeability' through the example of a mass-produced car: Thus, 'virtually any mechanical part from any 1956 Cadillac Eldorado (e.g., a carburettor) can be substituted for any other 1956 Eldorado without disturbing the functional unity of the overall mechanism' (1986: 20). Or, to take another example suggested by Gendron, the speakers from one stereo system can be replaced by others and the system will normally still work. Part interchangeability is very important to rationalized industrial systems, although manufacturers often try to ensure that, in order to keep the market demand for their parts buoyant, only their own parts can be used in their products. Hence, it is possible to substitute a particular part from one Ford Fiesta for that in another Fiesta, but not to place that part into a Renault Clio. Nevertheless, certain parts are more likely to be interchangeable, such as the tyres.

Adorno calls the type of variation that exists between such standardized products, 'pseudo-individualization'. Such variations do not alter the basic structure of the product, as they represent only surface changes. For example, the addition of racing stripes to a Ford Fiesta may affect its appearance to the taste of its owner, but they will not alter its performance. Adorno suggests that the variations in popular music are of this type. The details of the popular song may be changed, but the essential structure or form remains the same. Goodwin gives an example of how these ideas of part-interchangeability and pseudo-individualization might be applied to the contemporary music scene:

> [P]op songs often utilize the same or very similar drum patterns, chord progressions, song structures, and lyrics while being distinguished by marketing techniques (the construction of 'personalities' involved in selling, say, New Kids on The Block, the makeup once worn by the rock band Kiss), performance quirks (Michael Jackson's 'hiccup', Madonna's 'controversial' videos) or rhetorical gestures (Pete Townsend's 'windmill' swing at his guitar, Chuck Berry's 'duckwalk'). (1992: 76)

Adorno's analysis of popular music is built upon a comparison of popular music with 'serious' music. He argues that it is possible to distinguish standardized popular music from 'serious' music, where the detail of a section of music only takes on meaning in relation to the piece as a whole and standardization does not exist in the way that it does in popular music. Adorno's argument about 'serious' music rests on the valuation of an intimate relation between the specific parts and the overall nature of the whole of a piece of music, which give the piece its own particular distinctiveness and individuality. Great works of music, like those of Beethoven, are distinctive and original. The parts of the piece come together to form a whole, which is not simply the sum of the parts. It is an artistic creation, which uses the parts to create an overall meaning. The substitution into the piece of a different part would seriously affect the meaning of the whole piece.

According to Jay (1973: 182), the distinction drawn by Adorno between these types of music relates to issues of the market and the context in which music is produced and consumed. It is not that Adorno was a conservative who simply liked classical music because it was better in an unexplained way. As Jay argues: 'The real dichotomy, Adorno contended, was not between "light" and "serious" music – he was never a defender of traditional cultural standards for their own sake – but rather between music that was market-oriented and music that was not.' The main features of popular and serious music as distinguished by Adorno are summarized in figure IN.1.

The Frankfurt School argued that the principles of mass production applied to the production of culture as well as the production of goods like motor-cars. In this view, popular music would be produced in an industrial way. However, Adorno's analysis ran into a specific problem at this point, as much pop music is not written on a production line but rather in what he called a handicraft fashion. Thus, the writing of a piece of standardized popular music might be carried out by a lone individual sitting at home with a pen and paper, who would not be

'Serious' music	'Popular' music
Every part/detail depends 'for its musical sense on the concrete totality and never on a mere enforcement of a musical scheme'	Musical compositions follow familiar patterns/frameworks: they are stylized
	Little originality is introduced
Themes and details are highly interwoven with the whole	Structure of the whole does not depend upon details – whole is not altered by individual detail
Themes are carefully developed	Melodic structure is highly rigid and is frequently repeated
Details cannot be changed without altering the whole – details almost contain/ anticipate the whole	Harmonic structure embodies a set scheme ('The most primitive harmonic facts are emphasized')
	Complications have no effect on structure of work – they do not develop themes
Consistency is maintained between formal structure and content (themes)	Stress is on combination of individual 'effects' – on sound, colour, tone, beat, rhythm
If standard schemes are employed (e.g. for dance) they still maintain a key role in the whole	Improvisations become 'normalized' (the boys can only 'swing it' in a narrow framework)
	Details are substitutable (they 'serve their function as cogs in machines')
Emphasizes norms of high technical competence	Affirms conventional norms of what constitutes intelligibility in music while appearing novel and original

Figure IN.1 The structure of production and consumption of 'serious' and 'popular' music

Source: Held 1980: 101

constrained by the discipline of producing standardized parts for a production line. For Adorno, this showed the remnants of an earlier form of production, which was not subject to capitalist work patterns. Despite this, he maintained that the popular music industry was industrialized in other very important ways. Most notably, it was promoted and distributed in accordance with industrialized principles, as well as being manufactured in such ways.

According to Adorno, the listener to industrialized popular music is caught up in a standardized and routinized set of responses. He argues that the listener is distracted and inattentive. In this sense, pop music is a part of the everyday background of contemporary social life. For example, we do not listen to it in the way that musical experts think that we should listen to a Beethoven symphony: that is, by sitting down and giving it all our attention (see, for example, Plotkin 2003) and seeing how the parts relate to the whole in creating the kind of meaning that Beethoven intended to communicate. In Adorno's view, the pleasure derived from popular music is superficial and false. Thus, the listener may be what he calls 'rhythmically obedient'. He or she is a 'slave to the rhythm', following the standardized beat of the song and becoming overpowered or conditioned by it. For Adorno, individuals who enjoy these pleasures are corrupted by immersion and are open to the domination of the industrialized, capitalist system. Another type of pleasure, which Adorno calls 'emotional', is, in his view, also dangerous. Feelings of emotion brought on by the popular song are false or immature, rather than deep or penetrating. There is no comparison between such feelings and the sorts of emotion that can be generated and expressed by the best forms of serious music. The distinctions that Adorno draws between the audience responses to serious and popular music are summarized in figure IN.2.

Adorno's argument implies that the production, textual form and audience reception of popular music are all standardized, revealing a similar essential structure. Industrial production in capitalist societies gives rise to a standardized product, which is used in superficial ways by members of the audience, who desire or express a wish for such industrial products because of their familiarity. Such a system reinforces the domination of society by those who control the industrial apparatus – the capitalist or bourgeois class – as the vast majority of the population is passive and falsely happy having been manipulated by the culture industry, which feeds them products that they think they want. The different aspects of Adorno's thesis are summarized in figure IN.3.

It has already been suggested that Adorno's approach attempts to characterize the nature of popular music, its production and consumption. Adorno wanted to develop a critique of this along the lines of a critical theory derived from Marx. As such, the theory covers a lot of ground and seeks to mount a critical attack on much contemporary music and culture, which would show how it was implicated in the oppression of the working class in capitalist society. Some of the problems with this account are examined in the next section.

Adorno and pop: key criticisms

In considering the criticisms that can be made of Adorno's thesis, it is important to recognize that his formulations seem to have some applicability to

'Serious' music	'Popular' music
To understand a piece of serious music one must experience the whole of it	The whole has little influence on reception and reaction to parts – stronger reactions to part than whole
The whole has strong impact on reaction to details	The music is standardized into easily recognizable types, which are pre-accepted/known prior to reception
Themes and details can only be comprehended in the context of the whole	Little effort is required to follow music – audience already has models under which musical experiences can be subsumed
The sense of the music cannot be grasped by recognition alone, i.e. by identifying music with another 'identical' piece	Little emphasis on the whole as musical event – what matters is style, rhythm (the movement of the foot on the floor)
Effort and concentration are required to follow music	Leads back to familiar experiences (themes and details can be understood out of context because listener can automatically supply framework)
Its aesthetic disrupts the continuum of everyday life and encourages recollection	A sense of the music is grasped by recognition – leading to acceptance
	Pleasure, fun gained through listening are 'transferred' to the musical object, which becomes invested with qualities that stem from mechanism of identification
	The most successful, best music is identified with the most often repeated
	Music has 'soporific effect' on social consciousness
	It reinforces a sense of continuity in everyday living – while its reified structure enforces forgetfulness
	Renders 'unnecessary the process of thinking'

Figure IN.2 Differences between 'serious' and 'popular' music in responses encouraged/demands made upon listener

Source: Held 1980: 103

contemporary music. Thus, there does seem to be a great deal of standardization of pop music around different forms and the commodity status of the product seems increasingly prevalent. However, a number of points can and have been made against the sort of approach outlined by Adorno. The more specific of these are considered first, followed by some more general considerations.

Gendron suggests that Adorno confuses what he calls functional and textual artefacts. An example of a functional artefact is a washing machine and of a textual artefact a compact disc. Gendron points to a key difference between text and

INDUSTRIAL PRODUCTION
(including promotion and distribution, though actual song production often takes a craft form)

↓

POPULAR MUSIC
(is standardized and contrasted with serious music)

↓

THE LISTENER
(is distracted and inattentive; obedient and emotional)

Figure IN.3 Adorno's account of popular music

functional artefact, when he says: 'A text (whether written or oral) is a universal, whereas a functional artefact is a particular. However, to be marketed and possessed, every universal text must be embodied in some functional artefact (paper, vinyl discs)' (1986: 27). Thus, when a person buys a compact disc, he or she is actually buying a combination of functional and textual artefacts. The universal artefact, according to Gendron, is the recording that appears on the disc, which is a product of the recording process, mixing and so on (dimensions of the recording process are considered at greater length in chapter 2). However, before it can be sold, this universal artefact needs to be 'embodied' in a functional artefact (even if it is embodied in a computer file). The extent to which both these dimensions are industrialized should be investigated, but it cannot be assumed that they are equally industrialized and rationalized in the same sorts of way. Thus, the universal artefacts that are the product of the music industry may be produced under industrialized conditions, whereas the actual recordings may not be, as was pointed out above, and recognized by Adorno when he talked of the handicraft nature of much song-writing. However, there are problems with this conceptualization of handicraft, as it does not in itself actually examine the nature of song production or the nature and extent of the technology that is used in the process. This suggests that sociological analysis of the production of music needs to pay attention to two different levels: the more macro-level structure of the pop music industry and the more micro-level of the social production of pop music itself, which takes place in the context of this organization of the music industry, but which is not simply determined by it.

Furthermore, Gendron argues that the part interchangeability of the functional artefact is largely a consequence of its being produced on an assembly line: 'In this system of production, every whole (e.g., the automobile) is assembled out of qualitatively different parts, each of which is taken at random from qualitatively indistinguishable batches' (1986: 26). However, in Gendron's view, the increased use of technology in the production of music actually *expands* the degree of variation possible. For example, this may be seen in the marketing of music in a number of different formats, which leads to greater availability of different forms. Further, the importance of the relatively cheap cassette tape also increased the variety of available music, which can also be copied by those who have bought the original tape, as does the availability of music to download from artists' websites and so on (see Kusek and Leonhard 2005).

Middleton makes a related point when he suggests that Adorno pays insufficient attention to the 'specificity of cultural goods', which he explains by quoting from Simon Frith that 'music can never be just a product (an exchange value), even in its rawest commodity form; the artistic value of records has an unavoidable complicating effect on their production' (1990: 38). In addition to not recognizing the specificity and variations in the nature of cultural production, Adorno does not pay enough attention to the struggles which take place between different cultural producers (Middleton 1990) and to the competitive market relations which prevail in the different sectors of the music industry. Thus, in speaking of the culture industry there is a tendency to neglect variations between different sections of that industry and the precise patterns of relations between different companies.

Another of the key problems in Adorno's approach is that he does not allow for enough diversity in the structure and form of popular music texts (Middleton 1990). Adorno wrote a good proportion of his work on popular music in the late 1930s and early 1940s. At this point, it may have seemed that the products of the popular music section of the culture industry were standardized. However, it is more difficult to sustain this thesis in the light of the current variation in pop music styles, though we may still wish to take seriously as matters for empirical investigation the extent to which this is true, rather than superficial variation. There is a problem here, however, in that it is not always easy to decide what is fundamental, and what is superficial, textual variation. This distinction might conceivably work for the very standardized songs produced from Tin Pan Alley in the 1930s, but it is not so easily applicable to some more recent forms, or to free-form jazz. The further elucidation and consideration of this point depends upon analysis of the structure of musical texts themselves and the tools that can be used in this exercise (see chapter 5).

In a similar way, Adorno's account of the reception of pop music is very unspecific. He makes a number of generalizations which are not backed up by evidence of a substantive kind. Before his suggestions can be accepted, it would be necessary to consider the different ways in which people actually relate to popular music. Thus, it might be difficult to argue that people respond to Madonna and Frank Zappa in similar ways. What is more, Adorno does not consider in enough detail the different sorts of pleasure that are a part of the consumption of popular music. Some forms of music may be valued because they are exceptionally good to dance to; others may invite contemplation – and so on. These pleasures are not all as superficial as Adorno seems to think.

These more specific criticisms can be related to the general nature and basis of Adorno's account, in terms of four areas.

1 *Immanent method.* Middleton (1990) suggests that many of the problems of Adorno's work stem from his initial focus on a particular type of musical work

itself. In his view, Adorno generalizes from within the Western tradition of 'serious' music, and compares other forms against this. These are then seen to be of less value. A more proper procedure would be to proceed in a non-judgemental way, rather than implicitly or explicitly comparing different forms of music against the ideal of aspects of the Western classical tradition. This involves the suspension of critical judgement about value. A similar point is made by Gendron (1986).

2 *Historical and social location.* Adorno's approach is too constrained by his own historical and social location, of being a highly educated, musically literate German intellectual of the mid-twentieth century. Owing to his lack of reflection on the effects this may have, his approach has many difficulties in coping with social and historical change in music-making, as he continued to value a particular and very specific form of music. However, as Gendron (1986) points out and as has been noted several times above, there are senses in which Adorno's theory does seem to explain features of contemporary pop music. The extent to which this is the case, for example in the kind of superficial variation identified by Goodwin (1992), and the extent to which his theory also illuminates aspects of contemporary pop needs consideration. A different view of this issue has been addressed by Robinson (1994), who argues that Adorno's understanding of jazz was critically affected by the way in which it was interpreted in Weimar Germany in the 1920s and '30s. For a variety of reasons, particular and distinctive forms of jazz, which were different from American jazz, developed at this point. While Robinson shows how this affected Adorno's analysis, he does not answer the question of why Adorno failed to take account of the different understandings of jazz that became available to him in later years.

3 *Innovation.* In a way related to these other general points, Adorno pays insufficient attention to the dynamic and changing nature of music. Popular music has developed considerably since he formulated his ideas, and consideration needs to be given to the issue of whether musical innovation and the development of new technologies actually alter aspects of musical production in quite significant ways.

4 *Analysis.* As Adorno's account is so general, it constrains detailed analysis of the specific nature of musical production, textual variation and consumption. My suggestion is that, as well as problematizing pleasure, Adorno's critical account militates against sociological exploration and analysis. In the terms set out at the start of this Introduction, critique overpowers analysis. Before the relevance of such a theory can be determined, there needs to be investigation of the changing nature of the music industry, the ways in which music is actually produced in different places and times, the specific political effects of music in different contexts, the extent of textual variation between forms of pop music and the different ways in which music is consumed and produces pleasure. We are now much more able to consider these issues, as there has been plenty of research carried out since Adorno's time, some of which is reported in this book. However, as a general theory, we have to ask if Adorno's account allows the kind of detailed analysis which is necessary for the proper evaluation of pop music in society.

Having made these points against Adorno, I want to consider the relevance of work on rationalization, influenced by Max Weber, to the contemporary study of music.

Rationalization and McDonaldization

A different and potentially illuminating approach to the place of music and culture in society derives from the approach of the German sociologist Max Weber (1864–1920) and in subsequent writers influenced by his work. Weber's sociology is based around a typology of different types of social action: rational action towards a goal, rational action towards a value, affective action and traditional action. One of the central themes of his work is that Western societies are becoming increasingly rationalized, as forms of rational action become more central. An example of this form of action and social organization is a bureaucracy. Weber's ideal type of this form of organization consisted of elements such as a clear hierarchy of positions, a division of labour, written documentation, promotion and recruitment on merit, government by rules, and impersonal relations between bureaucracy members and clients. Bureaucracies were becoming increasingly common, and in important ways society was bureaucratized and rationalized. This was not necessarily a bad thing in Weber's mind, though his work did also have a pessimistic tone and he talked of becoming imprisoned in the 'iron cage' of bureaucracy.

Moreover, this would seem to be even more likely, and depressing perhaps, if many other areas of social life were being organized along the lines identified by Weber. A contemporary argument that this is clearly the case has been made by the American sociologist, George Ritzer (1993). Ritzer suggests that the dominant form of organization of social life is not bureaucracy as identified by Weber, but the similar type of rationalization exemplified by the McDonald's fast-food restaurant chain. Ritzer argues that a large number of other social enterprises are being organized along lines similar to the fast-food restaurant. He calls this 'the McDonaldization of society'. Thus, sport, education and medical care, to take just three of the examples examined by Ritzer, increasingly exhibit features similar to McDonald's. The main dimensions of this sort of organization are efficiency, calculability, predictability and control (see figure IN.4). They aim to deliver their goods in an efficient way, eliminating wasteful operations in the working practices of staff and not keeping the customer waiting for long periods. Every aspect of the production and delivery of the good is measured and calculated. Hence, the burgers and rolls in McDonald's restaurants are of a precise size and are cooked for an exactly measured period of time. The products and surroundings in

- efficiency
- calculability
- predictability
- control

Figure IN.4 Dimensions of McDonaldization

Source: Ritzer 1993

McDonaldized organizations are standardized and predictable. The idea is that a hamburger will look and taste the same in New York, London, Paris or Moscow (despite the planned variation of the type discussed by the two main characters played by John Travolta and Samuel L. Jackson in Quentin Tarantino's film, *Pulp Fiction*). Finally, the processes in organizations like McDonald's are controlled with clear lines of management.

Ritzer suggests, rather like Weber, that despite the rationalization processes involved in McDonaldization, such organizations can be irrational and inefficient. For example, we may have to queue for a relatively long time for a hamburger and may find the lack of variation in the quality boring and unexciting. Further, other types of organization develop, which attempt to produce experiences that are not routinized and predictable in the McDonaldized fashion.

An important aspect of Ritzer's argument is his suggestion that our leisure time has become rationalized. Hence, not only are the production of goods and the places where we consume them rationalized, but so also are our time and wider leisure activities. The places where we might have escaped from office or state bureaucracies in earlier times have themselves become organized along the rationalized, McDonaldized model.

It has been argued that these processes of rationalization are applicable to pop music. Weber (1958) identifies the particular nature of the rational structure of Western music and his argument suggests that: 'The value of musical rationalization is the transformation of the process of musical production into a calculable affair operating with known means, effective instruments, and understandable rules. Constantly running counter to this is the drive for expressive flexibility' (Martindale and Riedel 1958: li). As Goodwin explains:

> It is suggested that just as capitalist societies need increasingly to rationalize production to bring order to the creation of commodities, so Western music also creates a network of rules for music making. Thus a universal notational system and precise measurement of tonal and rhythmic differences comes to define what music is. (1992: 76)

In an argument which is examined in more detail in chapter 3, Goodwin finds evidence that the development of new forms of technology and their application to music involve the rationalization of the nature and production of musical texts along Weberian lines. He identifies three dimensions to this: 'harmonic rationalization, temporal rationalization, and timbral conformity': 'Harmonic rationalization occurs partly, for instance, through the elimination of microtonality that is involved in many modern synthesizers. This has implications for the globalization of music because many non-Western musics depend on microtones that are difficult to achieve on Western synthesizers' (1992: 83). Thus, there is a limiting of the range of tones that we might expect to hear in music. Temporal rationalization occurs through technology, such as the drum machine, which can produce a precise number of beats per second, thus structuring the overall nature of a piece of music. Timbral conformity occurs through the ways in which the sounds from synthesizers are often pre-set at the factory which means that 'the new machines produce the same sounds whoever plays them, whenever and wherever they are played' (ibid.: 84).

On a Weberian interpretation, production in the music industry might increasingly be organized along rational lines. Thus, different aspects of a piece of music may be constructed in different places and brought together for completion if they have been recorded at the same rate of beats per minute. This increases the importance of the beat, which structures the whole piece of music. Moreover, tracks can be constructed from a limited range of sounds in a rapid fashion, by people skilled with computers rather than musical instruments. A further discussion of the use of new technologies in this process can be found in chapter 2.

In addition, the delivery of the musical product increasingly takes place in large leisure stores and supermarkets such as Tesco that used only to sell groceries, as well as online (from suppliers such as Amazon). In supermarkets or shops such as HMV in the centre of Manchester, the music is lined up in tidy boxes and packets, self-selected by the customer and taken to a till to be paid for. There are relatively few staff in evidence and they mainly interact with customers only to take their money. By contrast, record shops more frequently used to be places where the potential purchaser could ask advice from the expert sales person who would allow the customer to listen to several records of his or her own choice before deciding on a purchase – or not, as the case may have been. Such modes of interaction would now only be expected in the increasingly marginalized specialist shops. Tables IN.1, IN.2 and IN.3 offer evidence of the increasing importance of the McDonaldized-typechains and supermarkets and the decline of the larger independent specialists in the retailing of recorded music in Britain. It should also be noted that more and more people are downloading music from the Internet (see also chapters 1 and 7). It has been suggested that both these developments have led to more women purchasing popular music.

Potential purchasers of such music are quite likely to work in organizations structured along McDonaldized lines, such as call centres. In Douglas Coupland's novel *Generation X* (1992), for example, the young characters have had a series of McJobs in the past, and at the beginning of the movie version of *Wayne's World*, Wayne describes his career in terms of lots of jobs which entail wearing a name badge and a hairnet. In themselves, the consumers of music might be affected by these same processes of rationalization.

Rationalization and McDonaldization: some criticisms

Since Ritzer's analysis was first published in 1993, it has been subject to much discussion and analysis. Ritzer himself updated the book (for example, see Ritzer 2004), while other authors have applied his analysis to a range of different areas of social life (see, for example, Ritzer 2002a) and there have been general and specific criticisms of his work (see, for example, Alfino et al. 1998). Ritzer has defended the overall outlines of his argument. He concedes that there is some evidence of countervailing tendencies to the success of McDonald's, which he label de-McDonaldization. Thus, he recognizes that the economic strength of McDonald's in the USA is under pressure (though it is still globally successful), that it has become a 'negative symbol' (2002b: 256) for a range of protesting groups, and that it is

Table IN.1 Number of shops selling recorded music, 1994–2004

	1994	1995	1996	1997	1998	1999	2000	2001	2002	2003	2004
Specialist chains											
HMV	88	95	99	106	109	120	125	134	155	155	194
Sanity	299	274	253	235	224	223	107	77	117	–	–
Virgin	27	46	67	80	85	88	88	86	89	86	130
MVC	na	29	34	47	61	83	87	89	85	85	82
Virgin Megastores Express	–	–	–	–	–	–	101	124	74	66	–
Music Zone	–	–	–	–	–	–	–	–	43	46	55
Now	na	31	28	34	44	38	–	–	–	–	–
Multiples											
Woolworths	788	774	784	788	789	798	812	817	825	825	823
W. H. Smith	372	328	309	353	406	520	519	519	533	530	525
Debenhams	–	–	–	–	–	–	–	–	101	101	–
Borders	–	–	–	–	–	–	–	–	17	24	26
Dixons/Currys	na	na	65	249	661	724	852	814	–	–	–
Blockbuster	–	–	–	727	727	680	669	–	–	–	–
Boots	235	207	207	207	164	156	81	–	–	–	–
Menzies*	163	156	143	144	123	–	–	–	–	–	–
Comet	–	–	–	–	–	–	–	–	–	246	–
Supermarkets											
Tesco	na	na	260	556	624	605	600	605	640	656	698
Sainsbury	na	na	202	376	386	416	425	405	442	477	520
Safeway	na	na	308	380	423	459	329	441	433	419	316
Asda	na	203	211	218	221	238	236	247	258	261	273
Morrisons	–	–	–	–	–	–	–	–	121	125	180
Other Supermarkets**	193	750	–	–	–	–	–	–	–	–	1,206

Independent specialists

Large	282	265	251	240	262	236	243	240	210	177	168
Medium	397	390	361	348	342	330	315	304	272	247	232
Small	601	605	595	497	460	420	409	399	407	370	374
Others (estimate)***	800	400	400	300	300	250	250	300	300	200	200
TOTAL	4,245	4,553	4,577	5,885	6,411	6,384	6,248	5,601	5,122	5,096	6,002

* Menzies' stores have now been incorporated into the W. H. Smith chain.

** Other Supermarkets figure has risen with the introduction of Somerfield/Kwiksave.

*** Includes motorway service stations, garages, small corner shops etc.

Note: Sanity previously traded as Our Price. Virgin Megastores Express also trade on some previous Our Price sites. Music Zone previously classified as Large Independents. Virgin Megastores Express stores have now been merged in with the Virgin figure.

na = not available

Source: BPI Statistical Handbook (2005: 65)

Table IN.2 Total singles sales by type of retailer, 1995–2004 (% down)

	1995	1996	1997	1998	1999	2000	2001	2002	2003	2004
Specialist multiples	40.2	45.7	48.3	49.6	49.5	50.7	49.6	45.3	50.4	50.9
General multiples	26.0	28.3	31.6	34.8	36.3	37.0	39.7	46.2	41.4	41.9
Independents	33.8	26.0	20.1	15.6	14.2	12.3	10.7	8.5	8.1	7.2

Source: BPI Statistical Handbook 2005: 68

difficult for any corporation to 'stay on top indefinitely' (ibid.: 257). While these may create difficulties for McDonald's, in Ritzer's view these are separable from the overall process of McDonaldization. What matters is the process of rationalization that has been given this label rather than McDonald's per se.

Ritzer then examines the threats to this process of rationalization. He considers that there are examples of new and successful small and local businesses. But these are either of relatively minor significance or, if successful, will become subject to rationalizing pressures. Further, while there are examples of McDonaldized businesses that produce a high-quality product (Ritzer examines Starbucks Coffee Company), these are successful because of the focus on just one product or a limited product range. Moreover, large companies may be producing an increasing range of goods (such as styles of trainers) but the processes of production are still McDonaldized. Thus, while suggesting that his analysis has to confront such issues, Ritzer remains confident of its overall thrust. However, some problems for the thesis remain.

As will be examined in more detail in chapter 2, it is not clear that rationalization is the only process at work in the production of contemporary popular music. Thus, some writers have argued that there will always be dimensions that are not rationalized and that musical production will escape from this kind of straitjacket. Frith captures several aspects of this notion:

> The industrialization of music hasn't stopped people from using it to express private joys or public griefs; it has given us new means to do so, new ways of having an impact, new ideas of what music can be. Street music is certainly an industrial noise now, but it's a human noise too so it is perhaps fitting to conclude that the most exciting and political music of the early 1990s should be the hip-hop sounds of young urban black bands like Public Enemy, groups that are heavily dependent on both the latest technology and street credibility. (1992: 74)

Goodwin suggests that rap and hip-hop music, whilst using technologies that might imply rationalization, have broken with conventionalized forms. He argues that 'what is really striking about the recent development of popular music is its progressive shift away from conventional tonality and structural conformity'. Furthermore, 'extremely avant-garde sounding recordings that thoroughly challenge the conventions of tonality and song structure have routinely charted' (1992: 92–3). Moreover, music producers using such technologies often experiment with them to produce new sounds that were not envisaged by the makers.

Table IN.3 Retailer album share by genre, 2004 (% down)

	Total	Rock	Pop	Urban	Dance	MOR	Classical	Country	Jazz/Blues
Music Specialists	44.9	54.9	29.8	53.8	49.9	33.2	47.6	69.0	46.7
HMV	22.6	27.9	16.6	29.8	24.7	16.7	22.5	29.1	23.7
Virgin	10.2	11.3	7.6	12.5	14.2	8.0	11.9	10.4	8.6
Music Zone	2.3	3.6	1.9	2.8	3.0	1.8	0.7	0.2	2.2
MVC	2.2	2.8	1.4	2.1	1.3	3.1	1.6	4.4	2.6
Fopp	0.9	1.7	0.2	0.9	1.5	0.1	0.0	3.7	0.1
Other Specialists	6.6	7.4	2.1	5.8	5.3	3.5	10.9	21.2	9.6
Supermarkets	22.8	17.6	32.3	22.3	24.5	32.5	13.0	7.8	22.1
Tesco	10.4	8.1	14.0	11.1	11.1	13.4	4.5	5.2	11.4
Asda	6.5	4.6	9.9	7.0	8.0	9.9	2.3	0.6	3.9
Sainsbury	3.0	2.6	4.0	2.7	2.8	4.3	4.1	0.8	4.5
Morrisons	2.4	1.8	3.5	1.4	2.4	4.6	0.7	0.7	1.6
Other Supermarkets	0.6	0.5	1.0	0.1	0.3	0.4	1.4	0.4	0.6
Chains / Multiples	16.5	13.3	25.9	14.3	17.7	20.8	8.6	8.2	9.0
Woolworths	13.2	10.4	22.1	11.4	14.2	15.7	3.4	6.9	7.4
W. H. Smith	3.2	2.9	3.7	2.8	3.5	5.0	4.6	1.2	1.6
Other Chains/Multiples	0.1	0.0	0.1	0.1	0.0	0.1	0.6	0.0	0.0
Internet	8.9	10.8	6.7	6.7	6.3	5.1	9.8	8.1	12.3
Amazon	3.6	4.9	2.6	0.3	2.7	2.9	2.7	3.5	6.3
Play.com	1.7	2.1	1.2	3.5	1.5	1.0	0.1	0.6	0.8
CD Wow	1.2	1.2	1.3	1.6	0.9	0.5	1.1	1.0	1.9
Other Internet	2.4	2.6	1.5	1.3	1.2	0.7	5.9	2.9	3.3

Table IN.3 (continued)

	Total	Rock	Pop	Urban	Dance	MOR	Classical	Country	Jazz/Blues
Mail Order and Clubs	3.4	1.3	3.4	1.9	0.7	3.5	11.5	1.5	5.4
Britannia	1.5	0.8	2.1	0.6	0.2	0.3	6.8	0.3	1.6
Other Mail Order	1.9	0.5	1.3	1.2	0.5	3.2	4.7	1.2	3.8
Other Outlets	3.4	2.2	1.8	1.0	0.8	4.8	9.6	5.5	4.5

Base: albums expenditure

Source: BPI Statistical Handbook 2005: 72

In addition, the consumers of this sort of music might try to escape from the structures of rationalization in which they are forced to work. The characters in *Generation X* seek escape from their McJobs and Wayne and Garth in *Wayne's World* develop their own forms of creativity by running their own cable-access television programme and in their appropriation of heavy metal music.

As with the account offered by Adorno, the arguments about rationalization seem over-generalized, again implying the need for a more specific and empirically based understanding and theorization of the precise nature of musical production, products and consumption. While general theories can provoke thought and may capture significant aspects of contemporary practice, they need to be evaluated in the context of the application of the theory to a range of different cases. This may often lead to a reformulation of the theory with more specific reference. The argument here is not about theory per se, but about the attempt to stretch a theory to cover all cases in different contexts.

Audience power and creativity

The two general accounts considered in this Introduction so far have stressed themes of commodification, standardization and rationalization. In different ways, they are both critical and pessimistic accounts of contemporary culture and popular music. Both theories continue to have influence upon interpretations and understandings of popular music. However, in recent years a number of writers have sought to understand the limits to the influence of mass culture and rationalization. This has often entailed a move away from consideration of what culture does to its audience towards an evaluation of the ways in which audiences use the products of the culture industries in their own lives. The contours of these developments have now been traced by a number of different authors (for example, McGuigan 1992), who show the way in which the sort of critique of the culture industries put forward by Adorno and Horkheimer was superseded by the theory of hegemony associated with the work of the Italian Marxist writer Antonio Gramsci (1891–1937). Hegemony is explained by Abercrombie in the following terms:

> In such a view, popular culture cannot be seen as a simple imposition of dominant ideology on subordinate classes. While cultural relations have to be understood in terms of the antagonistic relationships between the bourgeoisie and the working classes, bourgeois culture is not simply dominant. One cannot speak of domination here but rather the struggle for hegemony – that is, moral, cultural and political leadership. For Gramsci, the bourgeoisie can achieve hegemony only to the extent that it can accommodate subordinate class values. The establishment of hegemony is thus a case of negotiation between dominant and subordinate values. (1990: 201)

Such an approach entails the attempt to understand how members of society negotiate with the products of the culture industries. These developments are reviewed at length in chapters 7, 8 and 9 of this book. However, one of the key suggestions of recent versions of this sort of approach is that audiences have power to negotiate with the texts of media products. Based partly in these theories of hegemony, the works of Hall (1980) and Morley (1980) argued that audiences could accept the dominant messages in media texts, could oppose them or develop a negotiated reading on them (see further Abercrombie and Longhurst 1998: 9–28). In adopting a particular variation of this approach, Fiske has argued:

> against the common belief that the capitalist cultural industries produce only an apparent variety of products whose variety is finally illusory for they all promote the same capitalist ideology. Their skill in sugar coating the pill is so great that the people are not aware of the ideological practice in which they are engaging as they consume and enjoy the cultural commodity. I do not believe that 'the people' are 'cultural dopes'; they are not a passive, helpless mass incapable of discrimination and thus at the economic, cultural, and political mercy of the barons of the industry. (1987: 309)

This leads Fiske to consider how audience members use media texts in different ways in their lives. For example, he writes of Madonna in the following way:

> The meanings of the Madonna look, as of the Madonna videos, cannot be precisely specified. But that is precisely the point, the pleasure that they give is not the pleasure of what they say, but of their assertion of the right and the power of a severely subordinated subculture to make their own statements, their own meanings. Madonna's invitation to her girl fans to play with the conventions of patriarchy shows them that they are not necessarily subject to those conventions but can exercise some control over their relationship to patriarchy and thus over the sense of their identity. (Ibid.: 233)

Fiske's subsequent work received a somewhat hostile reception, one criticism being that it leads to a simple celebration of popular culture and suggests that opposition to domination can be found in all its forms. It may be that, in attempting to focus attention on the different ways in which products of the culture industries can be used, Fiske (and others like him) have played down the dimensions of the culture industry identified by Adorno. However, this does not mean that the implications of this work should be ignored, and the ideas of activity and creativity on the part of the audience need to be considered in empirical terms alongside those of commodification, standardization and rationalization.

A framework for analysis

The implication of the discussion in this Introduction so far is that there is a need to pay detailed analytical attention to the different dimensions of research on production, the nature of the product and its consumption. The field of popular music studies (in the wider context of the study of a range of media) has developed in precisely these ways. To reflect this and to structure such consideration in this book, I have organized the discussion according to a scheme of production, text and audience. In its essentials this scheme is very simple. It argues that any cultural object, such as a book, play, film, television programme or record, should be thought of as a text. These texts do not come into existence spontaneously, but result from production processes that involve various different institutions. In

PRODUCTION	TEXT	AUDIENCE
P_____	T_____	A

Figure IN.5 Production, text and audience scheme

some cases, such production may be relatively simple. Thus, when I write a lecture, I may sit down at a computer or with a pen and paper and write a text which is then delivered orally to an audience sitting in a room. In other cases, production is exceedingly complex. Thus, a recording will be the outcome of a complex set of procedures involving different people and social processes, including musicians, recording engineers, record producers, playing instruments, interaction in a recording studio, mixing tapes, the manufacture of CDs in a factory and so on. Such cultural objects are not only produced, they are also consumed, or read, by an audience or audiences, and it is necessary to study the processes that occur here. This scheme can be represented diagrammatically, as in figure IN.5.

This scheme leads to at least five sets of issues or questions that need to be examined in sociological analysis. First, there is a set of concerns raised by the consideration of what is meant by production and producers. Here, it is important to examine the way in which producers such as musicians or novelists are located within a range of contextualizing social institutions. For example, musicians may be contracted to a multinational corporation with interests in many different fields, or they might publish material on their own website or write music for their own interest and never have it published or performed. It can be suggested that most cultural production takes place within an economic context where the profit motive is paramount, and this will have effects, however mediated, on the text.

Second, it is important to consider precisely how production takes place. It is important to examine not just who produces, and the wider economic and institutional contexts for such production, but the actual nature of the processes of production themselves. Therefore, it will be necessary to consider whether people collaborate in the production of the text. Also, whether one organization, or group, has the power to prevent another group or individual from developing ideas: for example, is one institution – such as the state – attempting to prevent another – such as a rock group – from recording certain songs? Furthermore, it is important to consider whether there are conflicts within a company or group involved in cultural production.

Third, there is a range of issues raised by the description of the cultural object as a text. One consequence of this depiction is that a text such as a pop record is thought to have a structure, which can be examined through analysis. In chapter 5 of this book a number of different concepts which are used in the analysis of texts are identified. It is also important to recognize that, at least partly because of the way in which they are structured, there can be different interpretations of texts and the meanings they contain.

Griffiths, in an insightful and polemical survey of the study of popular music as music, has identified three positions that have been adopted, which have tended to operate in the critical mode. For Griffiths, the 'high analysis of low music' can be typologized into 'earnest onlooking', that pursued by 'street fighting men' and the approach of 'the managers'. The earliest stage is the first and really begins the serious study of popular music (if not its sociology). This approach is 'serious and lacking irony, morally purposeful, slightly awkward in relation to the object of study' (1999: 398). With the next group 'popular music literature really takes off' (ibid.: 400). This approach is heavily influenced by sociology and cultural studies and is heavily politically engaged in its discussion of popular music. As will be considered in chapter 5 and elsewhere, the work of Middleton (1990) was central in this move. As Griffiths argues:

> Studying Popular Music stands at the cusp of where an engaged literature of the left, outward-looking and able firmly to articulate its intent, turns in to the text itself. The book's method, which is effectively to try to wrap every literature in the language of critique, endlessly deferred, seems to me its most enduring display, and right now its most important legacy and challenge. (1999: 407)

The final group of writers – termed the 'managers' – engage in the theory of popular music, which appears very complex. As Griffiths suggests, this sort of approach 'appears characteristically where an observation concerning technique which is, be honest, dead easy, suddenly requires a load of graphs' (ibid.: 409). Whether or not this is 'dead easy' is for debate (especially for those of us without musicological training), but there is a shift from the politics and influences of the second type of approach.

Fourth, returning to the production, text and audience scheme, there are issues deriving from the idea of an audience and what is meant by this term. Thus, the particular make-up of the audience for any particular text should be investigated and we may want to consider the way in which a text or set of texts is used by different social groups. For example, do contemporary heavy metal fans listen to Black Sabbath or Led Zeppelin differently from rock fans from the late 1960s and early 1970s? Also, it is important to consider the ways in which texts produce certain identifications for us when we watch, read or listen to them. Thus, when some people listen to guitar-based music, they pretend to be playing the electric guitar themselves, thus in some way identifying with the guitar player. This is similar to identifying with the hero of a narrative, and it is no accident that players like Eric Clapton and Jimi Hendrix were known as guitar heroes.

Fifth, it is important to consider how it is that a text is consumed. This may involve examination of whether music is listened to on an iPod, Discman, Walkman, a small stereo or a system costing thousands of pounds, as these may alter the ways in which the text is understood and the forms of pleasure that are derived from it. Does an individual listen to a text on his or her own in the bedroom, or dance to it in a club? The detail of social context can have a great effect on meaning and form of appropriation of a text. These different aspects can be mapped onto the basic production, text and audience scheme, as shown in figure IN.6.

Popular music can be examined in the context of such a production, text and audience scheme and the development of the field that is surveyed in this book reflects it. In what follows, this framework is adopted to structure the presentation of material. In chapter 1, the wider institutional and economic context of popular music production is considered. This includes a discussion of the patterns of

PRODUCTION	TEXT	AUDIENCE
Takes place in a wider economic and institutional context	Is structured	Reads the text in a social context

Figure IN.6 Developed production, text and audience scheme

ownership in the pop music industry, an examination of the nature of the markets for the products of that industry, details of the income derived from rights in the industry, the effects of digitization and consideration of the ways in which 'globalization' of the music industry is occurring.

In chapter 2, on the social production of music, more 'micro' and detailed aspects of musical production are considered. This includes examination of the subcultures of musicians, the social backgrounds of pop musicians and the detail of more 'amateur' musical production in local contexts. The chapter includes discussion of the changing division of labour in the popular music production process and the effects of technological change on these processes.

In chapters 3, 4, 5 and 6, attention moves from the production of texts to issues raised by the nature of texts themselves. Chapter 3 considers a range of material and issues deriving from the history of popular music, its political orientation and connections with sexuality. Included in this chapter is a discussion of pop, postmodernism and fragmentation.

Chapter 4 develops the discussion of these matters through an analysis of 'black' music. This includes examination of the problems of attributing music to different racial groups and includes three case studies of the genres of blues and soul, ska and reggae, and rap and hip-hop. Again, these discussions involve consideration of some of the different dimensions of the debate around postmodernism and fragmentation in contemporary culture.

Chapter 5 focuses on the structure of texts and how they convey meanings. It begins with a discussion of the limits of musicology in the study of popular music, before considering different aspects of musical meaning. This involves the introduction of some key terms from structuralism and semiotics. The chapter continues with an examination of the debate on the relative importance of words in the creation and communication of musical meaning, before analysing the debates on music and visuals, particularly through music video.

Chapter 6 analyses a range of issues that derive from the fact that popular music is performed. Drawing on the work of Judith Butler and Pierre Bourdieu, a number of different aspects of dance are examined, as are processes of collecting and karaoke. There is also an examination here of processes of distinction in popular music and how taste operates.

Chapters 7, 8 and 9 consider different dimensions of the audience for popular music. Chapter 7 looks at some of the most important recent accounts of text/audience relations, then goes on to consider some data on the trends in consumption of different musical texts by different parts of the audience. This is followed by a description of some of the main contours of the examination of music as it is used and developed by different subcultural groups. Chapter 8 considers the literature on fans and summarizes the most important accounts that have been produced on the attachment of fans to individual groups and artists and some of the recent theorizations of fan activity in general. This involves consideration of some theorizations of celebrity. This is followed by an examination of the debates on the increasing difficulty of defining the relations between production and consumption in the sphere of popular music, returning in conclusion to some of the issues raised by the studies of local music-making described in chapter 2. These issues are further explored in chapter 9 via a consideration of recent work that has developed the idea of subculture in new ways in the light of the sort of issues considered in chapter 8. Chapter 9 also considers the idea of scene and the argument that cultural tastes have become more omnivoric. It concludes with an examination of different aspects of audience and everyday life.

The production, text and audience scheme thus structures the presentation of the material to be examined in this book. There are a number of different sociological dimensions to the analysis which run through the application of this scheme. Thus, attention is paid at different points to dimensions of class, gender, race, age and place. Any sociological analysis worth its salt has to do this. The utilization of these dimensions as threads running through the book does mean that there is no chapter entitled 'Women and Pop', for example, and no chapter on young people and music – and so on. However, examinations of both of these dimensions (and the others) will be found in various different places. As I have suggested, the approach of the book is sociological, drawing on media and cultural studies. This means that the emphasis is less on the musicological, though key aspects of this are discussed in the book.

There are also a number of specific concepts and issues examined in this book, which are important in contemporary cultural studies and the sociology of culture. These have to do with, for example, the value that is placed on particular pieces of music and the struggle which take place between different social groups around music. The salience of these issues is identified as they are introduced in particular contexts, so as to avoid overburdening the discussion at this introductory stage.

Summary

This chapter has considered:

- the differences between critical, celebratory and analytical approaches;
- Adorno's account of popular music and criticisms that can be made of it;
- the Weberian account of rationalization and its development through the thesis of McDonaldization by Ritzer;
- some criticisms of the rationalization idea;
- recent work which has moved beyond Gramsci's account of hegemony to emphasize audience power and creativity;
- the production, text and audience framework for the analysis of culture and the issues it raises;
- the structure of the remainder of the book.

Part I

Production

1

The Pop Music Industry

This chapter covers five main areas. First, it characterizes the economic structure of the contemporary popular music industry, examining patterns of market domination, relations between the structure and wider social and economic change, and employment patterns. Second, it outlines the data on the material production of the industry, summarizing the information on what the music industry produces and where it is sold. Third, the chapter considers the income derived from the ownership of rights in the music industry. Several authors (for example, Frith 1987; Marshall 2005) have pointed to the centrality of such rights to the contemporary music industry. The nature of copyright is explained and the different rights in the music industry distinguished. The idea that the industry is moving away from the exploitation of rights to the use of trademarks is considered. Next, the contemporary and potential effects on the music industry of digitization, downloading and so on are discussed, before the chapter concludes with an examination of some of the issues raised by the contemporary globalization of the music industry. Consideration is given here to the ideas of cultural imperialism, transculturation and glocalization.

The economic structure of the pop music industry

As was explained in the Introduction, all pop music is produced within a social context, and a great deal of it is produced from within an industry attempting to generate profits. This being the case, how is the pop music industry currently structured?

At the time of writing, the popular music industry is dominated by four companies: Vivendi Universal (henceforth Universal), Sony/BMG, Time Warner and EMI, which produce 75 per cent of recorded pop music (Bishop 2005: 443). Two of these companies (Sony/BMG and Universal) are parts of other larger companies, whereas two (EMI and Warner) are music companies outside a wider conglomerate structure (Burkart 2005: 493).

The music industry is therefore concentrated in and affected by conglomerates. Concentration refers to the fact the ownership of an area of production is concentrated in the hands of a small number of companies. Concentration can

Table 1.1 Number of firms and market shares in the weekly Top 10 of the popular music single record market, by year

Year	Labels	Firms	Firms with only one hit	Concentration ratio	
				4-FIRM	8-FIRM
1948	11	11	5	81	95
1949	9	8	3	89	100
1950	11	10	3	76	97
1951	10	8	2	82	100
1952	12	11	5	77	95
1953	12	11	3	71	94
1954	13	12	4	73	93
1955	16	14	7	74	91
1956	22	20	10	66	76
1957	28	23	8	40	65
1958	35	31	19	36	60
1959	46	42	29	34	58
1960	45	39	20	28	52
1961	48	39	16	27	48
1962	52	41	21	25	46
1963	52	36	15	26	55
1964	53	37	17	34	51
1965	50	35	16	37	61
1966	49	31	13	38	61
1967	51	35	15	40	60
1968	46	30	17	42	61
1969	48	31	14	42	64
1970	41	23	5	51	71
1971	46	21	7	45	67
1972	49	20	5	48	68
1973	42	19	4	57	81

Source: Peterson and Berger 1990: 142

be discussed across an economy as a whole or in terms of specific sectors. It is often expressed by what economists call the *concentration ratio*, 'which measures the degree of concentration within a particular sector by taking the proportion of the market controlled by the top five firms in the sector' (Murdock and Golding 1977: 23). On the figures given by Bishop (2005), the concentration ratio for the music industry would be over 75 per cent.

The music industry has been concentrated for much of its existence (Negus 1992). However, it is important to recognize that concentration ratios and the precise nature of the relationship between companies vary historically. For example, in their discussion of 'cycles in symbol production' in the American pop music industry, Peterson and Berger (1990) demonstrate significant variation in the four- and eight-firm concentration ratios between 1948 and 1973, as is shown in table 1.1. The American industry was most concentrated in the early 1950s, with the four-firm concentration ratio varying between 71 and 89 per cent. It was least

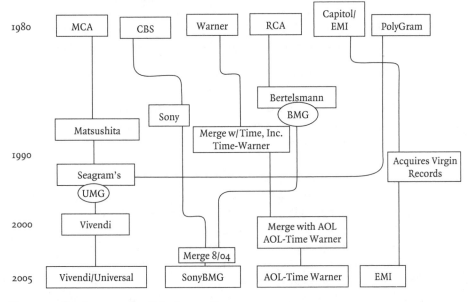

Figure 1.1 Industry consolidation, 1980–2005

Source: Bishop 2005: 448

concentrated in the early 1960s, before becoming more so in the early 1970s. Some further discussion of the factors behind these changes can be found in the examination of the development of rock and roll in chapter 3. Moreover, as Bishop (2005) shows, over the past 25 years the relationship between the major players in the music industry has itself been subject to a series of take-overs and mergers. This process is shown in figure 1.1.

The parent companies of two of the producers, which dominate the pop music industry, are also active in other sectors of the economy. They are conglomerates with a wide range of interests, which focus in the media field. In an influential examination of the structure of contemporary media industries, Murdock and Golding (1977) suggest two reasons for this historical process of diversification or horizontal integration across different spheres on the part of the conglomerates, which produce a range of different products. First, they argue that such strategies facilitate the maintenance of overall profits even when individual sectors suffer from a lack of potential for expansion as a result of falling demand; and second, that the process provides the opportunity for one sector to 'cushion' another where profitability has declined because of other factors. However, it is clear that at some points this diversification can produce an unstable compromise, which can then lead to the parent company divesting itself of a specific area of operation. Thus, in the case of music, EMI was recreated as a music company in 1996, moving away from Thorn EMI, and 'Time Warner sold Warner Music to an investment group led by Edgar Bronfman Jr. in 2003' (Burkart 2005: 493–4). A current example of a horizontally integrated company is Bertelsmann (Bishop 2005: 447). As box 1.1 suggests, this is a fluid situation.

An alternative, but sometimes related, historical strategy is that of 'vertical integration', where 'oligopolistic concentration of the record industry was

Box 1.1 Duet in the offing

Will EMI take over Warner Music? Or will it be the other way around?

For years, EMI and Warner Music, the two smallest recorded-music majors, have been circling each other, talking in private and public about merging. Last year, Sony united its music business with Bertelsmann's in a 50/50 joint-venture, creating a firm that rivals Universal Music, the biggest. The next merger will surely be EMI and Warner Music. Both companies, of roughly equal size, are desperate to be the one that takes over the other. The music industry is waiting to see which of them has the nerve to pounce first.

Earlier this year it looked like Warner Music, an American firm owned by a group of private-equity investors, would come out the winner. In February, EMI, a slightly larger company listed in London with a market capitalisation of £1.8 billion ($3.1 billion), issued a profit warning, partly because of delays on albums from two of its biggest bands, Coldplay and Gorillaz. Its shares fell by more than 15%, and it looked vulnerable. In the following months EMI watched nervously as Warner Music prepared for an initial public offering (IPO), aided by a wave of optimism about the prospects for digital-music sales. In the end, however, Warner Music's IPO did not go as well as expected. Merrill Lynch dropped out as an underwriter because its analyst, Jessica Reif Cohen, told the firm's bankers that the IPO was overpriced. Warner Music has to cut the price from $22–24 to $27, and its shares have since fallen to below that level.

EMI's shares, on the other hand, have more than doubled since a low in 2003, and it recently issued a strong trading statement. Some people in the music industry reckon that the British firm is ready to seize the moment and that it will bid for Warner Music before the end of the year. This month, Warner Music's post-IPO lock-up period for insiders comes to an end, meaning that its private-equity investors can sell the rest of their shares. Its biggest private-equity shareholder, Thomas H. Lee Partners, has lost hundred of millions of dollars on Refco, a futures and commodities broker that went bankrupt last month, and may therefore be more interested in selling its stake in Warner Music.

Warner Music and EMI came close to merging three times between 1997 and 2003. In 2000 the European Commission blocked a deal on competition grounds. But the regulators might take a more forgiving approach next time. Even though a merger would reduce the number of music majors from four to three, competition authorities might well accept that the recorded-music industry is in retreat because of falling sales and has no option but to consolidate.

The two companies certainly have complementary businesses: EMI has a particularly good international repertoire, whereas Warner Music is strong in the huge American market. A merger could bring about £100m–150m of savings a year, according to Morgan Stanley, even though the companies have already cut deeply in the last few years. A merged EMI/Warner Music would be better placed to compete with Universal Music and Sony/BMG, whose broader range of artists gives them far greater leverage with radio stations and big retailers.

But a public struggle at Sony/BMG's joint-venture, where Bertelsmann is trying to get rid of Andy Lack, Sony's chosen chief executive, will have impressed upon Warner Music and EMI that mergers of equals tend not to work – one side or the other has to be in charge. When EMI bids for Warner Music, or vice versa, the battle is sure to get nasty. There is little love between two management teams that have different philosophies. EMI prides itself on its strong record in finding and developing new talent. Warner Music, on the other hand, has pared back its spending on finding new talent to nearly half of EMI's, according to a report from Ms Cohen. Whereas EMI has a broad roster of international artists, Warner Music concentrates on American and British musicians.

Warner Music's big advantage is its shareholder structure: its private-equity owners may be able to move more quickly and aggressively than EMI's diverse institutional shareholder base. EMI's weak presence in America, where it had an 11% market share at the end of October, compared with 17% for Warner Music, is also a serious drawback. The fight, when it comes, will be a close one.

Source: The Economist print edition, 10 November 2005

maintained by control of the total production flow from raw materials to wholesale sales' (Peterson and Berger 1990: 143). For example, an artist might record in a studio owned by a company which manufactures a disc from the recording at one of its plants, and which is then reviewed in a magazine owned by that company (which may also include a review of the film made by the artist for a film company owned by the same conglomerate) and sold to the public in a shop owned by the company. Aspects of Bertelsmann are also vertically integrated in this way (Bishop 2005: 448).

The concentrated nature of the pop music industry has led to complaints that the dominant companies can use their power against the interests of consumers. An example of this arose in Britain during 1992 and 1993 over the pricing of compact discs. The House of Commons Committee that investigated this matter suggested that prices of CDs were too high in Britain, especially by comparison with the United States. Leaving aside the merits of the arguments from the different protagonists, it is clear that there was resentment against the concentrated nature of the market and its dominance by conglomerate concerns, as is shown by the article reproduced in box 1.2.

Another very important and more recent area where the interests of the large companies have been contrasted with those of consumers is with respect to the downloading of music and the closure of Napster in 2000. This episode is discussed further below in the context of copyright, digitization and downloading.

Box 1.2 Monopoly inquiry into UK music industry

Britain's £1bn-a-year music industry is to be referred to the Monopolies and Mergers Commission in a decision likely to cause a political furore and deep divisions among government ministers.

Sir Bryan Carsberg, Director-General of Fair Trading, has privately told industry leaders that he believes 'a complex monopoly' exists in the supply of compact discs and that competition has not been working effectively. Artists such as Mark Knopfler of Dire Straits have also complained about the price of CDs.

An announcement is due to be made on Thursday, shortly after the Commons National Heritage Committee publishes a damning report on the price of CDs.

Sir Bryan's decision flies in the face of his predecessor, Sir Gordon Borrie, who said last year that there were no grounds for an MMC inquiry. Ministers at the Department of Trade and Industry are believed to oppose interference with one of Britain's most successful industries and biggest export earners, but are powerless under the Fair Trading Act to contest Sir Bryan's decision.

The MMC will be given nine months for the investigation. It is to be asked to concentrate on the application of copyright laws to the music industry, which MPs on the national heritage committee believe keep CD prices artificially high and prevent an inflow of cheaper imports.

Maurice Oberstein, executive vice-president of PolyGram, said any meddling with the copyright laws would be 'a hugely dangerous enterprise' that would almost certainly backfire and destroy a thriving industry. It would also have profound implications for other successful British industries such as pharmaceuticals and publishing. 'I can tell you right now that it would have hardly any impact on the price of CDs, but would be highly destructive of smaller independent record producers and retailers. Why are they picking on us? Copyright exists in all kinds of industries and it applies all over the world. We are not allowed to export our product to the US. If we could, the price of CDs would be lower.'

He also claimed that 'almost all of us lose money on our UK trading. We make money out of our overseas royalties, which is a huge benefit to the UK economy, but it is a total red herring to say we are profiteering at the British consumer's expense.'

Mr Oberstein, whose comments were echoed by Rupert Perry, UK chief executive of EMI Records, said he found it 'simply incredible' that Sir Bryan had 'caved into the rantings' of the Commons select committee.

'I could have told you what that committee was going to write before they even sat down to think about it. They wouldn't listen to our arguments. They wouldn't look at the figures.'

The British market in CDs is dominated by just four players: PolyGram, Thorn EMI, Warner Records and Bertelsmann Group. Though Sir Bryan accepts that no evidence exists of a cartel, he is concerned that copyright laws and binding contracts between artists and music companies have the effect of creating a 'complex monopoly'.

They also, he believes, severely restrict imports of cheaper CDs from the US. According to the industry, there is no significant difference between the wholesale price of CDs in Britain, which averages about £5 per disc, and its US counterpart.

Much of the blame for high CD prices, the industry claims, lies with retailers. It says prices are lower in the US largely because of the economies of scale that US producers enjoy.

Source: Independent on Sunday, 9 May 1993. Author Jeremy Warner

Within this overall picture of a market dominated by a small number of very large companies, attention has often been drawn to the innovative role of small 'independent' record companies. Thus, Peterson and Berger (1990) argue that a period of concentration in the music industry is followed by a burst of creativity when the previously unmet demand on the part of the public for different sounds is unleashed and fed by smaller innovative companies. They suggest that this happened during 1955–9 after the advent of rock 'n' roll in 1955. A similar case can be made for the effects of punk in Britain during 1977 and subsequently, as well as for dance music in the late 1980s, though it is important to recognize that demand itself may be influenced by shifts in consumer preferences, which are related to wider changes in consumer culture. Similar sorts of argument have been made by Kusek and Leonhard about music-making in the digital age, with large music companies being depicted as 'conservative' forces in resisting change wherever they can. Thus, writing in a context where they see demand for digital music sharing on the part of consumers to be building up, they say that: 'Just about every new transformative technology was fought, tooth and nail, until it could no longer be contained, discredited, or sued out of existence, and only then it was reluctantly embraced, its providers acquired and controlled, then put to work to bring in the bacon' (2005: 140).

This perceived situation has led some journalistic and academic writing to focus on the creative stance and effects of small, 'independent' record companies such as Atlantic (Gillett 1988), Stax (Guralnick 1991) and Chess (Cohodas 2000), which are perceived to have produced particularly distinctive and interesting music. It is suggested that the smallness and intimacy of such companies facilitated the production of particularly innovative sounds, which broke free from the standardized products of the dominant record companies. Furthermore, it is argued that such companies were better able to represent the aspirations and feelings of their artists and audiences than the large corporations.

Negus offers a critique of such approaches. He maintains that a dichotomous distinction between the large, conservative conglomerates and the small, innovative independents is misleading, as the recording industry is actually 'a web of major and minor companies' (1992: 17). Thus, larger companies will, for example, fund smaller ones to develop particular artists, set up 'independent looking' companies of their own and adopt small group working practices which resemble those in smaller companies. More recent academic writing has similarly pointed to the complexities of the relationship between the 'independents' and the majors (for example, Lee 1995; Hesmondhalgh 1997, 1998; and in general for the cultural industries, Hesmondhalgh 2002).

It is illuminating in this respect to consider the example of 2 Tone Records. As the detailed discussion reproduced in box 1.3 explains, the first record on 2 Tone,

---

Box 1.3   The birth of 2 Tone Records

This further stamp of approval from John Peel only added to the circus of record company suits that turned up at every gig, along with the likes of new wave fave Elvis Costello, who was an early convert to the 2 Tone sound. A & M, Arista, Island, CBS, Virgin, Warner Bros. They were all sniffing around, offering larger and larger amounts of money to get the hottest property on the market at the time. Christ! Mick Jagger was turning up in person to represent Rolling Stone Records! The band couldn't believe it was all happening to them, but rather than get carried away with it all, they knew exactly what they wanted out of any deal. A distribution deal for their 2 Tone label, giving them the freedom to record what they wanted and to sign other groups of their choice.

At the end of the day, it was Chrysalis who finally got the Special A.K.A. to put pen to paper by agreeing to their demands. . . . The stumbling block with other labels had been 2 Tone. Everyone wanted the Specials, but nobody wanted the label. At Chrysalis too, there were some arguments over creating a separate label identity, but in the end it was agreed to do just that because the band were too good to lose.

The 2 Tone idea might have put the others off, but the extra money involved turned out to be peanuts. 2 Tone was allowed to record ten singles a year by any band and Chrysalis were obliged to release at least six of them. The budget for each single was only £1,000, and so it was just like giving the Specials another ten grand advance with the added bonus of the chance to discover new talent and more chart success. For that, the Specials signed a five album deal, with options up to eight LPs. With most bands doing well if they are still in business after the 'difficult second album', Chrysalis were certainly taking no chances about losing their new signings half way along the road to Beatledom.

2 Tone was never a separate entity from Chrysalis, although those directly in control decided what was released on it. In effect it was just a trading name for Chrysalis. There were no fancy 2 Tone contracts and bands on 2 Tone were actually signed to Chrysalis. For this, Chrysalis paid 2 Tone a 2 per cent royalty on top of that offered to the bands.

2 Tone might have been a revolutionary challenge to what had gone before, but when all was said and done Chrysalis still held all of the aces.

Source: Marshall 1990: 17

Gangsters by the Specials, was recorded 'independently' and then manufactured and distributed by Rough Trade, an 'independent' record company. Radio airplay and live appearances by the Specials led to record industry attention and an interesting deal with Chrysalis Records.

Negus draws attention to the webs and networks that operate in the music industry:

> These organisational webs, of units within a company and connections to smaller companies, enable entertainment corporations to gain access to material and artists, and to operate a coordinating, monitoring and surveillance operation rather than just centralised control. The corporation can still shape the nature of these webs through the use and distribution of investment. But it is a tight-loose approach, rather than a rigidly hierarchical form of organisation; tight enough to ensure a degree of predictability and stability in dealing with collaborators, but loose enough to manoeuvre, redirect or even reverse company activity. (1992: 19)

In more recent work (1999) Negus has considered the place of specific genres within large record companies. A good example of some of the complexities involved is that of rap and hip-hop (see also chapters 2 and 4). Negus points out that this is more often considered 'as an aesthetic form of African-American expression: a resistant, oppositional, counter-cultural style created via the appropriation of technology and existing musical signs and symbols (scratching, sampling, mixing), drawing on a long tradition of diasporic creativity' (1999: 82). Negus adds consideration of the music industry. Thus, the music industry develops and uses rap and in turn the music has been very successful commercially. Divisions have been set up within major companies to deal with genres like rap (and country and salsa), and these divisions are themselves reorganized as musical genres are reconstituted. The major companies have also formulated relationships with smaller ones. However, the use of rap and hip-hop has generated a range of issues concerning copyright (see below) as 'rap is perceived to be less attractive in terms of the criteria through which long-term catalogue value is accorded' (ibid.: 94).

The interconnections between the small and the dominant companies in the music industry can be characterized in a fashion which reflects the influence of writers who maintain that Fordist methods of mass production (so called after the model of Ford's development of the mass production of cars) are increasingly being replaced by post-Fordist (or flexible) ones in contemporary capitalist societies. The differences between these regimes are summarized in figure 1.2. According to Bagguley, the 'central element of a Fordist economic structure is mass production articulated to mass consumption' (1991: 154). Thus, the characterization of the culture industry produced by Adorno, which was considered at length in the Introduction, could be said to depict a Fordist structure. Standardized goods would emerge from production lines, under the control of a hierarchical management, to be consumed by a public with very little choice over what was available to them. In a post-Fordist system, there would be far more flexibility in production: work groups would often be organized into teams with a variety of tasks, a move towards the production of a greater range of goods

Fordism	Post-Fordism
Mass consumption	Fragmented niche markets
Technology dedicated to the production of one product	General flexible machinery
Mass, assembly-line production	Short-run batch production
Semi-skilled workers	Multiskilled workers
Taylorist management strategy	'Human relations' management strategy
General or industrial unions	No unions or 'company unionism'/ no-strike deals
Centralized national bargaining	Decentralized local or plant-level bargaining
Geographically dispersed branch plants	Geographically concentrated/new industrial districts/flexible specialist communities

Figure 1.2 Ideal types of Fordism and post-Fordism

Source: Bagguley 1991: 155

addressed to different markets, with the aim of giving consumers a wider choice. For the post-Fordist industry, 'the emphasis is on breaking down rigid job classifications both horizontally between functions and vertically within the hierarchy of authority, implying "multiskilling" on the one hand, and participation on the other' (ibid.: 157).

Hence, it can be argued that working practices in a small company might not be that different from those in a small team in a much bigger one which has moved away from Fordism and bureaucracy. Negus (1992: 14–16) argues that this process has occurred in the music industry, resulting 'in a proliferation of project groups and team-based working practices' and contributing 'to a blurring of previous hierarchical distinctions' (ibid.: 15). This is reinforced by the fact that even very large companies are divided into divisions often based around different genres with degrees of autonomy.

However, there are a number of criticisms that can be made of this idea of post-Fordism. Bagguley (1991) suggests that it concentrates mainly on the manufacturing industry to the neglect of services, that it tends to ignore divisions of race and gender and to overestimate the extent of the spread of post-Fordist practices, which may be confined to a relatively small number of industries in specific locations in the world. Such developments have also complicated the arguments about cycles of concentration and innovation in the music industry that were first articulated by Peterson and Berger (1990). In carrying out an analysis of the USA between 1948 and 1973, Peterson and Berger argued that they had shown 'a link between market structure and musical diversity and musical innovation' (Ross 2005: 477), which involves the following:

> Changes in market concentration lead to diversity in musical form, which in turn leads to musical innovation; this musical innovation leads to market competition, which results in further musical innovation as each record company attempts to find a new musical form to stimulate consumer demand; innovation slows down as record companies strive to gain the largest share of the market for the most popular new musical form

(secondary concentration) and finally, this market concentration starts the cycle over again. (Ibid: 478)

Since Peterson and Berger's paper was first published in 1975, a number of researchers have extended the analysis. Most straightforwardly, this has meant updating the time span beyond 1975, but it has also led to significant refinement of how the processes identified by the two authors are measured. Thus, for example, Peterson and Berger examined musical diversity through the number and variation in singles reaching the *Billboard* weekly chart. While this captured diversity well in the 1960s, when singles charts were very significant and sales of singles were high, it is not such a useful indicator in the twenty-first century. Moreover, as pointed out above, large companies have diversified their output partly by introducing large numbers of different 'labels' (which may look like 'independent' companies to the casual consumer). Thus, while advocates of the approach suggest that the cycles idea has much to recommend it, as it captures in general terms some plausible relationships, it needs to recognize the new modes of delivery of music (for example, via downloading) and the way in which large companies have diversified their activities over time. Thus, even if these companies do control 75 per cent of recorded output, it might be thought to be less significant if that output is much more diverse than it was 20 or 30 years ago.

A connected development in the culture industries has been a shift in authority from those people directly concerned with production to those who are essentially concerned with other aspects of the company. Marketing and finance departments grow in importance by comparison to those concerned with production (Abercrombie 1991: 177). The different dimensions of what this actually means for the working practices in a record company and the promotion of artists is examined in more detail in chapter 2. However, it has been argued that rises in employment in the marketing and administration areas of the music industry have sometimes offset falls, which have taken place in employment in manufacturing. An example of this occurred in 1988 in the United Kingdom, when there were: 'a number of pressing plant closures and although the continued buoyancy of the retail market continued to increase employment in marketing and administration, the size of the fall in manufacturing employment reduced total estimated employment in the recording sector by around 150 to just over 9,000' (*Cultural Trends* 1990: 39).

In this chapter so far, attention has concentrated on the most important general aspects of the music industry. The next section considers some different dimensions of the objects that the industry actually produces.

Products of the music industry

The main functional artefacts (Gendron 1986 – see my Introduction) produced by the music industry are CDs, DVDs and tapes. As is shown by figure 1.3, the most important markets for these products are in the United States, Japan and Europe.

Hung and Morencos have usefully shown the fluctuation in the history of sales for the record industry worldwide. In discussing the period 1969–89, they examine three phases. The first phase, from 1969 to 1978, involved expansion with the value of retail sales increasing from 'USD 2 billion in 1969 to USD 10.2 billion in 1978'

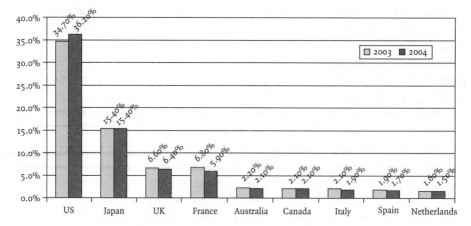

Figure 1.3 Leading world markets as a % of world sales

Source: BPI Statistical Handbook 2005: 103

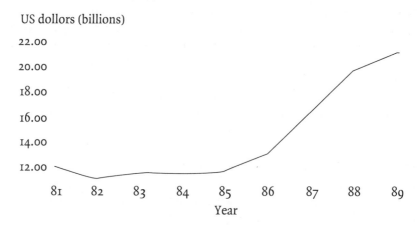

Figure 1.4 World sales of sound recordings, 1981–9

Source: International Federation of the Phonographic Industry 1990

(1990: 64). The second phase, a recession from 1979 to 1984, corresponds to the general world recession and the increased effects of home taping made easier by the market penetration of cassettes. The third, recovery, phase developed from 1985, and the value of sales of sound recordings increased from 1985, as shown by figure 1.4. Hung and Morencos expected that this expansion would continue. Thus, the value of world music sales in 1992 was US$28,893 million, compared with US$26,361 million in 1991. CDs were increasingly important in these sales figures. For example, their worldwide sales value increased from US$975 million in 1991 to US$1,163 million in 1992. However, once the effects of the CD boom began to wear off, sales began to contract, and the retail value of world sales fell from US$39,716 in 2000 to US$33,614 in 2004. Over this period, sales of CDs fell from 2,454 million units in 2000 to 2,111 units in 2004, while DVD sales went from 12 million units to 180 million units over the same period (British Phonographic Industry 2005: 102). Other aspects and trends in sales are considered in chapter 7, from the point of view of the consumption of music. The substitution of the purchase of CDs by downloading practices is addressed later in this chapter.

Three important themes can be noted from the review carried out in this section. First, the market for records and tapes is concentrated in the USA, Japan and Europe, though the value of the markets in other areas of the world can be expected to grow rapidly. Second, there have been significant fluctuations in the value of the market. Third, the value of sales is significantly affected by technological change and innovation in the ways in which music is carried. However, it is very important that other means of the generation of income are examined, as these can be seen as increasingly salient, and the chapter now turns to this area.

Income from rights

The manufacture and sale of discs, DVDs and tapes are obviously major sources of income for the popular music industry. However, income derived from rights is also very significant and 'a considerable part of the turn-over of the music industry is now being derived from "the exchange of immaterial items" based on the rights to produce a musical work or its performance' (Fabbri, 'Copyright: The Dark Side of The Music Business', *World Beat*, 1991, pp. 109–14, as quoted by Negus 1992: 12). Frith contends that:

> For the music industry the age of manufacture is now over. Companies (and company profits) are no longer organised around making *things* but depend on the creation of *rights*. In the industry's own jargon, each piece of music represents 'a basket of rights'; the company task is to exploit as many of these rights as possible, not just those realised when it is sold in recorded form to the public, but also those realised when it is broadcast on radio or television, used on a film, commercial or video soundtrack, and so on.
> (1987: 57)

In the context of the music industry, copyright centres on intellectual property right, which is 'the right given to the creators of original literary, dramatic, musical and artistic works, and [which] also extends to the creators of original sound recordings, films, broadcasts, cable programmes and the typographic arrangement of published editions' (*Cultural Trends* 1993: 56). In addition, 'The concept of copyright embodies the further principle that although the creator of the work may want to retain the copyright, he may allow others to use his material providing they pay him for it' (ibid.: 56). As is shown in figure 1.5, *three* types of right can be identified, which are collected on different bases. Frith shows that these rights are subject to international variations. Thus, 'France and the USA, for example, have never acknowledged a performing right in records as such (and it was not until the 1976 Act that jukebox operators in the USA had to get a license from ASCAP/BMI for their use of songs as songs)' (Frith 1987: 58; for more detail, see also Marshall 2005). A problem for the individual copyright owner is the collection of the income which should stem from the ownership of such rights. Therefore, income from these rights is collected on behalf of copyright owners by collecting societies.

The three types of right identified in figure 1.5 are sometimes further grouped into performing and mechanical. The Performing Right Society (PRS), which was founded in 1914, is the principal collecting agency for performing

Right	Basis for collection
Performing	'for use of the musical material . . . collected on behalf of writers and publishers when music is performed or broadcast'
Public performance	'paid for the privilege of broadcasting or playing the actual recording (rather than the song) in public'
Mechanical	'paid to the copyright holder every time a particular song or piece of music is recorded'

Figure 1.5 Rights in the music industry

Source: Negus 1992: 13

rights in Britain. Its membership is split between writers, publishers and copyright owners and successors. In 2005, there were 36,748 writer members, 2,261 publisher members and 1,813 successor members. The distributable income of the society in 2004 was £256 million (see <www.mcps-prs-alliance.co.uk>).

Phonographic Performance Limited (PPL), which was founded in 1935, collects royalties for record companies and artists in the United Kingdom. There are 3,000 record company members and 30,000 performer members of the society, and revenue is of the order of £80 million per annum (see <www.ppluk.com>).

Mechanical copyright income is collected in Britain by the Mechanical Copyright Protection Society (MCPS), which was founded in 1924. 'The MPCS represents some thousands of composers and publishers of music in the UK, and agreements with reciprocal companies overseas effectively give it representation of over one million composers and music publishers around the world' (*Cultural Trends* 1993: 60). In 2005, MCPS had 13,314 writer members and 4,921 publisher members. In 1998 MCPS and PRS formed an 'operational alliance' under one management team (see<www.mcps-prs-alliance.co.uk>).

Frith has further argued that the contemporary music industry is beyond this world, where exploitation of rights is central, to a different structure:

> In this multi-media setting the relationship of intellectual and industrial property is once more confused, and it increasingly seems that pop stars are better thought of as designer goods rather than as creative artists. The importance of image for sales – whether specific images like A-Ha or corporate images applied (as with Duran Duran) to every aspect of 'company' product (records, posters, tee shirts, videos, etc., etc.) – puts musicians under the protection of trade mark and registered design rather than that of copyright. (1987: 72)

As Lury explains: 'A trademark provides a legal shield around the name, slogan, shape, or character image and, in conjunction with product licensing, makes it possible for the original proprietor to transfer this sign to second and third parties for a limited period of time in exchange for royalties' (1993: 85).

It has been suggested that such developments are taking place across a number of different media. Indeed, it may be that they enable performers to move between different media more easily through the transfer of their image, and thus to break down the divisions which exist between media. What has been termed 'branding' – 'the forging of links of image and perception between a range of products' (ibid.: 87) – facilitates the development of images that are transferable between different media and into increasingly diverse spheres of consumption. For example, Kusek and Leonhard argue:

> Hip-hop culture has become a de-facto part of mainstream culture through the combined power of music, merchandise, and marketing. Brands such as Baby Phat, Roc-A-Wear, Sean Jean, Phat Farm, Shandy, and Snoop Dogg are among the leading brands of hip-hop inspired clothing and merchandising businesses and are making many of hip-hop's smartest artists very wealthy. According to Simons Lathan Media Group, 45.3 million consumers worldwide spend $12.6 billion annually on hip-hop media and merchandise. The hip-hop success formula has a lot more to do with creating far-reaching musician business than just selling CDs. (2005: 118)

Such transferability of images means that the music industry is increasingly connected to other media industries. This process is clearly speeding up under the impact of the digitalization of cultural goods, where boundaries between CDs and DVDs are being eroded and television, radio, MP3 and telephones are being integrated. As is discussed elsewhere in this book (especially chapters 2 and 5), one of the implications of these developments is the increasingly prominent view that the music industry should not be examined primarily in terms of *manufacturing* but in the context of the promotion of images and signs. Thus, it may be equally seen as a *service* industry, where the product is an experience. In important respects, advertising and promotional practices (Wernick 1991; Lury 1993) are central to contemporary culture. They are not simply added on to a previously produced product. Promotion of goods across different sectors is increasingly important. Madonna is not simply a recording artist, but an image that connects a number of different areas of culture. Of course, problems arise for the images and the companies whose profitability is connected to it when the personal life of the real person affects the image.

If the image definition of such products or brands is clear enough, they can be sold all over the world, without alterations for different cultures and markets, rather like Coca-Cola, for example. This sort of characterization leads to three important issues: the way in which media are converging, the effects of new technologies on the protection of rights and the globalization of the music industry and its products.

Digitization and downloading

It is clear that the development of digitalization is leading to the convergence of technologies; for example, CDs are now often sold with a 'bonus' DVD, DVDs are increasingly sold in stores that were previously devoted to music and music is available on mobile phones. This process is likely to continue to break down the 'barriers' between the different products and further facilitate the sort of branding described by Lury. Second, the advance of computer-based technology has major

Box 1.4 'Music industry scuppers pirates'

'Online legal downloads have risen tenfold in the past year'
Owen Gibson
Media correspondent

The music industry yesterday claimed that it was winning its global battle against online piracy as it revealed figures showing that legal downloads had risen tenfold during the past year.

Trade body the International Federation of the Phonographic Industry, said that music fans in the United States and Europe downloaded more than 200m tracks during 2004, up from about 20m over the previous year.

The digital music industry is now worth £177m in Europe a figure expected to double this year. Some record companies estimate that the digital market could be worth 25% of total sales by 2009, compared with the present 1.5%.

After being caught out in the late 1990s by the rapid rise in online piracy, record executives said the tide had turned during the last year through a combination of legal action against pirates and the widespread availability of around a million tracks through legal services such as Napster and Apple's iTunes Music Stores.

Barney Wragg, vice-president of the eLabs division at Universal Music, said that in the coming year labels would come up with new ways of marketing digital music online, such as releasing songs exclusively on the web, and start to exploit their back catalogue of deleted albums. The biggest selling single over the internet last year was Vertigo by U2. The majority of existing CD catalogues released by the major tables, with the notable exception of The Beatles, is now also available online.

The number of websites offering legal music around the world has also mushroomed in the past year, more than quadrupling to around 230. Apple's iTunes, buoyed by the success of its digital music player the iPod, remains by far the most popular way of legally buying music online. In the largest market, the US, the Californian company has a 70% market share.

'At long last the threat has become the opportunity', said IFPI chairman and chief executive John Kennedy, and pointed to new research showing that for the first time as many people were downloading music legally as were copying it for nothing.

An IFPI survey showed that 44% of people who downloaded now did so legally, while the same proportion continued to use illegal services. The number of illegal files downloaded fell by 30m to 870m.

But Mr Kennedy said that the industry would keep up the legal pressure, both on individual file sharers and the companies behind the peer to peer software, which allow users to swap pirated tracks.

Trade bodies around the world sued 7,000 people during 2004, including the first cases brought in the UK. 'There is more litigation to come in more countries in 2005. It's necessary and while it's not always popular we have to carry on,' said Mr Kennedy.

A crucial test case against file-sharing service Kazaa in Australia concluded at the end of last year with a decision expected in April. An application against a similar operation, Grokster, will be considered by the US supreme court next month. Record companies are also planning to step up their campaign to persuade Apple and Microsoft to come to an agreement over their competing standards for downloads.

At present owners of Apple's iTunes can only download songs from the company's own online music store. Microsoft's technology, used by most other download sites including Napster, works with a range of players manufactured by Apple's rivals but not with the market-leading iPod. Mr Wragg said the labels were doing 'everything they could' to encourage interoperability between the sites.

Source: Guardian, 20 January 2005, p. 23

implications in the context of rights. The development of file-sharing technologies and their promotion by companies such as Napster led very rapidly to legal action by the music industry in 1999. Napster closed in 2000. Since then, the culture industry has developed the 'legal' system of paying for downloads (the new 'legal' Napster opened in 2004 in the UK). It is very likely that this mode of distribution will continue to develop in importance (see box 1.4 and also chapter 7). It is a significant next step in the process described by Frith, as there is no purchase of a physical object. McLeod argues that this is very good news for the big companies, as '[i]n the world of digital distribution, there are few costs associated with manufacturing and distributing a physical object, whereas costs are built into getting CDs into stores' (2005: 526). This reinforces the general point about the significance of rights, which have always been tightly policed by the industry. While concerns about physical piracy are still high on the agenda (for a detailed consideration, see Marshall 2005), it is likely that new issues will continue to arise in this context with the advance of technology.

While there is much room for speculation about current changes, there seems little doubt that there is potential for significant transformation to be brought about through such technological and practical shifts. This is likely to reinforce the historical significance of the rights, brands and trademarks described so far. While detailed academic study of this area is currently in train, there has been speculation (akin to a form of futurology) about what this might mean for the industry (and for audience practices – see chapter 9). A readable example of such speculation can be found in the work of Kusek and Leonhard. A significant part of their argument concerns the popularity of music and the growth of music consumption in the broad sense (one aspect of this is an increase in the revenue gained from live performance of music). They argue that in the future music will be like water, i.e. 'ubiquitous and free flowing' (2005: 3). Music will be available on-stream, as it were, like water from a tap. It will be consumed via technologies that allow enhanced listening on the move and while engaged in a range of everyday activities. It could also be paid for as a form of subscription (like paying a quarterly or monthly water bill) and therefore turned on and off like a tap. Despite the irony of this comparison at a time when, in Britain, the London-based media have been full of periodic concern about drought and water shortage, the specific dimensions of this model bear further consideration.

A key aspect of the idea is that forms of music sharing, as in peer to peer networks (P2P) and downloading, are popular with consumers and that these practices and the technologies that support them are throwing the music industry into crisis. Thus, despite the development of the 'legal' Napster and other such services:

> Using approaches similar to Napster, but technically and legally more insidious and clever, companies and P2P file-sharing systems including Kazaa, Morpheus, Grokster, iMesh and Limewire have grown stronger than Napster ever was. It is estimated that hundreds of millions of copies of these free software applications have been downloaded, and that millions of people are online trading music files every minute of everyday around the world. No wonder the record labels are worried. (Ibid.: 5–6)

However, while the sales value of CDs has declined, there is not a simple substitution going on. Kusek and Leonhard's argument here is rather similar to some of those considered earlier in this chapter, namely that CDs have been expensive, range has been reduced in retail outlets and there has been a lack of innovation on the part of the music industry – and so on. Kusek and Leonhard argue that instead of trying to fight the developments in downloading techniques, the music industry should accommodate them by introducing a new approach to copyright. Given what has been shown in this chapter so far, that the protection of rights has been central to the music industry, the music industry is unlikely to relinquish this very significant income stream. However, it is possible that new modes of delivery and protection can be developed. In Kusek and Leonhard's view, this should mean that the interests of musicians are protected, as 'once the mechanisms of performance royalty collection are adapted to address the new modes of song usage, music "renting", and distribution, performance royalty collection and publishing will take the lead as the primary source of compensation for musicians' (ibid.: 26). Moreover, 'ultimately, publishing will, by default, become inseparable from distribution' (ibid.).

What is needed then in this view is for the music industry to adapt to the new consumer and technological realities, and to incorporate the new practices: 'Just as ASCAP or BMI collect blanket licensing fees from radio stations, so could similar organizations collect blanket licensing fees from the P2P companies or ISPs, who could in turn charge the customers for access via their systems' (ibid.: 128). While there is much scope for speculation about these changes, there is no doubt that significant shifts are in train. These issues are reinforced by the impact of globalization.

Globalization and the transmission of music

It was explained earlier in this chapter that the main markets for pop music products are in the United States, Europe and Japan. The United States and Britain

Figure 1.6 Cultural exchange

Source: Wallis and Malm 1990: 173; first pub. in Wallis and Malm 1984

have in turn dominated the production of popular music for sale in the world market (Negus 1992; see also Burnett 1996). It seems likely that world markets will be increasingly opened up to the products of these music industries. Though often relatively small in terms of size, the markets in many of the countries outside the established main markets are among some of the fastest growing in the world. These include countries in Latin America (e.g. Bolivia and Chile), Eastern Europe (e.g. Poland and Hungary), Africa (e.g. Nigeria), the Middle East (e.g. Israel) and Asia (e.g. Taiwan). It seems obvious that the nature of domestic music production may be affected by the attempts of the big music companies to sell in these markets.

Such a process is but a specific example of the process that has been characterized as 'globalization'. There has been a major debate concerning this idea (and, in a wider sense, considerable political protest around it) since the late 1980s (Robertson and White 2005). It was argued that new modes of global connection had been developed on the basis of a range of economic and political processes such as state deregulation and economic restructuring. While at one point it seemed possible to suggest that such a process was likely to lead to the obliteration of 'local' cultural forms, writers on globalization realized that this was not happening in any straightforward sense. To take account of this process, the concept of 'glocalization' was coined by Robertson (1995) to capture the way that globalization was producing new modes of local attachment (for further discussion of these issues, see Savage et al. 2005).

In such a globalizing context, Wallis and Malm (1990: 173–8) have argued that patterns of cultural transmission can be classified into four types: 'cultural exchange', 'cultural dominance', 'cultural imperialism' and 'transculturation'. In cultural exchange (see figure 1.6): 'two or more cultures or subcultures interact and exchange features under fairly loose forms and more or less equal terms' (ibid.: 173). An example of this process would be the (illegal) copying of a CD which is exchanged on a reciprocal basis with a friend. In more global terms, it could entail the ways in which reggae adopted elements from American soul groups which have then been fed back to African forms in subsequent years (see, for example, the work of Cheikh Lô).

In cultural dominance (see figure 1.7), by contrast, one form of culture is imposed by a powerful group on a weaker one. For example, in school we may be forced to listen to particular forms of music to the exclusion of others because the approved forms were perceived to be proper music. Such a process occurred on a wider scale in Africa, where 'missionaries working in Kenya and Tanzania supported by a colonial administration exerted pressure on local culture. Schools were established at mission stations where native pupils were taught a mixture of European and Christian values and music' (ibid.: 175).

Culture 1

Culture 2

Figure 1.7 Cultural dominance

Source: Wallis and Malm 1990: 174; first pub. in Wallis and Malm 1984

Culture 1

Forms of culture ┊ Money resources

Culture 2

Figure 1.8 Cultural imperialism

Source: Wallis and Malm 1990: 175; first pub. in Wallis and Malm 1984

In cultural imperialism (see figure 1.8), 'cultural dominance is augmented by the transfer of money and/or resources from dominated to dominating culture group' (ibid.). Wallis and Malm suggest that 'examples of the money transferred are profits made by subsidiaries of record companies belonging to the dominating culture, or copyright money. The resources can be gifted musicians, pieces of music, or unique traditional musical instruments which are removed to museums in a dominating culture area' (ibid.). It has been argued that the dominance of the United States in the transmission of music represents a form of cultural imperialism. This was a great concern in Britain in the 1950s when commentators such as Richard Hoggart (1958) were appalled by the prospect of the Americanization of British popular culture by rock 'n' roll and other American cultural forms (Hebdige 1988).

Garofalo has pointed to three main problems with this thesis of cultural imperialism. He argues, first, that it tends to underestimate the amount of resistance to domination that can occur, even in subjugated cultures. Second, he maintains that it tends to 'conflate economic power and cultural effects' (Garofalo 1992a: 4). It is important to recognize in this argument that cultural dominance does not simply follow economic dominance. Third, he contends that the cultural imperialism thesis often rests on the premise that unspoilt cultures of the dominated are corrupted by the imposed cultures from the west. In criticism of this aspect of the cultural imperialism thesis, Collins argues that the forms of 'Western' music that are influential in South Africa are actually developments of forms which were earlier exported from Africa in the days of slavery. These forms are being reclaimed in interaction with music developed along a different route in Africa itself. Collins argues that:

· 20th century African popular performers have found three ways of circumventing the problem of 'cultural imperialism' and producing a viable

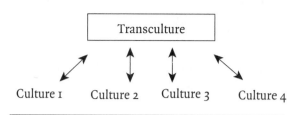

Figure 1.9 Transculture

Source: Wallis and Malm 1990: 177; first pub. in Wallis and Malm 1984

contemporary art form in touch with the common person. These are
through the progressive Africanisation or de-acculturation of genres which
were initially modelled on foreign ones, by the creative use of the black
dance-music 'feedback' from the New World, and by continuing the old
African tradition of protest music. (1992: 194)

Garofalo's view is that reality is more complicated than the thesis of cultural
imperialism allows and that the complexities may be better understood through
the concept of transculturation.

'Transculturation' is the result of the worldwide establishment of the
transnational corporations in the field of culture, the corresponding spread of
technology, and the development of worldwide marketing networks for what can
be termed transnationalized culture, or 'transculture' (Wallis and Malm, 1990: 176;
see figure 1.9). The emergence of 'world music' could be seen as an example of
this process. Another term which therefore could be used for this sort of culture
is *global* culture. The music of Madonna or Michael Jackson might be said to be
transcultural, or a form of global culture. As Garofalo argues: 'Can it be that the
25 million or so people outside the United States who bought Michael Jackson's
Thriller were all simply the unwitting dupes of imperialist power? Or, is it
conceivable that Jackson produced an album which resonated with the cultural
sensibilities of a broad international audience?' (1992a: 6).

The effects of this process may be leading towards the creation of what
Appadurai has called 'mediascapes':

'Mediascapes', whether produced by private or state interests, tend to be
image-centered, narrative-based accounts of strips of reality, and what they
offer to those who experience and transform them is a series of elements
(such as characters, plots and textual forms) out of which scripts can be
formed of imagined lives, their own as well as those of others living in other
places. (1990: 299)

Thus, it may be that globally we are witnessing the creation and expansion of
mediascapes made up of a variety of elements which are used in alternative ways in
different places by particular groups of people. Furthermore, such mediascapes
would not be the product of one group or controlling organization, but involve
complex negotiations and struggles around the placing together of different
elements. The mediascape is like a landscape, in that it can be seen in different

ways from alternative perspectives and is relatively open to different uses. The idea suggests that configurations of media are very complex, and that whilst they are affected by the operation of power, they are not simply subject to the whims of powerful corporations or governments. A landscape may be affected by the decisions of the powerful – a motorway may be built through it for instance – but such decisions may be fought, or parts of the landscape may come under the control of smaller owners, and so on.

In this sort of approach the attempt is made to move away from more simplistic accounts resting on notions of the overpowering strength of a few capitalist corporations who can do more or less as they want. It suggests that more attention should be paid to the production (and consumption) of music in specific local contexts, as part of a consideration of the interaction of the global and the local. However, it is important to recognize the leading role of large corporations and to study their aims and the potential effects they can have in a detailed fashion.

Three summary points can be made. First, these processes are dynamic and contradictory. As can be argued, globalization does not mean that everything is becoming the same. As Tomlinson suggests:

> From the instrumental point of view of capitalism, then, connectivity works towards increasing a *functional* proximity. It doesn't make all places the same, but creates globalized spaces and connecting corridors which ease the flow of capital (including its commodities and its personnel) by matching the time-space compression of connectivity with a degree of cultural 'compression'. (1999: 7)

What is occurring is what Tomlinson, following Robertson, terms 'unicity' – 'a sense that the world is becoming, for the first time in history, a single social and cultural setting' (ibid.: 9). In one sense this defines the nature of the transculture discussed in this section so far.

Second, different aspects of globalization are connected. Thus, the consumption of a CD as part of a way of life of an individual (see chapter 9) will depend on the social interaction of those who made it (see chapter 2), who may be globally separated, the political processes that facilitate trade and the economic patterns of production and organization that led to it being produced and marketed (see chapters 2 and 3).

Third, the practices of globalization are contested This may be the overt struggle that has led to violent and explicit confrontations around specific meetings of the global elite, the organization of pop/rock concerts, and so on. However, the practices of hybridization also involve modes of contestation as well as accommodation and the production of new forms through collaboration.

Thus, Appadurai's approach (see also Appadurai 1996) is very important as it draws attention to how people reconstruct their patterns of local living as they confront a range of other people and processes, as well as how they imagine other places and processes to be (see further Savage et al. 2005). A number of studies of musical reconstitution in different parts of the world can be seen as offering evidence for the complex reconstitution of cultural forms rather than the obliteration of one by another (Taylor 1997; Bennett 2000).

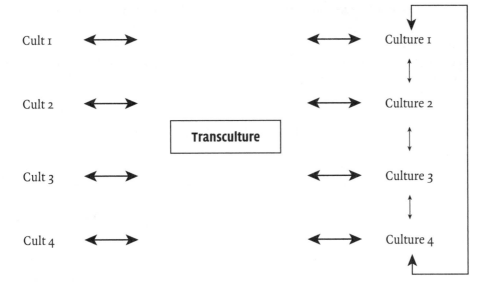

Figure 1.10 Glocalization

Ho (2003) shows how the development of Cantopop in Hong Kong (music that is sung in Cantonese) emerged in the 1970s as a 'local' form in response to the desire for music in the local language rather than in English or Mandarin Chinese. This is termed a process of localization. However, as time passed, Cantopop has itself been promoted by the large record companies, and has been influenced by musical innovation in other parts of the world. In this sense, Ho argues, it is multicultural. Indeed, as the need to increase market share has come further to the fore, Cantopop artists now sing in Mandarin as well and have explored a range of different genres, not just 'formulaic romantic ballads and brain-dead dance tunes' (ibid.: 151). Hong Kong pop has thus been influenced by music from the USA and Britain, as well as Japan, China, Taiwan and Korea. In the production of 'new creative fusions', '[t]he story of Hong Kong pop in its global–local interaction is not only a case of cultural (western) imperialism and the Asianisation of Asia, but also involves a process of negotiated cultural identities as expressed in the language of Cantonese and other representational means' (ibid.: 154). Similar sorts of argument can be made about the effects of rock in China (de Kloet 2003).

As such ideas progress, it can be suggested that a new stage of development has been reached in addition to that discussed by Wallis and Malm. As well as producing a transculture and feeding back to it, local cultures are also relating to other cultures and how they are imagined to be. Such a characterization can be represented diagrammatically, as at figure 1.10.

Summary

This chapter has considered:

- the current patterns of ownership and control in the pop music industry, pointing to the concentration of the industry by conglomerates;

- the status of 'independent' record companies and the ideas of Fordism and post-Fordism;
- the nature of the markets for the products of the pop music industry;
- the importance of copyright, distinguishing different types of right, the value of the income they generate and the membership of the collecting societies in the United Kingdom;
- the possible replacement of copyright by trademark;
- arguments concerning the potential impact of digitization;
- some characterizations of processes of cultural exchange and transmission, including a discussion of the thesis of cultural imperialism and trends towards transculturation, globalization and glocalization.

The Social Production of Music

This chapter examines a number of different aspects of the production of music. The components of such production are set out clearly in box 2.1. Some of the aspects of the industry referred to in the box have already been examined in chapter 1, especially lesson 4 on publishing. This chapter focuses on the more 'micro' aspects of the production of music. It begins with a discussion of the most important sociological studies of musicians. Without musicians there would be no music – and consequently no music industry at all. However, it has been argued that, as a result of technological advance, the musician is being replaced by machines. This chapter considers this argument, especially in the final section on the issue of the effects of technological change.

Box 2.1 The music industry in 10 easy lessons

1 *The band* A group of hopefuls, longing for a hit record, for fame, fortune, and *Top of the Pops*.
2 *The manager* The manager's role is to mother the band, to organize their day-to-day life, to negotiate work and contracts. A manager's primary function is to take care of business and finances. 'Super-managers' such as Simon Napier-Bell (Marc Bolan, Wham!), who help create their acts and often manage a whole stable of artists, still exist, as do management agencies; but more often they are simply friends who become involved. More and more women are entering this area.
3 *The A & R department* Unless they want to produce their record completely independently, a band's first aim is to get a record contract. Every company has an A & R (Artists and Repertoire) department. A & R workers – most of whom are men – go out to gigs and listen to tapes that are sent in. If they like a band or artist, they will usually commission a demo-tape to be made fairly quickly in a small studio; if that turns out well, the act will be signed to the label.

The A & R department is sometimes known as 'Um & Ah', due to its indecisiveness.

4 *Publishing* Every time a song is played on the radio or TV, or is performed by someone else, royalties are due to the writers. Their collection is dependent on the song having been published, and most record companies now have their own publishing companies. A group writing their own material may choose to set up their own company or to sign to someone else. Publishing companies spend their time looking for potential hit song writers. Like A & R, they are responsible for signing new names, and they also collect royalties from cover versions and plays of work published by them.

5 *The studio* The control-room is run by two, sometimes three, people. The *producer's* job is to direct the overall sound. Some, like Phil Spector, impose their ideas on artists who are there simply to make the basic noise he wants. Most, however, work with the artists, offering criticisms and suggestions until both sides are reasonably happy. The *engineer* makes the machinery do what the producer wants, getting the required effect out of the equipment. Increasingly, producers and engineers are working together as a permanent team, moving together from studio to studio to do different sessions, although all studios still have a resident engineer, and sometimes even a house producer. The *tape op*, or second engineer, is essentially a luxury employed by larger studios to help the engineer, set up equipment, make tea, etc. Producers, engineers and tape ops are nearly always men, as are the technicians and studio managers; studio bookings are invariably handled by women.

6 *Production, packing and sales* From the studio, the tapes are taken and made into masters, the mould from which records are pressed in the factory. A sleeve is designed and printed, the records are put inside them, and they are then packed and sent out to the shops. Dealers can phone in with orders, but chainstores such as Our Price and W. H. Smiths will negotiate huge bulk orders of records they think will be popular. Records are also sold by reps, who go round shops trying to persuade managers to buy their product. Though the travelling reps are usually men, most of the work involved in getting a record from cutting to shop is done by women. The larger the company, the more likely it is that all the work will have been carried out by their own staff: smaller companies will employ outside agencies or pay multinationals such as EMI to press, pack, distribute or market their records.

7 *Promotion* When the record is released, the priority is to get it played on the radio. This is the job of the promotions department, whose 'pluggers' try to persuade radio-show producers and DJs to give their songs airplay (by taking them out to dinner, for instance). This department also ensures that record shops have advertising posters and display their records, and that the shops are provided with tour programmes and other promotional material. The artist and/or their publishing company may also decide to employ independent pluggers to push certain records.

8 *Press* Meanwhile, the press department is working hard to get our budding stars splashed all over the media. They liaise with the media, commission photo sessions for publicity shots, try to get records and gigs reviewed, send out press releases to tell everyone what artists are doing, dream up gimmicks, 'leak' gossip, and approach editors with ideas for stories. Most of this work is done by women and within the record company, although some people prefer to hire their own publicists/agencies.

9 *Touring* In general, the bigger the show, the bigger the entourage. Any tour will usually have roadies to move and set up equipment, lighting crews, sound crews, and an engineer to mix the sound live. This area, again, is almost exclusively male.

10 *DJs and journalists* These play an essential part in getting a record across to potential customers!

Source: Steward and Garratt 1984: 60–1

The review of the sociological studies of musicians begins with a consideration of those accounts that focus on groups of musicians, particularly the pioneering work of Howard Becker. This introduces a number of themes concerning the relationship between making music and being artistic. These are considered in more detail through the work of Frith and Horne (1987) before the section concludes with a review of some of the most important studies of music-making in particular local environments.

The next section looks at the most important aspects of what goes on in record companies and the recording process itself. A particular focus here is on the changing role of the producer and the nature of social processes in the studio. The third main section in the chapter picks up the issue of the role of technological change in some detail. It first considers the more general relations between technology and society before applying these themes to contemporary pop music.

Musicians: culture, social origins, and performance

Jazz musicians

One of the earliest and most important discussions of the culture of a group of musicians was written by the American sociologist Howard Becker (1963). Despite having worked as a jazz musician himself, Becker was primarily interested in jazz musicians as a 'deviant group' in connection with his revision of the sociology of deviance vis-à-vis the thesis of labelling, rather than with detailed investigation of their occupational culture. Basing his account on the participant observation of jazz musicians in Chicago, Champaign-Urbana (Illinois) and Kansas City (Missouri), mainly in 1948–9, Becker focused on the following points:

(1) the conceptions that musicians have of themselves and of the non-musicians for whom they work and the conflict they feel to be inherent in

this relation; (2) the basic consensus underlying the reactions of both commercial and jazz musicians to this conflict; and (3) the feelings of isolation musicians have from the larger society and the way they segregate themselves from audience and community. (1963: 83)

He argued that these jazz musicians explicitly differentiated themselves from the rest of society, calling non-musicians 'squares'. The musician, as an artist, was expected to deviate from conventional ways of behaving. The 'square' was ignorant of the ways of musicians, but was also feared as 'the ultimate source of commercial pressure' (ibid.: 90). Thus, the musician wished to follow his or her artistic sensibility and expression, but was in danger of being forced along the lines of commercialism by the dictates of the tastes of the 'square'. The musician reacted to the pressure generated by this situation in one of two main ways: either by remaining within the jazz community and attempting to stay true to his or her artistic beliefs, or by compromising and going commercial. Both reactions were based on dislike of the 'square', which could lead, according to Becker, to the attempt on the part of the musicians to separate themselves physically from the audience.

Becker also discusses the nature of the career of these sorts of musician, extending his analysis to suggest that: 'The antagonistic relationship between musicians and outsiders shapes the culture of the musician and likewise produces the major contingencies and crisis points in his career' (ibid.: 102). He shows how the career of the jazz musician was based on an informal network of connections that made it easier to secure employment. However, those who controlled the most important cliques had adopted the commercial orientation. This further exacerbated the pressure of commercialism and the market on the jazz musician, who sometimes responded by adopting 'the orientation of the craftsman' (ibid.: 112), where the musician was not interested in the music actually being played, but focused on performing in a proficient or correct manner. In summary, with regard to the musician's career, Becker maintains that:

> [T]he emphasis of musicians on freedom from the interference inevitable in their work creates a new dimension of professional prestige which conflicts with the previously discussed job prestige in such a way that one cannot rank high in both. The greatest rewards are in the hands of those who have sacrificed their artistic independence, and who demand a similar sacrifice from those they recruit for these higher positions. This creates a dilemma for the individual musician, and his response determines the future course of his career. Refusing to submit means that all hope of achieving jobs of high prestige and income must be abandoned, while giving in to commercial pressures opens the way to success for them. (Ibid.: 113–14)

Becker argues that the family acts a constraint or 'problem' for the male jazz musician, whose desire for freedom often clashes with the views of parents for the younger musician, and of wives for older players. The jazz musicians therefore expressed, and attempted to live out, a particular type of masculinity, based around notions of freedom of artistic expression and liberation from family ties. The centrality of this to male musicians is brought home by the analysis of women musicians by Bayton (1990, 1998), who shows that women musicians had to cope with the demands of children and family life in a way that male musicians did not. Thus, babysitting arrangements would be the woman's responsibility and children and babies would often have to be taken to band practices, something that was never the case for male musicians.

Becker's work is important because it identifies some key aspects of the culture of this group of musicians, including the difference between art and commerce, and the dislike of the audiences who do not understand 'art'. However, it may not be possible to generalize from this group, which was studied at a particular time and place. It is important therefore to broaden this analysis by bringing it up to date and by examining other forms of music.

Christian (1987) and White (1987) also examined and observed the nature of jazz by themselves playing in jazz bands. White studied a professional band's engagement at a jazz club in Zurich and Christian researched various semi-professional bands in the English Midlands. White echoes many of Becker's points in his discussion, noting, for example, how some jazz musicians suggested that he should learn to read music, as 'you can do the shows and the cabaret thing – there's a lot of bread in all that game' (White 1987: 199). Furthermore, he argues that the lack of stability in the lives of the male jazz musicians interfered with the possibility of a stable family life (ibid.: 212).

The musicians studied by Christian had avoided the pressures of commercialization by not becoming, or attempting to become, full-time jazz musicians. They earned small amounts of money, which were normally sufficient only to cover their costs and expenses (and in some cases not even these). The groups were subject to the market but mainly in the form of ensuring that they had a place to play. As Christian explains:

> [There is a] precarious and fluctuating balance between, on the one hand, efforts to maintain musical integrity as expressed in the values and conventions held by most jazz musicians – that their music is not primarily a commercial commodity but a creative artistic activity – and, on the other hand, the need to operate within a market situation in order to find opportunities to play . . . compromises have to be made, sometimes in terms of what they play but more often in terms of the level of payment they can expect . . . most semi-pro jazzmen would rather not play at all than completely sell out to popular taste. (1987: 238–9)

The two main themes revealed first by Becker have been reinforced through this brief review of contemporary jazz musician culture: first, the way in which musicians distinguish commerce from art; and, second, the desire for the musician to be perceived as an artist, rather than subservient to commercial goals (see also autobiographies and biographies of jazz stars that have much to say on these dilemmas: e.g. Carr 1999; Cole 2001; Davis 1990). These themes also run through much contemporary rock and pop music, where they have been confronted in alternative ways by musicians in different social circumstances, as is shown in the next part of this section.

Art and pop

The most comprehensive tracing of the interconnections between art and pop music can be found in the work of Frith and Horne. Developing some aspects of the work of Becker, they are interested in 'how, in art schools, a particular tension between creativity and commerce is confronted and how pop music works as a solution' (1987: 3). They identify the structure and changing nature of the place of art schools in the English education system, and show how attempts to make the art schools more vocational and responsive to the needs of industry have run up against the widely held conception of what it means to be an artist (ibid.: 30). The 'romantic' notion of the artist as a 'bohemian' entails ideas about individual creativity, freedom of artistic expression, the conflict between true art and the market, and so on.

From the late 1940s and early 1950s, when they connected to and bred a mode of appreciation of black American jazz, the art schools went on to attract and produce a significant number of the most important and influential rock musicians of subsequent decades. Frith and Horne identify three main waves of musicians: the rock bohemians, who 'simply picked up the bohemian attitude and carried it with them into progressive rock' (ibid.: 100), the pop art bands 'who applied art theories to pop music making' (Frith and Horne 1987: 100) and the pop situationists, who were central to the development of punk rock in the late 1970s. Some of the musicians and colleges involved are listed in figure 2.1. The art colleges provided spaces for these bands and musicians to rehearse and practise, and often their first audiences from other students at the college. The later musicians and bands, as well as some of their managers, wanted to put into practice some contemporary ideas about the relation between art and society and the political role of art through pop music. The art education of Malcolm McLaren, the future manager of the Sex Pistols, which is set out in box 2.2, is illustrative of some of the main themes outlined by Frith and Horne.

The earlier rock bohemians espoused notions of artistic freedom and individualism, which developed into their own attempts to produce pieces of rock art, often 'complex' in form. It was possible at that moment to sell lots of records (as albums) and still not be seen to be 'selling out' to the marketplace, thus 'solving' the dilemma of the jazz musicians identified by Becker, by integrating art and commerce. The later situationists were more aware of the intertwining of pop, commerce and art. They didn't see the need to be 'authentic' artists and, as such, above commerce, since, as far as they were concerned, art and commerce were inextricably linked and art could not exist without commercial relationships, which were not necessarily to be criticized. The art industry could be exploited from within; there was no need to attempt to create a 'pure' space outside it.

In his book *Lipstick Traces*, Greil Marcus (1993) points to the interconnections between the Dadaist art movement of the Cabaret Voltaire in Zurich in 1916, the Lettrists in France in the 1940s and '50s, the Situationists in Paris in the 1950s and '60s and punk rock in Britain in the 1970s. Such interconnections between art and pop music are also traced by Savage (1991) and for American punk by Heylin (1993). They came to the fore in the 1970s and have remained there ever since,

College	Musician
Liverpool	John Lennon, Deaf School, Orchestral Manoeuvres in the Dark
Newcastle	Eric Burdon
Sidcup	Phil May, Dick Taylor, Keith Richards
Ealing	Ron Wood, Pete Townsend, Thunderclap Newman, Freddy Mercury
Kingston	Eric Clapton, Keith Relf, Sandy Denny, John Renbourne, Tom McGuiness
Camberwell	Syd Barrett
Wimbledon	Jeff Beck
Hornsey	Ray Davies, Roger Glover, Adam Ant, Viv Albertine, Mike Barson, G. Lewis, Rob Gotobed, Lester Square, Steve Walsh
Croydon	Mike Vernon
Sutton	Jimmy Page
Harrow	Charlie Watts, Marco Pirroni
Hammersmith	Cat Stevens
Newcastle University	Bryan Ferry
Ipswich/Winchester	Brian Eno
Royal College	John Foxx and Ultravox
St Martin's	Glen Matlock, Lora Logic
Central	Lene Lovich, Les Chappell, Joe Strummer
Epsom	Richard Butler
Northampton	Kevin Haskins and Bauhaus
Coventry	Hazel O'Connor, Jerry Dammers, the Specials, Selecter, 2 Tone movement
Leeds	Marc Almond and Soft Cell, Green Gartside, the Mekons
Manchester	Linder, the Ludus
Edinburgh	Joe Callis, the Rezillos
Sheffield	Richard Kirk

Figure 2.1 Art schools and pop musicians in Britain

Source: Adapted from Frith and Horne 1987

Box 2.2 The art school career of Malcolm McLaren

In autumn 1963 [aged 17] Malcolm started evening classes in life drawing at St Martin's School of Art on Charing Cross Road but his mother objected to the nudes on display, so, still under the thumb of his family he transferred to 3-D design and graphics. To be accepted by the new system of art education, Malcolm needed two extra O levels, and enrolled in an Edgware school for a booster course. He passed, but was in the wrong educational area for St Martin's: instead, he was accepted by Harrow Art School to begin a Dip.AD in autumn 1964 . . . which, in his account of McLaren's early life, Fred Vermorel describes as 'the centre for miles around for Bohemian frenzy, mixing the local gay community with beatniks, drug pedlars, sexual delinquents and Mods'. . . . By degrees Malcolm began to see himself as an avant-gardist, searching for a key with which to unlock his deep anger and resentment. Between 1965 and 1968, he passed through a number of art schools and polytechnics (Reigate, Walthamstow, Chelsea, Chiswick) under a series of names falsified for the purpose of getting grants. Throughout this period he took up and discarded ideas from ideas then in currency. . . . Common to these was the idea of art being indivisible from everyday life, indivisible particularly from commerce and the environment. . . . Malcolm had entered Croydon [Art School] in the autumn of 1967: the course provided him with more freedom than hitherto and, as importantly, a community of peers . . . all were involved in a sit-in that developed in Croydon a week after the famous Hornsey Art School action. On 5 June [1968], the art students barricaded themselves in the annexe at South Norwood and issued a series of impossible demands. . . . After the Croydon sit-in, Malcolm Edwards entered Goldsmiths' in autumn 1968 to study film and photography.

Source: Savage 1991: 18, 23–4, 26, 28–9, 37

reconstituting some of the dilemmas about being an artist and earning a living expressed by earlier generations of musicians. Commentators continue to show the role of arts education in popular music in the UK (see, for example, Harris 2003; Reynolds 2005).

The studies considered in this section so far have focused in the main on more professional musicians. However, music is also made, in the local context, by those who do not, in the immediate future anyway, expect to make a living from it. It is important therefore to consider the social processes at work in this realm. Furthermore, it is important to remember that the musicians discussed by Becker and Frith and Horne will have started their careers by playing in local groups.

Local music-making

One of the most comprehensive and important studies of the nature of local music-making can be found in *On Becoming a Rock Musician* by H. Stith Bennett (1980). While Bennett's study is based mainly on fieldwork done between 1970 and 1972 in the US state of Colorado, its general themes have applicability beyond that place and time. He divides his analysis into four main parts: 'group dynamics', 'rock ecology', 'mastering the technological component' and 'performance: aesthetics and the technological imperative'. Following the approach developed by Becker, Bennett traces the process through which a person becomes a local rock musician and plays to an audience. He identifies a number of stages in such a career, which are summarized in figure 2.2.

The budding rock musician has first to acquire an instrument. Most often, the first source of an instrument is the musician's parents. However, theft has also been used as a way of developing an individual's or a band's resources. There are well-documented cases of this in rock journalism. For example, Savage (1991) describes how Steve Jones of the Sex Pistols stole equipment in the early days of the band, and Rogan (1993) alludes to the illegal activities of Johnny Marr of the Smiths in the pursuit of a new guitar and amplifier. According to Bennett, the

Stage

1 acquiring an instrument
2 finding someone to play with and a place to play
3 increasing skills and forming groups
4 getting songs
5 working-up or 'getting-down'
6 structuring the set
7 finding a gig
8 getting to the gig
9 playing the room

Figure 2.2 Stages in the local rock career
Source: Adapted from Bennett 1980

problems involved in the acquisition of instruments and equipment represent economic barriers to becoming a rock musician.

After the instrument has been acquired, the beginner often attempts to learn to play on his or her own. This might involve attempting to play along with some favourite records. However, most beginners realize that they can learn only so much in this way and begin to seek other musicians to play with. This can happen in different ways, but it often involves contacts with friends or friends of friends, who might form the nucleus of the beginner's first group. Groups form and re-form very quickly and can often be very loose in membership. Further, groups can often re-form out of pools of musicians who have been in a variety of groups. Bennett suggests that this is also often based on networks of friends and acquaintances. However, bulletin boards in colleges, for example, were also significant. In other contexts, advertisements in music papers have brought band members together. After people have come together to form a budding group, it is important for them to find somewhere to practise. Given the space needed and the noise produced by using electric instrumentation, this can often be quite difficult. Garages and basements were the sorts of places often used by the bands studied by Bennett. These factors constitute a social barrier for the budding rock musician.

As has already been noted, Bennett points to a rapid turnover in the membership of groups. He suggests that the relationship between the skills of the individual relative to the rest of the group is very important in this process (summarized in figure 2.3). Bennett gives as a graphic example a 'musical status degradation ceremony':

> We had picked Mike up in Denver where he was sorta hanging out after his group in Texas broke up. For a while there everything was cool and we were playing steady, but we were progressing too . . . you know what I mean? . . . playing new songs and doing originals and getting our sets really together. Then you'd start hearing these mistakes in the bass, it was really ragged . . . just sorta falling apart. The thing is Mike was getting hung up on speed. First he was just popping and finally he was shooting up every morning. And he just looked like shit warmed over. Finally we just had to get rid of him, he was bringing the whole group down. (Piano player, quoted in Bennett 1980: 33)

Individual skills	Group skills		
	decrease	same	increase
decrease	3	4	5
same	9	2	6
increase	8	7	1

Situations 1, 2, and 3 are stable group configurations.
  1 = a 'good' group: the beginning of steady gigs
  2 = a transitional stage: the end of steady gigs
  3 = a disintegrative stage: 'natural death'

Situations 4, 5, and 6 are unstable group configurations which result in 'firing and hiring' – the individual is displayed by the group: an individual status degradation ceremony, or a group status enhancement ceremony.

Situations 7, 8, and 9 are unstable group configurations which result in 'quitting and looking' – the group is displaced by the individual: an individual status enhancement ceremony, or a group status degradation ceremony.

Figure 2.3 The levelling process of attributed musical skills in rock groups

Source: Reprinted from On Becoming a Rock Musician, by H. Stith Bennett (Amherst: University of Massachusetts Press, 1980: 31), copyright © 1980 by The University of Massachusetts Press.

In the main, the sorts of group studied by Bennett were 'copy' groups who relied on non-original material. This meant that group practice and rehearsals mainly involved the 'getting' of songs from a record. The groups did not use sheet music or musical notation in this process, but developed their material by a process of trial and error from the recorded form. There are important issues here concerning the way in which a recorded form, which might involve extensive multi-tracking and over-dubbing, is transformed into something that can be played live by a small group of four or five musicians. Bennett argues that the local musician listens to the recordings with a 'recording consciousness' (1980: 126), which enables the musician to hear the different components of the recordings and the technical aspects of its construction, and to translate them into practical ways of playing in the local group. Furthermore, he suggests:

> [A]fter a song is gotten it must be transformed into a performable entity. After a song may be known in its individual parts it cannot be said that the group knows the song until the process of working-up (which is not so ironically also known as getting-down) has been concluded. (Ibid.: 145)

This involves repetitive practice. The next stage in the process is the organization of the worked-up songs into a set or sets, which often entails thinking through the pacing of the performance and trying to produce an overall effect out of the discrete elements which have been learned as separate songs.

The groups have first to find gigs and then get to them. As this normally involves transporting themselves and the equipment, access to a van is very important and a musician with a van might be accommodated within a group in preference to a more accomplished player without one. Bennett divides gigs into four main categories: social (including sponsored ones with free admission, breakeven and fundraising types), which 'refers to situations which are concerned with pure sociation events, gatherings, which are primarily ends in themselves' (ibid.: 85); ceremonial (for example, weddings); bar; and concert. Concert gigs are relatively rare and are normally played by the local group as a support for the more well-known group. The bar gig is very important to the local group (which, given the male nature of most bars, will affect the potential for participation of women). As Bennett says in general about the bar:

> The economic mainstay of local groups is the local bar. A bar gig is a more complex economic event for the group than either the social or ceremonial one-nighter – it could mean 'Friday and Saturday nights' or 'six nights a week' depending upon the clientele the bar services, but it always means a performance reality which is purchased as entertainment in the same way as mixed drinks and bar chatter. Bar owners and managers consider the group an economic investment which draws customers to the site; from their viewpoint they are paying the group for the number of bodies it pulls through the door. (Ibid.: 91)

The group has to adapt and set up its equipment to play the room, which can affect the nature of the performance and the musical event in different ways. The physical make-up and acoustics of rooms can have effects. There are also important differences between playing inside and outside.

Bennett's book is important in illustrating many different aspects of the local musician's life and career and, like Becker's work, for illuminating some of the dilemmas in the local musician's life: finding someone to play with, deciding what to play, agreeing on the time to practise, and so on. However, despite its continuing general pertinence, it is subject to some limitations: first, it is now rather dated; second, it discusses rock music of a particular type and period; third, it is located in one place in the main; and fourth, the musicians considered are mainly men and Bennett plays little attention to the issue of gender. It is important, therefore, to examine some other, more recent, accounts of local music-making to extend the scope of the approach pioneered by Bennett.

A more recent study of the making of rock music in a local context can be found in *Rock Culture in Liverpool* by Sara Cohen (1991). Cohen spent a year between October 1985 and October 1986 carrying out unstructured interviews and participant observation on 'bands without record contracts that therefore functioned on the margins of the industry' (ibid.: 5). The sorts of band she studied had mostly been together for between two and three years, and consisted of four or five white men aged between 20 and 30. The pattern of instrumentation in the groups tended to be similar, being guitar- and drum-based. Cohen focuses on two of these bands in particular: the Jactars and Crikey it's the Cromptons!

Cohen makes a number of important points about the bands and different aspects of local music-making, some of which echo, in a rather different context, the themes developed by both Becker and Bennett. First, she shows how the groups are based in particular social settings and how important their participation in one studio was – Vulcan Studios in Liverpool – as they tended to interact with other bands based at the same studio. Second, she examines the issues around how the band acquired their instruments, based on the difficulties they had in securing the necessary finance.

Third, she discusses the way in which the bands developed their own songs. The bands studied by Cohen were primarily interested in writing their own material. They would play the occasional cover version, but an important aspect of their self-perception as musicians was their originality. This contrasts with the copy groups examined by Bennett. Cohen points to 'four main themes implicit in the music-making of the Jactars': an 'emphasis upon natural talent', a 'simple and clean sound', 'originality', and 'musical incompetence as style', which were shared by Crikey it's the Cromptons! (1991: 169). There were differences between the bands in the ways in which they developed their material, but they had similar notions of creativity and originality. In part, this stemmed from a post-punk ethos of creativity, to be developed outside what the bands themselves saw as the established sounds of a mass culture.

Fourth, despite this anti-commercialist ethos, the bands were interested in getting record deals. Cohen describes in some detail the reactions of record companies to the material sent to them by the bands, and the bands' attempts to get record companies to listen to their music. Thus, the bands were seeking success even if this was defined in terms that did not include doing anything to sell records. Likewise, more than 50 per cent of the wider sample of local bands studied by Cohen had some kind of management (ibid.: 59). However, despite this, legal and financial affairs remained difficult and were often implicated in the break-up of bands.

In addition to the factors noted so far (and there are other aspects which make Cohen's book useful in the developing literature on local music-making), it is the fifth factor that is the most important: the bands' masculinity and attitudes towards women. Cohen notes how the relations between different bands tended to resemble gang rivalry (ibid.: 35). Furthermore, the band was a social unit: being in a band was a 'way of life' (ibid.: 38) for the male members, and the only woman member of one of the bands was systematically marginalized. These practices and attitudes were reinforced by the performances of the bands. Women were seen in terms of visual image (ibid.: 81), not as musicians, and were hence involved as 'mostly backing singers and non-instrumentalists' (ibid.: 206). In Cohen's account, at gigs 'the community and solidarity the bands strove for was predominantly masculine. While women generally liked to dance, their male counterparts were reluctant to do so' (ibid.: 101). Women were seen as a problem for the bands and were 'actively excluded'. This reinforces the theme identified by Becker, where wives and families were seen to be a 'problem' for the male jazz musician, and also the gendered nature of music-making identified by Bayton (1990, 1992, 1993, and 1998).

Bayton discusses these themes comprehensively in *Frock Rock* (1998), which examines female music-makers in the 1980s and mid-1990s. She shows that women still comprise only around 15 per cent of musical performers (ibid.: 23) and even those who do perform tend to be written out of the histories of music, apart from those who reach star status. Bayton asks: 'why have there been so few women playing instruments in bands?' (ibid.: 25). She shows that there are a number of constraints on women engaging in music-making (some of which will affect men, though in different ways). She divides these constraining factors into two broad types: material and ideological. The material factors include the need to secure equipment and transport, the necessity for space and time to practise and the way in which female leisure time is constrained by parents and partners. Male musicians often exclude female players and the rock musical style is masculine, which is further explored by Bayton in terms of the construction and reproduction of ideologies of femininity, which are class differentiated in some respects.

Despite these significant material and ideological constraints, some women do become involved in music-making. Bayton offers an analysis of the 'routes into rock' by which this can be facilitated. She discusses the parts played by having a musical family, being classically trained, having an art education, being involved in drama, gender rebellion, having boyfriends or husbands who are musicians, attending higher education and having female role models. Bayton argues for the importance of punk (and what is now most often termed post-punk; see, for example, Reynolds 2005) in the late 1970s in creating space for more women to be involved in music-making at local levels (1998: 68). This was also significantly affected by the feminist and lesbian politics of the time, which encouraged female creativity and provided places for practice and performance. These points are summarized in figure 2.4.

Bayton then analyses the nature of the processes that confront women once they have begun to get involved in music-making. Again, some of these are similar to those discussed by authors like Bennett (1980) and Cohen (1991), but Bayton draws out some of the particular processes that affect women, such as the fact that they are more likely to join a band at an earlier stage of learning an instrument, and are less likely to practise in the parental home. The all-women bands considered by Bayton tended to be more democratic in operation than those examined by Bennett, and to be more involved in writing original material. Once they start playing in public, there are further issues for women to confront, such as sexual harassment at a number of levels, the image and style that is to be projected, and so on. Some of the dilemmas involved here are captured in box 2.3, which can also be read in the context of semiotics (see chapter 5). Women also have to confront the sexism of the music industry and while some practitioners and commentators perceive that there have been some improvements for women since the 1980s, Bayton argues that there is still a long way to go before 'there as many women playing in rock bands as men' (p. 209).

A very comprehensive study of local music-making was undertaken by the anthropologist Ruth Finnegan (1989) between 1980 and 1984 in Milton Keynes. In *The Hidden Musicians*, Finnegan describes seven musical worlds which she found in this English new town: classical, brass band, folk, musical theatre, jazz, country and western, and rock and pop. She draws a series of contrasts between the worlds (which can often overlap, as members can belong to more than one) in terms of how the playing of music is learned, how it is performed and how it is written. She identifies a number of different social institutions which support music and the patterns of organization of the musical worlds and, in general, points to the importance of music to everyday life in Milton Keynes in providing pathways for

Constraints	Escapes
childhood femininity	gender rebellion
family	unusual/musical family
technophobia	unusual family/school
	women's music projects
teenage femininity	bohemian/artist
(via mass media and female peer groups)	rebel identity
material constraints:	feminist collectives
equipment space, money, time	political collectives
	women's music projects
	unusual boyfriends and husbands
ideological constraints	feminism
(dual standard of morality etc.)	lesbianism
	Riot Grrrl
	Girl Power
exclusion by male music-making peer	women's music projects
groups and by male bands	women's bands
exclusion by promoters	DIY feminist venues
male-dominated gigs	
hostile male audiences	women-only gigs
sexploitative managers	DIY administration
	supportive husbands/managers
sexist PA crew	DIY feminist PA
	feminist courses in sound engineering
female compartments	punk, Riot Grrrl, and feminist
alternatives in the record promotion	DIY record production and distribution
industry (esp. light pop/vocals)	

Figure 2.4 Constraints and escapes for women musicians

Source: Bayton 1998: 190

Box 2.3 Dilemmas of dress for female performers

SHAREEN (Ms45): I have to think too hard. I shouldn't have to. All female dress is drag. All female dress is some kind of signifier and the thing that pisses me off as a band is if we showed up in a little gold lamé dress and false eyelashes we would be heard differently than if we show up in jeans and t-shirts. And, goddamn it, there are some days that I want to wear a gold lamé dress and false eyelashes. Then there's the ridiculous cat fight mythology. If one of them is wearing a pretty little gold lamé dress and the other one's wearing jeans, they say, 'Oh, that's the pretty one and that's the dykey one.' And it's like, 'What? No, I really want to wear comfy shoes today. Give me a fucking break.' . . . Since clothing is such a signifier, I'm trying to figure out ways that I can have a better sense of humour without putting myself into the Barbie category. That's taken some manipulation.

Source: Bayton 1998: 112

urban living. In this respect, Finnegan's detailed empirical study suggests that music is a core activity in the structuring of contemporary social life: an argument that has been made in far more theoretical terms by writers like John Shepherd (for example, 1991). It is also an important part of those works that consider the role of music consumption in everyday life (e.g. DeNora 2000; Laughey 2006: ch. 10).

Finnegan shows the large number and variety of bands that were active in the pop and rock world at this time. She divides them into three main categories. First, there were 'the young, relatively inexperienced and recently formed bands' (1989: 110), often formed by people still at school. Second, there were the groups 'who had left school and were beginning to perform in local clubs or youth clubs for a small fee' (ibid.: 111). Third, there were those bands which 'had established a secure position in pub and club circuits, outside as well as within Milton Keynes, played in upwards of 50 or 100 performances a year, and, while still towards the amateur rather than the professional end of the scale, brought in substantial fees' (ibid.: 114). Despite the existence of these different types of band, some overall patterns were identified. First, the groups were predominantly made up of men; second, they aimed at giving live performances; and third, they wanted to be paid, though remuneration varied greatly.

Finnegan uses her detailed research to confront some of the main themes arising from the literature on pop music. First, she argues that pop music cannot be simply seen as the music of youth, since the category of youth is cross-cut by many other social divisions and youth is actually a fairly wide category, encompassing people of a variety of ages: 'Youth predominated, for even mixed audiences also included young people, but family audiences were nothing unusual and it would be misleading to conclude – despite the widespread image – that rock bands played exclusively to either teenagers or young people under 25' (ibid: 123–4). Second, she examines the view that pop music is produced by those who are uneducated or unemployed and again finds this assumption to be unwarranted. She suggests that the picture on education was mixed and that, 'of band members who gave details nearly two-thirds were in jobs' (ibid.: 124). This figure in particular might not hold for other times and places, as at this point Milton Keynes could be said to be relatively prosperous. Third, Finnegan examines the idea that pop music expresses a form of rebellion. This is a theme which is treated at greater length in chapter 3, though Finnegan suggests that evidence from her study makes it difficult to generalize about this, and the idea of protest was not 'generally borne out by this study' (ibid.: 127).

Finnegan argues that there were a number of common themes running through the rock and pop music world. First, the musicians in this world tended to possess less knowledge about other players in it, compared with members of other musical worlds. However, certain individuals would be well known. Second, there were shared ideas about playing and learning. Echoing the account of Bennett (1980), Finnegan shows that the pop musicians were self-taught and joined bands in the early stages of learning an instrument. Moreover, there was a common pattern to the instrumentation in the bands, where 'the standard combination was guitars (rhythm and lead), bass guitar, and drums, together with vocals' (Finnegan 1989: 129).

The most important common feature of the pop musician's world, according to Finnegan, was 'their interest in expressing their own views and personality through music-making' (ibid.). She argues that this is a 'stress on individuality and artistic creation which accords ill with the mass theorists' delineation of popular music' (ibid.). However, for the mass theorists like Adorno, this may be a 'false' individuality and creativity, and they would not necessarily accept the participants own view of their creativity.

According to Finnegan, such creativity was often expressed in the musicians' desire to compose their own music, where: 'playing in a band provided a medium where players could express their own personal aesthetic vision and through their music achieve a sense of controlling their own values, destiny and self-identity' (ibid.: 130). This brings the discussion back to the themes raised by Becker in his account of jazz musicians, as the notion of self-expression repeats the idea of the artist, above commerce, at the core of the jazz musicians' beliefs. However, it should be remembered that these ideas of artistic achievement and autonomy may be more wished for than actually achieved. Moreover, it may be easier for the local musician to remain relatively separated from the music industry, as he or she may not have to deal with it to any great extent. This becomes more difficult as the artist seeks to earn a living from his or her activities and this, in turn, raises issues of the extent to which the musician can remain authentic as an artist, in the way that many musicians express, rather than 'selling out'. This theme will be returned to in this book, but, before it can be considered, attention needs to be given to some of the processes at work in the institutions which these musicians confront, and which some of them will become part of. In many ways, as the discussion continues, it should become clearer that the opposition between creativity and industry is oversimplified.

In this context, Toynbee (2000) offers a useful framework for analysis of the dynamic of such creativity. Toynbee argues that those who make popular music can be defined as creators, who operate in a field that places some limits on the nature and extent of their creativity. This may involve a range of roles, as Kusek and Leonhard suggest:

> What this means is that a musician does not have to be a recording artist or a performer to thrive in today's music industry. It means that you may be, at different times, a songwriter, lyricist, performer, band member, entertainer, promoter, entrepreneur, fashion designer, producer, teacher, or small business manager. Being 'creative' in the music business often means wearing several hats, doing several things at the same time, and picking up new skills on the fly. (2005: 21)

However, the 'freedom' in such a situation should not be overestimated. In Toynbee's words, 'the unit of creativity is a small one' (2000: 35). Musicians work in a context of 'possibles', where possibility of innovation is subject to some constraints. What can be analysed is the selection of possible modes of innovation, or the likelihood of the selection of ways forward. Patterns of possibles once established can then be pursued over a long period of time. Toynbee suggests that the career of the Rolling Stones is a good example of this. Other artists shift ground more rapidly and explore a wider range of possibles. An example of this might be the work over time of an artist like Elvis Costello, who, for example has worked in a new wave/punk context, country styles, with a string quartet and in producing ballads with Burt Bacharach. Costello's initial commercial success expanded the musical fields in which he could subsequently work, or expanded his range of possibles, while still allowing him to make a living. This contrasts with the constraints on Becker's jazz musicians. Moreover, as is shown in the study of three different young bands making music in contrasting localities in Sweden, such creativity and learning is a crucial aspect of the many dimensions of the pleasures and motivations of playing music (see Fornäs et al. 1995).

The pop process

Negus (1992: 38) suggests that all record companies share a division of labour of the type shown in figure 2.5. This section examines these different places in the division of labour, how they interconnect, and the different contributions they make to the overall musical product.

The Artist and Repertoire (A & R) division or staff have primary responsibility for the signing and development of artists at the record company. However, in accord with the general points made by Abercrombie (1991), which were outlined in chapter 1, Negus suggests that other divisions and groups of staff, especially marketing divisions, have increased their influence over these dimensions in recent years (1992: 50; see also Negus 1999). Despite this, A & R remains very important and, according to Negus, has continued to work along principles set during the 1960s, when the 'rock tradition' developed. He suggests that six criteria are used in the assessment of potential artists:

1   the live, stage performance;
2   the originality and quality of the songs or material;
3   the recorded performance and voice;
4   their appearance and image;
5   their level of personal commitment, enthusiasm and motivation;
6   the achievements of the act so far. (1992: 53)

The reference points for the predominantly male A & R staff, who may previously have worked as 'music writers, disc jockeys, musicians promoters and sales' (ibid.: 56), or have come into the industry from the 'college rock tradition' (ibid.: 57), are the stars of the Anglo-American rock tradition. There is a certain antipathy to the video and more image-based pop bands which fall outside this tradition. This may

---

directors

president or managing director

artist and repetoire   marketing   public relations
publicity and press radio   and television promotion
business affairs/finance and legal   manufacture and distribution
administration and secretarial

Figure 2.5 The division of labour in a record company

Source: derived from Negus 1992: 38

be because an album band may have a longer life and can be expected to reap more consistent rewards for the company over a longer period of time. Moreover, in accord with this 'rock' tradition, importance is placed on the quality of live performance. This relates to the idea that rock is a public or 'street' form. Within rock and pop music, as in other areas of social life, the street has been seen as an area of male dominance and camaraderie. This is illustrated by a comment from a rare female worker in A & R, quoted by Negus:

> I'll tell you why I think there are not many women in it. Because, number one, it's a very chauvinistic industry, it really is. Number two, the A & R lifestyle does not suit the majority of women at all. The fact of going out every night to clubs, being up all night in sleazy, dodgy clubs or whatever. (Ibid.: 59)

Once it has been decided that an act should be signed, it has to be developed and marketed from within the company. The interaction here between the A & R and marketing departments is central (ibid.: 63). The image of the group or artist is developed, with attention being paid to current trends. There may be an attempt to 'brand' the artist, in line with the general developments outlined in chapter 1. Thus, one executive interviewed by Negus:

> spoke of attempting to 'brand' artists. By this he meant that the unique quality of an act would become instantly recognisable and condensed into a specific image which could become a trademark. This director referred to the presentation of U2, who were not signed to the company he worked for, but whose marketing he spoke of with great admiration. (ibid.: 71)

It is important to understand that this process of 'branding' does not simply occur with the more recognizably 'pop' acts, such as Kylie Minogue or Girls Aloud, but is applicable to rock acts like U2 or Bruce Springsteen, who are often thought to possess more 'authenticity'. These distinctions between pop and rock and their accrued meanings will be discussed more fully in chapter 3 and the ways in which artists are branded as stars in chapter 5. The A & R and marketing departments both have their roles in the development of the product to be sold in the rock/pop marketplace.

Negus examines the different aspects of these departments of the record company. For the most part, he emphasizes the collaborative nature of the interaction between these different activities (1992: 134). However, he also points to significant conflict in this domain. He maintains that A & R staff have become increasingly resentful of the intrusion of the promotional staff at earlier stages in the recruitment processes. The importance of marketing and promotion means that these activities are important in the shaping of a sound and image. Hence, in Negus's view: 'Many companies, responding to an increasing emphasis on marketing in the wider global economy, have attempted to make the informal dialogue between marketing and artist and repertoire more explicit by providing marketing with a formal veto on the artists who are signed' (1992: 148). The development of pop videos as promotional devices and their importance during the 1980s attests to the increasing importance of marketing and promotion and to their role within the creative process. Increasingly, promotional and marketing strategies are formulated at an earlier stage of the creation of a musical product, where a number of processes and tasks such as producing, engineering and mixing have been examined.

The producer tends to have overall control of the recording process, and he or she may be seen as filling the same sort of role as a director in film production. The A & R department will often try to match the artist with a producer who may have been successful with particular types of act and music previously. In the past, the producer may have been contracted to a particular company and worked with a large number of that company's acts. However, by the early 1960s producers were becoming akin to artists in their own right and some were known for their own sounds. A well-known case of this is Phil Spector, whose 'wall of sound' is still instantly recognizable and seen as Spector's invention, based on his orchestration of musicians and skills in the recording studio. A similar, but less well-known, example from the early 1960s in Britain can be found in the work of Joe Meek, whose sound, which can be found on records like Telstar and Robot by the Tornadoes, still has devotees. Today, some producers are as well known as artists.

A similar movement towards greater importance can be traced for some record engineers. The distinction between the producer and engineer is put neatly by Negus when he explains that: 'while the producer works as director of proceedings, the engineer is involved in technically finding the combination of settings to create the sounds required' (ibid.: 84). Some engineers have become quite well known, though they would normally be ranked below the record producer in importance. However, it should be recognized that the process by which some more established acts have become involved in the production of their own music facilitates the development of the role of the engineer, who would assist the group in putting into practice their own ideas: a role filled by some producers in the past. Furthermore, this points to some fluidity in the tasks performed by different components of the recording process over time.

The process of development of occupation of the 'recording engineer' or 'sound mixer' has been traced by Kealy (1990). He suggests that there are three modes of collaboration in pop music production: 'craft-union', 'entrepreneurial' and 'art'. He characterizes these modes in terms of a number of different dimensions, as shown in figure 2.6. The content of these dimensions in the different modes is shown in figure 2.7. Kealy traces the development from the craft to the art modes of production. In the craft mode, which was dominant in the immediate post-war period, the recording engineer was expected mainly to use the acoustic properties of the studio to attempt to create as far as possible a 'realistic' reproduction of a concert-hall sound. The occupation was organized around trade unions, and relationships in the studio were formal and demarcated, with little overlap between tasks. Kealy suggests that:

> The basic standard used to judge a sound mixer's work was whether the sound was 'in the grooves'. The good mixer-craftsman would make sure that unwanted sounds were not recorded or were at least minimized, that the desired sounds were recorded without distortion, and that the sounds were in balance. The recording technology itself, and thus the sound mixer's work, was to be unobtrusive so as not to destroy the listener's illusion that

- technology of recording
- recording aesthetic
- social organization of studio collaboration
- job responsibilities of the mixer
- occupational ideology of sound mixing

Figure 2.6 Dimensions of the modes of pop music production

Source: derived from Kealy (1990)

	Technology of recording	Recording aesthetic	Social organization	Job responsibilities	Occupational ideology
Craft	acoustic properties	realism	professional/ unionized	formal/ impersonal	'in the grooves'
Entrepreneurial	tape	hit sound	fluid	open	selling
Art	multi-track	art	collaboration	rapport	expression

Figure 2.7 Craft, entrepreneurial and art modes of collaboration in popular music production

Source: Constructed from Kealy 1990

he was sitting in Philharmonic Hall rather than in his living room. The art of recording was not to compete for the public's aesthetic attention to the art that was being recorded. (Ibid.: 211)

The entrepreneurial mode of sound recording developed during the 1950s. The introduction of tape for recording facilitated the introduction of new aesthetic and social relations. Smaller studios developed which wanted to create sounds that would be hit records; they were not concerned with the reproduction of concert performance. The social organization of the studio loosened and the responsibilities of the mixer/engineer opened up, with the previous modes of craft unionism and professionalism breaking down. The studios became concerned to sell their sounds, especially in terms of the labels that were often based in a small studio, such as Sun, based in Memphis, which first recorded Elvis Presley in the mid-1950s, and Stax, also located in Memphis, which recorded a large number of soul singers and groups in the 1960s. There was a new entrepreneurial spirit, often based around the owner of the label, who was often directly involved in record production. Examples include Sam Phillips at Sun and Ahmet Ertegun at Atlantic.

The art mode of sound recording developed in the 1960s. Technology had further developed, with the introduction of multi-track recording. The concern of many pop artists, and associated mixers and engineers, was how to produce an artistic statement, which might be an experiment in sound. The engineer or mixer moved into a more collaborative relationship with the artist working in the studio, and there was a desire to establish a rapport between the engineer and the artist which would enable the collaboration to express themselves in the resulting music.

While these modes of organization can be seen as developing in a chronological fashion, it is important that they also be treated as ideal types. It can further be suggested that one does not necessarily replace the other. For example, it may that bigger studios still operate in accordance with the craft mode, whilst smaller studios are predominantly in the entrepreneurial mode.

A related, but different, view to that of Kealy is expressed by Struthers who distinguishes between 'three rival aesthetics of recorded music' (1987: 255): 'realism', 'perfectionism' and 'performance'. He suggests that realism was the earliest aesthetic, based in the idea that: 'recordings should strive towards a faithful reproduction of the original performance' (ibid.: 242). Such realism became increasingly untenable, as 'using multi-track magnetic tape recording, the final recording is assembled and "reconstructed" from a number of fragments, and so there is no "original" of which that published recording can be a reproduction' (ibid.: 244). This leads to the perfectionism of which Struthers writes. The final aesthetic, performance, places emphasis on the performance of the musician, and his or her expressive qualities, which are captured in the recording.

The ways in which these different roles might be changing in relation to the introduction of new technology is considered in the next section. However, before this, I want briefly to consider some other dimensions to the pop production process. The places in the division of labour in a record company were summarized in figure 2.5 above. I have already examined the role of A & R and mentioned the importance of the marketing department and its close relationship with A & R. Negus (1992) points to the importance of a number of the other dimensions of the process, examining the intimate relationship between publicity and the music press, despite the critical reactions of artists like Pat Kane of Hue and Cry as illustrated by box 2.4.

Like many other areas of society, pop and rock music can be seen as an aspect of a 'promotional culture' (Wernick 1991), where principles first formulated in the

---

Box 2.4   Rock criticism in the music press

'The bulk of pop writing at any time is embroidered press office material; the majority of pop writers end up subbing advertorial for aftershave.' Rock musician Pat Kane takes rock critics to task.

Rock criticism? An oxymoron. The only truly critical acts in popular music are musical ones: I don't like the noises I hear around me, so I'm going to make or choose better/different ones. If rock 'n' roll is 'democracy in action – anyone can do it' (Lester Bangs), then why read others' opinions when you can make your own sounds, or choose your own soundscape? Your ears never tell you lies: rock critics *always* do.

And rock critics? For the most part, poxy morons. The bulk of pop writing at any time is embroidered press office material; the majority of pop writers eventually settle for their own dusty little corner of a Condé Nast office, subbing advertorial for aftershave. The most interesting writers are the ones who endure, year after year, on magazines like NME or *Melody Maker*: forever foaming wildly at the next bunch of sallow-cheeked musical youth to come round the bend. They are particularly despicable. But at least they have their reasons.

Consider the basic lot of the long-term professional pop scrivener. It (I use the preposition wisely) is usually highly educated, yet utterly impoverished – a dangerous, distorting mixture. Despite years of training in the humanities, it finds itself reduced to a form of aesthete's beggary. The need to blag trips to Antwerp with Anthrax, or stuff down the crepes at some corporate mega-babe launch, reduces that precious critical distance to almost nil.

The reviews that result from this feudal employment are either slavishly reverential – which at least ensures that PR departments will keep the home-phone ringing. Or they're venomous and excessive – fuelled by self-loathing at continual compromise, and a kind of reckless bedsit nihilism.

I'll concede that these pressure-cooker conditions (young men and women writhing in the steam of their own insecurities and inadequacies) can make for some precocious writing. But it's a long trawl: and I usually just skim the pages looking for abusive references to a certain West-of-Scotland pop-soul duo by the name of . . .

Alright, I have an axe to grind: well, perhaps a machete to swing indiscriminately. My loathing of all rock critics – other than the self-evident pantheon (Marcus, Savage, Marsh, Bangs) – partly comes from having been at the end of some of their pathological attacks over the last eight years of my own career.

The golden rule that we broke at the start of our career and suffered for ever since was this: never give a more intelligent justification of your own music than the critic is able to. By doing so, you remove their whole raison d'être. Play the noble savage, hide your erudition under a comely fuzziness of mind, and the five-star ratings will be yours for as long as you want them. But push your own critical intellect too far and you will see the whites of their eyes.

A cursory flick through my cuttings renders up many such jewels of pundits-in-pique. 'May the bargain-bin save us from Sociological Pop Stars . . . Smart-Alec paranoid Scots, with gap sites where their shoulders should be . . . Tortuous lyrics, overripe melodies and everything framed in quotation marks. Don't they ever get tired of themselves?'

All this merely adjectival abuse – right down to the level of 'I've seen more soul in a billiard ball' and (I kid you not) 'Fuck off and die' – runs like water off a rocker's Gaultier. One can feel a certain empathy with the scattier rock critics; at least their writing displays a passionate, bilious commitment. Much more worrying is the advent of the Quality Music Establishment – represented pre-eminently by Q magazine but backed up by beanfeasts like the Mercury Music Awards (the 'Booker' of the pop world).

If the inky critic acts like a drunken gatekeeper between audience and artist – whose erratic behaviour at least allows the rocker all the random luck of schizophrenic reviewing – then the Quality Police are fully armed border guards. Only artists with corporate passports can get past them into the glare of public approval these days.

In an age of supposed relativism of taste and judgment, the presumption of Quality Rock-Crit is breathtaking: Q magazine proclaims its albums guide to be 'the best in the world', Professor Simon Frith, chair of the Mercury judging panel, has predicted that one day 'the endorsements of rock critics will have as much influence as the blurbs on book covers.'

What's behind this elevation of critical reasoning, of talk-about-pop music, is a major marketing crisis for the music business. Teenage singles buyers no longer lead musical taste, no longer create lasting stars: their rap and rave purchases have almost no connection to mainstream tastes in the album charts – the area that makes the corporations money. Over-25s mostly stick with established artists in their CD buying. So how do you get a 30-year-old married couple to risk their recession surplus on new releases?

Through elitist pop discourse, of course: the deliberate manipulation of status and credibility. If you're buying any new albums, intones the deep ideology of Q and the Mercury Awards, buy the ones that the experts say really matter. Rock academics and broadsheet scribblers, solicitors after the financial health of globe-straddling multinationals: same as it ever was. Only worse.

And the saddest thing about this current critical situation? That musicians and record companies are now looking for, or looking to be, 'Q-type' or 'Mercury's' artists: pointlessly chasing after criteria of excellence which these new, pumped-up commissars of rock can't even be consistent about themselves.

When pen-pushers start interfering with sound-makers – when the power of their response even shapes for a single second what musicians do musically – then the whole situation is completely upside down. They know the way, said Kenneth Tynan, but they can't drive the car. Music critics, get back under the Rock. And stay there.

Source: Guardian, 6 September 1993

advertising of goods such as soap powder are increasingly applied to spheres like politics and university life. Pop and rock are heavily promoted forms and it can be argued that many of their meanings derive from their image in a marketplace. Music is promoted and analysed in the press, the music press and in music magazines. Further, music is promoted through the music video or 'promo'. There is an extensive literature on video, which will be considered in chapter 5. Another important mode of advertising of musical wares is radio. A general examination of music and radio is beyond the scope of this book, being a topic in its own right. Such a general account can be found in the work of Barnard (1989). An extended consideration of the role of pirate radio in the 1960s is given by Chapman (1992) and an introductory account of radio in general can be found in Crisell (1994). More recent examinations of radio have pointed to the fragmentation of contemporary radio into a number of different specialist stations (Barnes 1990). It seems likely that radio will remain important in generating record sales even if the stations become increasingly specialized, especially with the impact of digital radio stations.

> ### Box 2.5   The other side of women in rock
>
> This is the invisible, decidedly unglamorous side of the industry, the places where many of the 'women in rock' work. Most of the major labels – and, indirectly, the independents – probably employ as many women as men, perhaps even more: 'tea ladies', secretaries, receptionists, canteen staff, cleaners, and almost anyone servicing the needs of people within the industry will be female. Women also do all of the menial work that cannot yet be done more cheaply by machines: they assemble the basic parts of instruments, solder the wires and chips of electrical equipment and, in the pressing and packing plants, it is women who check the quality of discs, put them in their sleeves and pack shop orders into boxes ready for distribution. They are anonymous factory-workers at the bottom of the company hierarchy, and almost every record is handled by them at some point. Which gives them, if they choose to use it, an enormous amount of power. . . .
> EMI's plant at Middlesex is, in fact, reputed to be one of the better factories: it is unionized, working conditions are fair, and the company was happy to let me visit. The manager . . . is a large, middle-aged, genial man who calls his staff 'girls' (some of them are grandmothers), and thinks his secretary is wonderful. He forgot to mention her name: he calls her 'Darling'. He meant well.
>
> Source: Steward and Garratt 1984: 63–4

Music companies employ secretarial and administrative staff, often in familiar gendered roles involving the support of male staff. The products of the musical process also need to be manufactured and distributed, and many of the jobs in manufacture are performed by women, as illuminatingly discussed in the passage reproduced in box 2.5.

Having examined the nature of the production process and the division of labour in the music industry, I now wish to consider the relationship between music and technology. particularly to see how this can be seen as repatterning some of the relationships so far described.

Pop music and technology

In considering the way in which technology interacts with pop music, there are two important matters which require immediate attention: first, the definition of technology and, second, the general nature of the interaction which is being suggested. I shall examine these issues before reviewing some of the particular roles of technology in the production of popular music.

MacKenzie and Wajcman (1985) suggest that there are three definitions of technology. First, technology may be defined as 'sets of physical objects', irons, buses, cars, CD players, tape recorders, and so on. Second, technology may refer to human activities as well as simple physical objects. These physical objects only become technology when they are used in human activity: 'a computer without programs and programmers is simply a useless collection of bits of metal, plastic and silicon' (MacKenzie and Wajcman 1985: 3). Third, there is the definition of technology as not only objects and activity, but as knowledge as well. In this approach, technology is not really technology without 'know-how'. When a lecturer uses an overhead projector, he or she has to know how to switch it on, how to place the overhead slide on the right way up and how to focus the machine on the screen, otherwise the overhead projector is simply an ugly box. These are relatively simple forms of knowledge and activity (though it is interesting to see how difficult many lecturers find them!), and many forms of technology require more detailed and expert knowledge and more complicated operations for them to function properly.

It is often assumed that technology is very important in affecting the nature and development of society. In its strongest versions this thesis is called *technological determinism*. In an important discussion and critique of this thesis, the cultural theorist and critic Raymond Williams suggests that:

> The basic assumption of technological determinism is that a new technology – a printing press or a communications satellite – 'emerges' from technical study and experiment. It then changes the society or the sector in which it has 'emerged'. 'We' adapt to it because it is the new modern way. (1983: 129)

In a similar vein, MacKenzie and Wajcman suggest that technological determinism 'is the theory that technology is indeed an independent factor, and that changes in technology cause social changes. In its strongest version, the theory claims that change in technology is the most important cause of change in society' (1985: 4). These writers argue that the thesis of technological determinism rests on two important premises: first, a prior separation of technology from society, where technology is at some point seen to be outside society; and second, that 'technical change causes social change' in a direct and unmediated sort of way.

There are two major problems with simple technological determinism. First, 'the characteristics of a society play a major part in deciding which technologies are adopted' (ibid.: 6). If this is accepted, it is hard to see technology as an independent factor. One point here is that technologies may be invented but not then developed, or they fail, for social reasons. Some technologies lose out for reasons that are not necessarily simply technological. Thus the cartridge lost out in a battle with the cassette and the Beta video system lost to VHS. Second, 'the same technology may have very different "effects" in different situations' (ibid.: 6).

On the basis of the discussion so far, it is difficult to sustain the thesis of clear or simple technological determinism. However, as MacKenzie and Wajcman show, this does not mean that technology is not important and they point to three areas where technology can have decisive specific effects. First, technology can be political, as technologies can be developed and designed to eliminate certain social developments and encourage others. Thus the 'New York builder Robert Moses designed road systems to facilitate the travel of certain types of people and hinder that of others' (ibid.: 7; see Rose 1994 and chapter 4 below for more on this and the development of hip-hop). Moreover, some technologies are more compatible with some social relations than others. Hence, it can be argued that 'basing energy supply around a nuclear technology that requires plutonium may enhance pressure for stronger state surveillance to prevent the theft of plutonium and help erode traditional civil liberties' (MacKenzie and Wajcman 1985: 7).

Second, technology can have long-term specific effects. Thus, for example, once a road is built or sited in a particular place, it is difficult to alter it. Critics argue that the decision to build the M25 around London has long-term effects on the habits of car-drivers and that it begins a process of expansion of the width of the road in a process which is supposed to ease congestion, but which actually turns out to be self-defeating as more traffic uses it at each stage of expansion. Third, technology can have very significant environmental and ecological effects, as the debates over pollution, acid rain and nuclear power demonstrate so clearly.

In this argument, technology is not independent and directly determining, but one of a number of factors which interrelate to produce specific results. Other factors which MacKenzie and Wajcman draw attention to are economics, gender and the state. Thus, technologies are invested in for particular reasons, often in the search for market advantage or profit. They are often related to particular conceptions of gender and the arrangement of households and finally are sometimes financed by the state for military reasons, among others.

Williams (1983) argues that technological determinism can often mesh with, and influence, forms of cultural pessimism, where, along with other factors, the development of new forms of technology is held to lead to forms of cultural decline. Thus the increasing development of computer technologies and games is thought, by some commentators, to lead to a decline in the ability of schoolchildren to concentrate on books, especially the sorts of book that are held to be of high standard. In the area of music it has been suggested that the introduction of new technologies leads to a decline in forms of previously established and valued standards of musicianship.

The discussion so far has raised a number of issues for consideration in the examination of technology and pop music. First, it is necessary to define the sorts of technology being discussed; second, to consider whether some accounts slip into a sort of simple technological determinism, where technology is seen to change social arrangements on its own; third, to consider the specific effects of technology; and fourth, to examine the other factors which are affecting social and technological change. A complete examination of the relations between different technologies and pop is a long way beyond the scope of this book and useful detailed and historical accounts can be found in the work of Steve Jones (1992) and Théberge (1997).

Toynbee (2000) offers a useful conceptualization. In accord with his idea of the selection of possibles discussed earlier in this chapter, Toynbee argues that there is what he terms a 'technosphere' – an area of 'imaginary possibilities and constraints which lies between performance on one side and the more or less remote reception of sound on another' (2000: 69). Thus, the technosphere may be more or less immediate and simple: the performer plays an acoustic guitar and people sitting in front of him or her hear it immediately; or exceedingly complex, for example where a track is made up of a number of different sections from a variety of sources recorded in different times and places, mixed in a several locations and then distributed over a range of formats, such as computers, CDs and DVDs.

Toynbee identifies three main 'tendencies' in the technosphere and the type of music involved. These develop in broad historical succession. First, there is the 'documentary' mode, where the idea is 'to carry the truth of an original unmediated performance event across the air to listeners' (ibid.: 70). This idea was dominant from the 1920s to the 1950s. Second, there is another approach that has existed through the twentieth century, which Toynbee labels 'ventriloquism'. Here, an instrument or the human voice becomes an extension of the body. The instrument and voice act as an intermediary between the body and the technosphere itself. Toynbee gives the following examples of this relationship: 'scat singing [as in jazz where the singer does not articulate words], the playing of the electric guitar, amplifier and effects, or scratching and editing tropes performed by the DJ' (ibid.: 70). Third, there is the strategy that develops from the 1950s onwards where the desire is 'to construct a sonic environment, a virtual dimensionality which never existed "originally"' (ibid.). This sort of approach has become more significant as advances in technology have opened new possibilities. Some of these important dimensions of technological change are the focus here. The extract from Jeremy J. Beadle's book, *Will Pop Eat Itself?* (1993), in box 2.6, details how computer technology can be used in the construction of music, pointing to the creator's lack of detailed musical or electronic knowledge.

In an important article also discussed in the Introduction, Goodwin identifies some technologies: the sequencer, the digital sampling music computer – the

---

Box 2.6   Making a record with the new technology

The equipment which was used in the process I'm going to describe was: an Akai S1100 digital sampler (there was an Akai S900, an earlier less-swish model in there somewhere, too, acting as a separate storehouse for spoken word samples); a mixing desk; Yamaha DX100 electronic keyboard; and an Apple Macintosh computer. The sequencer software package we used was Passport Mastertracks. Also helping things along was an Opcode Studio 3 Synchronizer and Midi Interface. I don't mention these names for reasons of commercial sponsorship, or because they were at the time of writing the last word in up-to-the-minute state of the art (which they weren't). In some ways we were operating relatively primitively. . . . The material I wanted to turn into a dance masterpiece included a bass line and rhythm culled from the twelve-inch mix of a British pseudo-soul hit of 1987, as well as the drum rhythm from the same disc. This second element turned out later to be too inflexible (a polite way of saying just too boring) and Rex elbowed it in favour of one of the most popular beat samples in the business (Bobby Byrd). I also had on my cassette of breaks and beats and other things a weedy but catchy synthesizer figure from a mid-1980s gay-club favourite . . . and some chords from another high-energy floor filler of that time, 'Ti Sento', by the Italian group Matia Bazar. These later choices were fairly unimaginative – early 1970s funk would have been much more useful. But the four truly distinctive elements I had to hand were: a Wagnerian tenor singing the four-note 'Blutbruderschaft' motif from the second act of Götterdämmerung; a three-note horn blast from the same source; a line of football commentary taken from a video of the TV coverage of the 1991 Spurs v. Porto match; and, best of all, a cartoon cat with the creepiest voice you ever heard enouncing the line 'But the third bowl of porridge was just right' . . .

Putting a track together differs from eating in many respects, but in this case the most significant was that the porridge had to wait until the end of the day. You start – well, we did – with the rhythm. And so the first rhythmic phrase I'd recorded was fed from the cassette into the sampler (in exactly the same way you'd record on to a cassette in the first place). There's always too much of what you record; as I've said, two bars of most beats or breaks is an extravagance. But this is where the sampler performs the first of its magic tricks, as an editing machine. In this case the bass figure was allowed to run twice before being chopped into two discrete phrases running alternately (so that the second could be made subtly different from the first in a way that it wasn't in its original form).

To help in editing, to make it virtually perfect and rhythmically exact (vital with 1990s techno-dance music), the sampler has its own small visual display, which portrays the sound as a graph. This display means that you can locate the precise beginning of each measure much more easily than by manipulating a reel of tape. You can see exactly what you're editing and be sure of precisely what you're doing. Recorded sound is reduced to basic, visible, separable units, and can be worked on almost the way you'd make a drawing more accurate or graphic. Even figures played on the Yamaha keyboard can be reproduced visually through another display produced through the sequencer, so that you can augment or diminish your chords and rewrite your music as if you were dealing with something written on manuscript paper, rather than something you may have plucked out of your head. This graphic aspect means, conversely, that you need never write anything down, or make the effort to remember anything you've played.

Once the figure is edited precisely it is retriggered on the sequencer. The result of this is that loop-like effect of endless repetition of the figure is achieved. I say 'endless', but in fact the sequencer is programmed to take the figure through 120 measures initially.

As you're editing, apart from sheer precision with the start and finish of beats, you also have the option of varying the tempo of the figure you're working on. For convenience, we opted for the standard 120 beats per minute (the usual 'four on the floor' tempo), but this is no way necessary. Varying the tempo raises or lowers the pitch.

There is another visual display involved which I've already mentioned – that produced on the computer VDU by the sequencer. Generally this display lists each track line by line, identifying each track – each element or figure that's been fed into the sampler – by name (a name which the producer/performer can assign according to his or her whim). After the sample has been fixed and played through, the display follows the tracks through all 120 measures, showing by means of a series of blocks whether or not each track is active in that measure – a black or filled block indicates that there is, a white or empty block that it isn't. This display is particularly helpful when editing the track (in the sense of song or number) as a whole, allowing you to work in unlooped variations in the various figures that have been sampled. After all, it's the unpredictable elements that tend to make even the most mundane of dance tracks memorable. But the elements which make up the rhythm track also need to have some kind of predictability about them to make dancing possible. Dance records with shifting rhythms have a limited appeal. The commonest and most effective way of putting variety into a rhythm track is to eliminate part of it momentarily, to take out the steady pulse of the beat for a measure or two so that only incidental percussion keeps the rhythm going in that time.

In the package that we were using, certain pre-sampled percussive sounds were available, saving us from the need to feed them into the sampler from outside. Many samplers come with a library of such sounds, or offer the capacity to retain such regular percussion features as bongos or tambourines on the machine's permanent hard-disk memory. There are, of course, separate digital drum machines, pioneered by Roger Linn (a standing joke on many Stock, Aitken and Waterman releases is that the drummer credit will go to 'A. Linn'). Such an instrument did not, however, feature in this day's work. When, after three beat samples had been fed in and doctored according to the method above, Rex felt that something lighter but sharper was needed to underline the beat, the percussion was added and edited like the other samples.

The keyboard turned out to possess power beyond my wildest dreams. Some of the time we used it simply as a synthesizer keyboard, and through it fed several 120-measure performances on to their own separate tracks. These tracks encompassed four completely separate styles, with varying instrumental sounds: rhythmically repeated minor triads, very common in much house music; frenetically repeated single notes, which form ideal complements to the triads; descending scales and similar figures; and finally the melodic line from the opening of Mozart's Piano Concerto No. 24 in C Minor, K.491, which is, after all, well out of copyright. The discrete keyboard performances were all separately edited. It turned out that the bottom notes of some of the triads had acquired, more or less by accident, a hollow tone, rather like the sound you get on a piano when one or two of the strings on a note have gone. This accidental sound was so pleasing that the bottom lines of the triads were separated out on to their own track, to give a separate sound timbre which could be used on its own. The triads and repeated notes had been recorded using a piano simulator (although the result didn't sound much like a piano to me, not even a fortepiano as beloved by the advocates of period instruments); the rest with a distinctly synthesized sound, to capture the 'techno' feel so popular in 1991 and 1992.

However, the keyboard had much more going for it than its role as a synthesizer. It also had its part to play in doctoring what had been fed into the sampler. At the simplest level, a note on the keyboard was designed to trigger the sample, particularly useful when editing the rhythm tracks. But this quality really came into its own when the two Wagnerian samples were thrown into the grand scheme. The sound of the hefty Wagnerian tenor crying 'Blutbruderschaft' . . . after it had been edited down to those simple four notes, was fed into the keyboard with the result that when you played the keyboard in certain designated areas, you got that note as though sung by the tenor in question backed by the Orchestra of the Met., with each group of four notes producing in turn each of the vowel noises of 'Blutbruderschaft' in the correct sequence. Obviously there was some electronic distortion on this . . .

After the tenor had been subjected to this treatment, the same thing was done with the three-note horn blast. This time I was more cautious at the keyboard, and in the end the horn blasts were used only singly or in groups of two and only towards the end of the track to provide some further unpredictable element of variety . . .

. . . to a computer-literate generation, this technology simplifies the concept of music-making. However much the punk ethos despised musicianship, it wasn't possible to get very far if you couldn't manage a few rudimentary chords on your guitar. . . . But even though you use keyboards which look something like the traditional piano/organ keyboard, in all this process you don't have to possess any knowledge of how to play it for real. It's just a way of controlling other people's music which you have fed in there. Again, real musical knowledge is an advantage but not necessary, providing you're not profoundly deaf. But if you edit properly, it's a question not of whether you passed Associated Board exams, but of whether you pressed the right buttons at the right time, with the right element of imagination. Music-making made supremely easy, if not supremely cheap . . .

Back in the studio, Rex decided to add some more 'pure' music to the proceedings, and plugged his guitar into the set up. The guitar figures he produced at strategic points as the whole track played back weren't put in the sampler. Having twiddled around at the guitar to his heart's content, he then ruthlessly edited what he'd played using the sequencer's graphic masterplan on the Apple Mac's monitor. Again, the point of the guitar was variety, surprise, so to keep it going all the way through would have been otiose and marred the impact . . .

At last it was time for the porridge. I'd been told . . . that it was possible to feed straight from the soundtrack of a video into a sampler, simply by plugging the video and TV into the general system. . . . Once the phrase 'But the third bowl of porridge was just right' had been captured inside the machine it could be edited and then messed around with like everything else. Although with a spoken phrase like this which was to recur at certain but by no means necessarily regular intervals, we used from a separate unit offering certain studio effects the tool of digital delay – the device which creates a stuttering effect with selected syllables or notes.

This was the first day's work.

Source: Beadle 1993: 131–8

sampler – and MIDI (Musical Instrument Digital Interface), which led the way in the development of electronic music:

> [Sequencers] automate the process of music making, allowing drum patterns, keyboard bass-lines, arpeggios, melodies, and so forth to be entered in 'real time' a musician actually hits pads, electronic drum surfaces, or a synthesizer (keyboard) in which the music is entered simply as information (with values such as the quarter note, for instance, or perhaps numerically constituted). The music can then be played back by the machine. It can also be manipulated by changing tempo, accuracy ('quantizing'), sequence, and sometimes timbre. (Goodwin 1992: 78)

A sampler, as its name suggests, is used to 'sample' sounds which can then be altered in different ways, as the extract in box 2.6 shows. MIDI allows the interconnection of different machines so that they can interact. As computer technologies have developed in recent years, there have been innovations that have led to the increased availability of prerecorded sounds and the programs to manipulate them. These are now commonplace on for example home computers and relatively inexpensive keyboards.

There are pessimistic, optimistic and more balanced views of these technologies and the ways they can be used. Pessimistic accounts suggest, sometimes in a technologically determinist fashion, that they will inevitably have negative effects, leading to the decline of musicianship, the end of true musical creativity and the development of a kind of 'programmed' music, perhaps along the lines suggested by the theories of Adorno which were examined in the Introduction. However, such accounts are difficult to sustain because of the general problems of technological determinism identified earlier: the technology is somehow seen as independent of society in the first place and technologies can have different effects in alternative social situations.

A far more complex, pessimistic account has been provided by Théberge (1989), who argues that the development of new technologies of musical production has led to increasing rationalization in the studio. This process is guided by the twin desires on the part of the producers for 'economic efficiency' and 'technical control'. Théberge maintains that this process involves the rationalization of music production along the Weberian lines outlined in the Introduction. The producer and the engineer take control of this overall rationalized process and 'enter directly into musical practice' (1989: 101). The producers do not engage in a dialogue with the musicians or carry out their wishes but are increasingly moving towards a situation where they are in control of the process, by which finished recordings are created from multi-tracks in the studio. As Goodwin argues:

Théberge sees the process of multitracking, then, as deeply ideological, creating an illusion of community and interaction, where in fact there is only a simulation created by the manipulation of separate, rationalized elements. These elements are apparently fused, partly through stereo imaging and the application of electronic reverberation (which can be used to construct the illusion that the individual parts were recorded in the same acoustic space) in the final mix. (1992: 82)

This pessimistic account expects music to be increasingly rationalized, programmed and controlled. More optimistic accounts suggest otherwise, arguing that the development of these new technologies can lead to more creativity (of the type shown in the account in box 2.6 perhaps) as difficult operations become more easy to perform. Further, it has been argued that there is a form of democratization involved in the process whereby the wider availability of these technologies leads to the possibility that more people can be involved in musical creativity. In a more balanced assessment, Goodwin enters two reservations about this sort of celebration. First, he suggests that there is a wide variation in the quality of the new technologies. The sorts of version of these machines that are put into record studios are very different from those used by budding music-makers in their bedrooms. It might be that such differences parallel those between the guitars often used by beginners and the quality instruments possessed by established rock stars. Second, Goodwin argues that more celebratory accounts tend to be gender blind, neglecting the point that it is men who are in control of such technologies. Goodwin's conclusion is important, as he suggests that:

There are clearly dangers in thinking about music as though it were a free-floating mystery, a social practice unconnected to actual conditions of production. As students of pop we need to know exactly how the means of musical production impact upon the sounds themselves. But in undertaking that task we have to recognize also that the definitions of music and musician can change. The new technologies of pop music have not created new music. But they have facilitated new possibilities. (1992: 97)

Such an approach suggests the need for complex sociological investigation, which locates the technology in context, and echoes the view of Steve Jones that there are new roles developing in the production of music. These involve a shift from the relationships and interaction between the musician, the producer and the recording engineer, which have characterized music production in recent years (and which will continue to exist in many areas), to those relationships which obtain between performers, programmers and performer-programmers (Jones 1992: 12). In this vein, Toynbee argues that 'technical and musical functions . . . have been completely elided. MIDI musicians are always programmers and technicians too' (2002: 94). This shows how the technical and the musical are intertwined, rather than one determining the other.

An excellent example of the complexities of this situation can be found in the work of Schloss (2004), who reports on an ethnographic study of the practices of the producers of 'sample based hip-hop' music. Schloss is interested in the way in which this hip-hop music is produced and the 'ethics' and practices around it rather than in the other dominant trends that have constituted the literature on hip-hop (see chapter 4). It is significant that this has much in common with the studies of local music-making considered earlier in this chapter:

> Most of the producers I spoke with worked long hours at mundane jobs, received the equipment as gifts from their parents, or were given used equipment by older siblings or peers who had lost interest in using it. In other words, the reality in most cases is precisely what hip-hop's critics would presumably like to hear; a story of hard-working, close knit families with a certain amount of disposable income and a willingness to invest that income in their children's artistic pursuits. (Schloss 2004: 30)

This music is based around 'beats' – 'musical collages composed of brief segments of recorded sound' (ibid.: 2). The producers sample music from pre-existing records. Their preferred way of doing this is to search out old vinyl records through their own endeavours. Schloss points to the significance of 'digging in the crates' for vinyl that other producers do not have for this musician subculture. In this respect, it has some commonalities with the record-collecting culture (ibid.: 58) and operates as a form of distinction (see chapter 6). Thus, while there are some producers who will use CDs to sample from, this is not the preferred medium. The producers have a clear sense of what sounds 'right' to them and this guides their aesthetic creativity – 'sampling is not valued because it is convenient, but because it is beautiful' (ibid.: 65). Furthermore, the producers have clear views about what should be sampled and what should not. For example, it should not be something that someone else has recently sampled and so on. Moreover, the technologically informed creative process of hip-hop itself takes place in the sort of social contexts described in this chapter and the previous one. A particular issue is the complexity of the clearance of copyright for sampled material. Schloss shows that 'a substantial number of people, including artists, lawyers, copyright holders, and their various representatives and assistants, must approve any given sample request – and any one of them can veto it by simply ignoring, forgetting or otherwise failing to respond to it' (ibid.: 179).

Thus this example brings together a number of themes from this chapter and the previous one, in emphasizing the complex practices of a group of music creators. This creation involves technological dexterity, but is not defined and determined by the technology as human beings are making deliberate choices about what sounds right to them.

Summary

This chapter has considered:

- some important studies of jazz musicians which point to issues of art and commerce in their lives;
- evidence of the interconnections between art and pop music-making;

- some important dimensions and accounts of music-making at the more specific and everyday level;
- the nature of some of the most important parts of the pop production process, including the changing role of the producer and the organization of the studio;
- the interactions between technology and pop production.

Part II

Text

History, Politics and Sexuality

This chapter is the first of four to focus on the texts of popular music. It begins the move away from the direct consideration of the production dimension of the production, text and audience framework outlined in the Introduction. However, in accord with the sociological orientation of this book, these texts are set in context. The chapter aims, first, to provide an account of the recent development of pop and rock music which locates the wider meanings of these forms in different political and economic contexts, developing some of the analysis from earlier chapters by including descriptive material on the development of contemporary pop music; second, to take up some of these wider meanings through an analysis of the interconnections between pop and political action and meaning; and third, further to consider some of these political and social meanings through discussion of pop's relations to gender and sexuality.

This chapter also introduces some themes which continue to resonate in the discussion of pop music. These include considerations of the value of pop music and why it is that some forms are valued more highly than others, and the extent to which forms of pop music are an authentic expression of individuals or social groups. These themes are further pursued in subsequent chapters.

The development of rock and roll

Richard Middleton has located the development of rock and roll since the mid-1950s in a wider historical context of musical and cultural change. He suggests that three 'moments' of important social change in music as a whole have occurred in Western societies, though at different points in time in different societies. The first of these, which Middleton calls a 'bourgeois revolution', occurred in Britain between the late eighteenth century and the middle of the nineteenth. During this period, a music industry developed which was dominated by the commercialism of the capitalist, or bourgeois, class and 'most musical production is in the hands of or is mediated by commercial music publishers, concert organizers and promoters, theatre and public house managers' (Middleton 1990: 13). By the mid-1850s, there was a 'congruence across a range of different musical practices, resulting in a not exactly homogeneous musical field but one clearly dominated by a bourgeois synthesis' (ibid.). As Middleton shows:

> With variants, this relative congruence of musical technique, repertoire and practice stretched across light opera, bourgeois domestic song, the brass band and mass choral movements and the now more rationally organized music hall; it even penetrated the broadside and orally transmitted song genres of the industrial areas. Street music was gradually banished, political song pushed tight proletarian enclaves, and the musical avant-garde characteristic of earlier in the century was either marginalized or assimilated, as brass bands played Wagner and parlour singers juxtaposed Schubert and Schumann with more commercial products. (Ibid.)

The second period of change began by the 1890s, when new forms of mass culture, generated by the new monopoly capitalism, appeared. Large corporations became more important in international marketplaces and American forms, such as ragtime and early jazz, became more popular, showing a tendency to overshadow national music forms. Middleton locates the third period of change after the Second World War, especially with the beginnings of rock 'n' roll, and argues that this was the 'moment' of 'pop culture'. At this point, there were the beginnings of increasing corporate domination, which coexisted with more local initiatives often based in particular sectors of the population. There were technological changes based around electronic systems and young working-class people became significant movers in musical creation. This system became relatively stabilized by the late 1960s when:

> new social patterns, technologies and musical styles had been substantially assimilated into a reorganized music-industrial system: a transnational oligopoly of vast entertainment corporations, supplied to some extent by 'independent' producers; serviced by mass audience radio and TV channels (with some 'minority' shows and channels), by a symbiotically pliant music press and by related leisure-products businesses; and directing itself at a series of separate audiences whose distinctness is less subcultural than a creature of market researchers' consumer profiles. (Ibid.: 15)

This view suggests that, despite the significant changes that are happening around digitization, contemporary music is dominated by the large corporations discussed in chapter 1. Small or independent companies feed the larger ones. However, as was noted in chapter 1, some writers have argued that 'independent' companies based in specific locations were central to the development of rock and roll. To consider such approaches it is necessary to examine the context in which rock developed. Gillett (1983) periodizes the development of rock in the way shown in figure 3.1. This periodization and terminology reflects a critical judgement of worth on Gillett's part which values the 'roughness' of rock 'n' roll over the later, blander, rock and roll. Rock 'n' roll is a hybrid which developed out of previous musical forms, most importantly black music, country music, folk music and previous pop forms (Frith 1983: 12–38). According to Gillett, it contained a number of different styles, which are listed in figure 3.2.

This diversity in rock 'n' roll reflected the internal diversity of some of its source materials. Thus, in discussing black music (a topic more fully explored in chapter 4),

Up to 1958	rock 'n' roll
1958–1964	rock and roll
1964–	rock

Figure 3.1 Periodization of the development of rock

Source: Adapted from Gillett 1983

1 'northern band rock 'n' roll' (for example, Bill Haley)
2 'the New Orleans dance blues'
3 'Memphis country rock (also known as rockabilly)'
4 'Chicago rhythm and blues'
5 'vocal group rock 'n' roll'

All 'depended for their dance beat on contemporary Negro dance rhythms'

Figure 3.2 The five styles of rock 'n' roll

Source: Adapted from Gillett 1983: 23

Gillett points to the number of different types of rhythm and blues music, which itself is an all-encompassing label used to categorize music produced for the black market. It replaced the earlier description of 'race music'. The different types of rhythm and blues music discussed by Gillett (1983) are the 'Dancehall Blues', the 'Club Blues', 'Bar Blues', Gospel and what he calls the 'Group Sounds'. Detailed discussions of these different styles can be found in Gillett's book.

The pivotal figure in rock 'n' roll is Elvis Presley. Gillett (1983) interprets the relationship of Presley with other musicians and the producer, Sam Phillips, in the studio in a way that brings out the creative roles of the participants in the new rockabilly or Memphis country rock. Some extracts from Gillett's interpretation appear in box 3.1.

So far, this brief consideration of the development of rock 'n' roll has centred on the transformations within the music itself, how it related to earlier, source, material, and some of the processes which went on in the studio at its creative moment. However, it is important to consider the social context in which rock 'n' roll developed in more detail. In his discussion of the development of rock 'n' roll in Memphis, Gordon (1995) shows the cultural importance of a wrestler (Sputnik Monroe) and a film Western hero (Lash Larue). In addition, like other commentators on Memphis, such as Guralnick (1995), he points to the importance of Dewey Phillips's radio show, where Elvis Presley's first records were aired. A key piece of sociological analysis of the wider context of the development of rock 'n' roll has been written by Peterson (1990).

Peterson asks the question 'why 1955?', that is, why was there such a fundamental shift in the nature of American popular music between 1954 and 1956? He suggests that previous analyses have tended to point to three main factors: first, the role of particular creative individuals, such as Elvis Presley; second, changes in the nature of the audience for popular music, in particular the influence of those individuals born after the Second World War; and third, changes in the media industries themselves.

Box 3.1 The development of rockabilly in Memphis

Presley was the most commercially successful of a number of Memphis singers who evolved what they themselves called 'country rock' and what others, record collectors and people in the industry, have called 'rockabilly'. Country rock was basically a Southern white version of 12-bar boogie blues, shouted with a minimum of subtlety by ex-hillbilly singers over an accompaniment featuring electric guitar, stand-up bass, and – from 1956 – drums, still taboo in Nashville. The style evolved partly from the imaginative guidance of a Memphis radio station engineer, Sam Phillips, who entered the recording business by supervising sessions with local blues singers and leasing the masters to a number of independent companies (Chess in Chicago, owned by the Chess brothers, or Modern/RPM in Los Angeles, owned by the Bihari brothers). The success of some of these singers, notably B. B. King and Howlin' Wolf, encouraged Phillips to form his own label, Sun, and two of the singers he recorded for his own label, Little Junior Parker and Rufus Thomas, had hit records in the Negro market.

The Memphis blues singers used small bands which featured piano, guitar, and saxophone. No particular dominant style linked them all, but common to many of their records was a kind of intimate atmosphere created by the simple and cheap, but unorthodox, 'tape delay echo' recording technique of Phillips. The singers invariably made their personal presence felt on the records, menacingly in Howlin' Wolf's case, impatiently in Junior Parker's. These recordings, and other more traditional blues, and rhythm and blues records issued by Sun, were known to a substantial number of white youths through the South, and presented a source of song material and stylistic inspiration that was in many ways more satisfactory than the orthodox country and western culture.

Jimmie Rodgers sang the 'white blues' in the twenties but Elvis Presley was the first to make it work as pop music. According to the legend of his recording debut, his discovery by Sam Phillips was casual and lucky. Presley is said to have attracted the attention of Phillips when he used Sun's studios to cut a record for his mother's birthday present; Phillips encouraged him to make a record with proper accompaniment, and the two men were rewarded with a local hit from one of the sides, 'That's All Right'.

The story of Presley's discovery has the elements of romance, coincidence, and fate that legends need, and in fact seems to be true, but it is likely that if Phillips and Presley had not met, two other such people would soon have done what they did – merge rhythm and blues with country and western styles and material, and come up with a new style. In the panhandle of west Texas, in Arkansas, in north Louisiana, and in Memphis there were other singers whose cultural and musical experience were comparable to Presley's; indeed, some of them followed him into the Sun studios, while others tried studios in Nashville and Clovis, New Mexico.

It is difficult to assess how great a part Sam Phillips played in influencing his singers – among other things, by introducing them to blues records – and how much they already knew. Presley told one interviewer:

> I'd play [guitar] along with the radio or phonograph, and taught myself the chord positions. We were a religious family, going round together to sing at camp meetings and revivals, and I'd take my guitar with us when I could. I also dug the real low-down Mississippi singers, mostly Big Bill Broonzy and Big Boy Crudup, although they would scold me at home for listening to them.
>
> 'Sinful music', the townsfolk in Memphis said it was. Which never bothered me, I guess.

In the same interview, Presley stressed the importance of Phillips:

> Mr Phillips said he'd coach me if I'd come over to the studio as often as I could. It must have been a year and a half before he gave me an actual session. At last he let me try a western song – and it sounded terrible. But the second idea he had was the one that jelled.
>
> 'You want to make some blues?' he suggested over the 'phone, knowing I'd always been a sucker for that kind of jive. He mentioned Big Boy Crudup's name and maybe others too. I don't remember.
>
> All I know is, I hung up and ran 15 blocks to Mr Phillips' office before he'd gotten off the line – or so he tells me. We talked about the Crudup records I knew – 'Cool Disposition', 'Rock Me, Mama', 'Hey Mama', 'Everything's All Right', and others, but settled for 'That's All Right', one of my top favourites. . . .

What Presley achieved was certainly not 'the same thing' as the men he copied. On 'That's All Right' and 'Mystery Train' (written and first recorded by Junior Parker for Sun), he evolved a personal version of this style, singing high and clear, breathless and impatient, varying his rhythmic emphasis with a confidence and inventiveness that were exceptional for a white singer. The sound suggested a young white man celebrating freedom, ready to do anything, go anywhere, pausing long enough for apologies and even regrets and recriminations, but then hustling on towards the new. He was best on fast songs, when his impatient singing matched the urgent rhythm from bass (Bill Black) and guitar (Scotty Moore). Each of his five Sun singles backed a blues song with a country and western song, most of them already familiar to the respective audiences; each sold better than its predecessor, and increasing numbers of people discovered Presley either through radio broadcasts or through his stage appearances.

But Presley did not reach the mass popular music audience with his Sun records, which sold mainly to audiences in the South and to the minority country and western audience elsewhere. Only after Presley's contract was bought by RCA-Victor did his records make the national top ten, and the songs on these records were not in a country rock style. At Victor, under the supervision of Chet Atkins, Presley's records featured vocal groups, heavily electrified guitars, and drums, all of which were considered alien by both country and western audiences and by the audience for country rock music. Responding to these unfamiliar intrusions in his accompaniment, Presley's voice became much more theatrical and self-conscious as he sought to contrive excitement and emotion which he had seemed to achieve on his Sun records without any evident forethought.

Presley's success for Sun, and later for RCA-Victor, encouraged Phillips to try other singers with comparable styles and material, and attracted to his studios young southerners with similar interests. Carl Perkins and Warren Smith from the Memphis area, Roy Orbison from west Texas, Johnny Cash, Conway Twitty, and Charlie Rich from Arkansas, and Jerry Lee Lewis from northern Louisiana brought songs, demonstration tapes, and their ambitions to Phillips, who switched almost completely from black singers to white singers once the latter became commercially successful.

Source: Gillett 1983: 26–9

Peterson criticizes both the first and second of these explanations. He argues that the first accords too great a role to the creative genius of particular individuals (though he does not suggest that these individuals were without talent). Rather, he maintains that at particular points in time certain individuals come to the fore because of a specific set of social conditions, which operate as a kind of pattern of selecting mechanisms. Peterson argues, therefore, that there are always more talented artists in existence than those who come to the fore at any one particular time. His argument against the second mode of explanation is more straightforward. He points out that in 1954, 'the oldest of the baby-boomers were only nine years old and half had not been born yet' (1990: 98). This leaves Peterson free to develop an argument that stresses the place of contextual factors in the development of rock. In general, he has been associated with the 'production-of-culture' perspective, which argues that there are six factors that 'shape' the development of culture: 'law, technology, industry structure, organisation structure, occupational career and market' (ibid.). In the main body of his article, he explores how these factors influenced the events of 1955.

Peterson begins with law and technology, which are thought to have a significant role in defining the ways in which the other factors operate. With respect to law, he identifies three important aspects: copyright, patent law and Federal Communications Commission (FCC) regulation. He argues that the main copyright collecting agency for public performance, the American Society of Composers, Authors and Publishers (ASCAP), which controlled the reproduction of music ensuring that only certain forms were allowed on the radio, for example, was challenged by a rival organization, Broadcast Music Incorporated (BMI), which had been formed by the radio networks when they had failed to agree over licensing fees. Because of ASCAP's control over more traditional radio-type material, BMI utilized other types of music which had previously been excluded from radio airplay. Thus, a struggle over rights revenue (see further, chapter 1) is seen as one of the contributing factors to the development of rock. However, this conflict occurred in the early 1940s, so it does not explain the outbreak of rock on its own. In terms of patent law, Peterson examines the struggle between different companies over the ownership of different record formats which led, by the early 1950s, to the existence of the long-playing 33⅓-rpm and the 45-rpm record. The latter was particularly important as it was aimed at the pop market and was far more robust than the fragile 78-rpm disc which it replaced. Thus, the 45-rpm record could be distributed much more easily by smaller record companies. Finally, in terms of FCC regulation, there was a great increase in the number of radio stations that were licensed to broadcast.

The introduction of the 45-rpm record was a form of technological innovation. Peterson draws attention to two other important technological innovations: the introduction of television and the development of the transistor radio. Television is significant, in the main, for its effects on radio. The big networks that had previously controlled radio moved into television, which they continued to dominate in the USA, where local television stations were affiliated to NBC, CBS or ABC. Smaller, more specialized radio stations were set up. Much of the traditional radio programming (for example, soap operas) moved over to the new television medium. Second, there was the introduction into America of cheap, portable radios from Japan.

In discussing industry structure, organization structure, occupational careers and the market, Peterson draws comparisons between the situation in 1948 and in 1958. He provides much detail in describing a movement over this 10-year period, from the control of the industry by a small number of companies which produced, distributed and manufactured musical products to relatively more diverse and 'entrepreneurial' situations (see also the discussion of these developments in the Introduction). As Peterson summarizes:

> In the early 1950s, the music industry was blind to the large and growing unsatiated demand for greater variety in music and deaf to the efforts of musicians that might have satisfied that demand. The music industry was financially as well as aesthetically committed to the big band-crooner style of popular music of the time, and, because of its oligopolistic control of the production, distribution and marketing of new music, was able to thwart the marketing of alternative styles.
>
> Then with the transfer of network radio programming to television, radio turned to playing records as the cheapest effective form of programming. The arrival of cheap transistor radios and the development of the top 40 radio-as-jukebox format meant that a much larger number and far wider range of music was exposed to the audience. Using the new durable 45 rpm records, and taking advantage of the developing network of independent record distributors, numerous independent record companies experimented with a wide range of new sounds in an effort to tap the unsatiated market demand. In a matter of two dozen months between late 1954 and early 1957 rock was forged in this caldron of entrepreneurial creativity. (1990: 113–14)

Peterson provides a very important and illuminating sociological account of the social context of the development of rock in the United States. However, it is important to note two problems with his approach. First, it is not always clear whether he is contextualizing the development of rock or explaining its development at a particular moment. At the beginning of his article, he stresses the explanatory. However, as the piece develops, he becomes more involved in drawing comparisons across time, which are not, in themselves, explanations, as it is not clear precisely what effects the factors are thought to have. Second, Peterson's focus is on the United States and his account is not necessarily very helpful in explaining the development of rock in other societies, such as Britain.

The latter has been examined by Bradley (1992) in the context of the 'composite account of rock 'n' roll'. His clear summaries of what he sees as myths about the development of rock are reproduced in box 3.2.

Box 3.2   The composite account of rock 'n' roll

It is possible to construct a sort of standard composite account of the main events and developments known as 'rock 'n' roll', based on the main texts discussed above and other similar books. It consists of a list of factors on which they more or less all agree, and on which they confer major causal status in relation to the rise of rock 'n' roll and beat music. It also involves a starting definition or delimitation of the body of musical artists, and records, radio and TV shows, which make up the phenomenon of rock 'n' roll and beat music.

The USA

The following is a summary of what might be called the standard view, the agreed wisdom, or the prevalent *myth* about early American rock 'n' roll.

1 'Popular music' already exists in the early and mid-1950s as an industry, with its 'major' and 'independent' recording companies, publishing houses, radio stations, etc. 'Live' venues exist in most towns and cities, while for records a whole infrastructure of distribution and sales outlets, as well as large chains of juke boxes, are well established. Trade magazines, magazines for listeners, and the charts or hit parades all serve promotional functions. The popular music audience already includes almost the whole population. Profits are high and, consequently, plant and other investments are expanding; this is especially true of record production, which, having all but died during the Depression and the war years, is growing dramatically, on the basis of improved and still improving materials (vinyl replacing shellac) and technology (hi-fidelity and, later in the 1950s, transistorization of radios).

2 'Popular music' also exists already as a *tradition* familiar to virtually all American listeners and musicians. Certain styles are nationally established as 'popular', others are more locally based (country music), or are

excluded, to some degree, from the national popular charts ('race' music, as gospel, blues and rhythm and blues were then called), though they are closely related to popular music, in being often catered for by the same companies, and in providing numerous popular artists. There are also several varieties of jazz, from 'traditional' to 'modern', each of which is less than fully familiar but by no means unknown to the 'mass' of the listening public. Both modern jazz and country music enjoy 'booms' in the late 1940s and early 1950s, but these are not on the scale of the rock 'n' roll developments which follow.

The presence of a black, working-class population in every major city of the USA by 1950, a result of migrations mainly from the First World War onwards, means that local radio stations and record stores almost everywhere reflect, to a significant degree, the tastes of these communities. And since neither radio-dial-twiddling nor shopping-around can be censored, despite the industry's compulsive categorizing, young white people in ever-increasing numbers do listen to the music which is becoming known as 'rhythm 'n' blues' and 'rock and roll' (or rock 'n' roll) in these years. Those local DJs, juke-box operators and independent record store and record label owners who are close to this development take note, and begin to consciously promote this music for white listeners.

Most of the authors agree, to some extent, that the 'boring', 'bland', 'sentimental' state of the nationally popular (among whites) music of the early 1950s, as a whole, contributes to the defection of these young white listeners, but they all argue this in a very generalized, sweeping way, and all argue for different exceptions. Their problems with regard to verbalizing musical meaning are clearly displayed in this difficulty or weakness which they all share.

3 A 'post-war boom' in the USA is the economic background to a new scale of working-class and middle-class 'affluence' in the 1950s. Both pocket money and widely available part-time work swell the disposable income of 'teenagers' at high school, while wages are often relatively high in the first years of work, in comparison with the 1930s and 1940s. The overall effect is to create a large group, throughout the country, of independent young or 'teenage' consumers, of relatively high spending power, even despite the rise in numbers staying on longer at school.

Most of the rock histories use the term 'teenagers' uncritically, ignoring the fact that it was a neologism of the late 1940s or early 1950s, replete with many new connotations. The connotations which are clearly retained in the rock historians' appropriation of the term are (a) a style of *leisure*, and of *consumption*, found among 'kids' from the ages of 13–14 to the early 20s, (b) a certain exuberance or rowdiness, which can become a threatening wildness, and which includes (c) a foregrounding of sexual practices (dating, going steady, courtship in general, and the 'threat' of 'sex before marriage'). Behind these implications of the term, we can also see clearly that the standard notion of 'the teenager' is usually of a boy, not a girl, and that the 'threat' of sex is a threat of boys *against* girls, as seen *by* parents, teachers, etc. These things, sadly, remain unsaid in the rock histories.

4 The search for 'novelty', derived from the competitive economic character of the pop industry, and in particular from attempts by 'independent' record companies to outflank 'majors', leads to 'cover versions' of dance blues and vocal group successes from the 'race' market, being offered on the mainly white pop market as a whole. In a sense, this is merely the equivalent of the raids on jazz and on country music of the same years, but partly it is also the result of an 'authentic' pressure from existing teenage audiences, as spotted by adventurous DJs and independent studio producers. These 'cover versions' are normally produced by 'acceptable' white artists, and involve some changes in musical style, and some cleaning up of lyrics on occasions, but none the less they have the side-effect, when successful, of arousing some interest in the originals, and the longer-term effect of familiarizing the white pop audiences with some of the conventions of the black styles. Some groups of white musicians actually begin to specialize in a 'half-way' style, notably Bill Haley and the Comets, whose 'Shake Rattle and Roll' is a cover version of a rhythm 'n' blues hit, while 'Rock around the Clock' is an original number modelled on the work of black artists to some extent.

5 A cluster of media events combines to shoot the Haley style, and that of some others, into national prominence, notably the use of the music in the sound track of *Blackboard Jungle*, a successful film about 'wild' adolescents, and subsequently the appearances of Elvis Presley on the Nashville TV show 'Grand Old Opry', and later on the nationally screened 'Ed Sullivan Show'. Later come other films, such as *Rock around the Clock* and *The Girl Can't Help It*.

6 At this point, the competitive logic of the industry once again influences developments, producing a race to imitate the initial successes and to promote the music with all the resources available. In particular, again, the 'independents' see their chance to compete on more equal terms with the 'majors', since both are relatively new to the style, and neither is very sure at first of how to predict who and what will be successful. Literally dozens of young artists are signed up, especially by independent companies, to produce rock 'n' roll; others are converted overnight, from aspiring crooners or country singers into imitation Elvises.

The very over-production and financial chaos which result help to ensure that this situation cannot last, and by about 1958–9 in the USA, the initial 'explosion' of production of, and enthusiasm for, rock 'n' roll is over. However, the consequences of this period of upheaval are that one or two independent companies do indeed establish themselves as small majors, that a new generation of producers, artists and song writers becomes established in the industry, and also that some black rhythm 'n' blues artists share in the explosion, singing their own music more or less as they would be doing anyway, but reaching young white audiences. Fats Domino, Little Richard, Chuck Berry, Jackie Wilson, Lloyd Price, Larry Williams and the Coasters are among those who owe their wider success to this upheaval.

Britain

Each of the rock histories devotes a section to Britain (though not normally to any other country), tracing the story of the impact of rock 'n' roll (and of the home-produced 'skiffle') and placing these events, usually, as 'background' to the Beatles and the 'beat-boom' years of 1963–6. I would argue very strongly that the view which sees the period 1955–63 in Britain as a mere 'background' to later beat, and other later styles, is heavily distorted by an almost fetishistic attention to the charts (i.e. the successes of the Beatles, etc.), and that, sales of records notwithstanding, the development of a 'youth culture' in Britain, and of a music *of* that youth culture, can only be understood by reversing that emphasis. In a very real sense, there is an element of *myth* in the way rock histories skip from one commercial peak to another, or from one 'great artist' to another, ignoring almost totally the social roots of both the music-making and the listening, which ought to be among their objects of study. Nonetheless, the main points of a composite account can again be enumerated, this time relying, however, on a slightly different list of books.

1 The pop industry is already international. American music already features strongly in British record stores, and on Radio Luxemburg, while the BBC allows a little of it into the major popular radio shows. British artists 'cover' most big US hits themselves. Equally, and very importantly, American films are readily available at British cinemas. Any BBC resistance to 'American trash' is out-flanked by the rise of records and by films; and when ITV comes along, it exhibits no scruples in adding to this trend with its pop shows. In any event, pop music coverage on radio and TV is on a very small scale in these years, by 1990s standards, and young listeners rely heavily on record buying and juke boxes.

2 The Teddy boys already exist, chiefly in London, before rock 'n' roll arrives in Britain. They probably originate (according to Hebdige) in the traditional working-class areas of South and East London in the early 1950s. Their style of dress is, in part, an imitation of the Edwardian man about town, but in other respects, they imitate American models. The interest in unusual clothes itself is odd (and new?) among male, working-class Londoners, as is the responsiveness to rapid change in fashions of music which follows in the mid-1950s. Hebdige calls this style 'a focus for an illicit delinquent identity' and points out its connection to a fantasy of America. The phenomenon apparently needs only publicity to spread: only later does commercial exploitation of the style move in.

3 The absence of a large black community with its own musical life (though this was beginning to take shape in the major cities), and also the resistance to pop and rock in general, and American pop and rock in particular, which is maintained by the BBC, combine to give the films which feature rock 'n' roll a greater importance in Britain than in the USA. The film *Rock around the Clock*, and its title song, are adopted by Teds in particular and teenagers in general all over Britain in 1955–6: various 'riots', and the occasional destruction of cinema seats to make room for dancing, gain the music and the audiences much notoriety, orchestrated by the newspapers into a full-scale 'moral panic'. This reaction tends to make rock 'n' roll a sort of badge of defiant identity, rather than just another fad of taste, for the kids involved.

4 Skiffle, a musical style taken initially from traditional jazz bands, coincides with this early rock 'n' roll enthusiasm and, being slightly more respectable in origins, is accepted as a quaint offshoot of jazz or folk music, even by the BBC, who launch '6/5 Special' as a TV pop show specializing in skiffle. One of the important things about this style is that its great simplicity, and the cheapness of using home-made instruments, lead to a wave of amateur and semi-professional imitations by the kids themselves. (What almost every account omits to mention, but is nonetheless true, is that it is *boys*, specifically and almost exclusively, who take up playing skiffle.) This craze lasts from 1956 to 1958 or so, after which amateurism continues, but now mainly in imitation of American rock and post-rock musics.

5 At the same time as amateurism becomes firmly established among teenagers, by about 1957 or 1958, the 'real' rock 'n' roll records from the USA dry up, and post-rock 'balladeers' and British artists exhibiting little or no rock influence come to dominate record sales and radio and TV shows, Tommy Steele, Marty Wilde and Cliff Richard perhaps being the most rock-influenced of these. Some of the new 'rock-pop' records lack the prominent beat of rock 'n' roll, and most are also highly 'arranged' products; on both counts they are not seen as good models by the teenage amateurs, who aim chiefly for a lively dance music. The result is that young audiences seeking live dance music turn away from the charts, just as some American teenagers did in the early 1950s. A live dance music style which becomes known as 'the big beat', and later as 'beat', develops, as does a standard group format of lead and bass guitars, sometimes a third ('rhythm') guitar, drums and vocalist(s), sometimes with a piano or organ, or a harmonica. This beat music thrives most strongly in the provincial British cities where the hit-making, and indeed, record-making, machinery is virtually non-existent (Liverpool, Birmingham, Glasgow, Manchester, Newcastle).

6 A somewhat more self-conscious movement of rejection of the charts leads to the British 'rhythm and blues' movement, chiefly in their milieux. Though this has much in common with the earlier and later jazz booms, in being mainly middle class and often idealistically anti-commercial, it also

resembles beat and rock 'n' roll in many ways: it is performed by small groups (four or five members, with guitars and drums the chief instruments), it uses electrical amplification, and it includes a lot of dance music with a strong beat. The Rolling Stones, the Animals and the Zombies are among many representatives of this movement who become pop successes, while other more 'uncompromising' groups have less success in the early and mid-1960s but strongly influence the later 'British blues', 'underground' and 'heavy' rock developments (John Mayall, Alexis Korner's Blues Incorporated, etc.)

Source: Bradley 1992: 9–14

Bradley identifies a number of problems with the 'composite account', which are also of general relevance to work on the history and meaning of rock. These are:

1   Many accounts neglect 'the problem of understanding and explaining the phenomenon of white kids responding to black styles' (Bradley 1992: 14). This is an area which is explored in chapters 4 and 6.
2   There is a tendency to neglect the phenomenon of the development of the group. Bradley suggests that the idea of a small group of musicians playing together is a new departure for white music in the 1950s.
3   There is a gender blindness in many of the standard accounts which neglects or plays down the 'maleness' of rock 'n' roll.
4   The accounts do not pay enough attention to the nature of amateurism in rock music production and the development of local pop music making in the 1950s.

Aspects of these sorts of criticism have been dealt with in some of the more recent work on rock and pop, which is summarized and examined at other points in this book. However, the discussion so far illuminates two significant factors that will continue to be developed through the rest of this chapter. First, there is the value placed upon particular textual forms of popular music by critics and commentators (see also chapter 5). As we have seen, Gillett conveys approval of a particular form through his use of the term 'rock 'n' roll' and his denigration of the more 'sanitized' 'rock and roll'. In this account, 'rock 'n' roll' somehow stands for freedom and expression and 'rock and roll' for constraint and manipulation. We shall see how rock came to have a particular meaning in the 1960s with connotations of opposition and resistance, especially when compared to pop music. Thus, definitions of textual types or genres are not just of academic interest, but also convey meaning to a much wider audience. This is often connected with politics in the broadest sense.

Second, there are the interconnected issues of gender and sexuality. Bradley (1992) comments on the maleness of many of the accounts of the development of rock. Related to this is the way in which pop music has often been seen as 'immature' or superficial because of its implied audience among young women. The femininity of pop is something implicitly problematic for male writers. Such themes can be explored as we take the story of the development of pop more up to date (see also, Chambers 1985; Reynolds and Press 1995).

Rock and pop in the 1960s and 1970s

The conventional account of the development of rock and pop sees a bland period between the late 1950s and 1963. This is the period where, according to Gillett, the excitement of rock 'n' roll is replaced by standardized music industry products such as Fabian in the United States and Cliff Richard in Britain. A perceived shift occurs with the rise to fame of the Beatles in 1963 in Britain and 1964 in the United States. Whilst in many respects the Beatles were partly located within more 'conventional' forms and packaged in a show business sort of way, their reappropriation of black music styles opened the way for a series of developments during the 1960s. Partly, they are important for the way in which they brought together different styles, integrating forms of black soul with rock and roll. They acted as a bridge between the rock 'n' roll of, for example, Chuck Berry and more pop-oriented material. It is possible to say that they integrated pop and rock and led the field in producing a kind of unified audience which was to exist for a good part of the 1960s. The suggestion here, then, is that there is normally recognized to be a difference between rock and pop which runs through the development of the forms since the 1950s. However, at certain points these forms are intertwined. Indeed, some writers, such as Grossberg (1983), have argued that in detail it is actually very difficult to separate them. In part, this has to do with the role of more detailed analysis of the actual nature of the sounds themselves. This is an issue taken up in chapter 5.

The Beatles opened the space for the development of rock music in the 1960s. There were many different strands of this. In Britain there were a number of groups that utilized blues-based themes and structures and a continuing appropriation of black American forms. Sometimes black American musicians developed the styles themselves, Jimi Hendrix being the most notable example. He played in r 'n' b groups in America in the early 1960s, before coming to Britain in 1966 to team up with two white musicians to form the Jimi Hendrix Experience.

Rock music sold in large quantities and was often seen by its producers and audience to involve the communication of authentic artistic consciousness and to have important things to say about contemporary events. At this time, there developed an audience for rock which seemed open to a number of different styles. Of course, this is not to say that there were not different tastes within the audience and different types of rock. There clearly were. However, by comparison with the polarization between different forms in the early 1960s and the increased separation of forms in subsequent years, these differences were not so clear-cut. There were perhaps more divisions in the United States, though it is possible to argue that forms of fragmentation of the rock pop audience really begin to appear around 1968 between west and east coasts, and forms such as 'Folk-Rock (1965–6), largely a phenomenon of New York and Los Angeles, and its wandering son, the San Francisco Sound (1966–7)' (Heylin 1993: 3) and the embryonic east coast scene centred around the Velvet Underground.

Throughout the 1960s in Britain there had been differences between the influence of more contemporary black sounds in the form of soul and earlier forms, like blues, which fed the more guitar-oriented rock bands. In the early to mid-1960s these could be integrated, as the extract from the journalist Cliff

White's diary from 1964 in box 3.3 shows. However, by the end of the 1960s and the early '70s, a greater degree of fragmentation had set in.

Looking back from the twenty-first century, it is possible to see the beginnings of forms which were to separate more and more as time went on. It has become increasingly common to date the beginnings of the genre of heavy metal to the work of Black Sabbath, Deep Purple and Led Zeppelin in the late 1960s and early '70s (Weinstein 1991; Walser 1993). Also, the 'pomp' or 'classical' rock of groups like ELP, Yes and Genesis can be clearly identified, as can the influence and popularity of some forms of British folk rock, such as Fairport Convention. Whilst the followers of all these forms may now see them as separate types, they might not have been seen thus in the early 1970s, when it was perfectly possible to be a fan of all three.

What did open up in a clear way in the late 1960s and early 1970s was a new divide between what was perceived to be the more serious – and, somehow, more

---

Box 3.3   Cliff White's 1964 diary

Fri	Oct 30	Jimmy Reed, Sugar Pie De Santo, The Dixie Cups on Ready, Steady, Go.
Sat	Oct 31	Saw Jimmy Reed at Club Noreik. Had to miss John Lee Hooker at Flamingo.
Mon	Nov 2	Saw Carl Perkins, Tommy Tucker, The Animals at Gaumont State. Had to miss Jimmy Reed at Flamingo.
Wed	Nov 4	Martha & Vandellas on Top Of The Pops.
Fri	Nov 6	Martha & Vandellas, Kim Weston on RSG.
Mon	Nov 9	My birthday. Still alive.
Tues	Nov 10	Martha & Vandellas on Pop Inn.
Fri	Nov 13	Saw The Isley Brothers at East Ham Granada. Had to miss The Soul Sisters at Flamingo.
Sat	Nov 14	Perkins, Tucker etc. at Finsbury Park Astoria.
Mon	Nov 16	Down to The Scene with the mob as usual.
Wed	Nov 18	Saw Jimmy Reed at Flamingo. Chatted with him for about an hour backstage. Great bloke.
Thurs	Nov 19	Took some records up to Jimmy's hotel and had breakfast with him. Geezer called Al Smith from Vee Jay was there. Nice enough bloke but seemed more keen to talk about Betty Everett than Jimmy.
Fri	Nov 20	Jerry Lee, Marvin Gaye, The Stones on RSG.
Sat	Nov 21	Saw Jerry Lee at Club Noreik.
Sun	Nov 22	Load of us went down to Brighton to see Jerry Lee again.
Mon	Nov 23	Saw Jimmy Reed at British Legion Hall, South Harrow. Had to miss Jerry Lee at Eltham Baths.
Thurs	Nov 26	Saw Howlin' Wolf and Hubert Sumlin at Marquee.

Source: C. White, sleeve notes for Jimmy Reed: Upside Your Head. Courtesy of Charly Records

CRB 1003, 1980

'authentic' – rock music and 'commercial' pop music. Devotees of rock could be scathing in their attacks on pop and commercialism, and criticism of groups seen to be 'selling out' became exceptionally shrill. This accusation, which continues to this day, despite the way in which Britpop musicians legitimated commercial success (Harris 2003), was regularly hurled at musicians like Marc Bolan, who stopped being a hero of the so-called underground when his singles began to sell on the mass market. It had of course been made against Bob Dylan when he moved from acoustic to electric instruments in the mid-1960s. Pop meant singles and chart success; rock meant albums and was serious. It is important to recognize that the distinction was not necessarily built around the size of the audience. The rock groups sold lots of albums, but their 'serious' intent and content seemed to protect them from the criticism of 'selling out'. The criteria of values did not depend on sales. There are political issues here that are considered in more detail later in this chapter.

There were forms that bridged this increasing divide between rock and pop in the early 1970s, in particular the association of different artists under the heading of glitter rock. Some of these bands were clearly seen to be pop groups oriented to top-20 success, examples including the Sweet and Gary Glitter; however, others straddled, and in lots of ways reconstructed, the divide between rock and pop, most notably David Bowie and Roxy Music. Both of these showed the influence of the later forms of connection between art and pop influence considered by Frith and Horne (1987), as discussed in chapter 2. This crossing and breaking down of the barrier which had been erected between pop and rock was to be influential on developments in both Britain and the United States in the mid- to late 1970s, where art, pop and rock intertwined to produce punk rock.

There has been a certain amount of rather nationalistic debate on the origins of punk. This was certainly an issue at the time when various factions wanted to claim punk as their own. However, it is more useful to see American and British punk as intertwined and interacting forms and to leave aside rather pointless debates about originality and ownership. The beginnings of American punk can be traced through from the forms of east coast rock art collaboration, of which the Velvet Underground is the clearest example (Heylin 1993). Such collaborations, together with the influence of glitter rock and the pub rock movement of the mid-1970s, combined to produce the punk and new waves of 1976 and 1977 (Laing 1985; Savage 1991). These often explicitly attacked the rock values, which were seen to have been corrupted through the 1970s as rock stars became richer and more detached from their audiences. However, most important for the present chronicle was the way in which punk attempted to draw on black forms, most notably the Jamaican one of reggae, in the production of something that was neither pop nor rock and which made no attempt to integrate the two. Thus initially, punk went against the album ethic of the rock bands and the kind of top-20 promotion strategies of the pop groups. Singles became important again, but they were to be produced in an 'independent' and amateur manner, even though, as was discussed in chapter 2, there are clear difficulties with the notion of independence used here. This integrative moment did not last very long before a new – and qualitatively different (on some accounts) – form of fragmentation occurred in the 1980s and 1990s.

Rock and pop in the 1980s and 1990s

Some see the punk period as a watershed. It represents an attempt, first, to regain the spirit of the early days of rock 'n' roll, in its desire for independence and the short three-minute song; and, second, to reintegrate the pop and rock forms which had increasingly split during the 1970s. It also marks an important point in the fragmentation that was to develop further during the 1980s and '90s. Thus in Britain, the early 1980s saw both the integration of punk and reggae in the 2 Tone movement (see chapter 1) which updated 1960s Jamaican ska with a punk framework and the development of new pop as represented initially by the groups labelled as the 'New Romantics'. Slightly later came the new 'rock' bands such as Big Country and, more enduringly and popularly, U2. During the later stages of the punk period, heavy metal reasserted itself in Britain and, subsequently, during the 1980s in the United States, where it has been argued that heavy metal moved to the centre of the popular music field (Walser 1993).

As the 1980s progressed, other forms, such as hip-hop from America, increased in importance and influenced white music in different ways. There has been the continued existence of what has been known as the independent or Indie sector, though, as has been noted at several points so far, it is not always easy to specify what this is independent of or from. All this has led to fluidity between the different types of music, where it has become, argue many commentators, more and more difficult to sustain the sorts of definition of rock and pop which seemed to have some analytic purchase in the 1960s and '70s. There has been a breakdown of barriers, it is suggested, so that it was, for example, possible for Michael Jackson to employ heavy metal forms as associated with Eddie Van Halen on his *Thriller* album of 1982. Furthermore, it has been argued that fragmentation into lots of different forms of music and the interactions between such forms represent postmodernism and the effects of this process in popular music. At this point, it is necessary to examine this concept in more detail, as this will then contextualize the discussion of musical forms that have developed since the 1980s in the rest of this book.

Pop and postmodernism

Postmodernism is a disputed term, which has been the subject of some of the most convoluted argument in the social sciences and humanities over the past 25 or so years. From its beginnings, as a categorization of new forms of architecture which broke from the regularity of the modern block of glass, 'postmodernism' has been applied to diverse cultural forms, intellectual activities and the nature of society itself. An introductory account, 'Postmodernism and Popular Culture' (Strinati 1992), has suggested that there are five main characteristics of postmodernism. These are listed in figure 3.3.

In this account, postmodernism entails a new fluidity between culture and society. Culture is not in some way separated from society or reflecting parts of it. Indeed, society cannot be defined without taking account of cultural factors. Style is central. It is not added onto an essential content as a secondary matter, but is often foregrounded over the meaning of a cultural form. Moreover, it may be

'1   the breakdown of the distinction between culture and society
2   an emphasis on style at the expense of substance and content
3   the breakdown of the distinction between high culture (art) and popular culture
4   confusions over time and space
5   the decline of the "meta-narratives" '

Figure 3.3 Elements of postmodernism

Source: Strinati 1992

argued that it is impossible to separate style from content. In earlier periods, it is maintained, such essential content to culture or art could be isolated and style was less important and seen as secondary. There is a new fluidity between forms of popular culture and high culture, which has led to difficulties in defining precisely what these different forms of culture actually refer to. For example, in the late 1960s, the artist Andy Warhol collaborated with the rock band the Velvet Underground, which itself included a classically trained musician (John Cale) and the more pop-oriented writing of Lou Reed. The resulting product is difficult to classify in either high or popular culture terms.

Further, there has been a breakdown of old feelings and experiences of time and space. People are less located in one place. They travel more and have wider experiences of other cultures. They can see events as they are happening on live TV, as in the reports on the bombing of Baghdad during the first Gulf War, and find the products of other societies for sale in local supermarkets and shops in a way that would have been unthinkable only 20 or 30 years ago. Finally, there are arguments that the grand narratives or ideas by which people led their lives have increasingly broken down. For example, Marxism, the official ideology of state communist societies, or a form of socialist ideology in the West, has collapsed, and alternative religions compete with more established or state-recognized ones. Some commentators maintain, therefore, that there has been a distinct shift in values in contemporary societies.

The discussion of postmodernism so far has been rather general, in that it is held to be a concept that applies across a range of developments in society, culture and philosophy. The term is also used in a more specific sense, to examine the nature of artistic change. Some writers have suggested that postmodernism is an explicit break from those forms of culture grouped under the heading of 'modernism', which was so influential in the arts during the twentieth century. Examples of modernism would be the paintings of Picasso and the novels of James Joyce. Some of the specific differences between modernism and postmodernism in the arts are summarized in figure 3.4, which complements the general account of Strinati.

Through this discussion, Featherstone (1988) illuminates clear differences between modernism and postmodernism. Postmodernism is more playful than modernism; it uses popular culture forms and is unafraid of suggesting that the artist is not a genius. Modernism tended to foreground the importance of the author and to separate high and popular culture.

There are difficulties with these general characterizations in that they often blur the specific development of particular forms of art and the differences between them. Thus, it may be that postmodernism in the novel is rather different from

Modernism
- Aesthetic self-consciousness and reflexiveness;
- A rejection of narrative structure in favour of simultaneity and montage;
- An exploration of the paradoxical, ambiguous and uncertain open-ended nature of reality;
- A rejection of the notion of an integrated personality in favour of an emphasis upon the destructured, dehumanized subject.

Postmodernism
- The effacement of the boundary between art and everyday life;
- The collapse of the hierarchical distinction between high and mass/popular culture;
- A stylistic promiscuity favouring eclecticism and the mixing of codes;
- Parody, pastiche, irony, playfulness and the celebration of the surface 'depthlessness' of culture;
- The decline of the originality/genius of the artistic producer and the assumption that art can only be repetitious.

Figure 3.4 Comparison of modernism with postmodernism
Source: Derived from Featherstone 1988

postmodernism in painting, or that modernism in the novel developed at a different time from modernism in architecture. However, it has been suggested that postmodernism has now become a 'cultural dominant' (Jameson 1991). If this is the case, it would affect popular music. It has been suggested by some analysts that the breaking of the boundaries between previously separated genres of popular music evidences the development of postmodernism. Likewise, the break with the narrative of the conventional song, in forms of hip-hop and rave music, could be argued to be postmodern. A related case has been made for the interconnection of music and image in contemporary music video, which some have seen as a postmodern form.

The important point to consider at the moment is the extent to which the seemingly increasing fragmentation and interconnection of pop and rock musics since the 1980s is an example of postmodernism, which can therefore be connected to other developments in different cultural and social areas (such as post-Fordism discussed in chapter 1). There is a certain amount of dispute around this issue and this can be followed up in the work of such writers as Stratton (1989), Redhead (1990) and Goodwin (1991). We shall return to some of the issues involved in the case study of Madonna at the end of this chapter. However, it is important to note that the debate on the nature and relevance of the concept of postmodernism has tended to take place at a high level of generality. Moreover, examples from different areas of culture are used as examples of postmodernism. The danger is that broad cultural changes are identified and examples then found to fit the overall characterizations. Furthermore, the focus on modernism and postmodernism obscures the continued importance of realism in popular culture in general and popular music in particular. The relations between these textual forms are considered at greater length in chapter 4. However, the potential benefits of a concept like postmodernism are that it illustrates the linkages and parallels between different areas of culture, which may be influencing each other, and facilitates the identification of overall trends in society and culture, showing in broad outline how society is changing.

The debate around postmodernism has often raised issues of politics (see in general, for example, Lipsitz 1994). In some accounts, the playful, anything-goes tendency within postmodernism is conservative, or deflects attention away from opposition to dominant groups through the celebration of individual actions. This raises more general issues of the connections between popular music and political intervention.

Pop and politics

Pop music has been seen as an important social force in many different ways. In this section, attention is drawn to the connections between pop and politics along three different dimensions. First, there is the way in which pop or rock is seen as in some way oppositional to established values in the broadest sense. Second, there are the interconnections between rock and politics, as understood in a more conventional way, as concerning political parties, the government, the state, and so on. Third, this leads to a consideration of definitions of censorship – how such processes should be understood and how they occur in different ways in specific contexts.

As was been discussed above, the development of rock 'n' roll in the 1950s is often presented as a kind of liberation from the dullness of American and British life of the period. It is seen to have opened up new possibilities for self-expression and to break down the conventions and stuffiness of everyday life. Rock was vibrant and something that authority did not like. In this account there is something inherently oppositional about rock. In the 1960s, ideas about the oppositional status of rock were entailed in its characterization as the music of protest, the 'movement' or the underground. A clear version of this argument has been expressed by Bradley, who argues that rock music is a 'collective, collectivizing, communal phenomenon' (1992: 118). Rock is produced in a communal fashion, in groups and bands for example, and is consumed communally at concerts, in clubs and so on. For Bradley, it was primarily the music of youth:

> Youth culture involves a resistance to atomization and massification, and to the boredom, the loneliness, the fear and the experiential vicariousness they produce. The unique position of post-war teenagers, physically adult yet excluded from adult roles and responsibilities, with considerable disposable cash, and familiar from early childhood with the products of the modern mass media, healthy, well-fed and energetic, yet involved in less hard physical work than many of their ancestors – this privileged, new position seemed merely to throw into sharp relief for them the limitations, frustrations and oppressiveness of their existence in other respects, and to give them the opportunity to respond in new ways to these conditions. Music-use became one of the main chosen instruments of their response. (Ibid.: 96)

In Bradley's account, rock music, therefore, is resistant. In its connections to youth culture, it resists and relates to feelings, about the family, school and the media.

Further, it is connected to issues of boredom and the attempt to overcome the mundane nature of society. Rock also resists the atomization or individuation of contemporary life in its construction of communities, which are often to exclude the adult world. All in all, in Bradley's phrase, rock involves a 'resistant communality' (ibid.: 131). Other aspects of the relation between rock and youth groups will be discussed in chapters 7, 8 and 9.

This sort of stance concerning the oppositional character of rock developed rapidly during the 1960s. However, the decline of some of the ideals of that period and the activities of some rock stars, which led them to be perceived as part of a capitalist commercial venture, threw the idea into crisis. In lots of ways, punk was built on that crisis and attempted to renew the idea that rock was an active political force. This occurred specifically through the activities of organizations like Rock Against Racism in the late 1970s (Widgery 1986; Frith and Street 1992), Red Wedge in the 1980s and in a broad sense through the opposition of some of the new groups to the established record industry by the ethic of do-it-yourself which punk spawned (see, more generally, McKay 1996). These raised expectations about the inherent oppositional nature of rock which have often, somewhat paradoxically, given rise to some of its strongest criticisms. Authors, who believed strongly in rock's oppositional stance, become disillusioned and then point to the role of the rock industry in the corruption of the original ideal. Thus, much writing on rock has characterized a cycle of supposed innovation and opposition being literally bought off by the activities of the big record companies and their agents. The writing on punk was no different. A number of these views are captured by Burchill and Parsons:

> In 1978 every record company is waking up to find a somewhat superfluous punk combo on its doorstep. Supply and demand? But you can't supply something that there's no demand for.
>
> Never mind, kid, there'll soon be another washing-machine/spot cream/rock-band on the market to solve all your problems and keep you quiet/off the street/distracted from the real enemy/content till the next pay-day.
>
> Anyhow, God Save Rock and Roll . . . it made you a Consumer, a potential Moron . . .
>
> IT'S ONLY ROCK AND ROLL AND IT'S PLASTIC, PLASTIC, YES IT IS!!!!!!
> (1978: 96)

The problem with this sort of approach, of seeing the music as 'corrupted' by the industry and consumerism, is that it is difficult now, and indeed it may always have been difficult, to suggest that rock or pop was ever outside the structures of the record industry and capitalism. If the arguments of Negus (1992) that the record industry is a web of connections between the small and the large, which were examined in chapter 1, are taken seriously, it is difficult to see where the pure spaces for creation outside the context of commercial relations exist. Further, the debate around postmodernism, discussed above, which argues that the boundaries between art and commerce are increasingly breaking down, also suggests that commercial relationships are unavoidable, but this does not necessarily make musical products corrupt, inauthentic or valueless.

There is another version of rock and the record industry which suggests that it was always a capitalist con-trick or part of an industrialized society anyway. Some of these general accounts have also been considered in the Introduction, where a number of the problems associated with them were identified. It is important to point out again that the examination of the politics of rock needs to take place in a more specific context, where the assertions are of a less general nature.

Grossberg has carried out an investigation of this kind. Building on a framework developed by Raymond Williams (1973), he argues that rock can produce three types of boundary between its followers and dominant culture: oppositional, alternative and independent. He defines these boundaries in the following way: 'Oppositional rock and roll presents itself as a direct challenge or threat to the dominant culture', whereas alternative rock 'mounts only an implicit attack on the dominant culture'. 'Independent rock and roll does not present itself as a challenge, either explicitly or implicitly, to the dominant culture although it may function as such' (1983: 110). Grossberg shows that there are crucial differences between different forms of rock with regard to their critical potential. He also identifies the way in which rock can be co-opted, which he examines at greater length in his book *We Gotta Get Out of This Place* (1992b) – an example of this could be the celebration of the Queen's Golden Jubilee in 2002, which included a large rock concert in London with established 'mainstream' stars. Moreover, there have been forms of rock that have expressed right-wing political views (see, for example, Barber-Kersovan 2003) and controversies over the politics of lyrics in forms such as death metal (Kahn-Harris 2003). This leads into the second part of this discussion of pop and politics.

The direct connection of rock with politics in the case of Rock Against Racism in the late 1970s and Red Wedge in the 1980s has already been mentioned. In the 1960s, rock was often seen as the music of protest continuing those 'folk' forms which had been connected with the working class, often by middle-class intellectual members of revolutionary political parties (Harker 1980). There have been various other direct connections between pop music and political activism, for example the free festival movement in the 1970s (Clarke 1982), which continued in the struggles around the festivals and activities of so-called new-age travellers in the 1990s. Groups on the right have also connected their politics to rock music. In the late 1970s the fascist right in Britain founded a group known as Rock Against Communism and the Oi Skinhead Rock of the early 1980s is also often related to fascist activity in various countries (Barber-Kersovan 2003). Rock and pop have been connected in rather different ways to politics since the 1980s through a number of charitable concerts such as Live Aid in 1985 and Live8 in 2005, and in more direct ways around the Nelson Mandela concerts in London.

Garofalo (1992c: 26–35) discusses four potential functions that such events may have: fundraising, consciousness-raising, artist activism and agitation. According to Garofalo, Live Aid in 1985 raised $67 million. Such events might raise the consciousness of the public about issues such as poverty and debt and political figures such as Nelson Mandela. Furthermore, they could deepen artist involvement in politics and contribute, perhaps indirectly, to political change.

In discussing such events, it is important to consider the issues and outcomes in a specific way. This has been done in other accounts of rock and politics and some of the most interesting connections drawn in the context of events in Eastern Europe in the late 1980s. Influential work by Wicke opens up the issues in a clear manner (see also on this topic, and the politics of rock more generally, Street 1986). Wicke (1992a, though see also, for example, Wicke 1992b and Wicke and Shepherd 1993) suggests that rock music played a significant role in the disintegration of East Germany in 1989. During September of that year musicians issued a statement which argued, from a leftist position, for greater democracy in East Germany. This had been prompted by the exodus of young people to the West via Hungary, which had been going on throughout 1989, and which the East German authorities had tried to conceal, though the information was freely available in the Western media. The musicians' statement was read out at numerous state-sponsored performances held to celebrate the 40th anniversary of the foundation of the German Democratic Republic on 7 October 1989. The attempts to prevent this by the state security forces led to conflict with audiences which continued after 7 October.

The fact that rock music could have such effects was based on three preconditions. First, East Germany's rock musicians had been organized by the state under the Committee for Entertainment Arts. This represented an attempt 'to render the musicians susceptible to forms of state-imposed discipline' (Wicke 1992a: 201). Second, the performances of the musicians provided a clear space for debates on political ideas, not least because other media were closed to such discussion. Third, the authorities interpreted lyrics in political terms, 'finding nearly every lyric to be politically disruptive' (ibid.). Audiences interpreted songs in this way as well, finding their own politically disruptive messages in them. Through these processes, rock music had become politicized by the state, the performers and the audiences.

Wicke argues that the state had been worried about the potential for opposition expressed by rock music since the middle of the 1960s, at first trying to argue that it had no place in a socialist society. This strategy was altered in the early 1970s to one that tried to incorporate rock music under the umbrella of state organization. However, this proved very difficult to sustain and by the mid-1970s the state was forced into a number of public struggles with rock musicians. By the late 1980s the state was attempting to split the musicians between the younger and older elements, in a strategy of 'divide and rule'. Thus, the state's own attempts to incorporate rock, to neutralize the threat that it was perceived to pose to the state, had actually led to the further politicization of the music, and indeed provided mechanisms for the expression of opposition from within state umbrella organizations themselves. Furthermore, once the state had fallen, the way was open to the influx of Western bands which has eliminated the indigenous rock music scene, showing the linkages between this form of rock and the state itself. In Wicke's words:

> But just as East German rock music was born and lived as an oppositional cultural and political force during Honecker's years in power, it is now in the process of dying with him. With the fall of the Berlin Wall has come a radical change in the music scene in the former communist territory. Having achieved their revolutionary cultural and political goals, German musicians

from the East have for the most part been quickly (and sadly) forgotten in the flood of commercial popular culture that has swept in from the West. (Ibid.: 206)

Pekacz (1994) has argued that accounts such as Wicke's have overestimated the role of rock music in political change in Eastern Europe and the extent to which it opposed the established regimes. She argues that, in fact, the government in such societies was much less monolithic and doctrinaire than is suggested by Wicke and that rock music entered into a number of everyday accommodations with it. Below the level of state rhetoric, rock musicians and state functionaries often shared common frames of reference. In sum, Wicke, in this view, romanticizes the oppositional role of rock partly by overemphasizing the unity of the structures it confronted. This is rather similar to those 1960s' accounts of the oppositional status of rock which saw it as fighting an all pervasive 'system'.

Other studies have explored the complexities of the 'censorship' process in societies like South Africa during the time of apartheid (Drewett 2003) and communist China (de Kloet 2003). In both these cases it is shown how artists and record companies sought to subvert the rules of censorship in a number of ways. One of these is by changing the lyrics of songs that were being sent to the censor for checking, so that the actual lyrics were covered up. This could be done by simple substitution of words, as Drewett (2003: 158) explains with respect to the sending of work to the South African Broadcasting Corporation (SABC): 'Many musicians tried to sneak controversial ideas onto radio using innovative methods. Keith Berelowitz of Carte Blanche revealed that they submitted counterfeit lyric sheets with albums sent to the SABC, replacing controversial words with ones that had a similar sound. In one instance they changed "policeman" to "please man"' (personal interview with Berelowitz, 15 April 1998). In 1985 Shifty Records released a compilation album of rebel rhythms called 'A Naartjie in Our Sosatie' ('A tangerine in our kebab'), a play on 'Anarchy in our society'. In other cases, such as Bright Blue, 'The group used symbolic lyrics to sing about a man living in fear within a heavily repressive society' (ibid.: 159). Similar processes happen in China.

To evaluate the political significance of rock, it is important to consider the way in which the different forms of music operate within specific constellations of political forces and how the impact of rock and pop musicians in mega events concerning issues such as world poverty continue to provoke debate about political effects. The third strand of this discussion, then, is that it is difficult to have, or develop, a general account or theory of the political nature of rock music, especially given the complexities of the situations. This sort of approach has been usefully developed by John Street, who suggestively points out that the politics of pop music are formed in the relationship between commerce and ideals. He uses the example of the 1970 Isle of Wight Festival to argue that:

The entrepreneurs, like the musicians, were caught between political idealism and commercial reality, between belief and the bottom line. Arguably, it is this tension which actually generates pop's finest moments and its truest politics. Utopian fantasies tend to issue in bland sounds, and self-righteous polemics in dull tunes. The politics of popular music are best animated by the attempt to combine commercial logic with romantic ideals. (2001: 244)

For Street, popular music has both 'the power to represent and the power to effect' (ibid.: 245), i.e. music can capture feelings and wishes and have influence. However, these are capacities rather than guarantees and the precise extent of representation and effect will depend on the specific context and the case.

This line of argument has been usefully explored by Cloonan, who explores the significant issue of the definition of censorship. This is done in the wider context of policing which is used 'to convey the variety of ways in which popular music can be regulated, restricted, and repressed' (Cloonan and Garofalo 2003: 3). Cloonan argues that it is important to explain what is meant by censorship. This is not straightforward: 'The essence of the problem lies in drawing up a definition which is narrow enough to exclude apparently frivolous examples but broad enough to include incidents other than overt attempts by governments and other agencies to prevent musical expression' (ibid.: 15). This leads him to the following definition: 'censorship is the process by which an agent (or agents) attempts to, and/or succeeds in, significantly altering, and/or curtailing, the freedom of expression of another agent with a view to limiting the likely audience for that expression' (ibid.). This allows a variety of activities to be considered under this head, from the 'market-based decisions within the music industry to the actions of official or state censorship agencies' (ibid.). This leads Cloonan to a useful categorization of the way that censorship can operate on a number of levels. He discusses three main levels: 'prior restraint', restriction, and suppression' (ibid.: 17).

Prior restraint involves a process like preventing a band from recording. Cloonan suggests that practices of the music industry (see chapters 1 and 2) can be seen as prior restraint:

> By not signing artists, record companies can effectively act as censors in the sense that, for whatever reason, they are acting to restrict an artist's audience. This is not to say that all decisions not to sign artists are acts of censorship, but rather that they can have censorial implications for the artists concerned. (Ibid.)

Restriction can be more visible and direct, as it involves 'the imposing of certain conditions upon the placement or ownership of products' (ibid.). Thus, 'In western Europe and North America, the most frequently cited examples of popular music censorship – banning of records from the radio – are examples of restriction' (ibid.). Finally, suppression involves 'attempts by a government or legal system to enforce a moral or political code' (ibid.: 18).

This sort of approach means that Cloonan is able to consider a range of processes of the policing for popular music, without necessarily suggesting that they involve the more overt forms of censorship. This means that a range of social, economic and political processes can be discussed in terms of how they affect the communication of a text to an audience (see the discussion of the range of factors in the case of the development of rock and roll above). Thus, while this involves the general definition of the processes involved, it also draws attention to the need to consider the specifics of the processes involved. It is not possible to see policing and regulation in China and the USA (Fischer 2003) in precisely the same ways, but having an overall framework enables these comparisons to be drawn in finer detail. This reinforces the critical comments on general accounts of rock discussed in the Introduction. Such accounts are further complicated when the relations between rock, gender and sexuality are considered.

Rock, gender and sexuality

It was suggested earlier that the more conventional accounts of the development of rock point to its initial power and resistance (in rock 'n' roll) which was transformed as the music industry moved in (producing rock and roll). Further, there was a clear barrier built between rock and pop at a later date. It has been argued that these accounts reflect hierarchies of gender in popular music and society. The most influential case for this interpretation has been made by Simon Frith and Angela McRobbie (1990). Frith and McRobbie's initial suggestion is that rock music cannot be analysed as either simply a product of the culture industry, and hence as a commodity which acts ideologically to incorporate its consumers, or in its subcultural consumption by different audience groups. They argue that rock's meanings, especially in the construction and representation of sexuality, are rather more complex than these rather general accounts allow.

Frith and McRobbie argue that male domination of the music industry leads to representations of masculinity in contemporary pop music. They identify two main types of pop music which they label 'cock rock' and 'teenybop'. Cock rock is 'music making in which performance is an explicit, crude and often aggressive expression of male sexuality', its 'performers are aggressive, dominating, and boastful, and they constantly seek to remind the audience of their prowess, their control', the 'image is the rampant male traveller, smashing hotels and groupies alike. Musically, such rock takes off from the sexual frankness of rhythm and blues but adds a cruder male physicality (hardness, control, virtuosity)' (Frith and McRobbie 1990: 374).

Teenybop, according to Frith and McRobbie, is consumed mainly by girls, whose teenybop idol's 'image is based on self-pity, vulnerability, and need'. This finds a different form of musical expression from cock rock: 'In teenybop, male sexuality is transformed into a spiritual yearning carrying only hints of sexual interaction. What is needed is not so much someone to screw as a sensitive and sympathetic soulmate, someone to support and nourish the incompetent male adolescent as he grows up' (ibid.: 375).

There are artists who seem to fit fairly clearly into these categories (many heavy metal groups have been seen as examples of cock rock and singers and groups such as Jason Donovan, Take That and Boyzone as teenyboppers), though Frith and McRobbie point out that there can be important crossovers between the two. Frith and McRobbie argue that these textual and performance types connect to different audiences. Boys, as the consumers of cock rock, are active. They attempt to follow guitar-playing idols into the music industry and attendance at the cock rock concert is active. Furthermore, suggest Frith and McRobbie, this attendance is collective. Boys are in and form groups. The female fans of the teenybopper are, by contrast, relatively passive and individual. They consume as individuals. Their aim as performers is to be singers, or else to face the kind of exaggerated aggression associated with such musicians as Janis Joplin, with the attendant dangers of self-destruction. In addition, Frith and McRobbie suggest that teenybop idols can be used in different ways by the girl audiences as a form of collective appropriation and resistance to school norms. Aspects of this will be considered at later points in this book.

In Frith and McRobbie's view the conventional accounts of the decline of rock 'n' roll are actually accounts of its feminization (ibid.: 383). Furthermore, they begin a process of attempting to look beyond the lyrics of a song to investigate its gendered meaning in musical terms. The vehicle for this is a comparison of Tammy Wynette's 'Stand by Your Man' with Helen Reddy's 'I Am Woman', which values Wynette over Reddy:

> The lyrics of 'Stand by Your Man' celebrate women's duty to men, implore women to enjoy subordinating themselves to men's needs – lyrically the song is a ballad of sexual submissiveness. But the female authority of Tammy Wynette's voice involves a knowledge of the world that is in clear contrast to the gooey idealism of Helen Reddy's sound. 'Sometimes it's hard to be a woman', Tammy Wynette begins, and you can hear that Tammy Wynette knows why her voice is a collective one. 'I am woman', sings Helen Reddy, and what you hear is the voice of an idealized consumer, even if the commodity for consumption in this instance is a package version of women's liberation. (Ibid.: 385)

In their article, Frith and McRobbie address a number of important themes. These include:

- the idea that it is important to go beyond a focus on the rock industry or the consumption of rock;
- a characterization of the music industry as male-dominated;
- the characterization of the different forms of masculinity entailed in 'cock rock' and 'teenybop';
- the interconnections between these textual and performance forms and audiences;
- the attempt to move beyond lyrics in the characterization of the worth of songs;
- the argument regarding the feminization of rock 'n' roll.

In a subsequent critique of this piece, Frith suggests that in 'a jumble of good and bad arguments', there was a confusion of 'issues of sex and issues of gender'. Sex was somehow seen as an essence, rather than something that, like gender, was subject to forms of construction. This argument rejects the idea that there is a core to sex, which was simply expressed in music. Music plays a significant part in the construction of gender and sexuality. However, Frith suggests that 'the most misleading of our original arguments was the distinction between male activity and female passivity when, in fact, consumption is as important to the sexual significance of pop as production' (1990: 422). The original article tended to emphasize the ways in which music was produced at the expense of its consumption. This is an important theme. The Introduction to this book suggested that it is as important to examine audience appropriations of texts as it is to look at their production, and this will be discussed at length in chapters 7, 8 and 9.

Another problem with Frith and McRobbie's argument is that it was originally written before the developments in pop music since the 1980s. In the next section, I want to examine some of these through a brief discussion of the most discussed pop figure of the period: Madonna.

Madonna: pop, politics, gender and sexuality

The ongoing Madonna phenomenon raises issues in the three areas that have been discussed in this chapter: the distinction between rock and pop; the politics of pop music and its connections with power; and gender and sexuality. These three areas will be considered in turn. (For extended examination of Madonna, see, for example, Schwichtenberg 1993, which contains a number of important contributions to the discussion here.)

First, there is the relationship between rock and pop. Early interpretations and accounts of Madonna tended to focus on her implication in the pop industry. She was seen as an inauthentic product of the culture industry, who was involved in the exploitation of others for the gain of that industry. Madonna was sometimes contrasted with another popular woman singer of the early and mid-1980s, namely Cyndi Lauper, whose work was seen to be more thoughtful and authentic. However, as time has passed these debates have been reconstituted. Partly in connection with the increased salience in popular culture of the debates around postmodernism, there has been a heightened recognition of the problems of the definition of authenticity and what this can mean in an increasingly commercialized, commodified and media-saturated society. Hence, whilst Madonna seemed to have begun from what would normally be seen as pop beginnings, her work, in some accounts, has been at the forefront of the breaking down of this particular barrier. Further, this could be seen as crossing the divisions between art and commerce in a way consistent with the development of postmodernism. However, Madonna has sometimes asserted her own rights and authenticity as an individual artist. An example of this occurs in the documentary film In Bed with Madonna (1991, aka Truth or Dare), in which she argues against the censorship of her show on the grounds of artistic freedom, using a notion of individual authenticity close to that expressed by rock artists (and expressed by the jazz musicians studied by Becker – see chapter 2), which itself derives from earlier conceptions of the nature of the artist. However, an alternative interpretation would stress that this is in itself a kind of pose for particular purposes, which has little to do with what Madonna really is, even if there is any point in exploring such an issue. It is significant that this produces ongoing tensions in Madonna's career. Thus, with the release of her CD Confessions on a Dance Floor in 2005, critics suggested that Madonna had returned to disco and dance music in an attempt to secure a larger (pop) audience in the wake of her more artistic attempts to convey 'authentic' personal and social messages in releases like Ray of Light (1998), Music (2000) and American Life (2003), though it is important to note that these releases in themselves depended on collaborations with other popular artists and producers of the time.

Second, there is the issue of politics. If Madonna can be seen by some as transcending debates about authenticity, she also connects to new ideas about a form of politics based in ideas of play, the 'freeing' and reconstitution of identity, again in ways connected to the advocates of postmodernism. In an introductory discussion of the idea of identity, Hall (1992) distinguishes three concepts of identity: 'Enlightenment', 'sociological' and 'postmodern'. The Enlightenment concept rested on notions of there being an essential core to identity which was born with the individual and unfolded through his or her life. The sociological concept argued that a coherent identity is formed in relations with others and thus develops and changes over time. The postmodern subject is thought to have no fixed or essential identity. In postmodern societies, identities have become 'dislocated'.

It can be suggested that earlier forms of politics could be related to the search for new forms of identity as the oppressed or dominated threw off those forms which implicated them in the operation of power. These forms of identity could be seen to be relatively stable and to enable the new identity to be expressed in new oppositional forms. In such accounts, one identity which colluded with oppression was replaced by a new one that opposed the dominant order. Thus, the standardized identity of the pop consumer as characterized by Adorno might be replaced with the more sophisticated identity of the follower of serious music who would recognize the way in which the culture industry used pop music to reproduce inequalities. This sort of politics can be seen to rest on a sociological concept of identity, where the subject can be changed, or switched over, as social conditions change.

Some more recent forms of politics, however, suggest that the stability of such identities is problematic in that they freeze the fluidity of contemporary identities and indeed often involve the privileging of one construction of identity over another. Thus, talking of a working-class identity might neglect the different identities of black and white workers, and, for example, subsume the black identity in the white one. Similar arguments have been made against forms of feminism that do not take account of the different identities of black and white women. In some recent forms of politics, there is a celebration of the idea that there is not a true or real identity but a multiplicity of identities, which operate in different circumstances. In these respects, Madonna has, it is argued, caught the notion that there is no real identity, no authentic way of being, and has become involved in the play of masks and surfaces, rather than in a search for the truth and the underlying reality. Thus the shifts in Madonna's representation of self – and indeed physical appearance – can be seen in this light. As she gets older, further layers have been added to this play, such as the roles of wife and mother, and the relationship between the USA and the UK. This allows further dimensions of activity to be brought to bear and in turn fuels debates on what Madonna is doing. This has one function of keeping her in the public eye and reconstituting the nature of her star text (see chapter 5) and the nature of her celebrity (see chapter 8).

Third, in relation to gender and sexuality, Madonna is held to have exhibited a form of play with gender roles which overcomes the privileging of one form of gender as that to be emulated and which represents a form of freedom from straitjackets. Furthermore, the sense that she is in control of her own destiny and image has projected the idea of her being a strong woman who is generally in control, rather than someone who is manipulated by the men who dominate the pop music industry. In terms of sexuality, Madonna has connected to forms of culture and politics which value the transgression of established sexual norms concerning violence and pornography. It is argued that her videos and books, such as *Sex*, bring forms of sexual representation, which had been hidden, into the mainstream. This process makes visible forms of sexuality that had been hidden away or denigrated by the mainstream culture. This may lead to greater tolerance of those who engage in what have been described as 'perverted' practices. Moreover, the representations associated with *Confessions on a Dance Floor* stimulated debates in the popular press about the appropriate forms of behaviour for a woman born in 1959 with children.

Furthermore, there has been consideration of the way in which Madonna serves as a hero to younger generations of women (the 'wanna bees') who are tired of the older forms of politics and of the sterility of their everyday lives. This might also now apply to older women. However, there are others who reject the idea of Madonna as an icon. Schulze et al. (1993) point to four critical accounts of Madonna among those who hate her. She is seen as the lowest form of culture, as 'the lowest form of irresponsible culture, a social disease', as 'the lowest form of the feminine' and 'as the antithesis of feminism'. They also suggest that these critics of Madonna feel that they are going against the dominant ideas of Madonna as a 'good thing'; they are, in the phrase of Schulze et al., 'resistive readers'.

This debate about the worth of Madonna and her connections to postmodernism has carried through into other dimensions of academic and popular debate, where, for example, the merits of boundary-breaking, transgression and play have been much discussed, often in relation to gender and race. This debate throws into sharp relief many of the issues examined in this chapter. First, the distinction between rock and pop has often entailed judgements of value and assumptions about gender. For example, the evaluation of rock has often involved the privileging of masculinity. Second, general arguments about the relation between pop and politics need revision if the ideas associated with postmodernism, fragmentation and cultural difference are taken seriously, as more needs to be made of the specific contexts in which political practices occur. Arguments about politics need to be considered with respect to particular cases, as the extended discussion of the East German situation in the 1980s showed. Third, while the approach pioneered by Frith and McRobbie is still illuminating in certain respects, contemporary gender relations and feminine identities are far more complex (McRobbie 1993). Issues of gender and sexuality need discussion in a way that recognizes such complexity.

While the theme of new ways of thinking about sex, gender and sexuality is taken up in detail in chapter 6, it can be argued that recent popular musicology (see also chapter 5) has explored a number of different dimensions of how study of female performers allows reconsideration of key issues raised in this chapter. For example, in her analysis of Madonna, Whiteley (2000b: 136–51) examines the textual strategies of Madonna's work in the context of the feminist theory of Luce Irigaray concerning 'plurality, play and difference' (ibid.: 150), which in the terms set out in this chapter can be seen as important postmodern themes. This is a specific example of how Whiteley combines analysis of the overall social context, feminist and cultural theory with the discussion of music, lyrics and visual representation to produce new insights into the way in which a range of female performers (for example, Janis Joplin, Joni Mitchell, Patti Smith, k.d. lang, Tracey Chapman and the Spice Girls) express and construct identities and different spaces for women to speak in a way that explores new political directions.

Summary

This chapter has considered:

- the development and meaning of various types of popular music, pointing to the location of the beginnings of rock and roll in a complex social context, and how the consideration of the contemporary trajectory of popular music involves consideration of the debates about postmodernism;
- discussions of the distinction between rock and pop and some of the implications of this;
- the politics of rock music in general and specific senses, raising issues of the extent to which pop music opposes a dominant culture and the connections of rock with the state;
- the interconnections between gender, sexuality and pop music, using early work by Frith and McRobbie to provide a springboard for debate;
- the Madonna phenomenon in terms of the issues raised by the chapter.

4

'Black Music': Genres and Social Constructions

This chapter develops some of the themes introduced in chapter 3, as ascriptions of value and claims about authenticity have run through debates about the implications and wider resonances of 'black music'. The chapter opens with a discussion of the important issue of how 'black music' is actually defined. This is important in itself as it introduces debates and raises concerns about the extent to which an 'essence' of black music can be defined in musical or sociological terms. Furthermore, it introduces issues concerning the political implications of black music, and the ascription of the label 'black'. This is followed by an examination of the development of blues and soul, which is used to point to some important sociological dimensions of the evolution of these forms. The discussion of the reggae tradition which follows elaborates on these themes, in a way that connects the discussion to the debates about modernism and postmodernism introduced in chapter 3. The implication of this section of the chapter is that the development of specific forms of reggae can be understood through the utilization of ideal types of textual forms, which are themselves to be understood in social context. This theme is followed through into a discussion of rap and hip-hop culture, which reviews some of the debates about this form, which have centred on ideas of resistance, space and place, expression and gender. The chapter is used to raise more general issues of how forms of music influence each other and how forms can be related to ascribed characteristics.

Defining black music

The concept of 'black music' has in the past and in everyday criticism been used in an unreflective way, where it is assumed that it is the music performed by black people. However, several questions have been posed to such a view. First, would a black musician performing a song by Lennon and McCartney count as black music? Or a black opera singer performing a piece from the European classical tradition? (Oliver 1990). Second, how is a black person actually defined and recognized? In some accounts of black music there was a danger of reproducing stereotypes of natural racial difference. From such a racist angle, black people are held to have natural abilities in music-making or dancing, and so on. However, as Oliver explains:

> To follow this argument through one has to confront the problem of genetic admixture through intermarriage and cross-fertility between races. The outcome of miscegenation between people of different racial stocks over generations inevitably leads to the diminution of some genetic traits and the dominance of others. They're expressed most visibly and physically in, for instance, lightening of skin hue, or differences in hair section and hence, changes in hair growth. If abilities are genetically related, the diminution or dominance of some would also seem to be the inevitable result of such racial cross-breeding, but the vast literature on race does not bear this out. Nor does common experience: in the jazz field, for instance, dark-skinned Louis Armstrong, Bessie Smith or Charlie Parker are not rated as being the musical superiors (or inferiors, for that matter) of light-hued Jelly-Roll Morton, Billie Holiday or Lester Young; at least, not on account of the presumed 'blackness' of their genes. (Ibid.: 6)

Furthermore, as Hatch and Millward have argued, blackness varied according to legal definition between different states in the United States:

> Legally speaking, the definition as to what constituted a black person varied from state to state under the 'Jim Crow' laws. In Alabama, Arkansas, and Mississippi, anyone with a 'visible' and/or 'appreciable' degree of 'Negro blood' was subject to segregational laws as a black person, whereas in Indiana and Louisiana the colour line was drawn at one-eighth and one-sixteenth Negro blood respectively. Clearly, then, it was possible to change one's status – and therefore legal rights – by moving from one state to another. (1987: 117)

On the basis of the argument advanced by Oliver and Hatch and Millward, it is difficult to maintain that there is a genetic or biological base to 'black music' which marks it off from other forms. A similar point has been made by Tagg (1989), who also suggests that it is difficult to find common features in what has commonly been classed as black music. He argues that four musical characteristics are often used to define 'blackness' of what is sometimes called 'Afro-American' music: 'blue notes', 'call-and-response techniques', 'syncopation' and 'improvisation' (1989: 288). Tagg maintains that none of these characteristics can be used to identify a discrete category of black music and argues that the term black music should not be used. He concludes by noting:

> Scepticism towards the supposed pair of opposites 'black' or 'Afro-American music' versus 'European music' has two main grounds: (1) musicological because no satisfactory definitions of any terms are provided and (2) ideological. The latter is particularly important because not only does the implied dichotomy pre-ordain certain sets of feeling and behaviour for one race and deny them to the other, it also turns the overriding question of class into a matter of race or ethnicity. (1989: 295)

Tagg argues for a position which can be seen as 'anti-essentialist' (Gilroy 1993), in that he rejects the idea that there is an essence to black music. Despite such criticisms, some writers have continued to argue that the concept of black music has some importance. In Hatch and Millward's account, the music made by black people is related to their oppression in the United States, and they point out that these oppressions and inequalities are often cut across by class, locality, and so on. They argue for a pluralistic account of pop music, which rejects the idea that some forms are more authentic than others. This allows for the study of the complexity of the relations between different textual forms of music and the inputs into them without prior suggestions that one is more 'true' or authentic than another. Thus, on Hatch and Millward's (1987: 120) account, 'pop music has always depended upon the interaction between white and black traditions', and they back up their argument with the example of the development of forms like the blues. They do not take this position in order to reduce the importance of black musicians vis-à-vis pop music: a position that they are keen to emphasize. However, they do suggest that there is no need to oversimplify and consider just one form of music to be authentically black.

Oliver also uses a pluralistic notion to form the basis for the investigations that make up his edited collection of articles on black music in Britain. He argues:

> '[B]lack music' is that which is recognized and accepted as such by its creators, performers and hearers . . . encompassing the music of those who see themselves as black, and whose musics have unifying characteristics which justify their recognition as specific genres: peculiar patterns of 'sonic order' in John Blacking's phrase. (1990: 8)

In this view, black music is that which is socially defined as such. This is a form of sociological approach that emphasizes the actor's own point of view, rather than adopting some 'objective' standard of judgement. However, there are problems with such an account, as there may be different or competing definitions of what black music is. The music of Michael Jackson, for example, might be seen as black by some but not by others. But it may also be argued that in sociological terms such disagreements over 'blackness' are relatively fruitless, as they will run into the sorts of difficulty already outlined above. More important, it may be suggested, is an examination of complex roots of Jackson's music (and indeed his identity) and how it is produced and consumed in particular ways. This is not to say that the attribution of blackness has no effect. However, this is most important in the discussion of how particular forms of music articulate and connect to political issues.

It can be argued, therefore, that context and political meaning are important in the discussion of 'black music', and that some of the more relativistic arguments might tend to neglect this. Consider, for example, Maya Angelou's account of attending *Porgy and Bess*, reproduced in box 4.1. Here, a clear expression of the pleasure in a 'black' performance can be seen, in a way that conveys how Angelou's eyes are opened, and how, as a result, a commitment to black culture and expression might develop.

The discussion so far has the following implications. First, it has been suggested that it is difficult to sustain the idea that black music is based in biological factors. Second, that in the development of many forms of popular music, the interaction between black and white has been crucial. Third, that this

---

Box 4.1   Maya Angelou at *Porgy and Bess*

If *New Faces of 1953* excited the pulses of San Franciscans, *Porgy and Bess* set their hearts afire. Reviewers and columnists raved about Leontyne Price and William Warfield in the title roles and praised the entire company. The troupe had already successfully toured other parts of the United States, Europe and South America . . .

I went to the theater ready to be entertained, but not expecting a riot of emotion. Price and Warfield sang; they threaded their voices with music and spellbound the audience with their wizardry. Even the chorus performed with such verve that a viewer could easily believe each singer was competing for a leading part.

By intermission I had been totally consumed. I had laughed and cried, exulted and mourned, and expected the second act to produce no new emotions. I returned to my seat prepared for a repetition of great music.

The curtain rose on a picnic in progress. The revelers were church members led by a pious old woman who forbade dancing, drinking and even laughing. Cab Calloway as Sportin' Life pranced out in cream-colored suit and tried to paganize the Christians.

He sang 'It Ain't Necessarily So,' strutting as if he was speaking *ex cathedra*.

The audience applauded loudly, interrupting the stage action. Then a young woman broke away from a group of singers near the wings. She raced to the center of the stage and began to dance.

The sopranos sang a contrapuntal high-toned encouragement and baritones urged the young woman on. The old lady tried to catch her, to stop the idolatrous dance, but the dancer moved out of her reach, flinging her legs high, carrying the music in her body as if it were a private thing, given into her care and protection. I nearly screamed with delight and envy. I wanted to be with her on the stage letting the music fly through my body. Her torso seemed to lose solidity and float, defying gravity. I wanted to be with her. No, I wanted to *be* her.

In the second act, Warfield, as the crippled Porgy, dragged the audience into despair. Even kneeling, he was a large man, broad and thick-chested. His physical size made his affliction and his loss of Bess even sadder. The resonant voice straddled the music and rode it, controlling it.

I remained in my seat after the curtain fell and allowed people to climb over my knees to reach the aisle. I was stunned. *Porgy and Bess* had shown me the greatest array of Negro talent I had ever seen.

Source: Angelou 1985: 126–7

Copyright © Maya Angelou 1976. Published by Virago Press 1985

---

does not necessarily denigrate or undervalue the contribution of black people to popular music. As Hatch and Millward argue, 'those designated as black have made the major contribution to the development of pop music from its earliest origins' (1987: 116). Fourth, that some, more relativist, writers have concluded that

- A critique of productivism: work, the labour process and the division of labour under capitalism.
- A critique of the state revolving around a plea for the disassociation of law from domination, which denounces state brutality, militarism and exterminism.
- A passionate belief in the importance of history and the historical process. This is presented as an antidote to the suppression of historical and temporal perception under late capitalism.

Figure 4.1 Core anti-capitalist themes in black expressive culture
Source: Gilroy 1987: 199

the term 'black music' should not be used, as it tends to imply the existence of a black musical or racial essence. Fifth, sociological investigation into the development of those forms that have been designated as black needs to examine the complex social contexts and locations which have led to the development of such forms. Sixth, that such investigation will often lead to consideration of the political meaning and roles of such forms, in both the general and specific variants identified in chapter 3. In a seeming paradox, this may lead to the reassertion of the importance of the ascription of the label 'black music'.

One of the strongest arguments along these lines has been made by Paul Gilroy (1987, 1993). He suggests that many discussions of black music downplay its political importance. He argues: 'There are three core themes around which the anti-capitalist aspects of black expressive culture have been articulated' (1987: 199). These are detailed in figure 4.1. Gilroy argues for an approach called 'anti-anti-essentialism' (1993: 102), which recognizes that a biological or natural core to black culture and black music cannot be found, but which argues against attempts to suggest that, because of this, there can be no such category as black culture. His notion of black culture is based in social practices and social definitions, though the process of call and response is seen as central to the structure of black music (ibid.: 78). It can be argued, then, that the identification of categories of black culture and black music is intimately connected to a range of social and political issues.

In order to examine these issues more closely – as well as those concerning the ascription of cultural value and authenticity – this chapter traces the development and meanings of blues and soul in the United States, the rise of ska and reggae in Jamaica and the implications of rap and hip-hop culture. This will involve elaborating on the histories and discussion of modernism and postmodernism introduced in chapter 3. The focus here will be on 'Afro-American' and 'Afro-Caribbean' music. It is important to note that there are many other forms of 'black' music which have been relatively neglected in the sociological study of pop music, or which have implicitly not been recognized as 'black'. An important exception to this trend is Oliver's edited collection (1990) where the contemporary development of styles like Bhangra is considered (Banerji and Baumann 1990). However, this does not overcome the fact that writing on black music, often by white people, has implicitly constructed a black tradition which tends to exclude 'Asian' styles (Sharma et al. 1996). This has been highlighted by the success of performers like Cornershop, Talvin Singh and Apache Indian, whose work foregrounds interconnections between different ethnic groups. Some have argued that rap and hip-hop music facilitates such developments, as will be examined later in the chapter. It also raises general issues of the ascription of ethnic identities and how people live them. This discussion should also be read in the context of the examination of globalization in chapter 1.

Blues and soul

In chapter 4 it was noted how rock 'n' roll developed in part from r 'n' b (rhythm and blues). Following Gillett (1983), five forms of r 'n' b can be identified in the post-Second World War period. These were:

1   'Dancehall Blues'
2   'Club Blues'
3   'Bar Blues'
4   Gospel
5   'Group Sounds'

Gillett's distinctions illuminate the diversity of r 'n' b, which encompassed a variety of different types of music, and the connections between these forms and particular social contexts. Gillett suggests that there are a number of musical characteristics of the blues or r 'n' b. First, all the forms of r 'n' b had a dance rhythm, which distinguished the form from post-war jazz, 'which was rarely recorded as dance music and which could therefore dispense with the convention of maintaining a particular beat throughout a song' (1983: 122–3). Second, Gillett suggests that:

> In rhythm and blues, the soloists were generally more 'selfish', concerned to express their own feelings, depending on the rest of the band to keep the beat going and the volume up while they blew their hearts out and their heads off. In jazz, there was usually more interplay between musicians, more exploration into melody and harmony, less reliance on the emotional force of the musician's tone. (Ibid.: 123)

Third, in Gillett's view, the blues entailed the communication of character on the part of the performers.

Having thus established the common features of r 'n' b, Gillett examines the nature of the five categories in some detail. He identifies three subtypes of the dancehall blues: 'big band blues; shout, scream and cry blues; and combo blues' (ibid.: 124). The dancehall blues were, as the name suggests, performed for large audiences as a backdrop to dancing. The large dance bands often contained a main singer and a saxophonist, whose roles became more important with the passage of time. The 'jump combos' were particularly important in the development of rock 'n' roll, leading to the popularity of performers like Bill Haley, Chuck Berry and Fats Domino. In Gillett's account, the jump or combo blues was an exuberant music, which 'served to express whatever confidence people felt on the [US] West Coast during and after the war, the quieter club blues expressed the more dominant mood there, one tinged with despondency' (ibid.: 142). One of the first to play in this style was Nat 'King' Cole.

The bar blues developed in US cities as rural blacks migrated. In particular, much of what is familiar as the electrified blues which fed into rock 'n' roll in the 1950s, influencing rock music in the 1960s, was associated with the movement of black performers from the Mississippi Delta in the South to cities like Memphis in Tennessee and especially to Chicago. As Guralnick explains, 'the blues came out of Mississippi, sniffed around in Memphis and then settled in Chicago where it is most likely it will peacefully live out the rest of its days' (1992: 46). This Delta style was distinctive, as Palmer suggests:

> The Mississippi Delta's blues musicians sang with unmatched intensity in a gritty, melodically circumscribed, highly ornamented style that was closer to field hollers than it was to other blues. Guitar and piano accompaniments were percussive and hypnotic, and many Delta guitarists mastered the art of fretting the instrument with a slider or bottleneck; they made the instrument 'talk' in strikingly speechlike inflections. (1981: 44)

The originators of the style tended to play and record for local audiences throughout the South, often living in a hand-to-mouth manner. They recorded their music for the local black market, though they were also recorded in a more anthropological way by 'field researchers' as representatives of a kind of 'folk music', which placed a particular connotation of 'authenticity' on music that was often commercial in its aims and context. The musicians entertained, and developed their skills, at parties and social gatherings on large southern plantations.

The style originated with Charley Patton and was developed by such figures as Son House, Robert Johnson and, perhaps most famously, Muddy Waters. Waters was born in 1915 in the Mississippi Delta, grew up in Clarksdale and played at fish fries for local audiences. He moved north to Chicago in 1943. He recorded for a label called Aristocrat in the late 1940s, which had been formed by the Chess brothers, who were immigrants from Poland. The label was subsequently renamed Chess, and in 1950 Muddy Waters had his first 'hit':

> [This] meant you sold probably 60,000 copies in the race market and almost exclusively around Chicago, Gary, St Louis, Memphis and the South. There was no distribution on the coast, there was no radio air play, and the money that was involved would certainly seem small by today's inflated standards. Even so it was enough to make Muddy Waters a star. (Guralnick 1992: 69)

Waters continued to have hits through the 1950s, though his star waned as the decade progressed. His work continued to influence white musicians and he was subsequently 'rediscovered' at many points. His career is important, as it illustrates a number of social processes: first, the origination of a style in a particular local setting, though the style may have been developed out of commercially available recordings; second, the way in which the music was performed in social contexts for the local market; third, the movement of the music to a different, more urban, social setting; fourth, the recording of that music for the local market; fifth, the wider taking up of the music at various points by different international markets. These are common processes in the development of black music, and they will be further considered in the discussion of reggae below.

Gillett's characterization of the nature of the blues as a musical form was introduced above. Other writers have suggested that it is less easy to define its essence than might be thought. Thus Guralnick argues:

> What is blues then? Well, it's a lot easier to keep on saying what blues is not. It isn't necessarily sad music. It doesn't tell a story. It neither makes nor alludes to minor chords. It is for the most part self-accompanied. It follows certain basic progressions (I–IV–V–IV–I or tonic, subdominant, dominant chord patterns). It is not a music of particular technical accomplishment. In the end you come back to the familiar conundrum; if you have to ask, well then you're just not going to understand. Because blues is little more than a feeling. And what could be more durable or more fleeting and ephemeral than just that? (1992: 41)

These difficulties are also brought out by the more detailed discussion of the musical structure of the blues in the extract from Hatch and Millward (1987) reproduced in box 4.2.

Box 4.2   Blues as a musical type

As a musical type the blues is not easy to describe. Traditionally, writers on the subject take the other, emotional, meaning of the term too seriously in attempts to delineate the genre. Yet for its fans the music is immediately recognizable, but via its structure rather than through its supposedly 'sorrowful' qualities. In fact, as a music the blues is no more sorrowful than, for instance, popular, art-music, hillbilly, or many 'folk' musics. Hillbilly music in particular, and especially the modern 'country and western' variety, has a far stronger tradition of overt expression of sad and sorrowful themes, in the manner of the 'tear-jerker'. Like most songs, blues reflects human life in general, though concentrating on the experiences relevant to the singer/composer and immediate audience. Blues songs are thus, not surprisingly, concerned with such topics as sexual relations, travelling, drinking, being broke, work and the lack of it, etc., etc. If there is one central emotional attitude typical of the music it is that of *irony*. And whether this represents a cathartic method for overcoming the 'blues', as many writers, including Southern (1983: 331), claim, is mere psychological speculation. For the number of psychological states involved in blues singing may well be as many as there are performers. Some undoubtedly did it for the money, a normal motivation for professional entertainers. Still others quite obviously saw themselves as 'artists' with something important to give to the world (among these we would count at least Skip James, Robert Johnson and Muddy Waters).

The ironic qualities of the music have always been enhanced by the prevailing musical structure of the blues: though this has very often been described as being, wholly or partly, in a 'minor key', that is, really not an adequate representation of the music's structural properties. The melodic patterns of blues very often look like minor tunes, particularly when transcribed. Yet the aural effect, which is far more important, is one closer to harshness than to the traditional minor effect of 'sad' sounds. Thus many European and Anglo-American 'folk' songs which contain minor intervals in their melodies often look, on paper, similar to blues songs, yet when heard they sound very different. In fact many of the musics, including country and western, which do specialize in sorrowful sounds, use certain major key melodic patterns to achieve the required 'sad sound'.

The 'harsh' tonality in blues is particularly apparent in what Robert Palmer, following Muddy Waters, calls the 'deep blues', i.e. those with their roots in the Delta. These have a structure based on the 'blues pentatonic'. This mode is composed of the first, fourth and fifth tones of the scale plus 'altered' (or 'accidental') thirds and sevenths. The altered thirds and sevenths constitute what have come to be known as the 'bluenotes'. Though the 'bluenote' phenomenon is difficult to describe within the terminology of western musical theory, it constitutes a tone in between minor and major tones. That is, the major tone is 'leant on', flattening it somewhat, or the minor is sharpened in the same manner. On the guitar this can be done by bending the strings with the left hand; and on the piano an equivalent effect can be obtained by means of 'crushing' the notes (that is by playing adjacent notes at the *same time*, so blending them). The techniques required for the vocal expression of the mode are more difficult to master than many people seem to realize, and little more than a handful of those who have been recorded can be considered virtuosos. Prominent among those are Bessie Smith, Robert Johnson, Muddy Waters, Elvis Presley, Ray Charles and Aretha Franklin.

As these and a few other artists have illustrated, blues singing requires vocal range, intensity and the most delicate control. But it also requires the ability to provide subtle melodic and rhythmic improvisation. Bessie Smith's 'Gulf Coast Blues' (1923) is a wonderful demonstration of these qualities, as is Robert Johnson's 'Come On In My Kitchen' (1936), in which he shows to perfection the technique of using the guitar as a 'second voice' by matching the tones and textures of voice and guitar. And Muddy Waters's recording of 'Long Distance Call' (1951) exhibits beautifully the subtlety of vocal mannerisms involved in all the most accomplished blues singing. This is especially apparent in the first line of the final verse, as he sings

Hear my phone ringing, sounds like a long distance call,

sliding effortlessly between the major and the 'blue' tones, with just the right mixture of hope and bitterness in his voice.

Elvis Presley may seem a surprising, even a perverse, choice to anyone who has yet to listen closely to his best work in the blues field, though few would deny the awesome qualities of his voice. Despite Presley's well-established brilliance on his *Sun* recordings, perhaps his most convincing performance as a blues vocalist is on his version of the Lowell Fulson number 'Reconsider Baby' (1960), cut during the sessions immediately following his army release.

Ray Charles and Aretha Franklin are better known as soul singers. Yet unlike many of the gospel-trained vocalists who stuck closely to the major scale in their secular performances, as in the case of Sam Cooke, Charles and Franklin have often recorded songs with melody lines based upon the blues pentatonic. Charles' 'What'd I Say' (1959) and Franklin's 'I Never Loved A Man' (1967) are perfect examples of this aspect of their work.

The melodic structure is the basic *musical* component of the country blues song. Of the three fundamental song components, *lyrics, melody,* and *harmony,* it is the last named that is of least importance to the genre. For country blues are typically constructed so as to maximize the compatibility of their lyrical and melodic components. Thus the central 'logic' of the music is that of 'horizontal' (i.e. melodic) rather than that of 'vertical' (i.e. harmonic) coherence. It is a particular feature of Delta blues, for instance, that vocal and guitar parts are sung and played in unison, especially in the case of recordings where the vocal part is accompanied by 'bottleneck' style guitar, wherein the voice and guitar 'echo' each other. Harmony in country blues is an embellishment, secondary to the melodic line, which has become more important as blues have increasingly been played in bands.

An all too common method of describing the 'fundamental' musical structure of blues, particularly by writers with a jazz or popular music background, is that proposing a 'typical' chord sequence. It is ubiquitously given as:

```
1st line      ------- | ------- | ------- | ------- |
chord symbols  I         I         I         I
2nd line      ------- | ------- | ------- | ------- |
chord symbols  IV       IV         I         I
3rd line      ------- | ------- | ------- | ------- |
chord symbols  V        IV         I         I
```

Thus the 'typical, twelve-bar' blues is commonly described, in shorthand, as being of an AAB, I–IV–V–IV–I, form (wherein the AAB shows that the first, lyrical, line of the stanza is repeated).

However, the descriptive outline given above seriously distorts the structure of country blues. For not only does it imply that a particular harmonic progression is a crucial part of the music's structure; it also ignores the phenomenon of 'bluenotes' in the music. The more enlightened commentators at least include in such outlines symbols such as I^{7dim} and IV^{7dim} to denote the use of diminished chords. Without the addition of diminished chords the outline resembles a boogie progression rather than that of a blues. And even as an outline of boogie progressions it is little more than a very basic, practical, guide, providing a simplified 'musical map' for those who wish to strum out a boogie pattern, for instance.

Given the fundamental *melodic* nature of blues structures, the outline does not even give an adequate guide to (chordal) guitar accompaniment.

Country blues often begin on the dominant (i.e. Vth) tone of the scale. Furthermore, the actual chord position used to 'cover' the vocal line can be one of several, including that of the Vth chord, confined in the outline to the third stanza. Many Delta and Chicago 'downhome' blues commence with a diminished seventh (7^{dim}) tone. These include the Muddy Waters recording of 'Long Distance Call', in respect of the stanza quoted above. A chord progression which conforms to the verbal part, as appearing on the record, could be:

chording: I^{7dim} ^{7ma} IV IV^{7dm} IV V
vocal: Hear my   phone ring——ing——
chording: V   V IVIV IV^{7dim} I   I
vocal: Sounds like a long dis——tance call

Beginning the verse on the diminished seventh, as Muddy Waters does here, is a common feature of Delta, and Delta-derived blues. Moreover, the melodic structure of the whole line is typical of that blues strain. Thus the tune of the first two lines of the verse is noticeably similar to those of, for instance, B. B. King's 'Rock Me Mama' (1961) and Robert Johnson's 'Rambling On My Mind' (1936). The line is composed of two musical phrases the progressive structure of which conform to typical phrases of Delta blues. And the construction of blues songs by means of stringing together a number of lyrical and musical phrases has always been the basis of both continuity and change in that music.

Source: Hatch and Millward 1987: 59–63

The fourth and fifth forms of r 'n' b discussed by Gillett (gospel and group sounds) fed into the development of soul music during the 1960s. As Guralnick (1991: 21) suggests, 'the story of soul music can be seen largely as the story of the introduction of the gospel strain into the secular world of rhythm and blues'. Soul was, in Guralnick's account, 'Southern by definition if not by actual geography' (ibid.: 6) and centred in three main cities: Memphis in Tennessee, Macon in Georgia, and Muscle Shoals in Alabama (ibid.: 8). A similar story can be told for soul as for the blues, with a movement from the local to the wider international market over a very short space of time so that figures like Otis Redding, James Brown and Aretha Franklin became international stars whose work remains enduringly popular.

As with other forms there is a variety of different soul styles, though some commentators such as Guralnick have pointed to common features. He suggests that 'soul music is a music that keeps hinting at a conclusion, keeps straining at the boundaries – of melody and convention – that it has imposed upon itself' (ibid.: 7). However, of importance from Guralnick's account is the following:

The one other irreducible component of Southern soul music was its racial mix, and here, too, opinion remains divided about its precise significance. To some it is just one more variation on the old racist story: black workers, white owners. I have spoken earlier of my own confusion and my ultimate conviction that here was a partnership. But it was a partnership with a difference: the principals brought to it such divergent outlooks and experiences that even if they had grown up in the same little town, they were as widely separated as if there had been an ocean between them. And when they came together, it may well have been their strangeness to each other, as well as their familiarity, that caused the cultural explosion. (Ibid.: 10)

This returns the discussion to the theme considered at the beginning of this chapter, concerning the difficulties of clearly defining and separating black and white musics. In this section, several points have been demonstrated. First, that forms of black music have tended to develop in particular local and commercial contexts (for example, dances and bars), where a number of influences were brought together, in performances for black audiences. Second, that such forms have then been transmitted to wider audiences where they are then developed in other ways. Third, that it is possible, though often relatively difficult, to convey the precise musical texture of these forms of music. These are themes to be taken up in the next section on ska and reggae.

Ska and reggae

Reggae developed in the 1960s in Jamaica from two previous related forms: ska and rock steady, which had themselves grown out of music popular in Jamaica earlier in the 1950s and '60s. These were the calypso-like mento form, the drum music particularly associated with country-based Rastafarian religious groups, and the American r 'n' b sounds that were available in Jamaica from radio stations based in the southern states of the USA (Clarke 1980: 57–8; Hebdige 1987: 23–70; Jones 1988: 18–23).

Ska and rock steady, like reggae, addressed themes of importance to the everyday life of those in a less well-off position in Jamaican society. For example, in the 1960s there was a cycle of songs, whose lyrics debated the rights and wrongs of the rude boy phenomenon. Musical argument about the rude boys of the West Kingston ghetto considered their morals and ethics as well as the extent to which their law-breaking could be seen as an expression of political and social protest, or whether they should be seen as murderers and thieves who were simply hurting their own people. Lyrics of the current songs took different positions on these issues.

Reggae as a specific form developed from rock steady. As Clarke explains:

In its formation, Rock Steady began to express the specifically Jamaican experience as diversely as possible. Political protest was on the increase, but songs speaking of other themes were also part and parcel of the music scene. By 1968 Rock Steady was evidently being overtaken by another type of rhythmic invention, Reggae, which was faster and a synthesis of both Rock Steady and Ska. (1980: 96)

By the late 1960s reggae existed as a distinct musical form. At this point it began to address, in a direct fashion, themes articulated in Rastafari. There were many precursors to the development of Rasta, but perhaps the most important, and the most celebrated in the 1960s and '70s, was the work of Marcus Garvey, a black Jamaican who formed the Universal Negro Improvement Association (UNIA) in both Jamaica and the USA in the early part of the twentieth century. Garvey and his organization stressed black pride and ideas of repatriation or return to Africa. He formed a company called the Black Star Line, which was to purchase ships to take those who had been forcibly removed by whites back to their African homelands.

Marcus Garvey is significant for his iteration of many themes that were to become part of Rastafari, such as black pride and the idea of Africa as a homeland. However, his direct significance is on a different level. As Clarke states: 'Garvey's main contribution to the birth of Rastafari, however, was his prophecy to "Look to Africa, when a black king shall be crowned, for the day of deliverance is near"' (1980: 38). The coronation of Ras Tafari (Head Prince) as Haile Selassie I of Ethiopia in 1930 was seen as the answer to Marcus Garvey's suggestion, though as Clarke notes, Garvey might have known rather more about the political and social situation in Ethiopia and Africa and the likely imminence of this event than some of those who subsequently followed his words.

Some of the key themes and features of Rastafari are listed in figure 4.2 (see also Owens 1979; Gilroy 1987). Rasta themes were increasingly articulated in reggae in the late 1960s and the '70s. However, it is important to recognize that there were different styles of reggae. Three different forms can be distinguished: the vocal group, the DJ/talkover and the dub. The vocal group style is perhaps the most familiar form of reggae; perhaps its most well-known exponents were the Wailers and the subsequent work of Bob Marley. The vocals are foregrounded,

---

1 The belief in the divinity of Haile Selassie I. The Rasta term for God is Jah, which some commentators see as derived from Yahweh.
2 The characterization of white-dominated society as Babylon. There are obvious biblical reference points. Babylon can stand for different conceptions of white society, ranging from the society as a whole to its manifestations in particular oppressive agencies such as the police.
3 The centrality of Africa, though there has been debate about whether repatriation to Ethiopia or Africa in general actually means physical repatriation or whether it can be seen on a more spiritual plane, connected to other movements of Pan-Africanism.
4 The use of marijuana (ganga) as an aid to discussion and 'reasoning'. Marijuana is a sacred or religious plant, and is used as part of the cleansing of the body.
5 Dressing in particular ways including the growth of dreadlocks for males, the wearing of headscarves by women. Also important is the display of the red, gold and green colours of Ethiopia.
6 The following of a specific diet. A taboo on pork is as important as the attempt to follow what, in other cultures, might be termed an 'organic' diet.
7 A particular system of language, including the use of I-words. Thus, 'I and I' used to mean we, with a notion of the individual consciousness within the collectivity being stressed. There are a large number of I-words. Other examples include stressing the 'I' at the end of Rastafari.
8 A division of gender roles. The 'elevation' of the woman as the 'Queen'.

Figure 4.2 Some key features of Rastafari

either those of the main vocalist or the harmony of the small group. The DJ/talkover style, where the DJ talks over the basic rhythm track, originated in the sound systems of Jamaica, where the record producer who controlled the sound system, providing the music at dances, produced a particular rhythm which the DJs talked over at the dance, supplying words addressing individual and social concerns. These were then subsequently recorded and issued as records in their own right. This form alerts us to the central importance of the sound system and the live experience in this form of Jamaican music, in a similar way to which the blues functioned in black communities in the southern states of the USA. In the dub form, the basic rhythm track is doctored by the producer, so that electronic tricks can be played with it. Again, this points to the importance of the record producer in Jamaican music.

Rasta themes were brought to wide prominence by the work of Bob Marley, though the mass circulation of reggae has been interpreted as another form of white exploitation of an indigenous black form. Thus Clarke quotes from an interview he conducted with a black record producer:

> Now, all this heavy Reggae music sells a lot in Afrika, but who gets the money? Virgin, Lightning. . . . There are millions of pounds that come out of Afrika, but whose pockets does it go into? The same white man that these Reggae artists sing about, that they are gonna cut his head off, down with colonialism, and up with Rastafari. Those white companies enjoy that, man, because they are using those same words to sell you and me (i.e. black people)! (1980: 168)

Reggae and ska had been popular with young white people in the late 1960s in Britain (see further, chapter 7), and the more developed, politicized and Rasta-influenced reggae was popular in the late 1970s with the followers of punk. Early ska records were reinterpreted by the 2 Tone bands in the late 1970s and early '80s leading to the blurring of the edges between punk and reggae. Thus, a form produced originally in a black local context achieved wide circulation. The implications of this require further consideration. This means elaborating some of the categories introduced in chapter 3.

Realism, modernism, postmodernism, folk culture and reggae

Chapter 3 introduced the concepts of modernism and postmodernism, and in this section these are supplemented by ideas of realism and folk culture. Realism can be defined as consisting of three elements (Abercrombie et al. 1992). First, realist cultural forms offer a window on some kind of other world. This does not have to be 'our' world and, indeed, very often it is not, but it is a world that has plausibility for us and is coherent in everyday ways. Characters have familiar motivations. Often the constructed world is related in some way to our own world. However, popular fictions construct their own world, which relates to ours, and within that world there is both coherence and plausibility. Second, realism mobilizes a particular kind of narrative which is constructed through cause and effect and which often consists of a beginning, a middle and an end. Third, realism conceals the process of its own production and the fact that it is a fiction. The audience is often encouraged to think that they have dropped in on a world that exists independently of them and the producers of it. We 'suspend disbelief', to employ the common phrase.

There are many different realisms which have developed on the basis of this essential structure. For example, in a discussion of the US television soap opera *Dallas*, Ang identifies an emotional realism which she contrasts with 'empiricist' and 'classical' realism (1986: 45). However, the basic structure of realism can be contrasted with modernism and postmodernism.

Modernism exposes a different world. Rather than acting as a window, it focuses or refracts to show different elements of a world in a new light. The familiar world is made strange; a deeper reality of a different kind is alluded to, or explored. As Featherstone (1988), in the discussion reviewed in chapter 3, explains, narrative is fractured and the familiar patterns of cause and effect are shattered or self-consciously set in juxtaposition to other forms. Modernism is authored in an important sense. The author is central as the manipulator of the language of the representation, and may be central as a site for the exploration of consciousness. Language and the play of language are central. Modernism in its classical development was a creature of high culture and the late nineteenth century, related to the city and particular forms of new 'border crossing' experience (Williams 1989).

As was explained in chapter 3, modernism differs from postmodernism. Postmodernism does not offer a window on a separate world, or encourage the search for a different reality; rather, it suggests that our own world consists of images and discourses that cannot be known in an independent fashion. Further, postmodernism suggests that the world has lost meaning, or is simply the site of a clashing of incommensurate discourses that can only be juxtaposed and not ranked in order of importance. There is no truth or reality to be found in this scenario. Narrative may be fragmented, construct a 'knowing self' or refer to a number of other texts or narratives (for example, to another film, book or record). Different elements from different discourses or genres are placed together in one work of art. Jim Collins discusses the novel *The Name of the Rose* by Umberto Eco as a postmodernist text in this manner, explaining that:

> The Sherlock Holmes story is only one of a wide range of discourses invoked by the text. Eco intersperses A. Conan Doyle with Roger Bacon, William of Occam, and a host of diverse medieval works, along with frequent 'flash forwards' to contemporary figures (e.g. the monastery's chief librarian Jorge of Burgos, or, Jorge Borges). But the single most important intertext is 'fictional' and ironically serves as the justification of the interpenetration of detective and philosophical discourses. The key to the mystery within *The Name of the Rose*, responsible for so much murder and mayhem, is Aristotle's legendary 'lost' study of comedy, and it is this fictive text which serves to accentuate the power of discourse in and of itself. (1989: 62)

Postmodernism also plays with ideas of production and authorship. An example of this is David Byrne's film *True Stories*, a fictional documentary about a

	Folk	Realism	Modernism	Postmodernism
World	'bounded' or local supernatural or religious	clear window secular	strange opaque	discursively structured
Narrative	episodic	cause and effect beginning– middle–end	fragmented	cause and effect with incorporation of other texts
Production	immediate – performance based	concealed	foregrounded	playful + problematic

Figure 4.3 Ideal types of folk culture, realism, modernism and postmodernism
Source: elaboration of Abercrombie, Lash and Longhurst 1992

Texan town. Byrne (who led the group Talking Heads) appears as narrator of the documentary, implying control over the narrative on his part. However, he often undercuts this by foregrounding his own lack of understanding of events or by forgetting information that he wanted to convey to the audience. At points, the film appears realist, but is revealed to have been produced by the use of devices such as having Byrne step through a scenic backdrop. Authorship and production are revealed in a jokey manner.

At any one time, these forms (or ideal types) of culture may be in conflict with each other and may represent yet another form of culture which it is important to consider. This is the concept of folk culture, which has been used in diverse ways in the study of music (Middleton 1990: 127–54). In the current discussion, folk culture refers to forms of culture that are tightly linked to particular social groups and which are not subject to mass distribution, even if they are electronically reproduced. In many respects they are not realist, as they do not open a window on a different world, do not use conventional narratives of cause and effect and do not conceal the production process. The reggae tradition can be examined through these categories, which are summarized in figure 4.3.

The pre-ska forms identified above were essentially folk forms. This does not mean that they were unchanging, 'traditional' or 'authentic', but that they were rooted in particular social groups and specific localities. Ska was important, as it began increasingly to address social and political issues in Jamaican society. The music itself was distinctive, with a new 'jerky' sound. In this form can be found the beginnings of social realism in music in Jamaica, for example, concerning rude boys and criminality, which was to be so important during the 1960s. This direct, documentary and declamatory realism was to carry on running through Jamaican music. Themes of love and romance were increasingly played down by contrast with the earlier American r 'n' b-influenced forms (Clarke 1980: 72). This social realism was to become increasingly pronounced in the mid-1960s. At this point the audiences for these forms were predominantly local or in the black Jamaican communities overseas, in particular in Britain. At this point, ska and Jamaican forms did begin to have a certain wider impact. For example, Chris Blackwell set up Island Records and Millie Small had a number one hit in Britain. However, despite this success, the main audience was not ultimately made up of whites but of blacks and, in particular, working-class blacks. The music addressed some of the struggles of these groups directly: against the police, the upper-class forces in Jamaica and gang leaders who preyed on the community.

The music was not 'owned' by the sorts of people who played it or were its main audience, as it was controlled by entrepreneurs who produced the records and employed the musicians in an exploitative manner. Within this context, the role of the male record producer as entrepreneur and businessman was paramount. The musician was an employee. The musicians themselves may have recognized their own skills and looked to the great figures of black American jazz for their inspiration, but their own social position resembled that of an underclass of employees with little hope of considering themselves as 'artists' in the 'romantic' or 'classical' sense. Their own struggles were with their employers, to whom they had to sell their labour power. One of the essential problems for the musician, that of earning a living, was solved through a clear set of industrialized social relationships.

As has already been suggested, sound systems were also important. The latest sound was prized (as it still is), as a means of establishing a distinctive or novel feel and reputation. Through the concealment of the source of the sound, there was often an attempt to prevent quick mass distribution, though, of course, record sales were important and could be stimulated once a following for a particular track had been developed at dances. At this point, whilst there had been some success in Britain, this was still a folk form in the way defined above, though the transition to realism was well under way.

The realist tradition in reggae developed during the 1960s. Importantly, the sort of social realism already discussed continued to develop as ska turned into rock steady and then into reggae. The reggae that was popular in Britain in the late 1960s was essentially a familiar sort of form. The lyrics tended to address themes of love and loss; the instrumentals were rather simple, albeit danceable, tracks that held few surprises. Themes deriving from Rastafari also increased in importance. In the early 1970s these different aspects of the form were combined in the work of the Wailers and, most importantly, in the figure of Bob Marley (Davis 1984; White 1984).

Marley and the Wailers brought together many of the different aspects so far discussed. In developing what can be called an 'international' style of reggae, the Wailers drew on Rastafarian themes and imagery and addressed social issues such as the illegality of marijuana, police harassment and the conditions of slum-dwellers, as well as the themes of love and romance. They represent the high water mark of reggae realism.

The Wailers' music opened a window on a particular, coherent world centred in black Jamaican life, rested on narratives about oppression, exploitation and love and increasingly concealed the manner of its own production, through more sophisticated recording techniques. The latter was aided by the process of international success. The smoothing off of the rough edges of the Wailers' music after they were taken up by Chris Blackwell and Island Records is well documented and is sometimes seen as a typical dilution of the music's power for commercial purposes. However, it can also be described as an essential part of the perfection of the realist reggae form. Furthermore, the music was packaged in a way that made it more acceptable to those who were used to the form and content of Anglo-American rock, which had itself moved through a realist phase in the 1960s (Goodwin 1991: 178).

A further important aspect of this process should be noted. Increasingly, Bob Marley was marketed as an international star, which no doubt precipitated the split of the original Wailers, as the other two founder members (Peter Tosh and Bunny Wailer) were left behind. This process rested on the promotion of Marley as an artist in a way that had been relatively unfamiliar in the reggae tradition up to that point, but which paralleled the usage of such ideas employed in Western art traditions. Marley was seen as the creative genius behind the originality of the Wailers music. During the 1970s various other artists were promoted in this way, which can be seen as central to the strategies of the international music industry as described in chapters 1 and 2, though many seemed rather uncomfortable in the role (for further discussion of the construction of pop music stars through video, see chapter 5).

By the mid- to late 1970s, reggae had taken off as a recognized international style that would be 'marketed internationally as reggae' (Gilroy 1993: 95), and it was particularly successful. It had moved into the album market and was integrated into the white mainstream. Its own concerns and focus were developed to the highest realist point. The texts sought to open a window on a particular world, utilized narrative lines that were structured by conventional understandings of cause and effect and which reached conclusions or closure, and which seemed to be produced in a seamless manner, concealing the complexity of production.

Such developments leave those who wish to innovate with two main options: either to carry forward the realist strategy that had been so successful for Marley, or to do something rather different. Some acts were promoted in ways that approached the former strategy, but innovators tended to move in the latter direction, extending developments which had been happening parallel to the consolidation of realism in reggae.

During the 1970s and into the 1980s various reggae artists developed modernist forms. These were often based in some aspects of the forms that predated the realist phase. From the centrality of the sound system developed the two forms that encapsulate the modernist movement in reggae: dub and the DJ talkover.

In the dub style, there is play with sound itself. Rather than being smooth and developing in a familiar fashion, the music became disjointed and 'difficult' in ways that paralleled similar developments in art forms such as the novel and 'classical' music. Attention is directed to the form itself. The familiarity of the reggae sound is made strange, and attention is drawn to the role of the producer in the production of such strangeness. It is the artist as expert with sound that is important rather than as the commentator on romantic or social issues. Artistic experiment with the form is valued for its own sake; like modernist art it is the form that is the focus.

The second style did similar things, though the focus was on the voice rather than the sound. The toaster would follow his or her inclinations in voicing over the often familiar rhythm track. These words possessed a degree of narrative, but key phases were often repeated and drawn attention to. Language itself became important rather than being a means to represent something else of political or emotional importance.

Neither of these styles constructs or represents clearly any particular world, and the previous worlds constituted by reggae were dismantled and made strange in important ways. Narrative was broken and cause and effect of the rational kind are downplayed. Production and the role of the sound or language artist moved to the forefront.

Modernism in reggae does not simply follow on from realism in a straightforward sense, as variants evolved simultaneously. However, it is important to recognize the role of social and cultural struggle in these processes. The reggae artist, like all cultural producers, needs money to continue in operation and, above all, requires an audience to sustain a flow of finance. There are different strategies available to gain money and an audience. One way is to try to do something different from that which is already being done. However, in some respect innovation has to be based on what already exists. In the case of modernist reggae, these include the resources of the tradition itself, the growing dominance of realist reggae and technical resource, such as the increasingly sophisticated recording technology. The modernist forms set themselves against the dominant realist tradition by using assets from the (folk) past, including key vocal phrases, biblical imagery and mythical themes filtered through the new technical developments. At this point, a reggae avant-garde developed which took forward the claims of reggae as experimental. It could then be claimed, as a form of legitimation, that this was a more real form of reggae than the increasingly mass-accepted international style popularized by Marley and the Wailers. In this way the notion of the real might be used to ground a form that was increasingly moving away from the currently popular realist conventions.

Since the 1980s, as with other forms of popular music, there has been a mixing of reggae styles with soul (Hebdige 1987: 153–6), with rock and with dance music, not in a way that integrates them harmoniously but in a manner that allows the different discourses they entail to intertwine. It would be possible to analyse records like Smiley Culture's *Cockney Translation* (ibid.: 149–53; Gilroy 1987: 194–7), which plays with the relationship between white cockney speech and black patois, in a manner similar to Collins's consideration of *The Name of the Rose* considered above. Increasingly, discourses clash and 'mix' without one being the master or claiming dominance in a straightforward fashion (Collins 1989). The world has taken on a new complexity and an external view is not constructed, the music is within discourses that do not reflect the determination of cause and effect, but which are multiplied and multi-accented. Different ideas are juxtaposed. Production is not directly revealed, or consciously elaborated, but is not concealed in the manner of realism either. Rather, there is a play with production which is almost taken for granted. As the audience has become more aware of the process by which texts are put together, there is more fun to be had by playing on that knowledge. The consideration of this mixing of discourses can be developed through the examination of the development of hip-hop music since the 1980s.

Hip-hop and rap

The example of hip-hop allows further consideration of a number of issues that have run through this chapter so far. Since the rise to prominence of hip-hop from the late 1970s, an extensive literature has developed on the form. This has been summarized in seven broad areas: the history of hip-hop; authenticity; space and place; gender; politics and resistance; technology; and the culture industries (see Forman and Neal 2004). In this section I follow this logic and address these themes. It should also be remembered that some of these themes have already been considered elsewhere (see chapter 1 for hip-hop in the music industry, and chapter 2 for discussion of the technologically informed nature of the making of hip-hop).

A particularly clear and influential discussion of the key issues around rap music has been written by Rose, whose contribution continues to be of ongoing importance. Rose's analysis is multilayered and examines a number of key issues already discussed above, but her analysis emphasizes three key themes. These concern, first, the social and geographical context of the emergence of rap and hip-hop in New York City; second, the way in which rap is a development of 'traditions' in black culture; and, third, how new technology has facilitated the particular inflections that appear in rap. However, rap is not a radical departure from earlier forms of black expressive culture. Its key features, such as the way that it breaks the flow of the music and vocal yet rebuilds it through the layers of its construction, build on such practices in other fields of cultural creation. Rose discusses how these processes of 'flow, layering and ruptures in line' (1994: 38) have been affected by the development of the sorts of new technology and processes discussed in chapter 2 leading to a number of stylistic innovations.

Rose also points to the work of a number of female rappers and discusses the importance of the way that rap and hip-hop consist of processes of dialogue between different points of view. At times, this can take the form of boasting, which in itself can have extremely violent consequences for participants in the process, as the history of murder around hip-hop culture demonstrates. These processes around the dialogic nature of black popular music and culture have been extensively surveyed by such as Neal (1999).

Hip-hop and rap music came to wider prominence in 1979, though its roots can be found in other black musics (Toop 1984). Rap and hip-hop musics were a part of a wider hip-hop culture in New York, which included particular modes of dress, language and so on. The music developed from DJs merging different records and sounds together in a way which seemed startling at the time but which now has become a part of everyday pop music, especially as it has been facilitated by the sorts of technology described in chapter 2. Experiments in sound and voice occurred in rap as well, in part influenced by the Jamaican developments (Cross 1993: 15). However, one of the things that is distinctive about rap is the eclectic mix of elements. Toop quotes one of the pioneers of the style, Afrika Bambaataa, on his mixing strategy in the illuminating passage reproduced in box 4.3.

Rap had been developing through the 1970s before the first commercial records were released in 1979. These were a surprise to those at the core of the hip-hop scene, who were themselves quickly taken up by record companies and had their own records released. One of the key records which exemplified the hip-hop cut-up style was 'The Adventures of Grandmaster Flash on the Wheels of Steel' by Grandmaster Flash (1981). As Toop explains, this is 'a devastating collage of Queen, Chic, The Sugarhill Gang's "8th Wonder", The Furious Five's "Birthday Party", Sequence and Spoonie Gee's "Monster Jam" and Blondie's "Rapture".

Box 4.3   Afrika Bambaataa's mixing strategy

When I came on the scene after him I built in other types of records and I
started getting a name for master of records. I started playing all forms of
music. Myself, I used to play the weirdest stuff at a party. Everybody just
thought I was crazy. When everybody was going crazy I would throw a
commercial on to cool them out – I'd throw on *The Pink Panther* theme for
everybody who thought they was cool like the Pink Panther, and then I
would play 'Honky Tonk Woman' by the Rolling Stones and just keep
that beat going. I'd play something from metal rock records like Grand
Funk Railroad. 'Inside Looking Out' is just the bass and drumming . . .
rrrrrmmmmmmmm . . . and everybody starts freaking out.

I used to like to catch the people who'd say, 'I don't like rock. I don't like
Latin.' I'd throw on Mick Jagger – you'd see the blacks and the Spanish just
throwing down, dancing crazy. I'd say, 'I thought you said you didn't like
rock.' They'd say, 'Get out of here.' I'd say, 'Well, you just danced to the
Rolling Stones.' 'You're kidding!'

I'd throw on 'Sergeant Pepper's Lonely Hearts Club Band' – just that drum
part. One, two, three, BAM – and they'd be screaming and partying. I'd
throw on the Monkees, 'Mary Mary' – just the beat part where they'd go
'Mary, Mary, where are you going?' – and they'd start going crazy. I'd say,
'You just danced to the Monkees'. They'd say, 'You liar. I didn't dance to no
Monkees'. I'd like to catch people who categorize records . . .

In the who-dares-wins delirium of the house parties, Bambaataa mixed up
calypso, European and Japanese electronic music, Beethoven's Fifth
Symphony and rock groups like Mountain; Kool DJ Herc spun the Doobie
Brothers back-to-back with the Isley Brothers; Grandmaster Flash overlaid
speech records and sound effects with the Last Poets; Symphonic B Boys
Mixx cut up classical music on five turntables, and a multitude of unknowns
unleashed turntable wizardry with their feet, heads, noses, teeth and
tongues. In a crazy new sport of disc jockey acrobatics, musical experiment
and virtuosity were being combined with showmanship. Earlier in black
music history the same potent spirit had compelled Lionel Hampton to leap
onto his drums, Big Jay McNeely to play screaming saxophone lying on the
stage and the guitar aces – T Bone Walker, Earl Hooker. Johnny Guitar
Watson and Jimi Hendrix – to pick the strings with their teeth or behind their
heads.

Source: Toop 1984: 65–6, 105

It also overlaid a Disney-sounding story, the source of which Flash is keeping a
firm secret' (ibid.: 106).

The sources of much of the material used in these records could be surprising.
However, Toop suggests that the strategies involved elaborated black traditions:

An underground movement indirectly inspired by a Cliff Richard percussion
break might give the impression of a lemming-like abandonment of black

traditions, but in a perverse way these cut-ups of unlikely records, whether by The Monkees or Yellow Magic Orchestra, were a recreation of the forthright emotion that at times looked like becoming a rarity in the mainstream of black music. They were a way of tearing the associations and the pre-packaging from finished musical product and reconstructing it, ignoring its carefully considered intentions and restitching it into new music. As the process of recording music became increasingly fragmented in the 70s – a drum track laid down in Muscle Shoals, a back-up vocal in California, a lead voice in New York – so the implication began to exist that consumers might eventually be able to rejig a track according to their own preferences. (Ibid.: 115)

At the same time as these experiments in sound and voice were taking place, there was a direct address to political issues in rap. As the name suggests, these were often raps about issues such as the denigration of black history and the current exploitation of black people (Gilroy 1987: 182–7). This had been a significant presence in American black culture from the late 1960s onwards. The soul tradition had taken such issues to wide prominence since the late 1960s, for example in the work of James Brown, and those artists politicized during the 1960s, such as the Last Poets and Gil Scott-Heron, directly confronted what were in their view the realities of black life. Thus, Scott-Heron's debut album, Small Talk at 125th and Lenox from 1970 contains some the themes that continued to run through his work subsequently in tracks like 'The Revolution will not be Televised' and 'Whitey on the Moon'. Scott-Heron's work was partly born from forms of oral poetry and the music in his early work was minimalist. However, as it developed it worked in soul and jazz genres rather than connecting to hip-hop.

The work of Public Enemy, especially the albums It takes a Nation of Millions to Hold Us Back (1988), Fear of a Black Planet (1990) and the track 'Fight the Power' (1989) directly confronted exploitation and oppression. For Dery:

> [This work is] haunted by the ghosts of slaves flogged to death, Southern blacks lynched on trumped-up charges of raping white women, civil rights activists killed by Klansmen, Michael Stewart beaten to death by New York City Transit Police, Michael Griffith chased into the headlights of an oncoming car in Howard Beach and Yusef Hawkins shot in Besonhurst. (2004: 408)

Moreover, as Rodman discusses at some length, this is also an attack on white music icons:

> 'Fight the Power' is nothing less than a call to arms – made by the most outspoken and militant rap group in contemporary popular music – against the ideas, institutions, and practices that maintain the political, social and cultural inequalities between whites and blacks in the US today. The song served as the musical centrepiece of Do the Right Thing (1989), Spike Lee's critically acclaimed film depicting twenty-four hours of racial tension in a predominantly black Brooklyn neighbourhood, and it subsequently appeared on Public Enemy's best-selling album, Fear of a Black Planet. 'Fight the Power' is probably the most widely known and recognized of all Public

Enemy's songs, and its most frequently quoted lyrics are undoubtedly those concerning Elvis:

> Elvis was a hero to most
> But he never meant shit to me
> He's straight up racist
> That sucker was simple and plain
> Motherfuck him *and* John Wayne. (1996: 44)

Perhaps the paradox here is that despite such sentiments (or perhaps because of them) this music has been very successful with young white people (see below).

As hip-hop developed, music from the West Coast of the USA, and in particular Los Angeles, became more prominent (Cross 1993). The success of Niggaz with Attitude (NWA) was a key moment in the development of hip-hop. Their album *Straight Outta Compton* (1989) was widely commercially successful and also led to many of the questions that have been posed about 'gangsta rap', in particular about the way in which social and political concerns of Afro-Americans were being examined in the form, the misogyny of the raps and the violence that was seemingly advocated by the participants.

These directions have continued as the form developed from the 1980s onwards, when it has been the lyrics of rap that have led to a range of controversies, especially over the way in which rap records have been held to promote violent solutions to black problems, to exhibit a kind of gang world-view and to denigrate women. This led to widespread news coverage of the music and the sorts of story reproduced in box 4.4, which have set many of the terms of mainstream debate about this type of music.

Box 4.4 Murder rap

He's armed and he's dangerous: Ice Cube's lyrics are about race hate, the Los Angeles gangs and the glory of the gun. He's America's worst nightmare. And he's over here.

'Rapper Brings Message of Hate to Britain,' howled a headline in the London *Evening Standard*. The accompanying story warned that the Los Angeles hip-hop baron, Ice Cube, famed for raps apparently condoning misogyny and extreme violence, was coming to the UK for three concerts. 'He is accused of glorifying rape,' the piece continued, concluding with the observation that four people leaving a recent Ice Cube gig in Seattle had been machine-gunned in a drive-by shooting.

Cube's third album, *The Predator*, sold 1.5 million copies in America within a month of its release last December. That makes him a big star – as big, in relative sales terms, as Madonna. His immense popularity dovetails with white America's perception of him as its worst nightmare made heavily-armed, foul-mouthed flesh.

Cube (born O'Shea Jackson in the Compton district of Los Angeles in 1968) owes his notoriety to 'gangsta rap', a hip hop variation that is the musical equivalent of aggravated assault. Gangstas, or 'gangbangers', are

America's indigenous terrorists – the drug dealers and gang-thugs whose lawlessness has made the inner cities fearsome no-go zones. Gangsta rappers are the oral historians, chronicling the life in graphic street language.

The first gangsta raps were recorded in Los Angeles in the mid-1980s, by a reformed burglar called Ice T (whose name was derived from Iceberg Slim, a pimp and jailhouse novelist). The genre came to wider attention in 1986, with the formation of the Compton hip hop crew, Niggaz With Attitude. Before Ice T and NWA, rap had been an East Coast phenomenon. 'Where New Yorkers would rap about parties and clubs, I would rap about car chases and guns and the shit I was living through,' Ice T has said. As NWA's main lyricist, Cube was responsible for tunes such as Gangsta Gangsta and Fuck Tha Police. Both were on NWA's epochal debut LP, *Straight Outta Compton*. Gangsta Gangsta found Cube snarling: 'Do I look like a motha-fuckin' role-model?' The album's multi-million sales made it clear that America's teenagers had decided he was.

That record and its 1991 successor, *Efil 4 Zaggin* (Niggaz 4 Life), charted the group's version of the Compton life cycle: from a bleak childhood in the streets of South Central Los Angeles (where the 1992 riot would occur) to 'living large' to, inevitably, prison or a violent death.

Several themes run through all Cube's lyrics: women exist to be abused (a typical verse: 'Tucked her in / pulled out my third leg, pumped it in / she said will you call me? yeah. I'll call you a bitch or a ho'): all police are white and racist: men are judged by the fire power they wield.

Guns figure in most songs, along with an array of vivid synonyms for 'to kill', such as 'dusting', 'smoking', 'wetting' and 'burning'. AKs and 'gats' are not just symbols of machismo but the means of evening the odds against the white establishment. 'I'm a nigger gotta live by the trigger,' runs one song.

For all his evident toughness, Cube (the name refers to his impassive demeanour) had a fairly cushy upbringing. His was a middle-class home with a strict father who steered him away from the gangs. 'I was more scared of my father than I was of the niggers on the street,' he has said. He earned a certificate in architectural drawing but, enterprising to the core, saw rap as a quicker and more satisfying route to success.

He began writing lyrics in his teens. He did not lack inspiration. 'Some of the people I grew up with, they're straight-up killers . . . the hardest motherfuckers have seen, or are going to see, many of their homeboys die. Boom, boom, boom.' Dead Homiez, considered one of his more compassionate tunes, is about the funeral of a friend who fell victim to the gang warfare that once plagued South Central. (A truce has been observed since the riots.)

In 1990, Cube left NWA. He and the group's manager, Jerry Heller, were in dispute about money. Cube claimed he had been done out of royalty and tour profits – after a US tour grossing $650,000 he received a pay cheque of just $23,000. Heller, a white Jew (this is an important distinction, given persistent rumours of Cube's anti-Semitism; he denies it), declared that Cube was merely jealous of his fellow NWA rappa, Eric 'Eazy-E' Wright, who had made a platinum-selling solo album.

'I knew I had talent and I wasn't gonna stay there and get fucked out of my money.' Cube has said.

He released his first solo album, *AmeriKKKa's Most Wanted*, in the spring of 1990. The record confirmed that there was a social conscience under the belligerence. Laddish braggadocio was tempered with politically charged observations on ghetto life and police brutality.

Song titles like 'Once Upon A Time In The Projects' and 'Endangered Species' signalled a shift in Cube's preoccupations. The large-living gangsta had discovered Nation Of Islam minister Louis Farrakhan, and was in the process of becoming an outspoken campaigner for black rights. His music was adored by black teenagers for its ferocious condemnation of police harassment. White teenagers liked it because it intimidated their parents.

It took his next album, 1991's *Death Certificate*, to properly rouse white America's ire. 'Black Korea', a track inspired by the shooting by a Korean shopkeeper of an unarmed black girl, for which the killer received six months' probation, got Cube accused of incendiary racism. A coalition of groups, including the Southern Christian Leadership Conference and the Simon Wiesenthal Centre, called for a boycott of the album because of its 'outrageously violent and derogatory lyrics, which promote an attitude of racial hatred and violence'. A sample: 'Your little chop-suey ass will be a target.' Cube's UK label, Island Records, released *Death Certificate* without 'Black Korea' and another controversial number, 'No Vaseline'.

The same year, Cube made his film debut in John Singleton's *Boyz N The Hood*. His portrayal of a teenage excon won high praise and talk of an Oscar nomination. Violence in which one person died and 30 were injured marred the film's premiere. He returns to the screen here in May [1993] with *Trespass*, an all-actioner in which he and Ice T star as supremely unpleasant gangbangers. Cube's fee was said to be $1 million.

Which brings us to his new album. It opens with a prison body-search and ends with the shooting of a policeman. Cube is on typical form, raging against the society that disempowered his race and seems determined to keep it that way. *The Predator* is his inquest into the riots, which he regards as having been long overdue. 'I loved every minute of that shit. When it happened, I set my guns on the bed and waited.'

Cube is a powerful spokesman. His relentless aggression bludgeons you into seeing his point. The violence he depicts on his records is not titillation but a barometer of black anger. It is a shame that Cube, so clever about other issues, is so stupid about women. Sorry, 'bitches'. Although he is happily married, his songs contain no hint of sensitivity or tenderness. The closest he comes on the current record is, 'Got a beep from Kim, and she can fuck all night.'

This attitude saturates hard-core rap. Quick as Ice T and Cube are to take umbrage at racial slights, they refuse to believe that their view of women is vilely offensive. Ice T chortles it off as feminist jealousy of 'feminine women'. He says: 'Girls don't have a problem with being called a bitch.' And gays? Cube knows where he stands: 'True niggas ain't gay / Ya fuckin' homo.' Well, that's that, then.

They get away with it because few interviewers are willing to contravene the code of right-on-ness and challenge them. Those who do, find the rappers intractable, unable to comprehend the other side of the argument. Yet Cube and Ice T are dedicated to 'the enlightenment and education' of African-Americans.

But their misogyny and homophobia are peripheral issues nowadays. Ice T is embroiled in a censorship controversy that has riven America. Last year his backing band, Body Count, recorded a song called 'Cop Killer'. In the wake of the South Central riots, it was considered so inflammatory that police organisations pressed for a boycott of all Warner Bros Records products. The New York Patrolmen's Benevolent Association prepared to sell its $100 million investment in Time-Warner (the label's parent company) shares, and General Motors withdrew a $53 million investment. Warner Bros employees received death threats.

Citing the First Amendment, Time-Warner supported Body Count's right to free speech. Eventually the group voluntarily pulled the song from their album.

However, Ice T recently ran into more trouble. Warner decided not to release his fifth album, *Home Invasion*: it felt the cover artwork was contentious (apparently, it showed a white boy surrounded by rap records and armed black boys). Ice T refused to change it, and he and the label parted company in January. *Home Invasion* will now be released by Cube's label, Priority. As for Cube, he is white America's bogyman. It is a role he relishes. But he realises the importance of reaching the other side. 'White listeners are real important,' he says. 'Those kids that are listening to my records are going to be the mayors and senators until [blacks] get our act together.'

Caroline Sullivan

Reckless rhetoric of a fairy-tale gangsta

While Ice Cube goes to great lengths to maintain his tough guy black militant persona, in reality he is taking advantage of the poetic licence allowed creative artists.

Cube is engaging in myth-making of a grossly self-aggrandising sort. He is neither a boy from the hood like Ice T, nor a militant activist organiser like Malcolm X. Cube is a poseur, a B-Boy Wannabe son of the black middle class masquerading as a street tough.

While Ice T recounts tales from his life on the mean streets of South Central, Cube must rely on artifice to compose his raps. Under ordinary circumstances, this would be a cause for applause; for it is in the nature of things that artists should rely on artifice. But in the case of hard core rappers, excessive reliance on artistic imagination is anathema, because authenticity is central to the legitimation of their views.

Hence a middle class black guy like Cube – who has been called 'soft' by his former collaborators in NWA – is almost compelled to go to extremes in order to prove how hard he is. Yet Cube is not alone in seeking to camouflage his true background to gain authenticity. The white rapper, Vanilla Ice's account of his hard life in the Miami streets has been exposed as a near total fraud.

Instead of frankly identifying the excessive posturing of hard core rappers like Cube for what it is – the testosterone-driven rhetorical aggressions of ego-manaical and intellectually under-developed young males – legions of misguided pop music critics have become willing apologists for their transgressions against reason, manners and civility.

A persistent theme in the arguments of those critics who insist that hard core gangster and porn rappers are making an important contribution to the public discourse is that their listeners are not moved to act out the scenarios they hear on records. Greg Wilder, a writer for *The Source*, America's leading rap journal, makes a typical comment: 'People go too deep into things as far as I'm concerned. These rappers are just making records, just rhyming words that fit, that's all! I contend that not one of the millions of people who listen to these records is going to go out and try to do the things he hears on them.'

Many Afro-American psychologists disagree with this cavalier dismissal of the negative effects of the violent imagery and decadent values of some rappers. Psychological researchers like doctors Niam Akbar, Amos Wilson and Alvin Poussaint, agree that violence-riddled raps like Cube's 'Gangsta Fairytale' can influence young people to engage in anti social behaviour and even push those who may be inclined to violence over the edge.

There is a real tragedy here because there are real issues of injustice that cry out for redress lurking behind Cube's reckless rhetoric. But he has neither the intellectual equipment nor the disciplined organisational experience to offer any viable solutions.

On the contrary, considering some of the feelings he's expressed about the rap 'We Had to Tear This MF Up', a commentary on the Los Angeles riot, one could argue that he is part of the problem rather than the solution. 'I did a song called "We Had to Tear This MF Up", because that's the only way that black people can get respect. We had to burn LA and put them out of business for three days and now they want to talk . . . But, you know, I love that shit. Every bit of it.'

Playthell Benjamin
Source: Guardian, 11 March 1993

It was not only the representation of violence and such attitudes that caused controversy but also the real violence that was perpetrated by those involved. The verbal feuds between East and West Coasts turned into real violence. As Kitwana argues:

Probably no other event in rap's history has received as much coverage in the mainstream media as the so-called East Coast/West Coast beef – imagined and real antagonism between rappers and fans on the East Coast (mostly New York City) and the West Coast (mostly rappers and fans in Los Angeles). The conflict, which in print often centered on rap labels Death Row and Bad Boy, climaxed with the gangland-style murders of Tupac Shakur in 1996 and Biggie Smalls in 1997. In the wake of their deaths, many rappers participated in efforts to end the seemingly out-of-control antagonisms. From a rapper summit called by Louis Farrakhan's Nation of Islam to rap lyrics denouncing the East–West feud, rappers like Nas, Jay-Z, Common, Snoop, and others succeeded in reducing East–West antagonism. (2004: 347)

A theme that this sort of dispute and representation captures well is that of place and space. As has been considered, many of the discussions of the early days of rap and hip-hop place it very clearly in New York City. For Rose (1994), for example, hip-hop emerges in the context of the deindustrialization of the inner city area of the South Bronx, which had also been significantly affected by the construction of new roads to facilitate commuting from the suburbs into the business and commercial areas of the city. This has been a continuing theme, as Forman suggests, 'a particular image of hip-hop has been circulated, one that binds locale, resistance, innovation, affirmation, and cultural identity within a complex web of spatialized meanings and practices' (2004: 155; and see more generally Forman 2002). Moreover:

The tales of originary sites of significance that describe local places and place-based activities emerge as crucial indicators for the shaping of attitudes and identities among hip-hop's entrepreneurs including Def Jam founder Russell Simmons, James Smith of Rap-A-Lot Records, or Bad Boy Entertainment creator P. Diddy as well as among artists such as Tupac Shakur or Eminem. Can Jay Z be realistically disconnected from Brooklyn or Queens? Can Snoop Dogg be comprehended without acknowledging his Long Beach, California, roots and can OutKast be isolated from Atlanta? Where these individuals are from is an essential element of who they are and what they project, whether in a broader regional sense of space or in more finely nuanced and closely delineated scale of place. (Ibid.: 155–6)

Space in general and specific places in particular are important as 'real' and as 'cultural' or imagined in hip-hop. Many of these meanings have been condensed in the idea of the 'hood' or 'neighbourhood'. This signals real places and forms of community and linkage as well as conflicts within local spaces. However, it can be asked how significant these specific meanings are as hip-hop has become globally successful. For example, while the meanings of OutKast may be linked to their origins in Atlanta, an album like *Speakerboxxx/The Love Below* (2003) was a top ten hit in both the USA and UK in 2003/4, as was the single 'Hey Ya!' that was on it. The album was reviewed in the UK as a significant double album, often related to Prince's *Sign o' the Times* (1987) as well as efforts like the Beatles' *White Album* (1968) and the Rolling Stones' *Exile on Main Street* (1972). Thus, this work is located in a much broader context of other black music (see below) and the canon of 'rock'.

This also raises issues of authenticity, connections between social groups and modes of expression. Stephens (1992) has argued that rather than advocating a kind of black separatism, rap actually creates a form of interracial dialogue. In Stephens's view, as whites and Latinos have become involved in rap-like forms, there has been the creation of new languages and a form of multiculturalism (see also Cross 1993; Bennett 2000). In advancing an argument that music cannot be seen as racially 'owned', Stephens notes the way in which black rap has borrowed from white sources and the pride in 'multicultural identity' advanced by Latino rappers. Stephens offers an optimistic account of the development of the rap form, which sees it as a kind of 'transnational', or 'transcultural' form. His conclusion captures the essence of this argument:

> 'Black' music acts like a 'wave' at sporting events: once the wave starts rolling, you can't ask people not to stand up. When the call-and-response starts cooking, you can't pick and choose who's going to answer. It seems to me that instead of trying to draw colour lines around our music, we ought to be proud that black grooves are writing the bass lines to a new multicultural song.
>
> In hip-hop, white rappers like Third Base and Tony D, biracial rappers like Rebel MC and Neneh Cherry, Latino rappers like Kid Frost and Black rappers like KROne, all use black music and liberation theory as a base. But they use this tradition inclusively. The outcrop can no longer be defined along colour lines. With this mutually created language, participants can engage in 'negotiation strategies' through which they can 'transcend the trappings of their respective cultures'. This dialogic discourse provides a model of our movement towards the cultural crossroads where we can truly come to know what diversity means. (1992: 79)

The success of white rappers such as Eminem, whose work was produced by Dr Dre, who had been a member of NWA, can perhaps be seen in these terms. Other examples that can be thought to illustrate these processes include the work of the Sudanese rapper Emmanuel Jal and the London-based MIA. In this sense, a form of music that was originally located in place and sought to address issues of that place has become a global resource for the articulation of other themes and connected to other musical traditions. The success of artists like 50 Cent, with connections to Dr Dre and Eminem, reinforces the point that while this music retains themes that would have been at home in earlier stages of hip-hop, it can sell in very large quantities to a differentiated audience.

In a more critical discussion, Irving has argued that 'much black music, which works to construct a space for the self-dependent black male subject, has excluded spaces for the construction of alternative femininities. This is especially true of rap music' (1993: 107). Irving argues that rap's exclusivity, which does not completely exclude white men, works against women. She contrasts this American situation with that found in contemporary British black music, which she suggests is far more open to a 'multi-subjectivity'.

For Irving, the sexist and misogynistic terminology used in rap enables white male critics to identify with the black male position: 'Over and over, rapping is described in violent and phallic terms and, amongst both critics and performers, the sexism is a deliberate ploy to keep women off the turf' (ibid.: 114). She argues that this sort of male exclusionary practice can and has been overcome through some female rap records, such as those by M. C. Lyte and Roxanne Shante, which construct different positions for women. Irving's paper is one of the most developed analyses of gender address and politics in this form of music.

In a rather more positive assessment of rap, Swendenberg (1992) argues that the form has been particularly successful in articulating a political message within the context of a mass-circulated form. In this argument, rap constructs and reconstructs a black community which reinterprets the pre-existing forms of culture, in a far more radical way than punk, in a widely circulating form of music. However, Swendenberg neglects the sorts of argument that have been made about gender identified above, as well as the homophobia which he finds in much rap music, which he sees as 'shortcomings'.

Such debates have continued as rap and hip-hop music have become globally popular, being taken up and sometimes reconstituted in a wide range of places and spaces (see, for example Bennett 2000: 133–65). Hip-hop has therefore moved far beyond its origins in New York City and its subsequent development in Los Angeles. It has become a resource for a range of different artists and approaches. Thus, in addition to the approaches of the female rappers considered by Rose and Irving, artists like Missy Elliott have been successful. In working with the producer Timbaland, Elliott has addressed a range of concerns in the context of music that has often been very innovative. Moreover, the work of a range of artists, such as Mary J. Blige, who in many respects develop the soul tradition, also incorporate aspects from rap and hip-hop.

While these moves have opened the way for various forms of rap and hip-hop, it has also produced debate about the way in which hip-hop and rap have been appropriated by the culture industries. This is a common theme in the discussion of popular music, as has been considered in this book. On one level, as Neal suggests: 'For some rappers, hip-hop's engagement with the mainstream has forced them to renegotiate between long-standing narratives within the black community that have equated mainstream acceptance with "selling out" and basic desires to craft a lifestyle out of their skills as visibility as rap artists' (2004: 494). However, with the further development of popular music artists as 'brands' (see chapter 1) they have further branched out into commercial activities (see Blair 2004). There has been discussion of hip-hop groups as corporate entities in this context. As Negus points out:

> Many rap musicians have recognized such connections and formed their own successful companies. Notable here is Wu-Wear, the clothing and accessory company established by the Wu-Tang Clan. This company have stores throughout the United States where you can purchase T-shirts, socks, baggy jeans, coffee mugs and key-chains, all featuring the distinctive Wu-Bat brand logo. (1999: 100)

The position of the texts of rap and hip-hop has therefore moved in a number of different directions. There has therefore been a clear sense in which hip-hop has become part of 'mainstream' musical and commercial culture. As Kusek and Leonhard suggest: 'Hip-hop artists Simmins, L. L. Cool J., Missy Elliott, Eminem, Ludacris, Nelly, Sean Combs, and Jay-Z have shown corporate America

that hip-hop can generate substantial dollars outside the recorded music industry'
(2005: 118).

Conclusion

The discussion in this chapter suggests that ideal types of different cultural forms
can be used in the analysis of black music. In particular, this was shown through
the example of reggae music. However, a similar narrative could be developed for
jazz. Thus, for example, Heble notes that:

> For example, jazz, developing from the early diatonic (and, if I can put it this
> way, realist) styles of ragtime, New Orleans, and Dixieland, has moved
> through the chromaticism of bebop and the modernism of atonality and free
> collective improvisation into what might be seen as more recent
> (postmodern) attempts at rehistoricization. (2000: 13)

In addition, Peterson, in an early article (1972), located the development of jazz in
the relationships between folk, pop and fine art musics (see also chapter 6).

The specific black forms were connected to social locations and social
movements (see also, for example, DeVeaux 1997). In these locations, distinctive
themes were often articulated, which express, according to Gilroy (1987), some
core aspects of black culture (see also, for example Heble 2000; and Neal 1999).
Such themes can sometimes facilitate dialogue between different ethnic groups,
leading to the generation of new musical forms, such as Asian rap. These forms
tend to have value ascribed to them because of their authenticity. However, this
does raise problematic issues concerning the extent to which any artist can speak
for a community. The discussion has been predicated on social definitions of
black, rather than essentialist ones, and has taken account of the wider social and
political meanings of blackness. There remain problems with such descriptions. It
may be that often used categorizations of black slide over and eradicate important
social and political differences between different racial and gendered identities.
The examination of rap brings some of these matters to the foreground, prompting
consideration, for example, of the relation between 'black' and 'chicano' and male
and female identities. In this respect, consideration of rap and the current fluidity
of the relations between different musical forms further illuminates the discussion
of postmodernism, politics and identity introduced in chapter 3 and exemplified
through the discussion of Madonna. The valuation of the 'black' identities
constructed for men by 'gangsta' rap or pornographic videos may be problematic
for women (of all races) illuminating the complexity of contemporary cultural
politics.

It is important to recognize that the discussion of 'black' music in this chapter
has shown the importance of the consideration of different genres, but also how
these genres have influenced each other. Thus, in his discussion of the group
God's Property in a post-industrial soul context, Neal argues:

> The group's mission was blatantly apparent on their first single release, a
> remix of the song 'Stomp' which featured a bass line appropriated from
> Funkadelic's 'One Nation Under a Groove' and liberal use of urban slang,

Christian doctrine, and the simulated gunshots, which had become popular in many Dancehall reggae recordings. (1999: 171)

This sort of context has increasingly informed the discussion of pivotal figures such as Miles Davis. Substantial considerations of Miles Davis's electric music from the late 1960s onwards (e.g. Tingen 2001; Freeman 2005) discuss it in relation to the work of Jimi Hendrix and Sly Stone, for example, and show that it moved well beyond the boundaries of jazz. In addition, there were attempts at collaborations between Davis and Prince: Davis's last album showed the influence of hip-hop, and so on. However, much of Davis's work was also carried out in collaboration with the white arranger Gil Evans and producer Teo Macero, and has been remixed by dance producers. It is significant that this music can increasingly be examined in such a wide context. In a number of ways this shows the progression of the study of popular music away from stereotypes to a situation where the specifics of contexts can be recognized.

Summary

This chapter has considered:

- the nature of 'black music' and some of the issues raised by the use of this concept;
- the textual development of blues and soul in the USA and the social contexts for these forms;
- the textual development of reggae in social context, utilizing distinctions between folk, realism, modernism and postmodernism, elaborating the arguments of chapter 2;
- the development of hip-hop in its social context and some of the issues raised by this.

5

Texts and Meaning

This chapter is concerned with the ways in which pop music creates and conveys meaning. This means examining: first, what conveys meaning; second, how meaning is conveyed; and third, who conveys meaning. These threads run through the chapter, which begins with a consideration of how the established discipline of musicology has treated pop music. This is followed by a discussion of the way in which concepts deriving from structuralism and semiotics have been used in the study of the texts of popular music. This leads into an examination of the relationship between words and music in the conveyance of musical meaning. Discussions of musical meaning and the visual have been extended by the appearance of music video in the 1980s. This is examined in some length in this chapter by contrasting the accounts of Kaplan (1987) and Goodwin (1993). In addition to introducing the topic of music video, this discussion therefore has more general provenance in the consideration of the relationship between music and visuals in the creation of meaning. The chapter concludes with a brief consideration of the role of the star in the creation of musical meaning.

Musicology and pop music

Several writers have pointed to the way in which musicology, because of its origins in the study of Western classical music, neglects pop music. Middleton (1990), in an analysis that remains of significant importance (Griffiths 1999), suggests three areas where musicology has problems with the study of pop music. First is the terminology used in the musicological approach. According to Middleton, musicology uses value-laden terms such as harmony and tonality to the neglect of ideas like rhythm and timbre. Furthermore, such terms are not used in a neutral fashion. In Middleton's view, a term like melody suggests something to be valued, whereas tune suggests an everyday banal form:

> These connotations are ideological because they always involve selective, and often unconsciously formulated, conceptions of what music is. If this terminology is applied to other forms of music . . . [for example,

non-Western or pop forms] . . . clearly the results will be problematical. In
many kinds of popular music, for example, harmony may not be the most
important parameter; rhythm, pitch gradation, timbre and the whole
ensemble of performance articulation techniques are often more important.
(1990: 104)

Second, Middleton argues that there are problems with methodology, particularly
in the use of notation in musicology. This leads to an emphasis on those parts of
music that can be written down using conventional notation. However, many non-
classical musics have features that cannot be expressed through the forms
generated for the notation of European classical music. Furthermore, the focus on
notation leads to the valuation of the score as representing what the music actually
is. Again, this is not applicable in a direct way to other forms of music, where a
score may not exist or where, as is the case with some pop music, the score is
created after the music has been recorded and marketed. Indeed, Middleton
suggests that:

Even in notated popular music – Tin Pan Alley ballad, music hall, vaudeville
and minstrel songs, ragtime and nineteenth-century dances – the published
sheet music, almost always for piano and voice and piano, sometimes
'simplified', acted to some extent as a prognostic device or a beside-the-fact
spin-off. (1990: 106)

The analyst who simply focused on the text of a pop song as written down with
notes on a score would miss a number of the different ways in which such music
creates meaning, including, for example, the nature of the performance given of
the song. A number of these different dimensions to the creation of meaning are
explored as this chapter progresses.

The third problem with musicology identified by Middleton concerns ideology.
Musicology developed in nineteenth-century Europe to examine European classical
music. While it has expanded its horizons somewhat, this is still its touchstone.
Therefore, the claims of a particular kind of music are valued above others in a way
that reproduces the tastes and practices of a particular powerful social group and
marginalizes those of weaker social groups. The means by which other forms of
music are judged against the classical European tradition leads the latter to be
valued in ways that prop up established ways of thinking of music. This is a similar
sort of point to that made by Middleton against Adorno, which was examined in
chapter 1. In a further discussion, Middleton has summarized the key problems
with 'the old-style musicological pop text' (2000: 4) in terms of the five points
listed in figure 5.1.

Given that '[t]he discipline of musicology traditionally is dedicated to the
painstaking reconstruction, preservation, and transmission of a canon of great
European masterworks' (McClary and Walser 1990: 280), the prospects for
developing a musicological study of pop music would not seem promising.
However, in recent years a number of writers have attempted to elaborate
approaches which recognize that an analysis of the music can contribute to the
study of pop music. For example, Middleton (1990: 117) suggests that the critique
of musicology which he so clearly sets out should not be taken too far, because this

What exactly is wrong with the old-style musicological pop text? There have been many critiques. Usually the problems are seen as lying in the following areas:

(i) There is a tendency to use inappropriate or loaded terminology. Terms like 'pandiatonic clusters' applied to pop songs really do tend to position them alongside Stravinsky, even though it is not at all clear that anything comparable is going on there, while, similarly, a phrase such as 'the primitively repetitive tune', for example, is weighed down with evaluative baggage.

(ii) There is a skewed focus. Traditionally, musicology is good with pitch structures and harmony, much less good with rhythm, poor with timbre, and this hierarchy is arguably not congruent with that obtaining in most pop music.

(iii) 'Notational centricity' (as Philip Tagg calls it) tends to equate the music with a score. This leads to an overemphasis on features that can be notated easily (such as fixed pitches) at the expense of others which cannot (complex rhythmic detail, pitch nuance, sound qualities).

(iv) The most common aesthetic is one of abstractionism. Musical meaning is equated with an idealized image of the 'work', contextualized process turned into abstract product. This procedure is at its most extreme in formalist modes of analysis, which tend to reduce meaning to effects of structure, ignoring emotional and corporeal aspects.

(v) Listening is monologic. What the analyst hears is assumed to correlate with 'the music', and the possibility of variable aural readings is ignored.

Figure 5.1 Problems of the old-style musicological pop text

Source: Middleton 2000: 4

would block the proper understanding of how pop music works as music. Moreover, it would specifically obscure the connections that exist between the European classical tradition and popular music. Thus, Walser (1993) has shown how heavy metal makes use of the Baroque tradition from classical music. In general, Middleton argues that:

> The 'critique of musicology', then, should take aim not at 'art music' or musicology themselves – separating popular music off from them – but at a particular construction of musicology, based on a particular subject, conceived in a particular, ideologically organized way. Once the musical field as a whole is freed from the distorting grip of that ideology, the ground is cleared for a useful musicology to emerge. The metaphor should be not one of opposed spheres, or of decisive historical breaks, but of a geological formation, long-lived but fissured and liable to upheaval: the task is to remap the terrain. (1990: 122)

McClary and Walser also want to reconfigure the musical study of popular music, suggesting that it is important to study those aspects of the music which 'trigger adulation in fans' (1990: 287) as these are central in the creation of meaning. Walser has expanded upon these points in his study of heavy metal music, where he argues that:

> The danger of musical analysis is always that social meanings and power struggles become the forest that is lost for the trees of notes and chords. The necessity of musical analysis is that those notes and chords represent

the differences that make some songs seem highly meaningful and powerful and others boring, inept, or irrelevant. (1993: 30)

If this sort of argument is to be followed, it is necessary to consider the ways in which it has been suggested that music conveys meaning and can be analysed as a textual form. These ideas are developed in the next section.

Aspects of musical meaning

Much recent writing on the way in which music creates meaning has been influenced by structuralism and semiotics (or semiology). One important source of structuralism came from the linguistic theories of de Saussure (1857–1913), which were developed in the 1960s by influential writers such as Althusser, Barthes, Chomsky, Foucault, Lacan and Lévi-Strauss. Keat and Urry (1975: 124–6) identify the following main features of structuralism:

1　Systems must be studied as a set of interrelated elements. Individual elements should not be seen in isolation. For example, in a set of traffic lights, green only means go because red means stop.
2　An attempt to discover the structure which lies behind or beneath what is directly knowable.
3　The suggestion that the structure behind the directly visible is a product of structural properties of the mind.
4　The methods of linguistics can be applied to other social and human sciences.
5　Culture can be analysed in terms of binary oppositions – for example, between good and bad.
6　The adoption of a distinction between synchronic (static) and diachronic (changing) analyses.
7　The attempt to identify similar structures in different aspects of social life. For example, the standardized structure of pop music may be the same as the standardized structure of society.

Semiotics – or semiology – is the systematic study of signs. To introduce some of the concepts and ideas associated with these approaches, we can consider the photograph reproduced with its caption in figure 5.2. Certain features of this photograph can be identified immediately. It shows two white women standing next to each other, one with dyed blond hair wearing a white dress and the other with short black hair dressed in black. The blond woman is holding a baby's bottle and appears to be offering it to the other woman. The photograph seems to have been taken at some kind of public function, as there appear to be people standing around in the background. In the language of semiotics, this is what the photograph denotes. We can understand, or decode, such meanings in a fairly straightforward manner, as they are relatively objective.

However, the possession of other knowledge may facilitate more detailed decoding of the photograph. Thus, the contemporary pop fan might recognize these women as Courtney Love from the band Hole and the Irish singer Sinead O'Connor. He or she might also be able to explain Love's possession of a baby's bottle from the knowledge that she has recently had a child. Further layers of

Here, this will put hairs on your . . . er . . . head. Courtney Love extends her mothering instincts to an undernourished Sinéad O'Connor at the MTV awards. 'It was *formula* milk, wasn't it Courtney? I mean, tell me, it was out of a tin wasn't it – *wasn't it???*'

Figure 5.2 Courtney Love and Sinead O'Connor, 1993 MTV Awards

© London Features International Ltd, photographer: Kevin Mazur/Lfi-UKM

meaning, or connotations, of this photograph are built up on the basis of this knowledge. These women are pop stars and the photograph conveys ideas or discourses about motherhood and nurturing.

Still further levels of meaning are generated when the photograph is considered in context with its caption. The caption both explains some other factors surrounding the photograph and conveys a joke. It explains that this is indeed Courtney Love and Sinead O'Connor and that the photograph was taken at the MTV Awards. It is assumed that the readers of the magazine from which this photograph is taken will understand what MTV stands for, though not everyone would know this. The joke depends on understanding that Love had a record of drug-use which might be passed on through her milk. O'Connor is interpreted as ensuring that her health will be protected. It is likely that the readers of *Vox* will be aware of this aspect of Love's life, as the magazine had previously published long extracts from a book about the band Nirvana, led by Love's husband Kurt Cobain, which contained extensive descriptions of the couple's drug-use.

The discussion of this photograph has introduced several important points:

1 That any image or text can be said to contain different layers or levels of meaning. In particular there is a distinction between denotative and connotative levels.
2 That the nature of such meanings will depend on the context in which they are contained, or the surrounding circumstances. Meaning is relational.
3 That some of the levels of meaning or codes are relatively neutral, or objective, whereas others will be saturated with social meanings or discourses.

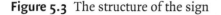

sign = signifier + signified

Figure 5.3 The structure of the sign

Figure 5.4 Language and myth
Source: Barthes 1976

4 That the recognition and elucidation of these different meanings involve analysis or decoding, which often depends on the nature of the knowledge and experience brought to the analysis.

Using the language of semiotics, the photograph can be said to be acting as a sign. The sign consists of two elements: the signifier and the signified. The signifier is a sound, printed word or image and the signified is a mental concept. This structure is represented in figure 5.3.

The semiotic approach, which was developed from the study of language by de Saussure, has been applied widely. Thus, the French theorist Roland Barthes (1915–80) argues: '[T]ake a black pebble: I can make it signify in several ways, it is a mere signifier; but if I weigh it with a definite signified (a death sentence, for instance, in an anonymous vote), it will become a sign' (1976: 113). Barthes shows how different levels of meaning are associated (shown in figure 5.4). This demonstrates the relationship between the denotative or connotative levels of meaning. Barthes also writes here about the distinction between language and myth. For him, myths shore up existing structures of power, which favour the bourgeois class. Myths make what is historical or changeable appear to be natural and static.

Signs are organized into systems which convey meaning; these systems are often called codes in structuralist and semiotic approaches (Fiske and Hartley 1978: 59). Middleton (1990) suggests that a number of different levels of code structure popular music (shown in figure 5.5). Thus, if a track such as 'Born in the USA' by Bruce Springsteen were to be analysed in these terms, we would see that the vocal, for example, contains characteristic figures of speech (or idiolects). We might argue that it was a rock song rather than a ballad. It might be Euro-American and be seen as a typical product of the 1980s, when rock took a particular direction – and so on, working up through the levels of code.

This sort of categorization can be used to inform discussions around the idea of competence. Middleton shows how Stefani distinguishes between 'high' and *langue*: a general Western music code, governing the territory, roughly speaking, of functional tonality (starting, that is, about the sixteenth century and still largely current today);

norms: e.g. the mainstream conventions *c.* 1750–*c.* 1900, or those governing the post-1900 period; within these

sub-norms: Victorian, jazz age, 1960s, etc.; and

dialects: e.g. European, Euro-American, Afro-American; within these

styles: music hall, Tin Pan Alley, country, rock, punk, etc.; and

genres: ballad, dance-song, single, album, etc.; within many of these

sub-codes: e.g. within rock, rock 'n' roll, beat, rhythm and blues, progressive, etc.; and

idiolects: associated with particular composers and performers; within these
   work and performances.

Figure 5.5 Musical codes

Source: Middleton 1990: 174

'popular competence' and ability in the understanding or decoding of the code. High competence 'treats music as highly autonomous', suggesting that there is a set of distinctive skills which are needed to understand it properly. In contrast, 'popular competence appropriates music in a more global, heteronomous manner' (Middleton 1990: 175), perhaps connecting it more directly with everyday life. Furthermore:

> Popular competence can attach itself to any kind of music – though musics themselves coded in an analogous way are the most likely. Similarly, popular music can be listened to according to high competence principles (as is sometimes the case with professional performers). But a preponderance of popular music listening does seem to be of a popular competence type. (Ibid.)

This suggests, for example, that a piece of classical music could be decoded for its melody, but this would neglect other features that would be identified through the use of high competence.

The idea of musical code has been used in other ways by recent writers on popular music. For example, Bradley (1992) draws a broad distinction between the 'tonal-European code' and the 'Afro-American code', which he suggests are merged in the development of rock 'n' roll (see further chapter 3). In identifying these codes, Bradley draws upon the work of Chester (1990), who distinguishes between the extensional nature of classical music and the intensional structure of rock and other non-European musics. Chester argues that in extensional classical music:

> Theme and variations, counterpoint, tonality (as used in classical composition) are all devices that build diachronically and synchronically outward from basic musical atoms. The complex is created by combination of the simple, which remains discrete and unchanged in the complex unity. Thus, a basic premise of classical music is rigorous adherence to standard timbres, not only for the various orchestral instruments, but even for the most flexible of all instruments, the human voice. (1990: 315)

By contrast, in intensional music:

> [T]he basic musical units (played/sung notes) are not combined through space and time as simple elements into complex structures. The simple entity is that constituted by the parameters of melody, harmony and beat, while the complex is built up by modulation of the basic notes, and by inflection of the basic beat. (Ibid.)

Another use of the idea of code can be found in the work of Sheila Whiteley (1992, 2000a) who mobilizes the idea of 'psychedelic coding' to study 1960s progressive rock. According to Whiteley, such coding of the music, which included 'the manipulation of timbres (blurred, bright, overlapping), upward movement (and its comparison with psychedelic flight), harmonies (lurching, oscillating), rhythms (regular, irregular), relationships (foreground, background)' (1992: 4), conveyed 'the hallucinogenic experience' in music.

The concept of style has been deployed in musicological discussion of rock by Moore (1993), who argues that it is possible to distinguish a general rock style, which includes a number of common features in areas such as rhythm and the voice, and a variety of different and specific styles within this general category of rock style.

The discussion so far has examined the ideas of sign and code, as they have been used in semiotics. Middleton (1990: 214–20) suggests four dimensions along which music can be considered in structural terms, which develops the structuralist approach. He sees each of these as a continuum. The four continua are:

1 Generative
2 Syntagmatic
3 Paradigmatic
4 Processual

Generative structure refers to the continuum between the deepest levels of the structure and those at the surface. This is similar to the idea of there being a hierarchy of codes, as considered above. Middleton's classification of generative levels is given in figure 5.6.

Syntagmatic analysis refers to the ways in which different musical units are combined to produce sequences of sounds. Thus, a pop song may be made up of a series of instrumental passages, verses, choruses, bridges, and so on. Likewise, to take another example, a meal may be thought of as a syntagmatic chain. In Britain, this might consist of a first course or starter, a main course and a pudding. Discussion of the precise contents of the different courses means moving the analysis onto the (third) paradigmatic level, as this refers to the alternatives that can be substituted for the different components of the syntagmatic chain. Thus, for example, a choice might be made between fish or meat for a main course.

Finally, Middleton considers the 'processual continuum'. He suggests that 'all musical events relate forward (through expectation and implication) and back (through memory), and their function and meaning change as the processual dynamic unfolds' (1990: 219). For Middleton, a full structural analysis has to consider the interconnections between these different dimensions.

1   General cognitive processes. Here, methods relating to the schemes of sensorimotor-affective organization and symbolic-behavioural logic would be appropriate (for example, principles of same/different, strong/weak, up/down, and of proportion, grouping, contour and gesture).

2   Culturally determined applications of (1), specific to musical materials (for example, note-frames, time-frames, patterns of tonal and harmonic relationship). Generative theories come in here.

3   Style-specific syntaxes constructed from (2) (for example, available scales, intervals, rhythms, parameter relationships; preferred formulae, modes of combination). Distributionist, commutational and paradigmatic approaches are appropriate at this level.

4   Intra-opus patterns: the individual piece in all its uniqueness.

Figure 5.6 Levels of generative structure
Source: Middleton 1990: 214

An issue that has come under close scrutiny in much consideration of the creation of musical meaning is the relationship between words and music. At this point, therefore, the chapter moves away from the examination of themes deriving from structuralism and semiotics to focus on the issues raised in the examination of this relationship.

Words and music

Much analysis of pop music has focused on the meaning of the words or lyrics. Early attempts to study pop music (see Griffiths 1999) often considered the lyrics as a form of poetry, suggesting that certain pop writers could be seen as poets. Much analysis of Bob Dylan was carried out along these lines. Lyrics have also been studied in other ways. In some cases, the focus has been on the content of the lyrics. Thus, in his book-length study of punk rock, Laing (1985) shows the difference in subject matter between punk and Top 50 pop songs through content analysis, as shown in table 5.1. Punk songs were less concerned than pop songs with romantic and sexual relations and focused more on the nature of sexuality. Social and political comment was far more commonplace in the punk song than in the pop song. According to Ball and Smith, content analysis involves six steps:

> (1) selecting a topic and determining a research problem; (2) selecting a documentary source; (3) devising a set of analytic categories; (4) formulating an explicit set of instructions for using the categories to code the material; (5) establishing a principled basis for sampling the documents; and (6) counting the frequency of a given category or theme in the documents sampled. (1992: 21–2)

As with all forms of content analysis it is important to see how the different categories of content are defined, to consider the basis on which the sample has been arrived at, and so on. Further details on these matters can be found in Laing's book. However, as Laing recognizes, content analysis is a rather crude form of analysis. It tends to abstract the specific content from its context and does not pay much attention to the detail of the modes of expression in the lyrics.

Table 5.1 The subject matter of the lyrics of five punk groups

	Punk	Top 50
Romantic and sexual relationships	21% (13)	60% (31)
Sexuality	15% (9)	–
First person feelings	25% (16)	3% (2)
Social and political comment	25% (16)	4% (2)
Music and dancing	7% (4)	18% (10)
Second and third person	7% (4)	3% (2)
Novelty	–	8% (4)
Instrumental	–	4% (2)

Figures in brackets denote the actual number of songs in that category
Source:
Laing 1985: 27; source for Top 50: *Star File* 1977

In an attempt to overcome some of the problems of content analysis, more recent analysis of the lyrics of songs has studied different modes of expression in lyrics and the ways in which the listener is addressed by them. One of the most consistent writers in this vein is Barbara Bradby (e.g. 1990, 1992; Bradby and Torode 2000), whose work is a form of discourse analysis. She suggests that lyrics and music construct and refer discourses in songs which have much wider significance. In the discussion of Madonna's 'Material Girl', which is reproduced in figure 5.7, Bradby lists the lyrics of the song as well as the discourses they refer to and construct. These include maternal, romance, everyday, money, school and teaching discourses. Further, she examines the pronouns (I, we, you, etc.) which address the other participants in the song's world and audience. This type of analysis goes well beyond the simplicities of content analysis. However, it does not overcome some of the issues raised by Frith (1988b) about the relations between words and music.

Frith notes the centrality of content analysis to early discussions of popular music, but argues that not only are such accounts overly simplistic, they also tend to relate the content of songs to general social attitudes or beliefs in a very straightforward fashion. Frith suggests that this neglects the sort of work that the song actually does through its lyrics and music. In his view, accounts which suggest that pop songs reflect the banality of mass culture are also prey to the same fault. Such a theory also occurred in rock music in the 1960s. He says: 'At its simplest, the theory of lyrical realism means asserting a direct relationship between a lyric and the social or emotional condition it describes and represents' (ibid.: 112). This theory of realism is different from that utilized in chapter 4. Frith uses the idea of lyrical realism to characterize those accounts that suggest a correspondence between the lyrics of a song and reality. The discussion of realism earlier referred to textual structure.

In lyrical realism, some songs are taken to be an authentic expression of social conditions or values, whilst others are inauthentic, but, in Frith's view, it is very difficult to establish the criteria on which such a judgement can be made. Furthermore, it is not always clear what reality the lyrics in the song are meant to be expressing. Frith's point is that simple links between the content of the words

[The figure] transcribes the lyrics of 'Material Girl', as actually performed on the record, which differs considerably from the neat verses reproduced on the inner sleeve of the album *Like a Virgin*. In addition, I have indicated the parts sung by the different voices in the performance, as follows:

Madonna as solo singer	= ordinary typeface
Madonna as girl-group, or female chorus, i.e.,	
using her own voice as backing vocal	= *italics*
MADONNA + MALE CHORUS OF THREE BACKING VOCALISTS	= CAPITALS
Madonna's voice as interrupting response	= {lyrics}
prominent electronic echo effects	= lyrics

Madonna, 'Material Girl', discourse analysis

	Lyrics	Discourses	Pronouns
Intro.	(4 lines rhythm alone, then 4 lines with prominent melody in the bass)		
Verse 1	Some boys *kiss* me, some boys hug me	maternal/romance	– me
	I think they're OK	everyday	I – they
	If they don't give me proper credit	money/school	they – me
	I JUST WALK AWAY	everyday	I
Verse 2	They can beg and they can plead, but	romance	they
	They can't see the light, {That's right},	religious/everyday	they
	Cos the boy with the cold hard cash is	money/romance	
	ALWAYS MISTER RIGHT		
Chorus 1	*Cos we're living in a material world*	material	we
	And I am a material girl	material	I
	You know that we are living in a material world	material	you, we
	And I am a material girl	material	I
Verse 3	Some boys romance, some boys slow dance	romance	
	That's all right with me	everyday	me
	If they can't raise my interest then I	money	they, I –
	HAVE TO LET THEM BE	everyday	– them
Verse 4	Some boys try and some boys lie but	teaching maternal	I – them
	I don't let them play, {No way},	maternal	
	Only boys that save their pennies	maternal/money	
	MAKE MY RAINY DAY	everyday	
Chorus 2	*Cos we're living in a material world*	material	we
	And I am a material girl	material	I
	You know that we are living in a material world	material	you, we
	And I am a material girl	material	I
Chorus 3	*Cos we're living in a material world*	material	we
	And I am a material girl	material	I
	You know that we are living in a material world	material	you, we
	And I am a material girl	material	I

Figure 5.7 Discourse analysis of Madonna's 'Material Girl'
Source: Bradby 1992: 80–1

	Lyrics	Discourses	Pronouns
Instrumental Break 1			
	(4 lines of bass theme from intro. + voice 'ah's ending in 'ouch')		
Chorus 4	LI – VING IN A MA-TE-RI-AL WORLD	material	
	<u>ma-te-ri</u>		
	LI – VING IN A MA-TE-RI-AL WORLD	material	
	<u>-al</u>		
	LI – VING IN A MA-TE-RI-AL WORLD	material	
	<u>ma-te-ri-</u>		
	LI – VING IN A MA-TE-RI-AL WORLD	material	
	<u>-a-al</u>		
Verse 5	Boys may come and boys may go and	everyday/romance	
	That's all right you see	everyday	you
	Experience has made me rich and	money/everyday	me
	NOW THEY'RE AFTER ME	everyday/romance	they – me
Chorus 5	Cos everybody's living in a material world	material	
	And I am a material girl	material	I
	You know that we are living in a material world	material	you, we
	And I am a material girl	material	I
Chorus 6	Cos we're living in a material world	material	we
	And I am a material girl	material	I
	You know that we are living in a material world	material	you, we I
	And I am a material girl	material	
Instrumental Break 2			
	(2 lines of bass theme from intro. + voice 'ah's, leading straight into)		
Voice	<u>a material, a material,</u>		
	<u>a material, a material,</u>		
Chorus 7	LI – VING IN A MA-TE-RI-AL WORLD	material	
	world <u>ma-te-ri</u>		
	LI – VING IN A MA-TE-RI-AL WORLD	material	
	<u>-al</u>		
	LI – VING IN A MA-TE-RI-AL WORLD	material	
	<u>ma-te-ri-</u>		
	LI – VING IN A MA-TE-RI-AL WORLD	material	
	<u>-a-al</u>		
Chorus 8	LI – VING IN A MA-TE-RI-AL WORLD	material	
	<u>ma-te-ri-</u>		
	LI – VING IN A MA-TE-RI-AL WORLD	material	
	<u>-al</u>		
[fade]	LI – VING IN A MA-TE-RI-AL WORLD	material	
	<u>ma-te-ri-</u>		
	LI – VING IN A MA-TE-RI-AL WORLD	material	
	<u>-a-al</u>		

Figure 5.7 (continued)

of a song and some reality which they are held to express are very difficult to establish. Because of this, he suggests, some writers have concluded that there is no need to pay attention to lyrics at all, also taking into account the evidence that the audience is very often not aware what the lyrics are meant to mean anyway, or produce rather different interpretations of them. However, Frith argues that words are important. He suggests that words should be examined, not as an expression of social conditions, social movements or the intentions of the great artist behind the song, but as a 'sign of a voice', as:

> A song is always a performance and song words are always spoken out, heard in someone's accent. Songs are more like plays than poems; song words work as speech and speech acts, bearing meaning not just semantically, but also as structures of sound that are direct signs of emotion and marks of character. (Ibid.: 120).

Frith argues that analysis of songs should proceed in three directions. First, attention should be paid to the ways in which singers sing the song, as it is not just what is sung that is important. The pop or rock song is a performance (see further chapter 6). Second, analysis should locate the song in a genre. Frith argues that different genres, by which he means forms like disco, punk, and so on, are understood in different ways by audiences and have different rules. Thus, 'The immediate critical task for the sociology of popular music is systematic genre analysis – how do words and voices work differently for different types of pop and audience?' (ibid.: 121). Third, detailed consideration should be given to how songs work. For example, this could involve analysis of words as a form of rhythm and sound.

Frith's conclusions are that audiences often feel words and music, and develop them in their imaginations. Thus, in his view, 'Pop love songs do not "reflect" emotions, then, but give people the romantic terms in which to articulate and so experience their emotions' (ibid.: 123). It could be said, therefore, that if this approach is adopted, those of us who listen to a lot of pop music have had our experiences and feelings couched in ways that derive from pop songs, and that our experiences are formed and interpreted in ways that are structured by the song. Thus, for example, I may be unable to divorce the experience of driving through America from my prior knowledge of all those songs that concern the American road. This would suggest an intimate relation between music and social experience, such that music structures our social life (Shepherd 1991; DeNora 2000).

Frith's suggestive analysis is based in the pioneering work on the voice carried out by Roland Barthes, which we considered earlier in this chapter. Barthes (1990) argues that it is possible to analyse the 'grain' of the voice, distinguishing the pheno-song from the geno-song. The extract in box 5.1 encapsulates his approach.

In Barthes' view, some singers go beyond the expressive level to produce the pleasures of 'jouissance' in the audience. This is a very difficult term to translate from French, but it is often explained by contrasting it to plaisir. Plaisir refers to structured pleasures and feeling, while jouissance refers to something like the pleasure of orgasm. Some singers take us into particular forms of pleasure not through what they express in language and words, but through the physical effect

Box 5.1 Pheno-song and geno-song

The *pheno-song* covers all the phenomena, all the features which belong to the structure of the language being sung, the rules of the genre, the coded form of the melisma, the composer's idiolect, the style of the interpretation: in short, everything in the performance which is in the service of communication, representation, expression, everything which it is customary to talk about, which forms the tissue of cultural values (the matter of acknowledged tastes, of fashions, of critical commentaries), which takes its bearing directly on the ideological alibis of a period ('subjectivity', 'expressivity', 'dramaticism', 'personality' of the artist). The *geno-song* is the volume of the singing and speaking voice, the space where significations germinate 'from within language and in its very materiality'; it forms a signifying play having nothing to do with communication, representation (of feelings), expression; it is that apex (or that depth) of production where the melody really works at the language – not at what it says, but the voluptuousness of its sounds-signifiers, of its letters – where melody explores how the language works and identifies with that work. It is, in a very simple word but which must be taken seriously, the *diction* of the language.

Source: Barthes 1990: 295, an essay published in *Image-Music-Text* by HarperCollins Publishers Ltd.

they have on us. I would argue that Otis Redding's voice, especially on 'I've been loving you too long', has this effect on me, which might have something to do with the content of the lyric, but has rather more to do with the effects of the 'grain of the voice'. More recently, the work of the 2005 Mercury prizewinner, Antony (see the album *I am a Bird Now* by Antony and the Johnsons), can also be seen in this light.

Middleton (1993) has also argued that music can be related to bodily experience. For example, it is possible to see the connections between dance and music. Thus, one of the most recent directions for musical analysis has been to consider in far more detail how music is used and how much of its meaning and pleasure is connected to physical activity (see further chapter 6).

Much recent analysis of the pop music text has developed the insights summarized in this chapter so far. Middleton (2000) suggests that three main directions have been followed, all of which in different ways relate music and music analysis more thoroughly to context. First, there has been more location of music in ethnographic-type studies (see, for examples, chapter 2 above). Second, building on the sort of approach discussed above with respect to Bradby and Frith, there has been a focus on discourse rather than on the structures and semiotics of texts. The implications of this sort of development are further considered via the work of Judith Butler in chapter 6. In addition, as Middleton recognizes, work by such as Walser (1993) and Brackett (1995) has advanced these sorts of perspectives helpfully. For example, Brackett combines discussions of the structure and meaning of the work of such artists as Bing Crosby, Billie Holiday, Hank Williams, James Brown and Elvis Costello with useful connections to contexts. Third, there have been approaches that emphasize the concept of mediation. These approaches explore the complex mesh of relations (or mediations) that connect music and define it in relation to many other mutually connecting influences and contexts: 'The musical worlds that we inhabit, then, are not clear sets, filled with autonomous entities which are foreign to each other and connected only via neutral "links": rather they are half-way worlds, without clear boundaries, filled with transient knots of variable meaning, practice and status' (Middleton 2000: 10). Negus identifies three main senses of mediation: (1) the 'idea of coming in between'; (2) 'a means of transmission' and (3) 'the idea that all objects, particularly works of art, are mediated by social relationships' (1996: 66). He argues that these ideas can be applied to the media in ways that illustrate some important institutional and textual processes.

In organizing a text that collects together a number of articles which can be seen as representing the progress of popular musicology, Middleton's edited volume (2000) includes chapters on the 'analysis of music', which look at the work of such artists as Randy Newman (Winkler 2000), Prince (Hawkins 2000) and Chuck Berry (Cubitt 2000). In addition, there is overview of the distinctive and influential approach of Tagg (2000). Another section examines the relationships between words and music. Here artists such as Peter Gabriel (Taylor 2000) and Bruce Springsteen (Griffiths 2000) are examined. Analysis is further broadened in a third section that brings in wider social contexts (for example, Whiteley 2000a, Moore 2000) and visuals (Björnberg 2000). Thus, this collection can be said to represent the state of an art that can be followed further in the pages of such journals as *Popular Music*.

This part of this chapter has explored a number of different dimensions of musical meaning. However, one dimension has been conspicuous by its relative absence in the discussion of the meaning of music so far: the visual. This dimension has been most recently considered in the context of the debate about music video, though this is only a specific textual form that combines music and visuals.

Music, visuals and video

As a number of writers have suggested, musical meaning has long been tied up with the visual. For example, Mundy (1999) explores the relationship of music to the visual in cinema, television and video. This view suggests that in both production and consumption, music and the visual are entwined. Thus, from the beginnings of the cultural industries as a modern phenomenon, the production of music and, for example, film have been connected, in the sense that the companies involved would often have interests in both, or would be looking to combine the appeal to the two senses. This is even the case with the so-called silent cinema (Mundy 1999). Moreover, the way in which audiences understand and access music is often connected to mass-distributed media forms. Bands will be seen first on television – and so on. It is therefore possible to consider how music and visual meaning have been connected in the history of the cinema (for example, through musical films), television (*Popular Music* 2002, in programmes such as *Top of the Pops* or *Pop Idol*), or in specific promotional forms like music videos that appear on broadcast and specialist TV channels like MTV.

Since the early 1980s a large literature on music videos has developed. A significant part of this focused on video as a visual text. One of the most important and comprehensive books which takes this approach is by Kaplan (1987). Kaplan makes two important points about music videos in general. She argues, first, that they abandon the 'traditional narrational devices of most popular culture hitherto' (Kaplan 1987: 33); and, second, that 'they are routinely, and increasingly, self-reflexive' (p. 34).

By the first point, Kaplan means that most music videos break with the relations between cause and effect, continuity, and time and space, which define the sort of realism described in chapter 4. Videos are edited in ways that differ from the classic conventions of the Hollywood film and thus disrupt our expectations of how a film should look. Furthermore, videos 'play off' earlier genres of film, such as the spy film, the Western or the horror film, as well as earlier familiar and popular movies. One of the most well-analysed and debated examples of this is the video for Madonna's 'Material Girl', which is a pastiche of the 1950s musical *Gentlemen Prefer Blondes*, which starred Marilyn Monroe and Jane Russell.

With regard to the second general point, Kaplan argues that music videos often turn in on themselves. She argues: '[W]e may see the video we are watching being played on a TV monitor within the frame; or the video sets us the production room in which a rock video is being made that turns out to be the one we are watching' (1987: 34). An example of this is the video for the Human League's 'Don't You Want Me?'. Videos, then, often expose the process of their making, something that most film and television in the realist mode seeks to prevent. Other videos comment on the nature of the music business, such as the video for David Bowie's 'Jazzin' for Blue Jean'.

Through such arguments, writers like Kaplan maintain that music videos disrupt the realist illusion that we are watching a familiar world, structured by a set of realist narrative conventions of cause and effect, where the production process is concealed. In these respects, music video texts are often seen as postmodern. Another way in which they are thought to be postmodern is through their location on MTV itself, which, by going against the established conventions of broadcast television, such as a variety in programming to cater for different tastes, breaks familiar patterns of television. It is suggested that the music videos on MTV run into each other and produce effects which blur the boundaries between different cultural experiences in classic postmodernist style.

Within this context, Kaplan identifies five main types of video, which are distinguished in figure 5.8. The first type is the romantic. In many respects this looks back to the 'soft rock' of the 1960s. Initially, it tended to be the province of female stars and was less prevalent than some of the other forms. However, since 1983–4 it has increased in importance and has been associated with more male groups and singers. As the title of the category suggests, the videos are often about romance, addressing themes of love and loss. They may feature a narrative, but this is relatively weak and the focus is on emotions. In some ways this parallels the discussion of 'emotional realism' in television soap opera by writers such as Ang (1986). The music in this sort of video tends to be tuneful and melodious rather than loud and overpowering.

		Modes (all use avant-garde strategies, especially self-reflexivity, play with the image, etc.)				
		Romantic	Socially conscious	Nihilist	Classical	Post-modernist
	Style	Narrative	Elements varied	Performance Anti-narrative	Narrative	Pastiche No linear images
Predominant MTV themes	Love/Sex	Loss and reunion (Pre-Oedipal)	Struggle for autonomy Love as problematic	Sadism/ masochism Homoeroticism Androgyny (phallic)	The male gaze (voyeuristic fetishistic)	Play with Oedipal positions
	Authority	Parent figures (positive)	Parent and public figures Cultural critique	Nihilism Anarchy Violence	Male as subject Female as object	Nether for nor against authority (ambiguity)

Figure 5.8 Five main types of video on MTV

Source: Kaplan 1987: 55

Kaplan argues that the socially conscious type of video retains elements of the critical rock stance that was supposedly at the centre of 1960s and '70s rock music. She suggests that this type of video is modernist in that it uses art to criticize established forms of authority and their associated forms of art. She argues that in the early 1980s three themes dominated this sort of video. First, there were anti-authority, anti-parental videos, which took a variety of different forms. Second, there were videos which concerned American foreign policy or 'specific social injustices, such as poverty' (1987: 75). These sorts of video were shown far less frequently than some of the other types. Examples include Bruce Springsteen's video for 'Born in the USA' as a critique of post-Vietnam America, and the Sun City video by Artists Against Apartheid. The third theme in the socially conscious category addresses 'women's oppression and the possibilities for female solidarity' (ibid.: 87). Thus, Kaplan argues that some videos address the problems faced by women in society and attempt to represent and construct forms of female solidarity.

This theme has been developed by Lewis (1993), who identifies forms of gender address to women in video. She argues that such videos use two distinct types of sign in particular ways. Thus: 'Access signs are those in which the privileged experience of boys and men is visually appropriated. The female video musicians textually enact an entrance into a male domain of activity and signification' (ibid.: 136). Discovery signs, by contrast, 'reference and celebrate distinctly female modes of cultural expression and experience. Discovery signs attempt to compensate in mediated form for female cultural marginalization by drawing pictures of activities in which females tend to engage apart from males' (ibid.: 137). Lewis finds evidence of these modes of address in videos by Cyndi Lauper, Madonna, Pat Benatar and Tina Turner. However, she maintains that these sorts of video are relatively few and far between.

Kaplan relates the nihilist type of video to the 'originally anarchic positions of recent punk, new wave and heavy metal bands' (1987: 60). On MTV this is mainly the province of heavy metal bands. These videos often feature live concerts or recreations of them. They rely on musical and visual shock. Sadistic and masochistic themes are often present, as are concerns with hate and destruction.

The classical video often relies on a more conventional, realist, narrative structure. However, they are also classical in 'retaining the voyeuristic/fetishistic gaze towards woman as objects of desire that feminist film theorists have spent so much time analyzing in relation to the classical Hollywood film' (ibid.: 61). Women are located in these videos to be looked at by men, both within the video itself and by the male spectator for the video. A second type of classical video takes on and uses classical Hollywood film genre, which moves it more towards postmodernism.

The postmodern form of video (Kaplan's fifth type) involves a large element of play with images. When we watch them we often feel that we have lost a clear position from which to view. They do not put forward a clear 'line' or point of view; positions are advanced at one point in the video and are then undercut at a later point. Whilst elements of this are present in all videos, they are exhibited to a far greater extent in this form.

Kaplan's account is one of the most detailed examinations of music video. However, there are some problems with it, the most important of which revolve around three issues: first, the nature of music video as promotion; second, the place of music in music video; and third, the nature of the audience.

The first point concerns the nature of the video as a promotional device. While Kaplan opens her book by examining the commercial base of MTV and locates it in an institutional context, as her analysis develops it increasingly centres on the nature of the music video text as if it were a separated art form. In some respects this is perfectly legitimate, as it is possible to study texts using, for example, structural and semiotic methods, but it is important to remember that videos are embedded in a commercial context. Videos are produced in a very different context from classical or even contemporary Hollywood films and cannot simply be studied using concepts and categories derived from film and television analysis, without consideration of the specific applicability of such ideas to different media.

Second, the musical dimension of music video often takes a secondary position in many discussions of music video. Kaplan's work develops out of her previous background as an analyst and theorist of film. Distinctions in the visuals are central, and musical differences tend to be discussed relative to these prior distinctions. In some writing, the music in music video has been almost ignored. Thus Frith criticizes the work of Browne and Fiske (1987) who, he says:

> compare Madonna's song-and-dance routine in the 'Material Girl' video with Marilyn Monroe's 'Diamonds are a Girl's Best Friend' in Gentlemen Prefer Blondes. 'The two songs', they assert, citing the lyrics in each case, 'are basically similar'. The differences are 'differences of tone'. Anyone who can

> hear a 1980s disco hit as 'basically similar' to a 1950s theatre song is
> obviously deaf. Alas, it has been the deaf who have dominated pop video
> theory. (1988a: 221)

Hence, our attention should be focused as much on music as on visuals and the
spoken word in videos, suggesting that it is the relationships between these
aspects that are important.

Third, Kaplan implies that the audience for the music video is of a particular
type. However, this is based on an analysis of the text rather than an investigation
of the audience itself (for more general discussion of this issue, see chapter 6).
Kaplan argues that, in the past, rock music addressed different cultural groupings,
but that MTV utilizes a mass address: 'I will be arguing that MTV reproduces a
kind of decenteredness, often called "postmodernist", that increasingly reflects
young people's condition in the advanced stage of highly developed, technological
capitalism evident in America' (1987: 5). And later, she states:

> MTV simply takes over the history of rock and roll, flattening out all the
> distinct types into one continuous present. The teenage audience is now no
> longer seen as divided into distinct groups addressed by different kinds of
> rock music, but is constituted by the station as one decentered mass that
> absorbs all the types indiscriminately – without noting or knowing their
> historical origins. (Ibid.: 29)

However, it is not clear how this sort of approach can be reconciled with Kaplan's
later comment that: 'Different groups of teenagers no doubt use MTV in different
ways according to class, race and gender' (ibid.: 159).

Goodwin's (1993) attempts to develop an analysis of video and MTV which
takes into account these sorts of problem together with the illuminating approach
taken by Kaplan. Goodwin stresses the promotional and industry context of music
video and MTV, emphasizing the way in which the different products of media or
cultural industries interlock in relations of multitextuality:

> [This process] was exemplified, for instance, in the selling of the 1989
> Warner Bros. film *Batman*, which involved tie-ins with the music industry
> (Prince's *Batman the Movie* LP, and the sound track from the film itself),
> publishing (including the Batman comic books, published by Warner
> Communications subsidiary D.C. Comics), television (through home video
> sales and rentals, and – eventually – cable and broadcast television rights),
> and merchandising (Batman bubble gum, breakfast cereal, and so on).
> (Goodwin 1993: 27; see also Wernick 1991)

Goodwin uses the ideas of the interlocking nature of the media industries and ideas
of promotion and rights which were examined in chapter 1 to contextualize the
development of music video. Video came about as a 'routine' way of promoting pop
in the early 1980s at the same time as the development of the post-punk New Pop,
which concentrated on issues of image and used new technologies in music-making.
Television itself was expanding and music videos were a cheap way of filling up
airtime. Furthermore, 'music television very precisely addressed two trends in the
1980s: the aging of the rock audience and the growth (at least in the United States)

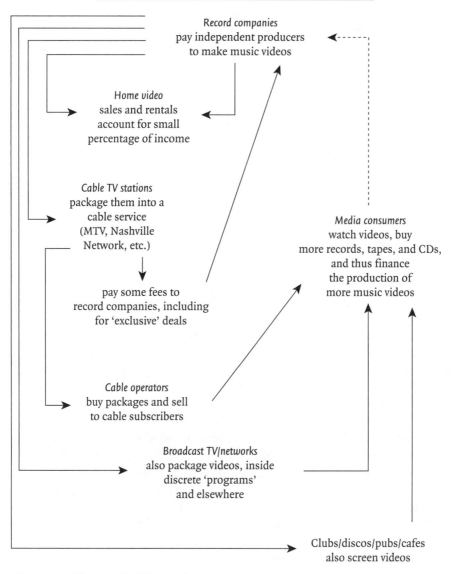

Figure 5.9 The music video cycle

Source: Goodwin 1993: 43

of a youth culture that was not centred on music' (ibid.: 39). What Goodwin terms the 'music video cycle' is reproduced in figure 5.9. One important point to note about this cycle is the relatively insignificant role of the sale of music videos as commodities themselves, as their main use is in the promotion of other goods.

Goodwin shows how MTV changed between 1981 and 1993, dividing its development into three stages: 1981–3, 1983–5 and 1986–93. The first phase was studied by some, such as Kaplan, who focused on the visual and postmodern nature of MTV. At this point, MTV did screen videos in a flow, and these videos themselves tended to break with narrative convention in the way identified by Kaplan (Goodwin 1993: 134). However, Goodwin maintains that developments during the second phase led away from this format. Most importantly, MTV was

7:00 a.m.	*Awake on the Wild Side*
9:00 a.m.	Music videos (Daisy Fuentes)
12:00 p.m.	Music videos (Andrew Daddo)
3:00 p.m.	*Spring Bread '91*
4.00 p.m.	*Yo! MTV Raps*
4:30 p.m.	*Totally Pauly*
6:00 p.m.	*Dial MTV*
7:00 p.m.	*MTV's Half Hour Comedy Hour*
7:30 p.m.	*Hot Seat*
8:00 p.m.	*Prime with Martha Quinn*
10:00 p.m.	*House of Style*
11:30 p.m.	*Bootleg MTV*
12:00 p.m.	*120 Minutes*

Figure 5.10 A typical MTV day in March 1991

Source: Goodwin 1993: 143

increasingly divided up into programme slots and the nature of the videos shown moved closer towards the performance type, with heavy metal music becoming ever more important. In August 1985 the ownership of MTV changed hands from the founders Warner-Amex to Viacom International, and from 1986 onwards the trends that had appeared during the second period were consolidated. There were more programme slots and different sorts of musical material appeared. A typical MTV day, in March 1991, can be seen in figure 5.10.

Goodwin contextualizes music video and MTV far more than other accounts have done. He also pays attention to the second problem that arises in accounts like Kaplan's, identified above: the relative neglect of music. Goodwin argues that it is important to recognize how musical and visual dimensions to video intertwine. Furthermore, he suggests that this is nothing new (see also Mundy 1999). Music has always made sense in relation to the visual associations that we in the audience give to it; hence certain forms of music suggest colours and images. Moreover, music has been connected with the visual through the media of film (early rock stars were promoted in film, especially Elvis Presley) and photographs. Goodwin's argument is that the 'visuals support the sound track' (1993: 70). Thus, for Goodwin, music videos are not films and there is a clear danger of 'misreading the generic conventions of the form by applying rules carried over from another (inappropriate) genre or medium' (ibid.: 77).

Goodwin maintains that music in pop videos tends to close off meaning in ways that other writers on the form have neglected. He argues that 'we can find three kinds of closure or coherence that introduce a high degree of stability via the sound track: repetition, structural closure, and harmonic closure' (ibid.: 79). Pop songs, he argues, are repetitive within themselves in alternating verse and chorus, for example. Furthermore, they resemble other pop songs (see the arguments of Adorno discussed in the Introduction), and are repeated across 'media sites', where the same song can be heard on the radio, TV, etc.

While such repetition might be held to suggest that pop songs do not resolve issues in the manner of the narrative realist text, Goodwin maintains that structural resolution does this in 'the way a song ends with the repetition of a chorus or refrain that "ties up" the song, perhaps as it fades out' (ibid.: 80). Such structural resolution is reinforced by 'harmonic resolution', which describes:

> the organization of the music itself around conventions of tonality and musical arrangement that both ground the music in a system of tonal relations that may be seen as the aural equivalent of the realist systems of 'looks' in cinema and often enable it to end with a musical 'resolution' which may be seen as the aural equivalent of a realist narrative reaching its conclusion. (Ibid.: 83)

However, despite his strong arguments for the centrality of music in the meaning structure of the music video, Goodwin recognizes 'that music video is relatively autonomous from the music, to a limited degree, in a number of ways' (ibid.: 85). He identifies and discusses four such ways:

1 The visualization of the song may go beyond its meaning.
2 The clips seek to provide pleasure (sometimes, but by no means exclusively, of a narrative nature) in order to keep the viewer watching and to encourage repeated viewings.
3 The clips might promote other commodities (such as films).
4 The clips might narrativize/display images of stardom that exceed any given individual song.

Like Kaplan, Goodwin points to the variety of different videos that are shown on MTV, and categorizes them as shown in figure 5.11. It is possible to see some overlap between these categories and the types identified by Kaplan. For example, Goodwin's social criticism category is not unlike Kaplan's socially conscious type of video, and Goodwin's category of self-reflexive parody is quite like Kaplan's postmodernist type. However, Goodwin points to the way that video is used as a promotional device for other texts. He suggests a number of different ways in which music and visuals interact in the music video. He also considers different visualization of videos by audiences. On the basis of a small-scale audience study, he concludes, first, 'that the vast majority of students in this sample were able to note down visual images associated with the musical extract'; second, that there was 'a high degree of consensus on the kinds of iconography associated with each extract'; and, third, 'while a variety of mass-mediated imagery is invoked in these accounts, a significant amount of this imagery does not derive from music video (at least not in any clear, literal sense), and a good deal of it is clearly triggered by personal memory' (1993: 55). Goodwin also suggests that the kind of intertextuality in videos such as Madonna's 'Material Girl' will not necessarily be recognized by the audience.

Goodwin's account is important, first, in developing a critique of the more unsubstantiated claims of those writers who have seen MTV and music video as postmodern in simple and clear senses; and, second, in providing a clear and historicized account of the promotional and industrial context of video. He alerts us to the interconnections of music and image in the way in which pop creates meaning. In more general respects, Goodwin's account explores a number of relationships that are not simply restricted to music videos. Thus, although the

Social criticism	Self-reflexive parody	Parody
SUN CITY (AAA)	DON'T LOSE MY NUMBER (Phil Collins)	BAD NEWS BEAT (Neil Young)
WAR (Springsteen)	JUST A GIGOLO (David Lee Roth)	LIFE IN ONE DAY (Howard Jones)
LIVES IN THE BALANCE (Jackson Browne)	THIS NOTE'S FOR YOU (Neil Young)	RIGHT ON TRACK (Breakfast Club)
TWO TRIBES (FGTH)	EAT IT ('Weird Al' Yankovic)	
RADIO CLASH (the Clash)	POP SINGER (John Mellencamp)	
JAMMIN' ME (Tom Petty)	ON THE GREENER SIDE (Michelle Shocked)	
SISTERS ARE DOIN' IT FOR THEMSELVES (Eurythmics)		
CULT OF PERSONALITY (Living Colour)		
ONE (Metallica)		

Pastiche	Promotion	Homage
RADIO GA GA (Queen)	A VIEW TO A KILL (Duran Duran)	DON'T GET ME WRONG (Pretenders)
THE ULTIMATE SIN (Ozzy Osbourne)	ABSOLUTE BEGINNERS (David Bowie)	CHAIN REACTION (Diana Ross)
MONEY FOR NOTHING (Dire Straits)	STAND BY ME (Ben E. King)	DR MABUSE (Propaganda)
MATERIAL GIRL (Madonna)	DANGER ZONE (Kenny Loggins)[a]	E = MC² (BAD)
THRILLER (Michael Jackson)	LAND OF CONFUSION (Genesis)[b]	TELL HER ABOUT IT (Billy Joel)
WHERE THE STREETS HAVE NO NAME (U2)	BATDANCE (Prince)	R.O.C.K. IN THE USA (John Cougar Mellencamp)
BIG TIME (Peter Gabriel)[c]	HEARTBEAT (Don Johnson)	
MEDIATE (INXS)		ROCKIT (Def Leppard)

[a] DANGER ZONE is especially interesting because it both promotes the film *Top Gun* and references (as pastiche?) the opening scene of Francis Ford Coppola's *Apocalypse Now*.

[b] LAND OF CONFUSION is not a move trailer, as the other examples here are, but it does indirectly promote the British TV series *Spitting Image*, through its use of puppets. It also contains pastiche, in its joking reference to the montage sequence in Stanley Kubrick's *2001: A Space Odyssey*, in which the chimp's bone becomes a spaceship (here it is transformed into a telephone receiver held by the Phil Collins puppet).

[c] BIG TIME uses a pastichelike reference to the television series *Pee-Wee's Playhouse* (through its distorted, playful *mise-en-scène*), but the complicating factor here is that this can be read as an auteurist discourse, since the clip's director, Stephen Johnson, has also directed that television program. Read in that light, the clip should more accurately be classified as (self-?) promotion or homage.

AAA	Artists Against Apartheid
FGTH	Frankie goes to Hollywood
BAD	Big Audio Dynamite

Figure 5.11 Visual incorporation in music video

Source: Goodwin 1993: 161

analysis of music video is marked by the influence of specific cultural theories (postmodernism) and particular ways of characterizing the social context (for example, as postmodernity), the institutional, textual and consumption relationships that emerge continue to have ongoing force. As Mundy suggests: 'It is quite possible to see what might be termed a "music video aesthetic" at work across a range of contemporary cultural forms, including television, cinema and advertising; even if much of the original enthusiasm for music video as distinct cultural form has itself lessened' (1999: 224). Thus, the link between the production of music and visual texts continues to work at a number of levels. For example, in terms of their pace and style, many contemporary movies have the characteristics of videos, and much contemporary TV is conducted to a beat. Moreover, these processes have impacted upon MTV, which has significantly changed its format: 'MTV has been forced to bend to advertising concerns and has changed its entire format, dropping music videos from a majority of its programming slots, and developing new show formats like *The Osbornes* to maintain or increase audience share' (Kusek and Leonhard 2005: 63). These relationships have involved the further development of modes of stardom, branding and celebrity, which have an ongoing impact on musical meaning.

Stars and meaning

Goodwin develops a number of aspects of the analysis of the importance of stars (see also chapter 8 on celebrity culture). In his examination of Madonna's video for 'Material Girl', he suggests, against a number of other writers, that the narrative is not actually very complex and that it moves 'through an initial lack, via action, to (romantic) resolution' (1993: 99). He reads this video in a way that draws attention to the 'star-text' – a concept introduced by Richard Dyer (see, for example, Dyer 1979 and 1987; Gledhill 1991). Goodwin interprets this video 'as if its central motif (the femme fatale who uses men to gain wealth and power) is coterminous with Madonna herself precisely because this is one of the many images Madonna has portrayed in the promotion of her music' (1993: 101).

Such an account connects to far wider themes concerning the ways in which stars function as trademarks that generate sales for the music business and the culture industries more widely (see chapter 1). However, it also raises issues concerning musical meaning. For example, it can be hypothesized that, in addition to focusing on the way in which the individual text can be shown to exist within a particular type (or genre), analysis needs to consider how the meaning of a text may relate to the overall meaning that has been created by a star. Thus, a new record by Madonna may be seen in the context of the various meanings of Madonna and not just, for example, as another dance or disco hit. Indeed, Madonna's album *Confessions From a Dancefloor* was reviewed in precisely these terms. In this respect, it is possible to draw attention to these two ways of grouping products: by genre (e.g. the rock song, the ska track and so on) or through the activities of the star whose music can change significantly over a period of time (Goodwin 1993: 103; Lury 1993: 92).

Goodwin adopts the view that has developed in the study of stars, especially by John Ellis, who has written extensively on film and television, that stars in the cinema express a form of incompleteness. He quotes Ellis as suggesting that: 'The star image is paradoxical and incomplete so it functions as an invitation to cinema, like the narrative image. It proposes cinema as the completion of its lack, the synthesis of its separate fragments' (Goodwin 1993: 117). This suggests that stars appeal because the audience wants to understand or fill in the knowledge that is missing. It may be that the fan of a star feels that only he or she can possess such knowledge. Goodwin argues that this kind of 'lack' is recognized by stars such as George Michael, who observed that 'It's not the something extra that makes the star – it's the something that's missing' (quoted in ibid.). Goodwin traces the development of Michael's career to demonstrate the changing nature of his incomplete star-text. Extracts from this informative discussion are contained in box 5.2.

It is possible to read Michael's disagreements in 1993 over his contract with Sony as another mutation in the development of his star-text. This case pits a

---

Box 5.2   Extracts from *Father Figure*: a case study

Pop star George Michael is someone who is capable of his own interesting and perceptive reflections upon stardom. During the 1989 MTV Video Music Awards program he observed: 'It's not the something extra that makes a star – it's the something that's missing.' Michael's star-text, which was initially constructed as one half of the duo Wham!, has exemplified the extent to which star imagery builds on vulnerability and ordinariness to establish points of identification for the audience.

. . . Michael became globally famous during his years with the British pop group Wham!, where, alongside childhood friend Andrew Ridgeley, he forged an identity that initially foregrounded fun and pleasure. The group's first release, 'Wham Rap!' was an ironic commentary on unemployment that became a hit in Britain only after its re-release (in February 1983) following the success of 'Young Guns (Go for It)' in October 1982. It is worth pointing out that in their early days Wham!'s image as young innocents confronting a sometimes harsh parental world was mirrored in the real-life drama of major conflicts with their record company, Innervision Records, with whom they had signed a contract that was exploitative to a degree that has become somewhat legendary (although it was by no means unique) in the music industry.

Wham! established themselves as fun-loving teen idols, with a string of hit singles over the next two years ('Bad Boys', 'Club Tropicana', 'Wake Me Up Before You Go-Go', 'I'm Your Man' etc.). . . . . In a 1984 interview, Michael presented fame as an especially pleasurable kind of work: 'Suddenly you're in a position where you have as much money as you need, you feel secure, and you have no one to answer to. It's absolutely brilliant! What better job could you have than that?' . . . . Wham!'s video clips tended to stress happy-go-lucky themes and to present George and Andrew as star-objects, rather than as musicians or people . . .

The issue of Michael as a solo artist was emphasized early in Wham!'s career, when it became apparent that band-mate Ridgeley actually contributed very little to the music. Before Wham! split up, in June 1986, Michael had already released two solo singles – 'Careless Whisper' (which earned him considerable critical respect) and 'A Different Corner'. Both songs are brooding, introspective ballads, and they highlighted both Michael's song-writing talent and the beginnings of an emerging star-text that became the vehicle for the subsequent marketing of George Michael-as-auteur.

The solo trajectory begun by George Michael during his career with Wham! is visually present in the clips themselves. The group's early videos were set either in everyday British locations (mum and dad's living room, the High Street, etc.) or in exotic places. 'Careless Whisper' is a transitional video-text, in that the colorful, romantic settings where we see the narrator's ex-lover contrast with the bleak, less colourful *mise-en-scène* where George Michael sings to us (backstage, on his own, surrounded by dangling ropes). Just as the singer is marked out from his more carefree past here, so is George Michael, pop star, isolated from the imagery of Wham! Indeed, the fact that 'Careless Whisper' was released as a solo project is revealing about the importance of the star-text in marketing music. Years later, Michael put it like this: 'We both had a definite attitude toward what a Wham! record should be about. Right up to 'Go-Go', they'd all been young and optimistic. It didn't seem right to abandon it for this one ballad' . . . . The promotional clip highlights that calculation and underscores the importance of star imagery as a site of fictional construction. (Similarly, the video for Wham!'s final single, 'The Edge of Heaven', includes extracts and multiple back-projection of excerpts from the previous videos – 'GOODBYE' runs across the bottom of the screen – and the line 'one day you'll wake up on your own' is thus unavoidably a comment on the fracturing star-text as well as a part of a romantic lyric.)

The bridge for the formal shift from Wham! to a solo career was a record George Michael made with Aretha Franklin ('I Knew You Were Waiting') in 1987. Simultaneously linking him with the authenticating power of classicism and soul (and indirectly with the word respect), this song foreshadowed his solo career, which was launched with the album *Faith* (Columbia Records) in the spring of 1987. 'I Knew You Were Waiting' also broke with the homoerotic appeal of the Wham! duo, being a romantic song whose heterosexual interpretation is buttressed through its performance by a male–female duo – a convention that has often been used in video clips.

The first single from *Faith* was the controversial song 'I Want Your Sex', which Michael was forced to defend as an ode to monogamy – the video clip had a closing shot added to it in which Michael writes 'EXPLORE MONOGAMY' on his lover's back, in lipstick, following criticism that the song and video promoted permissive (and, by implication, dangerous) sexual behavior. 'Father Figure' was released in February 1988. In May, *Faith* became the first release by a white artist to top *Billboard*'s Black Album chart. Michael also received an award as best soul/rhythm and blues act of the year at the American Music Awards (organized by the Recording Industry Association of America).

The context for the 'Father Figure' video was thus one in which George Michael's image was undergoing considerable change, as he was established as a heterosexual solo artist (a key component of success in the United States) and as his music was increasingly associated with notions of authenticity, as opposed to the discourses of irony (the first three singles) and triviality (most of the subsequent releases) that dominated the music of Wham! The shift is apparent, for instance, if we compare two widely circulated long-form videos: *Wham! in China: Foreign Skies* (CBS/Fox Video, 1986, directed by Lindsay Anderson) and *George Michael* (distributed in video stores by CBS Music Video and made by London Weekend Television for *The South Bank Show* in 1990). Where the tone of the first documentary is partly that of a travelogue, with a commentary about Wham! as 'ambassadors' for British pop and perhaps even Western youth culture (material that is also deployed in the clip *Freedom*, which includes extracts from the film), the film offers an uncritical celebration of stardom that inevitably reverberates with the numerous clips in which Wham! appeared as young jet-setting pleasure seekers ('Club Tropicana', 'Last Christmas'). *George Michael*, on the other hand, utilizes the conventions of the art documentary in its mostly reverential delineation of his artistic development, which is elaborated in an interview with Melvyn Bragg, and offers the star's own self-consciousness thoughts about stardom and his distance (as he sees it) from the world of Madonna and Prince . . .

Structurally, 'Father Figure' is both complex and extremely simple in terms of narrative organization. The complexities arise from its confusion of time frames and because of uncertainty about the point of enunciation in some segments. For instance, in shots 1.7 and 1.9 we see George Michael pinning up a photograph of the model *before* he has met her. Since this is also the last shot, it seems reasonable to speculate that these images occur (in 'story time') later than they appear (in 'discourse time'). It also remains unclear whether in fact he has had an affair with the model, or whether some parts of the narrative might be taking place in his imagination, a parallel with the pop fan's real-life obsession. Since Michael is seen by the model when they are not alone (for instance, in shot 6.10) it becomes clear that the events really occurred, but that the time frame has been mixed up in ordering the narrative.

Rather than attempting to make sense of this narrative definitively in immanent terms, however, it is more appropriate to consider its relation to the sound track, the song and the star-text. Visually, an important element running throughout 'Father Figure' is the prevalence of slow-motion imagery, and the use of dissolves to link most of the shots gives the clip a languid mood, underlining its subtle eroticism and illustrating the music itself, which is slow and understated. Structurally, the video text offers a complete, self-contained televisual 'segment', one that illustrates Ellis's . . . approach to broadcast television narrative as well as my argument about the image and its relation to a three-minute song. The music itself returns to a moment of completion in its final chorus and coda, and the clip climaxes through two devices: first, sections 10 and 11 have more frequent cutting (during the choruses) and then, via a fade to black (shot 11.12), settle (like the music) on a single, final image (of the model). Second, the last sections are more repetitive than the rest of the clip, reviewing the plot and returning the George Michael character to where he began . . .

. . . 'Father Figure' cashes in two symbols that have run from the earliest days of George Michael's career. The first is the black leather jacket – a familiar sign of rock rebellion that was originally worn with some irony (*Wham! Rap, Bad Boys*) and then became an integral part of Michael's iconography as a solo star. The BSA jacket, with its 'REVENGE' insignia, is the key visual *motif* of *Faith*, and in a later clip ('Freedom 90') it is this jacket that bursts into flames. Second, there is George Michael's beard – often worn as low-level stubble, a trendy version of 'five o'clock shadow' first popularized by Don Johnson on *Miami Vice*. Again, this symbol made an earlier appearance in the days of Wham! ('A Different Corner'), but in the context of a bright, lively *mise-en-scène* that is quite different from the dark, almost monochrome tones of 'Father Figure'. It is the new, brooding image of an unshaven Michael (often in dark glasses) that adorns the sleeve of *Faith* and is used repeatedly for advertising imagery and press photographs.

Taken together, the leather jacket and the stubble (along with the dark glasses and cigarettes) are not just character appropriate for a Hollywood version of a taxi driver; more important, they established 'classic rock' imagery for George Michael at a time when he was seeking mass acceptance in the United States. In fact, it would be more truthful to say that the characterization offered in 'Father Figure' is secondary to these aspects of the star-text – it was probably chosen for that reason, not the other way around.

Source: Goodwin 1993: 117–30

representation of Michael as an artist against the representation of the highly exploitative Japanese record company, which has only commercial aims. We might read the sober, but trendy, appearance and dress of Michael in court in relation to this narrative of stardom, which would potentially affect the meanings derived from his music (see figure 5.12). Subsequent developments in his career have also added new layers of complexity to this star-text.

Goodwin's argument, therefore, is that video texts need to be read in the context of the overall development of the star-text, as well as in their own narrative or musical terms. Likewise, it can be suggested that the video or musical texts themselves contribute to the changing development of that star-text, and can signal key moments of change in it very clearly. Hence, one way to map Madonna's changing star-text is through the different images and meanings contained in her videos (in addition to other forms through which the star-text is developed – films, interviews, photographs in the press and celebrity magazines, etc.).

Figure 5.12 George Michael arriving at the High Court, 23 November 1993 Reproduced by permission of The Press Association; photographer: Stefan Rousseau

Other writers have suggested that contemporary stardom is actually rather different from that displayed in the classic Hollywood cinema. Lury, for example, argues:

> At the same time a new kind of star is emerging; these stars are sustained through the strategic and self-conscious manipulation of performative intentionality across media; their appeal derives from their capacity to make the actual virtual and the virtual actual, and their radiance flickers with an oscillation between two and three dimensions. Jack Nicholson, Madonna and Arnold Schwarzenegger are the most obvious example of this phenomenon. Within this mode of stardom, the 'value added' from an artist comes not from the management of the distance between their image and their creative abilities, but from its collapse.
> (1993: 71)

This contributes to the process of 'branding' discussed in the Introduction, where the music industry (in common with other media industries) forms 'links of image and perception between a range of products' (ibid.: 87). Stars as brands (Michael Jackson, Madonna, Prince, Eric Clapton, Bruce Springsteen, Guns 'n' Roses, U2) have become, on the basis of this sort of argument, a very important focus of musical meaning. Good examples of the analysis of different constructions of stardom and the artist can be found in the work of Brackett (1995), especially in his discussions of the meanings of Bing Crosby and Billie Holiday, and how these contribute to the interpretation of the meaning of their texts on a number of levels.

This chapter has identified a number of different aspects of musical meaning. It seems clear that the overemphasis of one dimension can lead to a slanting of the analysis which neglects the potential effects of the others. However, the discussion of meaning leads into the ways in which meaning is understood or created by in performance. This is the topic of the next chapter.

Summary

This chapter has considered a number of different areas of study and issues raised through the investigation of musical meaning. These include:

- the critique of traditional musicology and contemporary arguments for the transformation of musicology to make it useful in the study of a variety of different forms of music;
- ways of studying musical meaning which derive in the main from the utilization of the approaches of structuralism and semiotics; important concepts discussed here include code, structures and denotation and connotation;
- the interconnections between lyrics, words and music;
- the interconnections between musical and visual meanings , using music video as a well-known example, where Kaplan's (1987) work was used to represent a more text-centred approach and was contrasted with the more contextualized perspective of Goodwin (1993);
- the potential importance of star-texts in the generation of musical meaning.

6

Performance, Dance, Distinction and the Body

This chapter explores a number of different aspects of the performance of popular music. It is significant that, despite the importance of performance to music (as opposed to the writing and reading of novels for instance), it is only relatively recently that performance has come under sustained academic scrutiny. In part this has stemmed from a more general and contemporary interest in how meaning is created in the modes of interaction that make up the performance situation. More specifically, the idea of performance has assumed a significant theoretical importance in academic work on culture and media. In no small part this has stemmed from the influence of the work of the American writer Judith Butler on performance, gender and sex. To reflect this importance, this chapter begins with an overview of the most salient parts of her work. One of the areas in which Butler has been influential is on theories and studies of the body. It can be seen that this is of specific interest given the role that dance has in relation to music. In addition to being a text that exists in various forms with the sorts of potential for study that have been overviewed in the previous chapter and chapters 3 and 4, music is danced to or – perhaps better, for reasons that are explored in this chapter – danced with. Again, it is rather surprising to note the relative neglect of this topic until comparatively recently in the study of popular music. To rectify this, to some extent, this chapter will consider some recent work that has studied and outlined theories that connect performance and dance with theories of the body. A specific area of consideration here will be the phenomenon of rave or, as it is now best known, dance culture, that has developed since the late 1980s. The examination of dance culture through the lens of performance, dance and the body also introduces two other themes that run through this chapter: distinction and identity.

One of the most influential academic studies of dance culture is Sarah Thornton's *Club Culture* (1995). This will form the base for the examination of dance culture in this chapter, in combination with other works that have usefully considered various aspects of the subject. In addition, this discussion introduces the important work on culture of the French sociologist Pierre Bourdieu. Bourdieu emphasizes the role of culture in the production and reproduction of cultural boundaries and hierarchies; his work in this area has assumed as much importance as that of Butler in recent years. It is significant that it has taken a lengthy period for these developments to be reflected in the study of popular music, and this aspect will be noted in this chapter. Ideas of distinction or, to use a Weberian formulation (see the Introduction), status are also played out in modes of consumption of popular music that involve its collection, and aspects of this issue are also discussed here (other issues of the consumption of popular music are further examined in chapters 7, 8 and 9). The issue of how collecting may contribute to the formulation and reformulation of identities is also a point of departure here.

Performance and identity issues have also come to the fore in the development and popularity of karaoke. This is discussed in this chapter, as, both in its Japanese origins and in its subsequent diffusion in a number of societies, it raises other questions of identity and performance. This examination of this area facilitates consideration of a number of other themes concerning the relationship between live and mediated performance and the nature of 'ethnic' identities.

A number of the themes of this chapter are brought together at its close in an examination of Frith's *Performing Rites* (1996), which focuses our attention on ideas of performance and taste in useful and thought-provoking ways.

Judith Butler: performance, performativity, gender and the body

Judith Butler is best known for her highly influential book *Gender Trouble* (1990; 10th anniversary edition, 1999), which radicalized discussions of sex and gender. Arguing against biological determinism in these areas, she considers the way in which notions of sex and gender are performed and how they are socially malleable. These arguments have been very important in promoting the ideas of performance and performativity, which have grown in significance in media and cultural studies in recent years. Butler (1993) also considers the social and discursive construction of human bodies. In more recent work (1997), she has examined the politics of speech and public utterances, which have been seen to be the cause of various forms of social harm. The discussion in this chapter will focus in particular on Butler's ideas of performance, performativity, gender, sex and the body, which are of most relevance to the nature of popular music performance.

Key aspects of Butler's approach are superficially relatively clear. As Bell puts it: 'gender, to cut a long story short, is an effect performatively produced' and 'identity is the effect of performance and not vice versa' (1999b: 3). In this view, identities such as gender are produced by discursive practice (Butler 1999: 184) and the performance of them in social processes, rather than being something essential that is given expression in action and practice: 'If gender attributes, however, are not expressive but performative, then these attributes effectively constitute the identity they are said to express or reveal' (ibid.: 180).

As Salih argues, this sort of approach 'has confused many people' (2002: 63). Salih demonstrates this by quoting the following from *Gender Trouble*: 'There is no gender identity behind the expressions of gender; that identity is performatively constituted by the very expressions that are said to be its results' (Butler 1990: 25), and she continues:. 'How can there be a performance without a performer, an act without an actor? Actually Butler is not claiming that gender is a performance, and she distinguishes between performance and performativity (although at times in *Gender Trouble* the two terms seem to slide into one another)' (2002: 63). This was recognized by Butler herself, and she sought to address the issue in subsequent work, as she says in the Preface to the tenth anniversary edition of *Gender Trouble*:

> Much of my work in recent years has been devoted to clarifying and revising the theory of performativity that is outlined in *Gender Trouble*. It is difficult to say precisely what performativity is not only because my own views on what 'performativity' might mean have changed over time, most often in response to excellent criticisms, but because so many others have taken it up and given their own formulations. . . . In the first instance, then, the performativity of gender revolves around this metalepsis, the way in which the anticipation of a gendered essence produces that which it posits as outside itself. Secondly, performativity is not a singular act, but a repetition and a ritual, which achieves its effects through its naturalization in the context of a body, understood, in part, as a culturally sustained temporal duration. (1999: xiv–xv)

In crude terms, performance can be said to involve intention and action on the part of a constituted and volitional subject, whereas performativity is the process that constitutes the subject (and the body of the subject: see Butler 1993). Butler argues that:

> gender identity is a sequence of acts (an idea that has existential underpinnings), but she also argues that there is no pre-existing performer who does those acts, no doer behind the deed. Here she draws a distinction between *performance* (which presupposes the existence of a subject) and *performativity* (which does not). This does not mean that there is no subject, but that the subject is not exactly where we would expect to find it – i.e. 'behind' or 'before' its deeds – so that reading *Gender Trouble* will call for new and radical ways of looking at (or perhaps looking *for*) gender identity. (Salih 2002: 45)

So even if there remain clear difficulties concerning how to distinguish between performance and performativity, Butler has drawn attention to how identities like those of gender are produced in the context of social interaction. This has been very influential in the study of gender, which then sees such identities as having some degree of fluidity and which can be subverted by forms of 'drag', for example, or through processes of queering (Brett et al. 1994). An even more controversial aspect of Butler's work has been her argument that the body (or sex) is also constituted through such performative processes. On the face of it, this seems a difficult argument to sustain. After all, is it not clear what sex we are from the body parts that we have? However, as Salih argues:

> A girl is not born a girl, but she is 'girled', to use Butler's coinage, at or before birth on the basis of whether she possesses a penis or a vagina. This is an arbitrary distinction, and Butler will argue that sexed body parts are

invested with significance, so it would follow that infants could just as well be differentiated from each other on the basis of other parts – the size of their ear lobes, the colour of their eyes, the flexibility of their tongues. Far from being neutral, the perception and description of the body ('It's a girl!' etc.) is an interpellative performative statement, and the language that seems merely to describe the body actually constitutes it. Again, Butler is not refuting the 'existence' of matter, but she insists that matter can have no status outside a discourse that is always constitutive, always interpellative, and always performative. (2002: 80)

According to this argument, the body exists, but it always exists within discourses that give it materiality. As with many other of Butler's formulations, this has caused significant debate. However, it should be recognized that, at the very least, it opens up space for the reconsideration of a range of interacting processes. Thus, the extent to which bodies are culturally and socially defined can be discussed, as can the extent and the ways in which gender is something performed (perhaps differently in different contexts) and debated. If this is the case, sex and gender are not essential, are not pre-given, which entails the adoption of a position rather like that reached in the examination of black music in chapter 4. A potential step on from an anti-essentialist position (such as Butler's) is to recognize the social, political and cultural construction and reconstruction of bodies and identities, without moving to complete relativism. This sort of approach is captured in a comment on Butler made by Gilroy (whose work we considered in chapter 4), when he suggests that 'what he would like to see is a way of complementing her enquiries into the histories of subjectivity with a kind of enquiry into the history of solidarity, and intersubjectivity' (Bell 1999a: 36). The idea is to study the social constitution of the body, subjectivity, identities and communities. It is useful that this sort of agenda has been taken forward in studies of dance and the body, to which it is now possible to turn.

The body and dance

In recent years there has been renewed consideration of the place of the body in social and cultural theory, one of the sources of which comes from Butler's work, as discussed in this chapter so far. However, there have also been a number of other influences on this process. While classical sociologists and anthropologists had interests in a number of aspects of the body, there has been a significant move to consider various dimensions of the social construction of the body in recent years. Such approaches to the human body 'identify a range of social and cultural influences that shape its appearance and activity'; although there exists a variety of social constructionist approaches, what they 'have in common is an opposition to simplified essentialist explanations, i.e. explanations of bodily appearance and activity that assign sole or major significance to biological factors' (Baldwin et al. 2004: 268). Many different aspects of body construction and reconstitution have been examined, including the ways in which the body is disciplined by power, body modification through diet and exercise, the gendering of bodies and the way in which the body interacts with technology to produce the cyborg (see ibid.:

267–315). Furthermore, the social constructionist 'body project' can bring the cultural theory of writers like Butler into dialogue with that of social constructionist sociologists, such as Garfinkel and Goffman (Thomas 2003). Despite the success of these developments in opening up new theory, it has been argued that, because of the way in which the body is seen as socially constructed, the material nature of the body disappears. As Thomas suggests:

> Recent developments in social and cultural theory, along with changes in the register of late capitalism, have been influential in bringing 'the body' out of the shadows and into the light of academe. But there has been mounting criticism, from a number of quarters, of the dominance of representational or discursive models at the expense of the lived body. (2003: 62)

If Thomas's argument is accepted, then there is a research agenda that combines the idea that the body (and its movement) is not simply a natural phenomenon, but is subject to modes of social and cultural constitution, with the idea that the body and its movement have a degree of materiality. Thus, educating the dancer involves training the body not only according to certain ideas of how it should move (it is thus constituted through discourse), but also in recognition of the fact that the body itself as a physical thing has to be altered. In pursuing this idea, Thomas argues that this opens the way for detailed ethnographic research on modes of dance.

To explore such possibilities, Thomas examines two modes of dance that can be seen as being at opposite ends of the spectrum of the disciplines of bodily movement: ballet and contact improvisation. Despite the fact that they share features in common, such as the fact that they 'are both products of the western cultural and artistic tradition' (Thomas 2003: 108), there are significant illustrative differences between these two modes of dance. However, both illuminate the ideas of discursive construction and physicality. Thus, 'the ballet body provides a striking example of this process of objectification through its celebration of the ideals of visualism and the pursuit of the mastery of the body over nature. It is an athletic, highly tuned instrument through which the dancer's inner expression is given an outward form' (ibid.: 108–9). Contact improvisation, the beginnings of which can be traced from 'the counter-cultures of the 1960s and in the emergent critiques of the star images, hierarchies and codified techniques of western theatre dance (ballet and modern dance)' (ibid.: 109), is different:

> The contact body directs attention inwards to the body of the self through touch and weight. The body is ideally the subject and the object of attention in contact, in contrast to ballet where the bodily focus is objectified and fashioned through its visual appearance and projections in space and time. While ballet conspires with the visualism of western culture, contact improvisation colludes with the 'truth of the body' ideology encapsulated in a range of alternative body re-education techniques, such as the Alexander technique, which gained some ground in the 1970s. (Ibid.)

In addition to her consideration of these modes of dance, Thomas shows, through a number of other examples, the value of a more ethnographically formulated approach to the study of dance. As she says: 'In dancing, as the case studies in this book hopefully show, individual embodied subjects/subjectivities enact and "comment" on a variety of taken-for-granted social and cultural bodily relativities' (ibid.: 215). However, despite the innovative nature of her work, Thomas tends to downplay the role of music relative to dance. One area where this can be explored in more detail is via the now quite heavily researched field of dance culture.

Dancing and raving

In the aftermath of the development of rave culture in late 1980s Britain, there developed both a journalistic (e.g. Reynolds 1998) and an academic literature (see below). One of the most influential studies of rave came in the work of Thornton (1995), whose work is also discussed in the context of post-subcultural studies in chapter 9 (on different aspects of rave, see also chapters 7 and 8). Thornton uses the work of the French sociologist Pierre Bourdieu as one of the sources for her study. In considering her work it is therefore possible to explore some important themes in dance culture, as well as to consider the work of this important sociologist, whose work will inform the consideration of ideas of distinction in this chapter.

Thornton argues that one of the salient features of dance culture (or, as she terms them, club cultures) is the way in which, within the culture, what she terms 'subcultural capital' is deployed. Some of the participants in this culture seek to advance their claims to being at the leading edge by being as 'hip' as possible to the most recent developments. In Thornton's argument, these are 'means by which young people negotiate and accumulate status within their own social worlds' (1995: 163). By defining themselves against what they perceive to be the 'mainstream', clubbers struggle over the capital that provides distinction in this area.

The framework for this argument comes from the sociologist Pierre Bourdieu (1930–2002). Bourdieu has been particularly influential in the English-speaking world through his work on culture and distinction (Bourdieu 1984). However, this work needs to be contextualized by his overall social theory. Bourdieu has been much concerned with a perennial issue in sociology, namely the relative weight to be accorded to the way in which human social life is determined by structural factors, such as the place of a human being in the class structure as defined by their occupation; or the extent to which individuals through social interaction have the power to create their own situations. Bourdieu addresses this debate through his idea of practice, which is captured in the notion of 'agents' engagement with the objective structures of the modern world, crystallized into those patterns of relations, with their specific determining force, that we call "fields" (economic power, politics, cultural production, etc.' (Fowler 2000: 1). Human beings internalize structures living within and producing what Bourdieu terms the 'habitus'. The habitus involves the habits that we develop, our disposition to look and classify the world in a particular way. It defines the world that we inhabit, but is not just about the knowledge of the world that we possess; it can be as much about our bodily habits, or the way in which we move our body. In Bourdieu's argument, class is very important to the habitus in which we live, but it can also be seen as conditioned by gender, ethnicity, region, and so on. In some respects there are clear parallels with Butler's idea of performativity as discussed earlier in this chapter (see Butler 1997: 127–63; Salih 2002: 113). The habitus has been a very influential idea in thinking through the ways in which our position in the world is structured and lived.

In addition, Bourdieu has been very important in expanding and developing the idea of capital and applying this idea in new ways. This has been a significant general movement in the social sciences, which has built upon the basic insights of Karl Marx. In Bourdieu's formulation, it is not only economic capital that derives from money, income, economic investments, etc., but also cultural, social and symbolic capital. In general, in this idea 'there is a class, capitalists, that controls the means of production – the process of pedagogic action or the education institutions (in homes, in schools, and so on). In addition, there is more attention to the more micro-social processes of capital deployment' (Lin 2001: 16). Cultural capital consists of such phenomena as knowledge, ways of life, ways of understanding the world and prestige. There are three main forms of cultural capital: embodied in 'long-lasting dispositions of the mind and body', objectified 'in the form of cultural goods' and institutionalized 'resulting in such things as educational qualifications' (Skeggs 2001: 296). Social capital is based in social networks, connections or relationships. Symbolic capital is 'the form the different types of capital take once they are perceived and legitimated as legitimate. Legitimation is the key mechanism in the conversion to power' (ibid.). Capitals can be converted from one form to another, might act in opposition to one another, or can be enclaved. Thus, for example, those with high economic capital (the wealthy) might purchase a high-status education for their children, which could then provide them with forms of cultural capital in educational qualifications and understanding of 'high' culture such as literature and art. Attending high-status (and costly) schools may also provide a network of contacts (such as the often cited 'old-boy network') that might continue at university and in future life. It can also be seen how this sort of 'conversion' might work in the production of popular music, which will require some level of economic investment, forms of knowledge and understanding of music itself, as well as a network of contacts.

The final idea developed by Bourdieu which has been of significance is that of the 'field'. A field is an area of social life that has its own set of rules and expectations. Some forms of capital may be very important in some fields, but are less important in others. However, it is possible to move between fields using the conversion of capitals. Thus, economic capital may be of prime importance in the economic field, but can be used to advantageous effect in the political field. For Bourdieu, then, these concepts are linked, as he shows in the equation reproduced in figure 6.1.

To return to dance culture, it can be seen that to be part of the dance 'world' is to be involved in a habitus, which may involve forms of knowledge (for example,

$$[(\text{habitus}) (\text{capital})] + \text{field} = \text{practice}$$

Figure 6.1 Bourdieu's formula

Source: Bourdieu 1984: 101

about clubs, DJs and records), ways of thinking (such as the idea that spending a significant period of time in a club is a good way to use time), ways of dressing (what are the appropriate clothes to wear) and ways of moving (as in the 'correct' modes of dancing). This habitus may be very significant in the dance music field, but less significant in others (the field of education, for example). Within the field of dance music, which involves a habitus that is likely to be shared by the participants, some may seek to be seen as leaders in the field. They might deploy their 'hipness' as subcultural capital in the way that Thornton describes. Moreover, their social contacts may be significant as well, as the extract in box 6.1 shows.

Box 6.1   A night of research

Saturday, 22 September 1990. Wonderworld, London W8, 11 p.m.

It's exactly eleven and I'm waiting for Kate. We've never met before, but she knows I'm researching clubs and has promised to show me 'how to have fun'. The 'hardcore techno-house' of the dance floor is just audible from here. Two women police officers patrol on foot. Mostly same-sex groups wear casual clothes and casual expressions; they walk slowly and deliberately until they've got past the door staff, then plunge down the stairs into the club. I feign uninterest because clubbing is the kind of activity that shuns official, parental, constabulary or even 'square' observation. Clubbers often voice antipathy towards the presence of people who don't belong and come to gawk.

   A few minutes later, Kate jumps out of a black cab. She's energetic and her immaculately made-up eyes gleam. Her brother runs this club, so she asks the doorwoman to 'sort us out'. The woman takes a pack of cards and hands me a three of diamonds, smiling: 'This will get you all the way.' We descend a flight of steps where a bouncer inspects my card, then ushers us in. The doorwoman insisted that this club, run by ex-rave organizers in rave style, has no door policy – absolutely anyone could come in. Nevertheless, the crowd looks pretty homogenous. They are mostly dressed in a late version of the acid house uniform of T-shirts, baggy jeans and kickers boots; they're white and working-class. There is also a handful of Afro-Caribbean men hanging-out near the door who look as if they might be friends of the entirely black crew of bouncers.

   We walk around the club. The venue is early-eighties plush, but it's transformed for tonight's club by large unstretched glow-in-the-dark canvases of surreal landscapes with rising suns and psychedelic snakes. A white boy, wired and talking a mile a minute, stops me in my tracks: 'Want some "E"?' He's referring to 'Ecstasy' and he's eating his words. The volume of the music is such that I can only catch bits of his sales pitch: 'I got burgers and double burgers . . . fifteen quid.' He is a poor advertisement for the effects of his wares. From his aggressive and jumpy delivery, I assume that he is really on some speed concoction or perhaps this is his first night on the job.

We descend some more stairs to the VIP room where another bouncer gestures for my card, then waves us in. No door policy upstairs, but an exacting one down here. This room is so restricted that, at this hour, there is no one here except the barmaid. But it's still early. We get a coke and a mineral water and sit down. It feels private. Kate is very much at home. 'Tell me about your research then.' She's genuinely interested in my work, but also probing into whether I can be trusted. Her brother is one of the original rave organizers, who began by putting on parties in barns and aircraft hangars, then went legit, organizing weekly clubs for ravers in venues around London. As Kate tells it, the police monitored all their parties from the beginning, but as soon as the 'gutter press' were hard up for a front-page story the scene got out of hand: 'Kids, who shouldn't have even known about drugs, read about the raves in the *Sun* and thought, "Cor – Acid. That sounds good. Let's get some", and loads of horrible people starting trying to sell "swag" drugs.'

During our conversation, the VIP room has filled up. Kate suggests I meet her brother who is sitting at the bar with a long blonde and a bottle of Moët et Chandon on ice. He is in his early twenties and wears a thick navy-and-white jumper, something which immediately distinguishes him from those here to dance. Kate tells him that I've never taken Ecstasy ('Can you believe it?') and tells him that we are going to do some tonight. He's not pleased. 'How do you know she won't sell this to the *Daily Mirror*?' he asks. Kate assures me that she's checked me out, that I'm all right. Later, they explain that they want someone to tell the 'true story' of acid house and that they'll help me do it as long as I don't use their names.

Kate pours me a champagne and takes me aside. A friend has given her an MDMA (the pharmaceutical name for Ecstasy) saved from the days of Shoom (the mythic club 'where it all began' in early 1988). We go to the toilets, cram into a cubicle where Kate opens the capsule and divides the contents. I put my share in my glass and drink. I'm not a personal fan of drugs – I worry about my brain cells. But they're a fact of this youth culture, so I submit myself to the experiment in the name of thorough research (thereby confirming every stereotype of the subcultural sociologist). Notably, there's 'Pure MDMA' for the VIPs and 'double burgers' for the punters. The distinctions of Ecstasy use are not unlike the class connotations of McDonald's and 'no additives' health food.

Source: Thornton 1995: 87–9

Thornton's study was one of the first extended academic discussions of the dance culture, and its deployment of the approach derived from Bourdieu has been influential. However, it has been subject to some criticism, as has some of the earlier work on rave culture that is discussed in Part III of this book. As Thomas explains, some of these studies actually neglect the nature of the dancing and therefore body movement that is such a significant part of the culture. She suggests that, 'despite noting the importance of Thornton's study to this emergent field of research, Malbon (1999) argues that she fails to attend to the experience of clubbing itself' (2003: 207). Furthermore, Thomas argues that more recent literature (for example, Malbon 1999; Bennett 2000; Pini 2001) on club/dance culture has a number of common themes, such as an ethnographic focus on the social patterns of club culture at a local level, an emphasis on the positive (and perhaps liberatory) aspects of dance culture and the way in which these processes can lead to the production of new identities for the participants (2003: 208–11). Such themes are also significantly present in the work of Jackson (2004).

Jackson also offers an ethnographic account of the clubbing experience, examining in some detail the following aspects: dancing, music, sex, dress, drugs and the 'vibe'. In this discussion, he is very upbeat and positive about the clubbing experience – it is painted in a very positive light. Part of the explanation for this enthusiasm is his argument that the experience of clubbing results in identities and ways of life that are not simply acted out in clubs, but which inform other aspects of clubbers' lives. This is significant, as Jackson differentiates his approach from some of the other academic work on dance culture on this basis. As he says:

> Now I want to examine the ways in which those club experiences move beyond the club space itself and filter out into that everyday world. This has been attempted before, but not altogether successfully because academics have tried to turn clubbing into other forms of knowledge. Redhead (1993) tried to politicise clubbing as a form of resistance, which just doesn't hold up in the long term. Thornton (1995) simply turned it into a field of consumption, which virtually ignores the experience itself. Malbon (1999) focused on the experience but couldn't move beyond the club space.
> (2004: 115)

Jackson goes on to say: 'My informants were adamant that clubbing had exerted a powerful influence on their lives and that this influence didn't just evaporate once the party was over' (ibid.). He suggests that the club culture experience can move individuals beyond their existing habitus and be a part of the constitution of a new mode of living and identity, and he argues that clubbers 'use the social, sensual and emotional knowledge uncovered via clubbing to generate a new bodily posture that re-orientates their relationship to and perspective upon the world that lies beyond clubs' (ibid.: 133). This has led, he suggests, to a more experimental approach to social life on the part of those who participate in the experience of clubbing.

It is significant that the two approaches to club or dance culture that have been considered at greatest length in this chapter both deploy (to different degrees, but significantly) the conceptual terms that have been developed by Bourdieu. While it can be seen that they take these terms in rather different directions, Thornton emphasizing the way in which club culture is internally differentiated around subcultural capital and Jackson arguing that club culture facilitates a move beyond the established habitus, it is important to note the purchase of this social and cultural theory on dance culture and vice versa.

Other work has related dance culture to a range of cultural theories even more directly. A good example of this sort of approach can be found in the work of Gilbert and Pearson (1999). In their view, dance culture has gone against some significant and dominant ideas that value particular types of music in Western culture. In broad terms, there has been a privileging of music that makes an appeal to the intellect (rather than being danced to – thus involving the body) and, with particular respect to popular music, is based around the human voice (rather than being around beat). Drawing on feminist and cultural theory, they argue how these dominant traditions are gendered and invoke particular pleasures (of meaning) rather than others (of bodily sensation). Thus, their work uses the sorts of distinction discussed by Roland Barthes (see chapter 5).

Gilbert and Pearson argue that while 'dance music and culture transgress prohibitions laid down by powerful western discourses' (1999: 179), its 'threat' in these terms has been countered in Britain by legislation such as the Criminal Justice and Public Order Act of 1994, which 'regulated' raves. However, despite this they suggest that dance culture has opened the way for new forms of sociality and community.

This section has explored dance and rave culture, as this has been an important episode in the history of popular music. However, the discussion of this form of musical culture has also furthered the consideration of cultural theories that are of relevance to the understanding of popular music, especially the work of the French sociologist Pierre Bourdieu. His work and that of other theorists can also be considered in the context of other music-related activity, such as record-collecting.

Collecting, masculinity and distinction

The phenomenon of collecting, like other modes of enthusiasm or fandom (see chapters 8 and 9), has often been viewed from two different perspectives. On the one hand, collecting is criticized as being a form of infantile (or 'nerdy') activity: collecting is for children (especially male children) and they should grow out of it, especially if they collect popular cultural artefacts such as comics or football programmes. On the other, collecting is seen as a worthwhile cultural pursuit if it is connected to the collection of valued forms, such as paintings or sculptures, as this can be seen as an activity rather akin to museum curation. As with work on fandom, recent scholarship has moved beyond such simplistic and politically charged representations of collecting (see, for example, the work of Belk 1995 and Pearce 1995). There exist the beginnings of a literature on masculinity and collecting that are relevant to the themes of this chapter on distinction and performance. A good example of this can be found in the work of Straw.

Straw suggests that record-collecting has both public and private dimensions: 'Record collections are seen as both public displays of power/knowledge and private refuges from the sexual or social world' (1997: 4). In this sense, collecting is like many other forms of cultural consumption (see Longhurst and Savage 1996). Record-collecting is usually seen as a male or masculine activity and Straw identifies different modes of masculinity that come into play. He distinguishes between three types: the dandy, the nerd and the brute. The dandy, who 'transforms cultivated knowledges into the basis of an ongoing public performance', is sometimes criticised on the basis that 'his persona is frivolous or depthless, reducible to the surface on which this mastery is displayed' (1997: 8). The nerd is opposite in the sense that he 'is noted for a mastery of knowledges whose common trait is that they are of little use in navigating the terrains of social intercourse'. The nerd's knowledge is 'a cause of performative social failure, blatantly indexed in the nerd's chaotic and unmonitored self-presentation' (ibid.). The brute is the 'male persona characterised by a pure and uncultivated instinctuality' (ibid.). Straw argues that while the brute might be thought to be a mode of masculinity associated with popular music, it actually carries the idea of being hip, which has most often been contrasted with the nerd. In this analysis of the hip (see also the discussion of Thornton above), Straw argues: 'Hipness almost always requires a knowledge which is more or less cultivated, but must repress any evidence that this knowledge is easily acquired in the mastery of lists or bookish sources' (ibid.: 9). This stance must seem to be easy and not contrived. Thus, while record-collecting can in a number of ways be seen as 'nerdish' – like other forms of male collecting – it also has significant hip aspects and can therefore be part of the performance of a mode of distinction. The interplay of these ideas then informs much representation of male collecting and acquisition. As well as continuing the exploration of distinction and performance, this example has also addressed issues of identity. A further example will allow the exploration of other aspects of performance and identity.

Karaoke: performance and identity

Karaoke is now a well-known practice, having originated in Japan in the early 1970s, where it is immensely popular. It consists of singing along to a backing track in public. The term is also used to refer to the technology that makes up karaoke equipment. It has been suggested that this is made up of five parts: a sound source, a visual source, a microphone, sound and visual distribution and accessories (Mitsui and Hosokawa 1998a: 8). As the technology has developed, these different components have increased in sophistication (see Mitsui 1998).

The success and popularity of karaoke in Japan is shown by the fact that in the early 1990s the turnover of the karaoke industry was around a third of that of the record industry in that country (Mitsui and Hosokawa 1998a: 21). There are different types of practice of karaoke in Japan, where specific markets have been developed for daytime participants – such as women and school students – and the night-time users. Karaoke also takes place in different places – such as bars, clubs and homes (Mitsui and Hosokawa 1998b).

While the basic idea of karaoke and its technology is common, the practices associated with it have evolved differently in different societies. This has much to do with previous traditions that have existed in any given society for singing in public (Lum 1998). Thus, the antecedents of karaoke in the UK include pub sing-alongs and audience participation in music-hall. In other societies there are different traditions (Mitsui and Hosokawa 1998b). In Japan, karaoke bars tend to be communal places, where there is more of an expectation than in other societies that all will sing along. This phenomenon was captured memorably for Western audiences in the hit movie *Lost in Translation* (dir. Sofia Coppola 2003).

While karaoke has taken different forms, the basic development of performing in public has become very popular. It is possible to suggest that this indicates the development of a context where public performance with respect to music has become a norm. Further, it may also be indicative of the way in which societies in a broader sense have become more performative (see further chapter 9). Thus, in important ways our sense of who we are is constituted by the performance of such activities as karaoke before an audience. Performing is not something that is done only by musicians on a stage or in a recording studio (for subsequent distribution to a mass audience), but is increasingly woven into the fabric of everyday life.

Studies of karaoke have importantly illustrated how karaoke is involved in the constitution and reconstitution of ethic identities. Thus, for example, Hosokawa (1998) has explored the way in which karaoke has mediated Japanese-Brazilian identities for Japanese immigrants to Brazil.

Popular judgements: performance, distinction and identity

So far in this chapter, a number of themes around performance, distinction, identity and the body have been explored. In an influential text, Frith (1996) has brought together a number of these issues. He is particularly concerned with the way in which judgement about music is made in the context of everyday life. He argues that we express our tastes for music very frequently, but that the academic study of popular music has tended to ignore such issues. This book, however, concentrates on the way that music is produced, structured as a text and consumed, rather than on our basis for making a judgement about whether music is good or bad (for an explanation of why this is, see the Introduction). Issues of this kind have come to the fore at several points in this chapter, especially when discussing the work of Pierre Bourdieu.

Frith argues that the basis for making judgements about popular music is no different from that with respect to other art forms. Thus, the grounds for considering whether a piece of popular music is good or bad are in principle no different from those about a piece of classical or 'serious' work (in contrast with the theories of Adorno discussed in the Introduction). However, this is not to suggest that judgement of value is straightforward, otherwise discussions of music would either be very short or would simply consist of direct expressions of preference of the type, 'I like this, I don't like that', and so on. Frith's argument is sociological in that he seeks to identify the different social contexts in which judgement can be made as well as the ideas (or discourses) that frame the way in which judgement is made. He identifies three different forms, or aspects, of the contexts in which judgement operates.

First, there are three key discourses about music that have been in play since the nineteenth century: art, folk and commerce. Despite the difficulties that might exist concerning the definition of these terms, they are all part of the context in which music is discussed. In simple terms, it could be argued that music is artistically worthwhile (for example, it is complex or original), that it is to be valued because it comes from, or expresses, the values of a particular social group (for example, poor black people from the southern states of the USA), or that it is devalued because it is simply produced for commercial gain. These are familiar strands of argument, but what is of most significance about Frith's argument is that he shows how they apply to a range of different musical forms ('high' and 'popular') at different times and in specific contexts.

Second, Frith demonstrates that such judgements are social in that they are made with reference to 'circumstances' of 'music making, selling and consuming' (1996: 95). Thus musicians express valuations of whether a performance is good or bad, as will the group that Frith terms 'producers' in quite a specific sense – 'to describe the broad range of people whose concern is to turn music and musicians into profitable commodities and to draw attention to the recording studio as the place where the most interesting and influential musical value judgements are made' (ibid.: 59). Furthermore, consumers themselves will make judgements. As Frith notes, with respect to music in everyday life (Crafts et al. 1993; see also chapter 9): 'What is striking about the accumulated voices of people talking about music is the sense that music matters not just because it is (like film) a powerful force for taking one out of oneself, but also because it can take one deep inside' (1996: 73). Music is thus about the body and identity.

Third, Frith points to the importance of genre in the contextualization of judgement. Usefully, he shows that genres are highly variable and are constructed according to a commercial logic of categorization, as well as aspects of the sound, who is playing the music, and so on.

In these ways, Frith shows that there are ideas and practices in society that contextualize the judgements we make about music. In addition, he shows that these judgements are made and deployed in the specific context of more micro-level social interaction. He shows this in a number of ways, but most illuminatingly in an analysis of his own place in a pleasurable evening's debate about taste. It can also be seen that evidence from group discussions can illuminate how taste is deployed. The extract from Carrabine and Longhurst (1999) in box 6.2 shows a range of grounds for taste given by participants of the type that Frith analyses. These include genre, that something is 'stupid', that someone has a wide taste, that something is a 'gimmick' and is thus commercial, and so on.

Box 6.2   Extract from focus-group discussion

Male A   I'll listen to anything, if I like it, I like it, whether it be rap, whether it be pop music, chart music, soul, house music, I'll go out and buy tapes that I consider to be like, I've gone out and bought . . . something like that, but at the end I really don't care because I think if I'm secure within myself of what is right and wrong and I'm certainly not going to hide all my tape that you don't approve of before you come round so.

What about everybody else?
Male B   What?

Do you think A had quite a wide range of music taste? Do you think you have?
Male B   I like anything, if I see a song that's just come out and I like it I'll go and buy the single or wait for the album to see that the rest of the songs are like, I mean if I like then, anyone, Seahorses,

anything like that I like it, you know, if I like the sound of it, if it appeals to me.

Female   I've got a particular taste because I don't really like Indie or anything I'm more into like the soul, I like soul.

What sort of soul?

Female   Erm, like Mary Jane B and things like that.
Male B   Oh I can't stand that.
Female   R. Kelly.

Is that R & B?

Female   Yeah.
Male B   Typewriter in it or something.
Female   Typewriter?
Male B   It goes PING!
Female   Everything?
Male B   Yeah stupid song.
Female   It's good!
Male B   Stupid, it's crap. I like Dodgy, Lightning Seeds and Seahorses and Skunk Anansie.

It's not soul though is it?

Female   No it all sounds the same to me, it's just a load of drums, it does!
Male B   I like the Beatles as well.
Female   Oh they are alright.

How do you get to hear it in the first place?

Male B   Just on the radio or friends given it to me or seen it on MTV.
Female   In the charts.
Male A   What's that new song by Cast that's in the charts, I heard that last night, that's beautiful!
Male B   Not heard it.
Male A   I can't really remember what it goes like but that's.
Male B   Like Teletubbies there's a big craze, people say they like the song or they like watching it because it's about nothing and they all go, again, and they can't speak properly, and everyone thinks they are great, it's just another gimmick like the Spice Girls but they've got better voices.

Male A opens this section of the discussion with a significant expression of his variety of likes. He is also at pains to point out that he is 'secure' in this respect and by implication is not affected by others. In this sense, his identity is confidently expressed. In response to a general invitation from one of the leaders of the focus group (the authors of this paper), male B expresses a similar view. The female participant who expresses a 'particular taste' for soul and a dislike of Indie disrupts the initial consensus. This leads to a rapid-fire exchange during which male B, who had started from the position of liking 'anything', opines that R. Kelly is 'crap'. In response the female participant takes a shot at Indie music before some level of agreement is re-established around The Beatles. Male A then points to the nature of an aspect of the contemporary mediascape (in this case the role of the Charts) with his comment about Cast, before the discussion turns to the Teletubbies.

Source: Carrabine and Longhurst 1999: 131, 135–6

It is important to stress that much musical judgement takes place in this way. A sense of self is being performed in front of an audience (in this case the other participants, but also the researchers who are focusing the discussion). This brings the discussion back to emphasize the key themes of this chapter. Music is part of the way in which judgement is performed in everyday life in a number of ways; but in dimensions that are further considered in chapter 9, as audience members, our identities are partly constituted and reconstituted through the sorts of discourse considered in this section. This leads to the discussion of the important topic of the audience, to be tackled in Part III.

Summary

This chapter has considered:

- the idea that sex and gender are constructed through performance;
- the social construction of the body and implications for dance;
- a range of different aspects of dance culture;
- identity with respect to record-collecting and karaoke;
- aspects of taste and distinction with respect to popular music.

Part III

Audience

7

Effects, Audiences and Subcultures

This chapter looks at the nature of the audience for pop music. It falls into three main parts. The analysis begins with a review of some of the different ways in which the relations between texts and audiences have been considered. This entails looking at contemporary debates on the social effects of popular music and specific examples are fed into this more general discussion. This is followed by an examination of the contemporary consumption of pop music (mainly at this point in terms of the sales of music), which provides a context for the more detailed examination of how pop music is actually used in contemporary society. This theme will be addressed through an evaluation of the literature that considers how music is used within different subcultures, which has been a dominant theme in the consideration of the consumption of popular music. The following chapters in this section develop this theme further.

The relations between texts and audiences

The earliest research on the mass media, in particular on film and radio, argued that there was a straightforward relationship between texts and audiences. The mass media were held to have great influence over the behaviour of members of the audience. In a commonly used phrase, they were held to act as a hypodermic syringe, injecting messages into the audience (Lewis 1991; Morley 1992; Moores 1993; Abercrombie and Longhurst 1998). The audience would accept such messages, often because they had no alternative sources of opinion, and would be 'brainwashed' by the media. Such a view was developed in the 1930s when fascist and totalitarian governments had come to power in various parts of Europe, partly, it was thought, through the use of propaganda. The earliest work of some of the writers of the Frankfurt School, including the work of Adorno considered in the Introduction, adopted a similar perspective. The mass media constituted a form of drug for the masses. Such a view of the media, and television in particular, is often voiced in popular criticism. For example, in the 1990s The Disposable Heroes of Hiphoprisy sang of 'Television, the Drug of the Nation' and in the 1970s the singer Gil Scott-Heron maintained that the revolution would not be televised.

Such characterizations of the relations between texts and audiences often see contemporary society as divided into a very small elite and a large mass. The vast majority of the population, consisting of essentially similar people, form the mass. The creation of such a mass was the result of the rise of industrialism, or industrial capitalism, in the nineteenth century, when people moved from their 'traditional' communities to the new industrial towns. There, they lived apparently uniform lives, working in large factories where they performed largely similar tasks.

Although it is recognized by such theories that the mass is made up of individuals, they are not seen to possess true individuality or discrimination. They are 'massified' in that the ties between them have been, or are in the process of being, broken down. Hence, old family or community ties from earlier days were held to be disappearing. It was argued that the development of such a mass society could have important ramifications. First, some writers suggested that the masses might challenge traditional or elite government, leading to its breakdown. This view, which was often expressed by conservatives, held that government by the elite benefited everyone in society and that democracy would lead to social breakdown and turmoil. Likewise, it was thought that the masses were calling into question 'good', 'proper' or previous 'folk' cultures. In such accounts, 'traditional' values were seen as threatened and under attack. Second, there was the fear that the masses would be manipulated by the mass media, helping the elite to retain its rule and propagate its views. In both these accounts the media are seen to be very powerful in affecting how and what people think and how they behave.

Similar accounts of the power of the media have held that people respond to it in a very direct fashion: the media act as stimuli to particular forms of behaviour. In accord with such a view, there has been a great deal of research into the effects of the media. This has clustered around a number of areas, including: the potential effects of representations of sexual activity and different forms of violence; effects on the attitudes and behaviour of children; the effects of media coverage on how voters behave in elections; and the wider ramifications of the media usage of stereotypes of race and gender. These sorts of approach have been represented in discussions of the effects of pop music.

In an examination of the case made against heavy metal music along these lines in the United States in the 1980s, Walser (1993) shows how the work of Tipper Gore (wife of ex-Vice-President Al Gore), who, along with other wives of members of the government, had founded the Parents' Music Resource Center (PMRC) in 1985, represented: 'heavy metal as a threat to youth, enabling her to mobilize parental hysteria while avoiding the adult word censorship. Objecting to eroticism and "lesbian undertones" in popular music, along with sadism and brutality, she conflates sex and violence, which have in common their threat to parental control' (1993: 138). In Walser's account, Gore accepts 'a "hypodermic model" of musical effects; music's meanings are "pounded" or "dumped" into listeners, who are helpless to resist. Young people in particular are thought to be more vulnerable, especially when repetitive listening and headphone use help create "a direct, unfettered freeway straight into the mind"' (ibid.: 141).

Walser argues that such writings are dependent on 'anecdote and insinuation' (ibid.: 142) and that none of the critics 'is able to connect heavy metal directly with suicide, Satanism or crime' (ibid.: 143). One important case discussed in

Figure 7.1 Hypodermic syringe or direct effect model

detail by Walser concerns the lawsuit brought against the heavy metal group Judas Priest, in which it was argued that subliminal messages in the group's music had led to the suicide of two fans called Vance and Belknap. The trial ended with Judas Priest being cleared of the charges, 'for the judge remained unconvinced that the "subliminal" messages on the album were intentionally placed there or were necessary to explain the conduct of Vance and Belknap' (ibid.: 146).

Walser does not argue that there are no representations of violence or, indeed misogyny, in pop music. However, he suggests that it is not possible to establish a direct link between such representations and the behaviour of pop music audience members. He argues that:

> [Critics of heavy metal] imagine that fans are passive, unable to resist the pernicious messages of heavy metal, and thus they themselves commit the sort of dehumanization they ascribe to popular culture. They make the fans into dupes without agency or subjectivity, without social experiences and perceptions that might inform their interactions with mass-mediated texts. (Ibid.: 144)

This argument is a particular example of the hypodermic syringe or mass society view. Powerful media performers or owners of the media place messages in texts which are accepted by the passive and gullible in the audience. Diagrammatically, using the Production, Text, Audience model, this can be represented as in figure 7.1. A simple version of such a thesis is relatively easy to criticize. First, it is important to remember that, in the main, people do not live as separated individuals. They are social beings living in groups that mediate media messages. Second, people question media messages: they do not simply accept them. Third, the message people receive from a text is not always the same as the one producers thought that they were putting into it: we interpret texts in different ways. In sum, such accounts rely on a very narrow and unsophisticated view of the individual.

Attempts to refine such a model included the two-step flow model associated with Katz and Lazarsfeld (Morley 1980). This model adopted a more sophisticated view of the audience than that found in the hypodermic account. Society is seen as consisting of groups, and our opinions, behaviour and attitudes are influenced by the membership of such groups and the relationships between them. We are not just 'bare individuals' but social beings. However, this does not mean that the mass media are unimportant; rather, that we are affected by the media in an indirect fashion. Thus, the majority of the audience will be affected by the views of opinion leaders. For example, in the case of music, we are all familiar with the way in which certain individuals will suggest that we listen to a particular record or go to see a certain band. This sort of approach begins to recognize the complexity of the composition of the media audience, and the nature of some of the social relationships between its different members. However, there are criticisms that can be made of it. First, it tends to divide the audience rather strictly between those who are active and those who are passive. Second, it is not clear why there should be only two steps. There might in fact be a whole range of steps and the relationships between the members of the audience might be extremely complex.

An approach that attempted to shift attention away from the effects of the media was called the 'uses and gratifications' approach. As the name suggests, the focus here is on the way in which the audience uses the media to gratify certain needs or wants. Such an approach is significant because it takes the everyday life of the audience rather more seriously than earlier approaches. For example, it would be possible, adopting such an approach, to argue that pop music can be used to satisfy a need for excitement or romance, and so on. However, there is a danger of allowing the audience rather too much freedom in the way they use the media. Thus, the nature of a text will constrain to some extent the uses to which it is put. For example, it would be unusual to satisfy a need to dance in a club with classical music.

Subsequent work on audiences argued that it is important to recognize the complex two-way relationship between texts and audiences. A text might be structured in a particular style, but is liable to be understood or decoded by the audience in ways that are not necessarily determined by the text itself. In a very influential study of the early evening television programme Nationwide, David Morley (1980), following the more theoretical work of Stuart Hall (1980), identified three categories of understanding of the programme amongst the audience. First, there was the dominant reading which followed the common-sense logic of the programme that had previously been identified by Brunsdon and Morley (1978). Audience members go along with and do not question the structure of the programme. Second, there was the negotiated reading. In this case, audience members would accept most of the message in the programme but would negotiate with it to some degree. The message would not be completely accepted: there might be misgivings about some aspects of it. Third, there were those audience members who opposed the programme altogether. They either saw it as a form of ideology, suggesting that it was putting forward a view of the world that suited the dominant class, or they thought that it had no relevance to their lives.

This study was influential for a number of reasons. First, it took audience reactions seriously and maintained that there could be rather different responses to the same programme. Second, these different responses were related to social background; they were not arbitrary or individualistic. Third, before doing this project, Morley had, with Brunsdon, carried out a detailed and sophisticated analysis of Nationwide. They argued that the programme tended to structure the viewer of the text in particular ways, so that it would not always be easy to perform an oppositional reading of the text. The relationship between the text and the audience was therefore a two-way one, as shown in figure 7.2.

A number of criticisms can and have been made of this influential study, including the relative neglect of how Nationwide was produced. The most important criticism for the purposes of the current discussion is that the research was rather

Figure 7.2 Two-way text–audience relationship

artificial: groups of people were brought together to watch particular editions of *Nationwide* and then asked to discuss them afterwards. It can be argued that this is not the way in which we normally watch television. This was a point recognized by Morley, and in subsequent research (for example, 1986) he situated television as a domestic medium, and examined the way in which it is watched and viewed in the home. Since the early 1980s, there has developed an extensive literature which attempts to study the actual ways in which television is viewed by audiences (for overviews, see Abercrombie and Longhurst 1998; Staiger 2005). However, there has not been such a corresponding expansion in the study of the audience for pop music, which would situate music use in the home, at concerts or dances, to take just three possible contexts (but see chapter 9 for consideration of some important studies that have investigated these aspects). One still useful study that did examine this topic was carried out by Dorothy Hobson (1980).

Hobson looked at media-use by housewives who were at home looking after young children. She found that the majority of those she studied listened to the pop station Radio 1 a great deal, using it as a background to their domestic work and as a way of structuring the routine of their days (see also, more generally, Longhurst et al. 2001). The disc jockey provided 'the missing "company" of another person' (Hobson 1980: 107), linking the women to others in the same position. In a sense, the male disc jockey would construct an 'imagined community' (Anderson 1983) between the women. The way in which daytime disc jockeys address their audience has also been considered by Rosalind Coward, who argues:

> Nowhere is sexual desire more obviously scripted and stage-managed than in the mishmash of music and chat directed at women during the day on popular radio. Sexual desire, attraction and love dominate not just as themes in the music but also make up a large part of the DJ's chatter. Forthcoming marriages, broken hearts, happy memories – these are the meat of radio discourse; relationships are at the heart of phone-ins; and radio dedications are from lover to lover. Popular music is broadcast into homes and workplaces during the day, presupposing a certain kind of predominantly female audience. The packaging of the music engages the emotions of this female audience, focusing attention on sexual relationships and in particular requiring the listener to think about her own sexual and emotional involvements. (1984: 144)

It is important to note that neither Hobson nor Coward pay much attention to the actual reactions of women to the music on the radio. Further, it is possible to speculate that the nature of daytime radio has changed somewhat since these studies were carried out, especially as daytime television has expanded. However, these studies do address important issues about how popular music is related to uses in everyday life.

The discussion of Madonna in chapter 3 has already pointed out that different groups respond to her videos in different ways. Other work has examined the way in which young people interpret the lyrics of songs. For example, Prinsky and Rosenbaum (1987) studied the interpretations of song lyrics by teenagers in the context of the concern articulated by parents' pressure groups in the United States in the 1980s, as discussed above. They administered a questionnaire to 266 students (55 per cent male, 45 per cent female), aged between 12 and 18, in four high schools in Southern California. In the questionnaire:

> The students surveyed were asked to list their three favorite songs and on the following page they were asked to describe the songs they had selected in about three sentences. Each song description was coded to determine if the interpretation fell into any of the four categories developed by the parents' Music Resource Center: sex, violence, drugs/alcohol, and Satanism. Three additional categories were included to allow for descriptions that were about love without being sexual as well as permitting respondents to find other themes or to say that they did not know what a song was about. These were love/feelings, other, and don't know. (Prinsky and Rosenbaum 1987: 386)

It was found that those respondents who did give descriptions of songs 'appeared to have only a superficial understanding of the lyrics' (ibid.: 387). They were not aware of many of the meanings that pressure groups found in the lyrics. Thus, 'teenage impressions of popular music in general reflect the interests of young people and are somewhat circumscribed by their lack of experience and limited literary abilities' (ibid.: 393). In addition, Prinsky and Rosenbaum show that young people use music in a number of different ways: for relaxation, entertainment, and so on. Furthermore, as was pointed out in chapter 5, lyrics may not be the most important aspect in creating musical meaning anyway. In some ways Prinsky and Rosenbaum's concise research returns us to the emphasis placed upon the uses made of the media in the uses and gratifications approach. More recent approaches, which emphasize the importance of studying media use in the context of everyday life, share some aspects of this (see chapter 9). However, it is important to bear in mind the complex nature of the interaction between what is in a text (as was demonstrated in chapter 5, there are a number of different dimensions to this) and what members of the audience make of it in the context of their social situation.

In making such points, it should not be thought that the role of the media in influencing forms of behaviour and attitudes is being played down. It may be that the media, including pop music, have long-term social effects, and it is important to recognize that the stereotypical ways in which women and black people are represented in pop music may feed into everyday understandings of race and gender, as the discussions of rap and hip-hop (see chapter 4) suggest.

More specifically, the approach known as cultivation analysis has argued that there are long-term effects of the media, maintaining, on the basis of several studies, that, 'the more TV you watch, the more likely you are to have a fearful or distrustful attitude to the world outside' (Lewis 1991: 19). Television is held to influence beliefs and behaviour over extended periods of time.

In recent years, writers interested in media audiences have begun to make greater use of the quantitative data produced from within media organizations themselves. Such data can be informative (though for a critical discussion, see Ang 1991) in helping to buid up a clearer picture of what the audience for pop music is like. In the area of music, this data refers in the main to the consumption of different forms of music and there are issues raised by the concept of consumption itself. These are examined in chapter 8.

Trends in consumption

Until recently, recorded music has been available in five main formats: singles, LPs, cassettes, compact discs and music videos (see below for discussion of downloading). The trends in consumer spending in Britain on these products are detailed in table 7.1. This shows the increasing popularity of CDs and music DVDs and the decline in LPs and cassettes. The overall number of sales of albums reached 239.4 million in 2004. Trade deliveries (i.e. sales of records, cassettes and CDs invoiced to dealers and distributors; Cultural Trends, 1991: 22) of recordings have fluctuated over the period 1978–2004, to a current peak, as is shown by figure 7.3. Again, this demonstrates the increasing centrality of CDs to the market.

The overwhelming majority of the albums sold in the United Kingdom contain popular music. As is shown in table 7.2, classical albums have tended to account for less than 10 per cent of trade deliveries, though there was a significant increase in 1990 and 1991, which has now tailed off. The international situation with regard to music sales is neatly summarized by Dave Laing in the piece contained in box 7.1.

It is important to move beyond such broad trends to examine the nature of consumption in more detail. The data reproduced in tables 7.3, 7.4 and 7.5 facilitate such a discussion. The percentages in tables 7.4, 7.5 and 7.6 sum horizontally. For example, 33.3 per cent of urban album purchases were made by those in the 20–29 age group and 11.4 per cent by those in the 40–49 range. A number of points can be derived from these data. For example:

1 Classical music, in the main, is the province of the older and the better off.
2 The purchase of rock music declines with age, though rock is not, on these figures, the music of youth, and more attention might be given to the middle-aged rock consumer by sociological research. It is important to note the success of magazines like *Uncut*, *Word* and *Mojo*, which are oriented towards this market.
3 Country and MOR music is most popular with older people, urban and dance with younger people.
4 Rock albums are more popular with men than women, the reverse being the case with pop albums. This seems to back up the arguments of Frith and McRobbie reviewed in chapter 3.
5 Jazz/blues and country albums make up a small proportion of sales.

The most significant contemporary change to this environment is coming through downloading. While data on this are only just beginning to be published, it is clear that there has been a significant impact on the singles market in the UK

Table 7.1 UK trade deliveries, 1978–2004 (millions)

	LPs		Cassettes		CDs		Total Albums		Music DVDs	
	Units	Value	Units	Value	Units	Value	Units	Value	Units	Value
1978	86.1	£163.2	20.6	£43.0	–	–	107.3	£207.1	–	–
1979	74.5	£161.5	23.5	£50.3	–	–	98.1	£211.9	–	–
1980	67.4	£148.5	25.2	£52.5	–	–	92.6	£201.0	–	–
1981	64.0	£145.1	28.7	£62.1	–	–	92.7	£207.2	–	–
1982	57.8	£139.2	31.5	£71.0	–	–	89.3	£210.2	–	–
1983	54.3	£138.0	35.8	£84.0	0.3	£1.5	90.4	£223.5	–	–
1984	54.1	£141.2	45.3	£104.0	0.8	£5.0	100.2	£250.2	–	–
1985	52.9	£145.4	55.4	£128.4	3.1	£19.2	111.4	£293.0	–	–
1986	52.3	£140.6	69.6	£152.1	8.4	£56.5	130.3	£349.2	–	–
1987	52.2	£146.6	74.4	£185.1	18.2	£116.5	144.8	£448.2	–	–
1988	50.2	£144.1	80.9	£224.8	29.2	£167.9	160.3	£536.8	–	–
1989	37.9	£118.0	83.0	£251.8	41.7	£230.7	162.6	£600.5	–	–
1990	24.7	£80.5	75.1	£246.2	50.9	£273.4	150.7	£600.1	–	–
1991	12.9	£46.4	66.8	£239.0	62.8	£345.5	142.5	£630.9	–	–
1992	6.7	£23.9	56.4	£207.0	70.5	£380.5	133.6	£611.4	–	–
1993	5.0	£16.3	55.7	£204.1	92.9	£480.0	153.6	£700.4	–	–
1994	4.5	£15.3	56.0	£200.7	116.4	£603.6	176.9	£819.6	–	–
1995	3.6	£11.9	53.4	£184.2	139.2	£708.4	196.2	£904.5	–	–
1996	2.4	£9.2	46.2	£158.9	159.7	£789.1	208.3	£957.2	–	–
1997	2.5	£9.9	36.6	£123.7	158.8	£785.6	197.9	£919.2	–	–
1998	2.2	£7.8	32.2	£109.4	175.7	£878.2	210.3	£997.2	–	–
1999	2.3	£7.1	18.4	£70.5	176.9	£914.7	198.0	£995.4	–	–
2000	3.2	£8.7	11.4	£40.8	201.6	£997.7	216.5	£1049.3	–	–
2001	2.6	£7.8	4.6	£15.0	218.6	£1099.4	225.9	£1122.7	–	–
2002	2.2	£6.3	1.9	£5.0	221.6	£1077.6	225.7	£1089.0	3.3	£23.5
2003	2.0	£6.0	0.9	£3.3	234.0	£1102.8	236.9	£1112.0	6.5	£46.6
2004	1.5	£4.3	0.5	£2.1	237.4	£1094.4	239.4	£1100.7	9.7	£60.7

Source: BPI Statistical Handbook 2005: 18

(see figures 7.4 and 7.5), where downloaded singles first topped the charts in 2006.

These figures on consumption are illuminating, but they still give only a rather broad picture of music use. One of the ways in which such use has been studied in most detail is through the concept of 'subculture' used in more ethnographic research.

Culture, subculture and music

Most of the research on subculture, which has focused particularly on youth subcultures, draws on two different meanings of culture. In the first, culture refers to the works and practices of artistic and intellectual activity. In this sense, music or a painting are forms of culture, but schoolwork, for example, is not. At times,

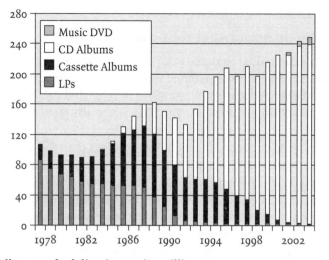

Figure 7.3 Album trade deliveries (units millions)

Source: BPI Surveys

Table 7.2 Classical trade deliveries, 1984–2004 (thousands)

	Total		% share of all albums	
	Units	Value	Units	Value
1984	7,864	na	7.8	na
1985	8,693	£26,366	7.8	9.0
1986	9,374	£33,527	7.2	9.6
1987	11,869	£43,028	8.2	9.6
1988	12,012	£42,243	7.5	7.9
1989	13,973	£47,066	8.6	7.8
1990	16,688	£67,335	11.1	11.2
1991	15,500	£63,574	10.9	10.1
1992	12,350	£50,938	9.3	8.3
1993	12,938	£53,697	8.4	7.7
1994	15,491	£64,384	8.8	7.9
1995	14,637	£62,680	7.5	6.9
1996	14,707	£62,386	7.1	6.5
1997	14,635	£64,519	7.4	7.0
1998	16,187	£73,076	7.7	7.3
1999	13,108	£58,630	6.6	5.9
2000	15,523	£66,524	7.2	6.3
2001	15,756	£70,313	7.0	6.3
2002	13,070	£59,905	5.8	5.5
2003	14,023	£64,979	5.9	5.8
2004	11,606	£50,178	4.8	4.6

Source: BPI Statistical Handbook 2005: 44

Box 7.1 World record sales 1992–2002

The retail value of global recorded music sales in 2002 was $31 billion. This total is published by the International Federation of the Recording Industry (IFPI) and is based on information supplied by large and small record companies in sixty-nine countries. The 2002 figure was almost 8% lower than the total of 2001 record sales. In terms of format unit sales, the number of CD albums sold in 2002 was 2.25 billion (5% less than the previous year), cassette album sales were 487 million (19% less), singles sales in all formats were 17% less at 265 million and vinyl LP sales were 8.5 million (28% less). Note that these are sales of new LPs only. The IFPI figures do not include the used or second-hand market, or the 'pirate' market whose sales are estimated by IFPI to have been $4.6 billion in 2002.

It is clear from the Table showing annual world sales since 1992 that the 2002 results confirm the existence of a long-term downward trend in the global record industry's income from sale of sound carriers. The value of sales has fallen in each of the last three years, but it is seven years since there was growth of more than 1–9.8% in 1995. It is worth adding that the early results for the first half of 2003 indicate that the downward trend is continuing. The Table shows that there was a sharp break in 1996 from the high growth rates of the previous four years shown in the Table and in fact several years before that. What are the reasons for the seven-year slump in recorded music sales?

Table: Annual world record sales since 1992

Year	Retail value ($ billions)	% change
1992	29.0	+ 12.4
1993	30.8	+ 6.1
1994	36.1	+ 17.4
1995	39.6	+ 9.8
1996	39.8	+ 0.4
1997	38.1	− 4.3
1998	38.2	+ 0.2
1999	38.5	+ 0.7
2000	36.9	− 4.5
2001	33.7	− 8.9
2002	31.0	− 7.9

Writing about the previous great slump in recorded music sales (1978–1981), Bruce Haring (1996) listed its causes as 'home taping; competition from video games, cable TV; youth unemployment; changes in radio formats with the rise of AC (adult contemporary) and country, genres whose audience were not record buyers on a large scale'. Although Haring was writing specifically about the USA, some of the factors involved in the late 1970s are of equal relevance over two decades later. The direct contemporary equivalent of 'home taping' is the burning of CD albums onto blank CD-R discs. Market research in Germany found that 260 million of the 486 million CD-Rs sold in Germany in 2002 were used to make copies of music CDs. This was greater than the 178 million pre-recorded CDs sold by German record companies. An equally – if not more – important form of 'private copying' is, of course, peer-to-peer file sharing (P2P) on the Internet. Although there have been many claims and counter-claims about the impact of such activities on purchases of CDs, it seems incontrovertible that at least some P2P participants are buying less music on CD than before.

The second factor mentioned by Haring is the competition for consumer spending from other entertainment formats. He mentions computer games and pay-television. In the contemporary market place, recorded music sales remain under pressure from games consoles and software, plus two more recent technologies: mobile telephones and DVD (Digital Versatile Disc). Japan is the most remarkable example of the popularity among young people of phones and their add-ons such as ringtones (from which the music industry derives a small amount in royalties). There, the market for singles has shrunk as phone sales have increased exponentially. And DVD has been the most successful new cultural product since the CD itself.

General economic circumstances must also play a role in the fortunes of the record industry. Having cited 'youth unemployment' as a factor in 1978–1981 and today's global economic stagnation makes the competition for entertainment spending more intense, according to financial analyst Helen Snell who has stated that 'historical trends confirm a strong correlation . . . between music sales and consumer confidence' (Snell 2001).

But perhaps the primary source of the current slump should be sought in the main reason for the high growth rate of recorded music sales in the late 1980s and early 1990s. This was what Snell and others have called the 'CD replacement cycle'. The term refers to the fact that new adopters of Compact Disc technology generally bought far more discs than their annual average purchase of music, notably in order to replace the LP versions of their favourite albums. This, and the fact that the CDs were expensively priced, led to a boom in retail spending on music. However, by the mid-1990s, all who wished to, or could afford to, switch to CD had done so and the boom was over.

It was this boom that led the record industry out of the 1978–1981 recession. Unless music DVDs achieve a popularity comparable to that of audio CDs, it is difficult to see another new carrier coming to the rescue of the industry this time.

References:

Haring, B. 1996. 'Off the Charts', in *Ruthless Days and Reckless Nights Inside the Music Industry* (New York).

Snell, H. 2001. 'Are Music Sales Recession-proof?', *Music & Media*, 20 (October), p. 8.

Source: Laing 2004: 88–9

Table 7.3 Average number of purchases per buyer per year, 1999–2004

	Total Albums						Total Singles					
	1999	2000	2001	2002	2003	2004	1999	2000	2001	2002	2003	2004
Total	7.0	6.8	7.0	6.9	7.3	7.5	5.8	4.7	4.8	3.8	3.8	4.0
Gender												
Men	8.6	8.4	8.6	8.1	8.6	8.9	6.1	5.1	5.2	4.2	4.6	4.3
Women	5.3	5.0	5.1	5.5	5.8	5.9	5.4	4.2	4.5	3.4	3.2	3.8
Age Group												
12–19	7.6	8.7	9.6	7.4	7.6	7.3	8.2	5.9	7.9	4.6	3.9	3.1
20–29	7.8	8.8	8.4	8.6	8.2	8.3	5.6	5.3	4.6	5.2	5.1	6.7
30–39	7.2	7.1	6.5	6.4	6.9	7.5	6.8	3.5	3.3	3.4	3.2	3.3
40–49	6.9	6.4	7.2	6.9	7.2	7.5	2.4	5.4	3.6	2.8	3.7	4.0
50–59	6.5	6.0	6.4	6.9	7.2	7.4	2.6	3.2	3.4	2.7	3.6	3.8
60+	5.6	4.4	4.2	5.4	6.8	6.0	1.2	0.9	0.9	2.5	2.5	3.6
Social Group												
AB	8.5	7.8	7.5	7.4	7.5	8.3	5.3	3.6	2.9	3.4	3.6	3.4
C1	7.5	7.1	7.3	7.0	7.9	7.3	6.6	5.2	4.3	3.5	3.0	3.1
C2	6.4	5.9	6.4	6.3	6.4	6.7	5.4	4.5	4.6	3.8	4.0	4.0
DE	5.8	6.6	6.9	6.9	7.0	7.8	5.5	4.8	6.7	4.0	4.4	5.0

Source: BPI Statistical Handbook 2005: 82

Table 7.4 Expenditure by genre. Albums (% across)

| | Gender | | Age Group | | | | | |
	Men	Women	12–19	20–29	30–39	40–49	50–59	60+
Survey Population	50.4	49.6	12.5	14.3	21.0	17.9	16.5	17.7
All albums	58.4	41.6	15.8	18.3	21.8	20.3	13.5	10.2
Rock	66.9	33.1	21.4	21.6	24.4	21.0	8.6	3.0
Pop	45.9	54.1	12.5	14.5	25.7	26.8	13.2	7.3
Urban	54.3	45.7	32.0	33.3	16.5	11.4	3.8	3.1
Dance	63.0	37.0	24.5	28.9	27.6	10.4	7.5	1.1
MOR	44.7	55.3	5.7	5.0	15.6	22.1	23.0	28.6
Classical	63.9	36.1	1.1	7.9	8.3	13.9	29.7	39.0
Country	66.7	33.3	4.1	7.9	14.5	22.8	38.8	11.9
Jazz/Blues	63.6	36.4	3.9	12.2	18.2	23.3	21.2	21.2

Source: BPI Statistical Handbook 2005: 83

Table 7.5 Choice of music by demographic group, 2004 (% across)

	Rock	Pop	Urban	Dance	MOR	Classical	Country	Jazz/Blues
Total	34.3	30.4	10.4	5.1	6.9	5.0	2.2	2.5
Gender								
Men	40.1	24.5	9.9	5.9	5.4	5.5	2.2	2.7
Women	26.5	38.2	11.1	4.1	8.9	4.3	2.1	2.3
Age Group								
12–14	45.8	27.3	20.1	3.9	1.5	0.0	0.0	0.8
15–19	44.8	22.0	20.3	8.0	2.6	0.5	0.0	0.9
20–29	40.6	24.0	19.0	7.6	1.9	2.3	0.4	1.4
30–39	37.5	34.9	7.7	6.9	4.8	2.0	1.9	1.7
40–49	34.4	38.8	5.6	2.6	7.3	3.0	2.2	2.3
50–59	23.2	32.1	3.1	3.0	12.5	11.6	3.4	3.7
60+	10.9	24.4	3.4	0.7	20.8	20.3	8.1	8.0
Social Group								
AB	38.5	24.4	9.6	3.7	6.4	9.2	1.8	3.3
C1	34.8	27.2	11.4	5.2	7.2	5.6	1.9	2.8
C2	35.5	34.0	9.6	5.1	7.3	2.5	1.7	1.5
DE	29.8	35.7	10.4	6.1	6.6	3.0	3.1	2.5

Note: Analysis based on 44 weeks data to year end
Source: BPI Statistical Handbook 2005: 84

this version of culture involves a judgement of value. Thus certain forms of music, for example by Beethoven or Mozart, are held to be proper 'culture', while works by such as Girls Aloud or Kylie Minogue are considered as trash. The second sense of culture is rather different, referring to the idea of culture as a 'way of life'. This more inclusive definition can be found in expressions such as 'the American way of

Figure 7.4 Weekly single sales, 2004

Source: BPI

Figure 7.5 Single track downloads as a percentage of all weekly sales, 2004

Source: BPI

life' or 'British culture'. These definitions both feed into the development of what has increasingly become known as British cultural studies (Turner 1990), and it is from within this context that many of the most important studies of youth subcultures and music have been carried out. The key definition of culture produced within this tradition explains that 'we understand the word culture to refer to that level at which social groups develop distinct patterns of life, and give expressive form to their social and material life experience. Culture is the way, the forms, in which groups "handle" the raw material of their social and material existence' (Clarke et al. 1976: 10). Clarke et al. relate three aspects of social life in this definition: social experience, social groups and patterns of life. In their account, social groups develop distinct patterns of life based on their own social experiences in relation to other social groups and forms of experience. Culture is both a level/area of society and the forms in which the raw material of social experience is handled.

The approach taken by Clarke et al. was greatly influenced by an earlier paper by Cohen written in the early 1970s (1980), who examined the nature of youth subcultures in the East End of London in the 1960s. He argued that after the Second World War, from the 1950s onwards, the East End working-class community was disrupted by three factors: migration out of the area; the redevelopment of housing involving the building of new tower blocks patterned on a middle-class nuclear family model, which destroyed the forms of communal space and the patterns of female support that had been so important in the area; and a series of economic changes. This led to a 'polarization of the labour force' (Cohen 1980: 80) between more specialized, 'high-tech' and well-paid jobs and more dead-end, unskilled labour.

One outcome of this process of dislocation was the development of youth subcultures, which opposed the working-class parent culture. In Cohen's argument, 'the internal conflicts of the parent culture came to be worked out in terms of generational conflict' (ibid.: 82). Furthermore, Cohen argued that youth subcultures 'express and resolve, albeit "magically", the contradictions which remain hidden or unresolved in the parent culture' (ibid.). Subcultures are ways of dealing with the difficulties that structural transformations in society have created in the parent culture to which they belong. Following the pattern of the polarization of the workforce between an upward and a downward social movement, Cohen argues that youth subcultures can express such routes in a variety of different ways. Hence, 'mods, parkas, skinheads, crombies are a succession of subcultures which all correspond to the same parent culture and which attempt to work out, through a system of transformations, the basic problematic or contradiction which is inserted in the subculture by the parent culture' (ibid.: 83). This sort of approach has been represented diagrammatically by Clarke et al. (1976), as shown in figure 7.6.

Cohen argued that there are two main components of the lifestyle of such youth subcultures, which he terms 'plastic' (dress and music) and 'infrastructural' (argot and ritual). Thus, music is an important part of the complex subcultural whole. However, Cohen paid relatively little attention to the detail of the music used by subcultures. Other writers who developed work within the 'Birmingham tradition' of British cultural studies, which was initiated at the Centre for Cultural Studies at the University of Birmingham, placed more emphasis on it. Some of the papers collected in *Resistance Through Rituals* (Hall and Jefferson 1976) consider this dimension, but most detail can be found in the work of Paul Willis (1978) and Dick Hebdige (1979).

Willis examined various dimensions of the lives of two youth subcultural groups in the late 1960s: the motor-bike boys and hippies. While these examples are rather dated, it is the nature of the link that Willis makes between music and other aspects of the lifestyle of these groups that resonated through work on subcultures. Willis argued that the musical preferences of these groups were intimately connected to the nature of their lives. Thus, the motor-bike boys' preference for early rock 'n' roll in a single format and the hippies' like of album-based progressive rock was no accident. Rock 'n' roll music matched the restlessness and mobility of the motor-bike boys' lives. Thus Willis argued:

> [T]his music allows the return of the body in music, and encourages the development of a culture based on movement and confidence in movement. The classical European tradition has steadily forced the body and dancing out of music, and made it progressively harder to dance to. The absolute

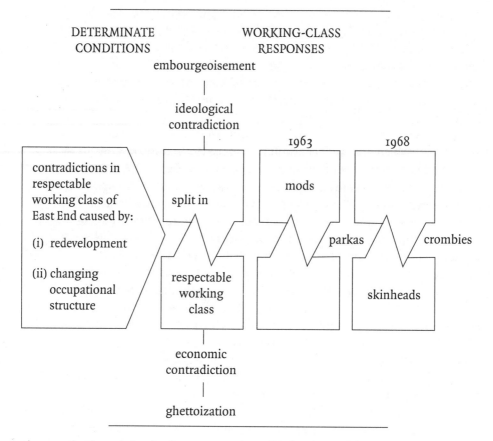

DETERMINATE   WORKING-CLASS
CONDITIONS   RESPONSES

embourgeoisement

ideological
contradiction

contractions in
respectable
working class of
East End caused by:

(i) redevelopment

(ii) changing
    occupational
    structure

split in

respectable
working
class

1963   1968

mods

parkas   crombies

skinheads

economic
contradiction

ghettoization

Figure 7.6 Class and subcultures: a version of Cohen's model
Source: Clarke et al. 1976: 34

ascendancy of the beat in rock 'n' roll firmly establishes the ascendancy of the body over the mind – it reflects the motor-bike boys' culture very closely. The eclipse of tonality and melody in the music is also the eclipse of abstraction in the bike culture. . . . [T]he suppression of structured time in the music, its ability to stop, start and be faded, matches the motor-bike boys' restless concrete life style. As we have seen, it is no accident that the boys preferred singles, nor is it an accident that the rock 'n' roll form is the most suited to singles and its modern technology (fading, etc.). Both the music and its 'singles' form are supremely relevant to the style of the bike culture. (1978: 77)

Willis mounts a similar sort of argument about the homologous relationships between different aspects of a hippie youth subculture (see especially ibid.: 168–9). In Hebdige's words, this expresses: 'the symbolic fit between the values and life-styles of a group, its subjective experience and the musical forms it uses to express or reinforce its focal concerns' (1979: 113). This means that, for Willis, subcultures are structured as different aspects of the lifestyle of the subculture fit together to form a whole. So, for the hippie subculture, there is a homology or correspondence between an 'alternative value system', 'hallucinogenic drugs' and progressive rock.

Subcultures express a response to a set of conditions and the different aspects of the subculture are tied together into structured relatively coherent wholes. A schematic version of this approach can be seen in the chronology of subcultures reproduced in figure 7.7.

Hebdige developed the idea of reading the nature of the style of subcultural groups by means of the structural and semiotic approaches that were introduced in chapter 5. He focused on the different dimensions of the style of subcultural groups. Using the general definition of culture proposed by Clarke et al., Hebdige argued that the styles expressed by different subcultures are a response to social conditions and experiences. Furthermore, he suggests that such styles often encode an opposition to the dominant or hegemonic forms of culture associated with dominant groups. Such challenges are often indirect and can involve the utilization and transformation of forms of culture that were previously the property of dominant groups. In engaging in such practices, subcultural members engage in a process of 'bricolage', responding to the world around them by improvising in a structured fashion, creating meanings that are different from those of the dominant or dominant groups. As Hebdige says about the style represented in figure 7.8: 'In this way the teddy boy's theft and transformation of the Edwardian style revived in the early 1950s by Savile Row for wealthy young men about town can be construed as act of bricolage' (ibid.: 104).

Hebdige argues that subcultures generally resist the dominant social order, albeit indirectly and in symbolic ways. However, he also argues that forms of subcultural expression are often incorporated into the dominant social order through two main routes. First, there is the commodity form, which involves 'the conversion of subcultural signs (dress, music, etc.) into mass-produced objects'. Second, there is 'the "labelling" and re-definition of deviant behaviour by dominant groups – the police, the media, the judiciary' (ibid.: 94) in a process of ideological incorporation.

This account of the ways in which subcultural groups produce new and resistant meanings, which are then bought off or incorporated by the capitalist system, is now relatively familiar. It entails the notion that there is a sphere where 'authentic' meanings are produced which is then corrupted. However, as has been pointed out in other parts of this book, this thesis has always been, and especially now, rather difficult to sustain. Nevertheless, it is also important to note that such characterization of the processes of change in social life is often produced by young music fans themselves.

On the basis of research carried out in 1972, Simon Frith (1983: 205–12) drew a distinction between 'sixth-form culture', based around progressive rock which stressed the individual nature of taste, and 'lower-fifth-form culture', made up of people who 'bought singles and watched Top of the Pops, went regularly to youth clubs and discos but rarely to concerts, emphasized beat and sound in their tastes rather than meaning, and identified with specific youth styles' (ibid.: 206). He also identified a group of prospective sixth-formers who had a 'missionary zeal for progressive rock and hatred of commercial pop' (ibid.: 207). This group was very assertive in its views about music and taste. As Frith explains:

> One of the paradoxes in my survey was that the group which most stressed individual music choice also most stressed the importance of shared

Date	Subculture	Class position	Style	Music	Shifts in post-war hegemony
1953–4	teds	unskilled	drapes		The construction of consensus Macmillanism
1955–6	teds	working class		rock 'n' roll	
1958–61	beats/CND	middle class	duffle coats, beards	jazz/folk	
1963	mods	semi-skilled	scooter of consensus	r 'n' b/Tamla	The construction of consensus Social democracy
1964	rockers	unskilled	motor-bike	rock 'n' roll	
1967–72	hippies	middle class/student	long hair, hallucinogenic drugs	progressive rock	Dissensus Protest and revolution
1967	rude boys	black underclass	hustling	ska	
1968–9	skinheads	unskilled	boots 'n' braces	ska	
1970	glams	working class?	bisexuality	glamrock	The Law and Order Society Authoritarianism and working-class resistance
1970	Rastas	black underclass?	dreadlocks	reggae	
1976–8	punks	working class?	absurdity	punk rock	
1978–81	mod/ted skinhead revivals				
1981	new romantics				
1982	?				

Figure 7.7 Chronology of subcultures

Source: Middleton and Muncie 1981: 90

Figure 7.8 Teddy boy, 29 May 1954
Reproduced by permission of Hulton Deutsch Collection Ltd.

musical taste for friendship – music served as the badge of individuality on which friendship choices could be based. One of the ironies was that because music was taken as a symbol of a cluster of values, the most individualistic groups were the ones most thrown by their musical heroes changing direction. This was particularly a problem for the hairies [long-haired followers of progressive rock] because they differentiated themselves from the masses as a self-conscious elite by displaying exclusive musical tastes. Their tastes weren't just a matter of identification; they also reflected a different – more serious, more intense – relationship to music. The hairies thought of themselves not as just another teenage style, but as people who had transcended the trivialities of teenage style. Their music meant something, and when one of their acts "sold out," became part of mass taste, there was great bitterness. (Ibid.: 208)

Frith tied age and class together, noting that the sixth-formers were more middle class than the more mixed younger groups. He also discussed some important gender differences, which will be addressed in more detail below. It is important to notice the clear distinction between rock and pop audience tastes which came out of Frith's study and the critique of commercialism expressed by the rock audience. It might be thought that such a division is now rather dated – after all, Frith's study was undertaken more than thirty years ago. However, it can be argued that the structure of the division continues to exist even if the contents of rock have changed. For example, it may be that the audience for 'indie' is rather like the one that used to exist for progressive rock, although some evidence suggests that there is also an allegiance to pop music within such subcultures. However, this is not the pop music associated with the top 40 charts (Kruse 1993). There certainly seems to be evidence for an 'oppositional' stance in the studies of local music-making by Cohen (1991) and Finnegan (1989), as discussed in chapter 2.

One of the most important problems with the literature discussed in this section so far is the fact that it concentrated almost entirely on boys or men. This was first challenged by Angela McRobbie in an article co-authored with Jenny Garber, in which they asked four main questions. First, 'are girls really absent from the main post-war subcultures, or are they present but invisible?' Second, where girls were 'present and visible, were their roles the same, but more marginal, than boys; or were they different?' Third, 'whether marginal or different, is the position of girls specific to the subcultural option, or do their roles reflect the more general social-subordination of women in the central areas of mainstream culture – home, work, school, leisure?' And, fourth, 'if subcultural options are not readily available to girls, what are the different but complementary ways in which girls organize their cultural life? And are these, in their own terms, subcultural in form?' (1976: 211).

In response to the first question, McRobbie and Garber argued that, at least partly because of the male bias of previous investigations, this was very difficult to answer. The men who had studied subcultures had not looked at girls' possible participation in them, and so girls' invisibility tended to be a self-fulfilling prophecy. In pursuing the second and third questions, McRobbie and Garber looked in more detail at the parts that women have played in three subcultures. First, they examined the rocker, greaser or motor-bike subculture as described by Willis. Here, they saw women as being in a very subordinate position: they were passengers on the motor-bikes – they did not drive them. Second, they considered the mod girls of the early 1960s, whom they saw as prominent within the mod subculture. Third, they examined hippie culture, identifying two particular roles for women: the earth mother and the pre-Raphaelite fragile lady. Furthermore, they suggested that this period saw the development of two particular styles for women in music: the introspection associated with singer/songwriter such as Joni Mitchell; and the boozy blues singer, as exemplified by Janis Joplin. These roles have continued to be important for women in rock music, where it might be argued that Beth Orton and Martha Wainwright are examples of the former and Courtney Love of the second.

McRobbie and Garber argued that the places for women in the subcultures so far described were related to their other roles in life. However, they also suggested that girls tended to organize their cultural lives differently from the boys, forming a more home-based, romantic or 'teenybop' culture. McRobbie developed this point and others in a subsequent critique of the male-dominated nature of research on subcultures (McRobbie 1980). She argued that there are two main approaches that can be taken vis-à-vis previous male-dominated writing on subcultures. First, such accounts can be dismissed, or accepted as applicable only to boys, and attention placed on the different nature of girls' culture. This extended the point made in the earlier article written with Jenny Garber. Second, previous accounts, such as those by Willis and Hebdige, can be read 'against the grain' to see what they can offer for

the analysis of masculinity, both in the nature of the subcultures and the writing on
them.

In developing her points about the different nature of girls' culture, McRobbie
argues that the street is a potentially dangerous place for girls and that 'younger
girls tend to stay indoors or to congregate in youth clubs; those with literally
nowhere else to go but the street frequently become pregnant within a year and
disappear back into the home to be absorbed by childcare and domestic labour'
(1980: 47). In her view, the use of drink and drugs can induce the same sort of
perils: 'it is clear from my recent research, for example, that girls are reluctant to
drink precisely because of the sexual dangers of drunkenness' (ibid.).

McRobbie suggested that the working-class girls she studied tended to form a
teenybop culture based around romance. These girls spent more time in the home,
at least partly because of the dangerous nature of public places like the street. Frith
(1983) added three other aspects to this when he argued, first, that girls are more
subject to parental control and discipline than boys and, second, that girls are
often expected to carry out work in the home, in a way that boys are not, a point
that was illustrated graphically by McRobbie (1978) when she pointed out that girls
were expected to perform large amounts of work in the home for very little
financial recompense. Frith's third point was that girls spend more time at home
getting ready to go out than do boys.

To summarize, this subculture of girls, identified in the 1970s, consisted of the
following features:

1 The centrality of the home and often of the bedroom. Girls tended to get
   together with other girls and listen to records by their favourite artists in each
   other's bedrooms.
2 Girls formed a teenybop culture, where there was a romantic attachment to one
   star or group. There is a history of different stars and groups that have filled
   such a role.
3 When girls did go out, it was most likely to be to a youth club. Though, as
   Robins and Cohen (1978) pointed out (see box 7.2), such youth clubs, like the
   one they studied in north London, could be a site of conflict.
4 Dance was important to girls in ways that it was not for boys. McRobbie (1984,
   1993) has continued to stress the importance of dance to girls (see also chapter
   6).
5 For the girls in McRobbie's study, the relationship with a best friend was very
   important and was more valued than their relationships with boys.
6 The idea of romance was very important. Many of the girls, despite at times
   showing a 'realistic' appreciation of some of the aspects of marriage, placed
   great stress on the idea of romance and the romantic attachment to one boy.
   This can be related to the continued existence of a sexual double standard,
   where girls could easily become known as 'slags' if they went out with several
   boys.
7 McRobbie argued that the girls she studied stressed some dominant ideas of
   femininity in an exaggerated fashion. This may form part of a culture which
   opposed the perceived school ethic of responsibility, hard work and
   seriousness. The girls spent much time talking about boys and wanted to bend

the school rules about dress and make-up in as fashionable a direction as possible. McRobbie argued that this culture, while it may oppose official culture in some ways, reinforces the culture of romance and the idea of femininity which is a part of this. This parallels the argument advanced by Willis (1977) concerning the way in which the exaggeration of masculinity among working-class boys, in opposition to school norms, suited them for manual labour.

The way in which this teenybop culture of femininity connects with music in more detail is discussed in the article on rock and sexuality by Frith and McRobbie (1990), which was reviewed in chapter 3. Various writers have identified some problems with this idea of the teenybop culture of romance. First, McRobbie may

---

Box 7.2 Gender conflict at a junior disco

So the demand for a junior disco was more complex than it first appeared. In fact it concealed two, distinctly antagonistic demands: the girls wanted to start a local chapter of the Donny Osmond Fan Club; the boys wanted a cross between an indoor adventure playground and the North Bank terrace at Arsenal. So when the doors were opened, the organizers found they had *two* distinct clubs which just happened to coincide at the one time and place. The boys swarmed all over the place, swung from the lights, held races across tables and chairs, savaged the football machine and had impromptu bundle fights on the floors, all this interspersed with much North Bank football chanting. They came in scruffy and came out looking – as one mum put it – 'like they've been put in a spin dryer'.

But the girls . . . ! Dressed to the nines in their best party clothes, and the latest teen fashion. Here and there a hint of eye shadow and deft application of mum's Chanel No. 5.

At the first bars of 'Long Haired Lover' they 'took' the dance floor, and remained there for the rest of the evening as if hypnotized, impervious to the boys' bedlam; ten-year-old seductive swaying bottoms, rolling hips – a completely convincing imitation of teenage disco sex. Mostly, the boys ignored them, but from time to time, the chant would go up from the North Bank: 'Donny's a poofta, Donny's a poofta.'* To which the girls would inevitably chorus, 'Charlie's a wanker' (i.e. Charlie George, the footballer).

Osmond-baiting was in fact one of the most familiar weapons used by older brothers in their continuous bickering with their younger sisters. A fourteen-year-old boy told how 'we went by the Rainbow [Theatre] once and we started screaming out the window, "Osmonds are bent, all queers", and they were lobbing everything that come in sight. You see one of them, she's in a state crying over the railing going "you bastards" and the next minute she picked up a bottle and threw it at the bus.'

Source: Robins and Cohen 1978: 52. Reproduced by permission of Penguin Books Ltd. Copyright ©
David Robins and Philip Cohen, 1978

have underestimated the participation and seriousness of the commitment of some girls to subcultural groups. Smith (1978) argued that the 'delinquent' girls she studied were heavily involved in the fighting that took place between subcultural groups. However, she also noted that girls were less committed to the groups in terms of length of time of membership. Second, Cowie and Lees (1981) found that girls had a more realistic appraisal of the potential problems involved with marriage than McRobbie found in her group. Cowie and Lees found far more emphasis on having a good time before marriage. Third, Cowie and Lees suggested that McRobbie's work tended to isolate a discrete female youth subculture, over-integrating and separating it off from the relations between men and women which existed in society more widely. Relatedly, they argued that too much emphasis is placed on the resistance entailed in the culture of femininity. Fourth, McRobbie's work concentrated mainly on white working-class girls, and more evidence is needed about black and middle-class girls for comparison. Furthermore, it might be that some of this work is now rather dated. This point can be considered through an examination of McRobbie's more recent work.

In her earlier work, McRobbie drew attention to the role of magazines in the culture of romance, demonstrating the difference between contemporary magazines like *Just Seventeen* and *Jackie*. She argued that romance had drastically declined in importance and that pop and fashion had become central, leading to a greater emphasis on image and the pop star: 'It is pop rather than romance which now operates as a kind of conceptual umbrella giving a sense of identity to these productions' (1991: 168). In such girls' magazines:

> [T]here is an overwhelming interest in personal information. The magazines increasingly play the role of publicist for the various bands who fall into the teenybopper camp. In return their pages are filled with glossy pictures and they can claim to have a direct line to the stars. This makes for cheap and easy copy. Three pages can be covered in a flash with the help of a transatlantic telephone call, a tape-recorder and a selection of publicity shots often provided by the record company. (1991: 169)

In McRobbie's view, pop music had become more important to girls than it had been in the 1970s. However, girls did not become involved only with pop music of the teenybop type; McRobbie has also drawn attention to their participation in rave culture. She argues that such culture can be connected to drastic changes in femininity over recent years in Britain, suggesting that 'girls both black and white have been "unhinged" from their traditional gender position while the gender and class destiny of their male counterparts has remained more stable' (1993: 408). In an article on rave culture, McRobbie reiterates some of the points already made about the changing nature of girls' magazines, but develops her arguments about dance. She points to the continuity of rave culture with earlier cultures in that 'dance is where girls were always found in subcultures. It was their only entitlement.' However, 'in rave it becomes the motivating force for the entire subculture' (ibid.: 419). The centrality of dance allows a far more important place for girls within such contemporary subcultures. In continuity with earlier work, McRobbie still sees the danger of these occasions for girls, even if at this later date it is as a parent rather than as a sociological observer.

At this point it is necessary to consider some of the main points made against the kind of writing on youth subcultures that has been discussed in this section so far. A very useful overall critique has been produced by Gary Clarke (1990), who makes a number of particular criticisms of work emanating from the Birmingham Centre for Contemporary Cultural Studies, such as that by Willis, Hebdige and McRobbie:

1 Much of this writing is imprecise on the nature of the 'structural location' of subcultures and the nature of the problem-solving involved in the subculture.
2 There is relatively little explanation of where the different subcultural styles actually come from.
3 There is a rigidity in the analysis, as the subcultures which are identified tend to be 'essentialist and non-contradictory', meaning that there is little attention paid to variations of style and commitment within different subcultures.
4 There is a lack of attention to the way in which individuals move in and out of subcultures. Thus, Clarke argues that 'Cohen, for example, classifies Crombies and parkas as distinct subcultures, but surely the only "problem" which distinguished them from skins and mods respectively was the need to keep warm' (1990: 82–3).
5 There is a tendency for these analyses to start from subcultures and work backwards to class situations and contradictions. This leads to a kind of 'freezing' of distinct subcultures.
6 There is a dichotomy between subcultures and the rest of the young people.

Clarke identifies three important consequences which stem from these criticisms. First, there is the lack of consideration of 'subcultural flux and dynamic nature of styles'. Second, there is the separation of subcultures from the rest of society which is incorporated into a 'consensus' or dominant social relations. Third, there is the point that a 'vague concept of style' is elevated 'to the status of an objective category' (ibid.: 84). Hence, he argues that there is a need to study what all categories of youth are doing, rather than just subcultures: 'It is true that most youths do not enter into subcultures in the elite form described in the literature, but large numbers do draw on particular elements of subcultural style and create their own meanings and uses of them' (ibid.: 92).

Furthermore, Clarke suggests that there are important differences between the early 1980s and the situation described in the 1960s and '70s by the classic writers from Birmingham. Thus, there was the combination of styles involved in movements like punk and 2 Tone, and the argument that 'new wave' broke the 'distinction between "teenyboppers" and youth' based around the distinction between LPs and singles. Thus, Clarke's general conclusion is that 'what is required is an analysis of the activities of all youths to locate continuities and discontinuities in culture and social relations and to discover the meaning these activities have for the youths themselves' (ibid.: 95). Some recent literature has attempted to take up this challenge and it is reviewed in chapters 8 and 9.

So far, this section has focused on class and gender in relation to youth subcultures and music use. There is also a developing body of literature which considers the ethnic dimensions of subcultures and music. Some general aspects of this have been considered in chapter 4, and at this point I consider one of the more specific studies of this topic which appeared within the 'Birmingham tradition' of studies of subcultures.

Simon Jones's (1988) book *Black Culture, White Youth* falls into two relatively discrete parts. In the first, he presents an overview of the development of reggae and its connection to forms of culture in Britain and Jamaica. However, it is the second half of the book, which contains an ethnography of black and white youth in Birmingham, which is of more interest for present purposes. Jones discusses the formation of identity in a multi-ethnic area of the city of Birmingham in the English Midlands. There, many white boys had adopted a form of culture that would, in more conventional analyses, be seen as black. 'Black' language was used to express opposition to authority on the part of white children (Jones 1988: 149). Reggae was adopted by the young white people growing up in this environment, and Jones shows how different themes from Jamaican music were adapted by young white men and women. He maintains:

> Black music generally and Jamaican music in particular have functioned as transmitters of oppositional values and liberating pleasures to different generations of whites for nearly three decades. They have consistently supplied white youth with the raw material for their own distinctive forms of cultural expression. Through the political discourses of Rastafari, reggae has provided young whites with a collective language and symbolism of rebellion that has proved resonant to their own predicaments and to their experiences of distinct, but related, forms of oppression. (Ibid.: 231)

However, Jones recognizes the contradictions that existed around these modes of appropriation: 'Powerful feelings of attraction to black culture could easily coexist with perceptions of that culture as threatening and with resentment and fear of black people' (ibid.: 216). He suggests that new forms of 'racial' identity are being formed in parts of Birmingham and other inner-city metropolitan areas, and he ends his book with a quotation from one of the people he studied which captures this:

> [In Jo-Jo's] eloquent conclusion is captured both the reality of the new 'England' that is already emerging, as well as the hope that such an England might itself not be 'recognisable as the same nation it has been', or perhaps, one day, 'as a nation at all':

> > Its like, I love this place . . . there's no place like home. . . . Balsall Heath is the centre of the melting-pot, man, 'cos all I ever see when I go out is half-Arab, half-Pakistani, half-Jamaican, half-Scottish, half-Irish, I know 'cos I am [half-Scottish-Irish] . . . Who am I? . . . Tell me? Who do I belong to? They criticise me, the good old England. Alright then, where do I belong? . . . you know, I was brought up with blacks, Pakistanis, Africans, Asians, everything, you name it. . . . Who do I belong to? I'm just a broad person. The earth is mine. You know, 'we was not born in England, we was born not born in Jamaica' . . . we was born here man! It's our right! That's the way I see it. . . . That's the way I deal with it. (Ibid.: 239–40)

Jones's discussion resonates with the arguments influenced by postmodernism, outlined in chapter 3, which suggest that there has been a 'decentring' of our identities in contemporary culture. For example, it has been suggested by a number of writers that we no longer have the same attachments to place as earlier generations did because we now live in a society where, in some respects, it is easier to see what is going on on the other side of the world through television coverage than it is to observe events at the other end of the street. Such themes concerning the study of youth culture were addressed by Steve Redhead.

Redhead (1990) criticized the idea of a neat fit between different elements of youth subcultures and music, which are entailed in the concept of homology used by Willis and Hebdige. He also suggests that it is problematic to see music as the straightforward expression of a subcultural community. For example, it is often difficult to specify what the community is of which music is an expression. This echoes the critique developed by Frith of the realist theory of representation in lyrics which was examined in chapter 5. Furthermore, the subcultures and communities from which music is often held to issue, or which put it to use, do not simply exist, but have to be examined within language and communication. They are, in important senses, constructed within writing about them, or, in other terms, discursively constructed.

Redhead considers whether the clear fit between music and subcultural use ever existed in the way identified by the Birmingham writers, or whether there has been a change in the articulation of music with subcultures in the period since punk rock in the late 1970s. In some accounts, postmodernism in pop developed through the 1980s, leading to the break-up of the forms of association identified by earlier writers. However, Redhead argues that in many respects pop music has always possessed some of those features that were held to be characteristic of postmodernism. He maintains that pop music has broken barriers between high and popular culture at different points. In common with theories of postmodernism, he argues that the best way to understand contemporary pop music is not through some of the conventional 'oppositions' which have often been used to study it, such as those between 'rock and pop', 'authentic and synthetic', 'true and false' and 'high and low', but through the distinction and relationship between the local and the global. Thus, 'world musics' are affecting local music-making in a number of complex and diverse ways.

Redhead's work raises a number of issues about the complex contemporary interaction between forms of cultural production and consumption of contemporary pop music. However, he does not provide, or attempt to provide, a blueprint for how these relationships should actually be studied.

Subsequent work considered different dimensions of contemporary music and youth. Rietveld (1993, 1998) examines a number of different dimensions of rave culture in the north of England in the late 1980s (see also, more generally, chapter 6). The account given of this form of culture is not dissimilar from that of the Birmingham writers. For example, with respect to rave culture, Rietveld argues:

> Not only the lack of finance, but also the intensive dancing and the use of the drug Ecstasy determined the style. It makes a person sweat, so baggy cotton clothing is the most comfortable to wear. Make up is useless in those

circumstances, because it would simply 'wash' off in a short time. The euphoria caused by the excitement of the rave events, the excessive body movement and drug use all interfere with a person's sense of balance: high heels are therefore definitely 'out of order' from a raver's point of view.
(1993: 53)

This is very close to the homology argument used by Willis which continues therefore to be influential.

There continues to be a focus on subcultures in the literature on popular music. However, this could be a problem, as the focus may be both too general and too specific. The general attention paid to subcultures might obscure the very particular uses that are made of music by individuals and even specific parts of subcultures. This is a problem that is beginning to be addressed in the more sociological literature on fans. The specific focus on subcultures may also be unhelpful in the consideration of how people more widely use or consume music. Both of these themes are picked up in chapter 8.

Summary

This chapter has considered:

- some different theories of the relationship between texts and audiences with particular reference to pop music; this included consideration of the idea of the 'effects' of pop, and the ways in which lyrics are understood;
- some of the different indicators of the consumption of pop music, illuminating patterns of contemporary consumption;
- a number of different studies of the way in which music is a part of youth subcultures; the class, gender and racial patternings of subcultures were addressed.

8

Fans, Production and Consumption

This chapter continues the discussion of audiences begun in chapter 7. Developing the points made at the end of that chapter, it starts with a discussion of the ways in which fans have been defined and examines some of the ways in which audiences as fans have related to different pop stars and groups. This is followed by a review of the general account of fan processes offered by Grossberg (1992a). This leads into an examination of work that has focused on the productive activities of fans. A particular issue, which runs through this discussion, is the extent to which social processes associated with fan activities characterize the relationship to the media of other groups. Therefore, the next section in the chapter broadens out the discussion to examine the ways in which young people relate to media in general, and pop music in particular. This leads into a more general discussion of the relations between production and consumption in culture. Reference is made back to the studies of local music-making which were introduced in chapter 2.

Fans and pop

The idea of fandom and fan processes can be approached from two broad directions. First, there is a literature on fame and celebrity that starts at a more general level through the examination of processes like stardom and reputation often through history or across societies. Second, there is work that starts from the cultural, social and psychological aspects of fan practices themselves. I open this chapter by considering some of the most significant aspects of these literatures for the discussion of popular music.

Fame and celebrity have a long history. In his examination of fame (Braudy 1997) points to a number of the processes involved. For him: 'fame is made up of four elements: a person and an accomplishment, their immediate publicity, and what posterity has thought about them ever since' (1997: 15). He examines the particular processes of fame related to a range of historical people. In particular, it is possible to trace a process whereby fame or celebrity have moved from being 'ascribed' to kings and queens, who were celebrities as a result of a particular place in the social order, to being 'achieved', in that they are dependent on action on the part of the celebrity (Rojek 2001). Two interconnected issues that Braudy introduces and explores are of particular significance. There is, first, the nature of the person and, second, that of the place of the audience.

A paradox of fame for the famous person creates a dilemma of what it means for the self. Thus, the famous person wants to be both celebrated and private. The celebrity has 'the desire to be different but familiar, famous but the kid next door' (Braudy 1997: 585). Second, there is the role of the audience. This is a process that Braudy draws attention to throughout his discussion. However, it has become particularly significant as the mass media have developed in the modern age. It is worth quoting a telling part of his discussion that concerns the Hollywood star, Clark Gable:

> As Clark Gable remarked to David Niven on hearing of the mysterious death of the actress Thelma Todd:
>
> > We all have a contract with the public – in us they see themselves or what they would like us to be. . . . They love to put us on a pedestal and worship us. . . . But they've read the small print, and most of us haven't. . . . So, when we get knocked off by gangsters, like Thelma did, or get hooked on booze or dope or . . . just get sold . . . the public feels satisfied. Yeah, it's a good idea to read that small print . . .
>
> Gable's opinion of the implicit contract between public person and audience may be excessively gloomy. But his basic insight remains: modern fame is always compounded of the audience's aspirations and its despair, its need to admire and to find a scapegoat for that need. (Ibid.: 9).

This argument is developed through the course of Braudy's book. He argues that there is an important interaction between media and audience which promotes fame and celebrity: 'But to be talked about is to be part of a story, and to be part of a story is to be at the mercy of story tellers – the media and their audience' (ibid.: 592). The pace of development of modern media (including popular music) and consumer culture has had an important role in accelerating and shifting processes of celebrity and fandom (ibid.: 595–6), as 'The media are no longer only what their name implies: intermediaries between events and audiences. Now, a metamedia has come into being, committed to, imprisoned by, and frequently bored to death by its own preoccupation with fame' (ibid.: 600).

Many of these arguments are further conceptualized in the more recent work of Rojek, who discusses 'celebrity as the attribution of glamorous or notorious status to an individual within the public sphere' (2001: 10). He also points to the problem or paradox of the nature of the individual for the celebrity and he constantly draws on the distinction drawn by the influential social psychologist George Herbert Mead, 'who argued that the split between the I (the "veridical" self) and the Me (the self as seen by others) is the human condition, at least since ancient times, in Western society' (ibid.: 11). Thus, a continuing issue for the celebrity, especially compounded in an accelerating media culture, is the nature of the relationship between the I and the me, as, for the celebrity, the me is increasingly subject to extensive media attention. This media attention is critical to the nature of contemporary celebrity and 'celebrity must be understood as a *modern* phenomenon, a phenomenon of mass-circulation newspapers, TV, radio and film' (ibid.: 16).

As I have partially introduced in a preliminary way above, for Rojek, 'Celebrity status comes in three forms: *ascribed, achieved and attributed*' (ibid.: 17). 'Ascribed status concerns lineage' (ibid.), 'achieved celebrity derives from the perceived accomplishments of the individual in open competition' (ibid.: 18) and attributed celebrity 'is largely the result of the concentrated representation of an individual as noteworthy or exceptional by cultural intermediaries' (ibid.). Rojek introduces the idea of 'celetoid' 'as the term for any form of compressed, concentrated, attributed celebrity. I distinguish celetoids from celebrities because, generally, the latter enjoy a more durable career with the public' (ibid.: 20).

Approaches to the study of celebrity, of which Rojek thinks there are three main forms – subjectivism, structuralism and post-structuralism – differ in the extent to which they accord agency and power to the audience. More structuralist accounts tend to emphasize the power of producers to affect the audience (thus celebrities will be sold to an audience), whereas other accounts allow the audience greater power in determining who becomes a celebrity and how enduring they are. In fact, as this book suggests, it is in the interplay between producers and consumers that the most suggestive analysis will be found.

Rojek explores a number of different aspects of contemporary fandom, including how celebrity is potentially a substitute for religion and why and how some celebrities fall out of favour. Moreover, he explores the different ways in which celebrity is constructed in ways that examine the processes that have been introduced via the idea of the star text, as discussed in chapter 5 of this book. However, it is significant that, because it focuses on celebrity and stardom, this approach to celebrity tends to reproduce a view of the fan as deranged and as a potential serial killer. Those fans that are considered are often those who have committed a criminal act against a star. Despite the many innovations in the book, it is limited by a lack of detailed attention to what fans do.

Another example of this can be found in the very sophisticated analysis by Elliott (1999) of the celebrity status of John Lennon. Again, this work could have figured at several other points in this book, most particularly in a discussion of how stars are constructed and narrated and how pieces of music can be discussed in relation to specific lyrical and musical themes that relate to the nature of the star as author. Elliott's examination of Lennon's track 'Mother' from his album *Plastic Ono Band*, is an excellent example of sustained insight. However, despite the many strengths of this analysis, it is almost inevitable that, because of the murder of John Lennon by the fan Mark Chapman in 1980, a particular version of fandom is deployed by Elliott. His discussion, which starts from a particular interpretation of the process, which he derives from Thompson (1995), centres on an analysis of Chapman. In many respects this is very insightful, as Elliott deploys sociological and psychoanalytical perspectives to good effect. However, a danger in Elliott's approach, and the way in which he starts, makes fandom at least potentially a 'problem'.

Fandom, as sociologist John B. Thompson has argued, involves wrapping up a significant part of one's self-identity in an identification with a distant other (the celebrity) and negotiating the necessary shifts between the world of fandom and the practical contexts of everyday social life (Elliott 1999: 136). While Thompson and Elliott (ibid.: 139) both recognize that fandom can have positive aspects, the weight of Elliott's discussion, as with Rojek, tends to suggest otherwise. There has also been a clear tendency for journalistic writing on fans and pop music to suggest that there is something wrong with being a fan. Fans are seen as fanatics (the origin of the term) and deranged (Jenson 1992: 9). Jenson maintains that the literature on fans has produced two models of the 'pathological fan'. First, there is the 'obsessed loner . . . who (under the influence of the media) has entered into an intense fantasy relationship with a celebrity figure. These individuals achieve public notoriety by stalking or threatening or killing the celebrity' (ibid.: 11). Examples might include Mark Chapman. Second, there is the 'frenzied or hysterical member of a crowd' (ibid.), shouting at a rock star or misbehaving at a sports match. Jenson argues that these models of fans relate to general characterizations of the nature of society, similar to the descriptions of mass society or mass culture examined with respect to audiences in chapter 7. As Jenson puts it:

> The literature on fandom, celebrity and media influence tells us that: Fans suffer from psychological inadequacy, and are particularly vulnerable to media influence and crowd contagion. They seek contact with famous people in order to compensate for their own inadequate lives. Because modern life is alienated and atomized, fans develop loyalties to celebrities and sports teams to bask in reflected glory, and attend rock concerts to feel an illusory sense of community. (Ibid.: 18)

Jenson contests this idea that there is something wrong with the fan by contrasting the traits of the fan with those of the high culture or academic 'aficionado'. Many academics form attachments to their favourite writers or theorists, which are just as obsessive as those the fan may feel for the pop star. However, the division of the world into fans and non-fans allows those who define themselves as non-fans to suggest that others are abnormal and thus to constitute themselves as the normal or the safe. For Jenson:

> Defining fandom as a deviant activity allows (individually) a reassuring, self-aggrandizing stance to be adopted. It also supports the celebration of particular values – the rational over the emotional, the educated over the uneducated, the subdued over the passionate, the elite over the popular, the mainstream over the margin, the status quo over the alternative. (Ibid.: 24)

He argues that characterizing fans as 'other' in this way blocks analysis and proper understanding of how people actually interact with the media in contemporary society. This means that the exploration of fan activity might have wider benefits in explaining the activities of the audience. For example, Fiske argues 'that fandom is a heightened form of popular culture in industrial societies and that the fan is an "excessive reader" who differs from the "ordinary" one in degree rather than kind' (1992: 46).

Work that has addressed fan response to popular music in a sympathetic manner is potentially illuminating. It has often come from people writing about their own personal experience of being a fan. The first illustrative discussion of this sort to be considered here is by Sheryl Garratt (1984).

Garratt uses an examination of her fan feelings for the Bay City Rollers in the 1970s to ground some general suggestions about the ways young girls relate to male pop stars. She argues that an important part of this phenomenon has little to do with the pop stars themselves, since what is most important to the girls 'is desire for comradeship' (1984: 144). Thus, what she most remembers from her fan days are the episodes of travelling to the concerts and discussing the band with other fans. She recognizes that there must be some reason why certain idols are chosen over others and she answers this by suggesting that women are attracted by androgyny: 'men they dress like and identify with, as well as drool over' (ibid.). Moreover, there is a an element of opposition in the process, as what is also important is other people's dislike of the teeny group that is the object of the girls' affection. This leads to the defence of the group against attack, as the passage reproduced in chapter 7 (box 7.2) makes clear. Garratt suggests that some aspects of this form of fandom make the girls a 'lucrative market' – 'how exploitable is this urge to collect not only the records, but the posters, tour programmes, fan club specials, books, magazines, and any other product companies wish to foist on them' (ibid.: 147). However, she maintains that the fans may recognize that much of what is written about their idols is fiction, and they are not necessarily 'taken in' by it. In general, she argues that the process of being a fan of the Bay City Rollers had relatively little to do with the Rollers and a great deal to do with the girls themselves.

Sue Wise (1990) has further documented the personal nature of the relation to a star. Wise examines her feelings for Elvis Presley in the context of her own development as a feminist. She argues that Elvis has normally been written about, by men, as a kind of 'butch god', whose 'expression of rampant male sexuality' was central to his appeal (1990: 391). This connected to boys' sexual fantasies, as 'his supposed ability to "lay girls" with ease and without consequence' (ibid.: 392) led to the celebration of the early Elvis by male writers. 'Although he had a career of over twenty years, male writers dwell upon only the first couple of these, when they can identify with the super butch sexual hero that they themselves have promoted and lauded' (ibid.). It is after this initial period that Wise's connections with Elvis began. She details how she collected pictures and cuttings about Elvis and how she created her own space within a crowded household through her immersion in Elvis. He acted as a friend. Wise suggests that her feelings for him were not concerned with sex or romance but rather with those of 'warmth and affection' (ibid.: 395): Elvis was like a 'teddy bear'. One of the general implications of Wise's discussion is that people might have related to Elvis Presley in a variety of ways. She argues that adopting such a 'relativist' view would go some way to overturning the dominant male ways of examining the meaning and audience appropriation of Elvis Presley. It is possible to recognize the complexity of these different appropriations and meanings through even a quick inspection of a book like Dead Elvis by Greil Marcus (1992), which identifies the ways in which numerous different images of Elvis continue to circulate in a variety of media. Furthermore, Elvis's death meant that images of him could multiply, since there is no longer a 'real' Elvis who has 'control' over them in any shape or form.

An important analysis of the different meanings of Elvis can be found in Rodman (1996). Rodman thinks that approaches that see the continuing popularity (indeed, perhaps the increased popularity) of Elvis since his death in 1977 as manipulation by the culture industries, as explained by studies of fandom or as a site to deploy versions of postmodern theory do not explain in themselves the Elvis phenomenon, since they only explain parts of it and do not account for the specificity of Elvis (ibid.: 18). The argument deployed by Rodman is based in cultural studies and he approaches Elvis from three main directions. First, he examines the way in which Elvis connects to a range of important mythological features of the USA. Second, he explores the way in which Elvis is spatially grounded in ways that make him different from other stars. Third, he discusses a range of features of what he terms 'Elvis culture'. As with many studies that are considered in this book, it is only possible to focus on some aspects of Rodman's sophisticated and wide-ranging discussion.

In particular with respect to the idea of myth, which Rodman defines as 'a narrative (or perhaps a cluster of related ideas) that people collectively believe (or believe in) independently of its "truth" or "falsity". The difference here is subtle, but important, insofar as a myth can in fact be partially – or even entirely true' (ibid.: 30–1), he shows that:

> Thus, it is more than just Elvis's status as a cultural icon that makes him such a ubiquitous presence across the terrain of contemporary US culture; more crucial to Elvis's lingering presence are the range and diversity of cultural myths surrounding him – not only today, but throughout his lifetime – and the multiple, even contradictory ways in which he is articulated to those myths. (Ibid.: 41)

In addition to the different aspects of gender that Elvis connects to, as introduced above, Rodman explores the differing views and discourses on Elvis and race and class. Moreover, he points out the interconnections (and contradictions) between these different emphases. He then explores the meanings of Graceland and how Elvis can be theorized in relation to different ideas of culture.

Like Wise's account, Rodman offers a critique of the idea that women's relation to the pop star is based around sexuality and sexual desire for the star. Several accounts have examined this dimension of the relation between the audience and the performer in more detail. Cline argues that one of the dominant ways of characterizing women rock fans is to see them as 'groupies'. However, 'most girl rock fans never become groupies' in the sense of sleeping with rock stars (1992: 81). Furthermore, Cline suggests that the term 'groupie' is often used as 'a putdown for any woman involved in the industry' (ibid.: 83). Cline concludes with the warning that 'it's well to keep a sharp watch on how the word "groupie" is bandied about' (ibid.). This is a description that is still applied by some to certain sections of women fans. For example, a number of 'conventional wisdoms' about fans in general and women fans in particular can be found in the article reproduced in box 8.1, which is taken from a 'quality' British Sunday newspaper.

A different view of sexuality is expressed by Ehrenreich et al. (1992) in a discussion of Beatles fans in 1964 and 1965 in the United States. They argue that the phenomenon of Beatle hysteria was a form of sexual revolution. It was a protest

Box 8.1 'More sex please, we're groupies – and proud of it'

Eighteen-year-old Jenny ('please don't use my surname') differs from most other fanzine editors in that she is not a shabbily-dressed, socially inadequate nerd. Written under her *nom de plume*, Magenta Placenta, her fanzine, *Slapper*, avoids the usual moronic menu of the fan's-eye view of the music world, all pious moralism and verbatim interviews with inarticulate rock stars. *Slapper* is Britain's first 'sexzine'.

Jenny is a student from Slough. She is also a groupie – a rock fan who has sex with her idols. Most male rock musicians and fans despise groupies, and misogynist tales of their humiliations fill rock folklore. Practising groupies are therefore keen to remain anonymous. Jenny has decided it is time for Groupie Liberation, and *Slapper* is the means to that end.

'It started out as a way of getting attention. The first issue was taking the piss out of groupies, I suppose,' she recalls. But then it got serious. Her heroes are The Plaster Casters of Chicago (legendary Sixties groupies who immortalised impressions of their heroes' most vital parts in dental plaster) and Pamela Des Barres, author of the best-selling autobiography *I'm With The Band*.

'I suddenly realised that these were amazing women. They use their initiative, they get things free, they have the most amazing lifestyles. People who think it's degrading are just ignorant.

'Talent is just as good a criterion for choosing sexual partners as any other, isn't it? You have a fantastic time, room service, free booze and great no-strings sex with incredibly talented people. Excuse me, but isn't that what rock's meant to be about? Groupies aren't the pariahs of rock 'n' roll, they're its lifeblood.'

When she was 10, Jenny daydreamed not of princesses or ponies but of 'hanging out' with the American heavy metal band Motley Crüe. Unlike most of her teenage female peers, she has no time for the pretty boys of manufactured chart pop bands such as Take That or Bad Boys Inc. 'I'm not after plastic hunks, I'm after real men, real rock 'n' roll men. Huge, hulking, big, hairy-chested, scowling, tattooed, formidable monsters. Phwooar!'

Jenny is adamant that she has no moral case to answer. 'These are grown men, no one's forcing them into bed are they? They can always say no. Aids? Use a condom, what's the problem?'

Slapper's messianic celebration of the joys of sex with stars contrasts strangely with the wave of fundamentalist feminism that recently swept through non-mainstream rock. The Riot Grrrl movement – represented by bands such as Bikini Kill, Dickless and Huggy Bear – has reinvented the feminist wheel and has no time at all for what it sees as the piggish horrors of 'boy rock'.

But other groupies have greeted *Slapper* with enthusiasm. 'It's a real breath of fresh air,' claims Phillipa. 'I mean, the fact that I daren't let you print my real name says it all, really, doesn't it? I shag pop stars – something most men would love to do, if they'd admit it.'

Jill, a university graduate, is typical of the new generation of groupies for whom *Slapper* is written. Espousing a philosophy that struggles to contain strands of bootstrap Thatcherism, feminism and good old-fashioned rock hedonism, she was, she claims, driven towards groupiedom by the effeteness of her male peers.

'Public schoolboys! Ugh! The relief that comes when you realise there's other sorts of men in the world than public schoolboys. Working-class boys know how to handle women and where do you find the best looking working-class boys? In bands. Dead simple really.'

Steven Wells

Source: © The Observer, 12 September 1993

by young women, if unarticulated, against the confines of the culture in which they were brought up. In their argument, Beatlemania was of a greater intensity than earlier female fan movements such as those directed at Frank Sinatra or Elvis Presley. Beatlemania broke out in a middle-class, white culture where gender roles were heavily structured and sex something to be confined to marriage:

> Intercourse was out of the question, so young girls faced the still familiar problem of where to draw the line on a scale of lesser sexual acts, including (in descending order of niceness: kissing, necking, and petting, this last being divided into "light" (through clothes and/or above the waist) and "heavy" (with clothes undone and/or below the waist. (Ehrenreich et al 1992: 93)

The authors argue that the appeal of the Beatles was that the young girl would never marry one of them, or probably even meet one of them: 'Adulation of the male star was a way to express sexual yearnings that would normally be pressed into the service of popularity or simply repressed' (ibid.: 97). This mode of sexual repression was one of the factors that made Beatlemania possible. The specific outbreak of fan interaction with these pop stars was fed, in this argument, by the development of a teenage consumer culture in the United States. Rock 'n' roll was at the core of this consumer culture, which marketed a form of 'hysteria', which could be used subsequently to sell fan goods. The arrival of the Beatles in America was accompanied by press and radio reports of the Beatlemania that had already swept Britain. However, Ehrenreich et al. argue that this consumer culture was double-edged: on the one hand it manipulated the consumer, while on the other it structured a teenage culture that was opposed to the adult world and which ran counter to dominant modes of sexuality (ibid.: 98–100). 'For girls, fandom offered a way not only to sublimate romantic and sexual yearnings but to carve out subversive versions of heterosexuality' (ibid.: 100). For these authors, the Beatles expressed a form of playful sexuality, which was shocking in the context of the dominant American codes. This opened the way for the development of alternative roles for women during the 1960s and subsequently.

The discussions considered in this section so far have tended to focus on the relation of fans to one star or group. Some general themes can be derived from these discussions. First, the relationship between fan and performer generated a great deal of emotion. Second, the process had a lot to do with the young women themselves. Third, the fan relationship needs to be interpreted in a social context. An attempt to take these sorts of factor into account in a general account of rock music fandom can be found in the work of Grossberg (for example, 1992a).

Grossberg maintains that the relationship between texts and audiences is an active one and that it cannot be understood as being determined by the nature of either the text or the audience alone, since it is the correlation between them that is important. Grossberg conceptualizes this relationship as 'sensibility':

> A sensibility is a particular form of engagement or mode of operation. It identifies the specific sort of effects that the elements within a context can produce; it defines the possible relationships between texts and audiences located within its spaces. The sensibility of a particular cultural context (an 'apparatus') defines how specific texts and practices can be taken up and experienced, how they are able to effect the audience's place in the world, and what sorts of texts can be incorporated into the apparatus. Different apparatuses produce and foreground different sensibilities. (Ibid.: 54–5)

Grossberg distinguishes between two types of sensibility. The first he calls the 'sensibility of the consumer', which 'operates by producing structures of pleasure' (ibid.: 55). This is the most widespread way of interacting with forms of popular culture, which is based on entertainment and pleasure. The second is engaged in by fans. Grossberg argues:

> The fan's relation to cultural texts operates in the domain of affect or mood. Affect is perhaps the most difficult plane of our lives to define, not merely because it is even less necessarily tied to meaning and pleasure, but also because it is, in some sense, the most mundane aspect of everyday life. Affect is not the same as either emotions or desires. Affect is closely tied to what we often describe as the feeling of life. (Ibid.: 56)

In drawing these distinctions, Grossberg adopts similar arguments to those advanced by Barthes in his discussions of the 'grain of the voice' (see chapter 5), where a distinction is drawn between the pleasure of communication and the feelings produced by the nature of the voice. This is based on the distinction between the 'rational' kinds of pleasure, or *plaisir*, and the explosions of jouissance (see also Gilbert and Pearson 1999: 64–8).

Grossberg argues that affect is very important: it matters to us. Affect helps us to live in contemporary societies. One of the important ways this happens is through the structuring of our identities. The prime way in which this is done is by the construction of differences between ourselves and others. Grossberg says:

> [A]s individuals and as members of various social groups, there are many axes along which we register our difference from others – some are physical categories, some are sociological, some are ideological and some are affective. We are women, black, short, middle-class, educated, and so on. Any particular difference, including that marked out by being a rock fan, is always augmented and reshaped by other differences. At different points

and places in our lives, we reorder the hierarchical relations among these differences. (1992a: 58)

For the fan, the different dimensions of popular culture matter enormously. Their identities may be most importantly structured by their affect for a particular type of music or a certain performer. According to Grossberg, 'Rock works by offering the fan places where he or she can locate some sense of his or her own identity and power, where he or she can invest his or her self in specific ways' (ibid.: 61). This commitment, or excess of commitment, is then justified or explained by the fan. Thus, rock fans often explain their commitment to particular forms of music through the idea of authenticity.

Grossberg identifies three ways in which authenticity is constructed. First, there is the argument that valued music articulates 'private but common desires, feelings and experiences into a shared public language. The consumption of rock constructs or expresses a "community"' (ibid.: 62). Thus the fan may argue that a particular performer expresses his or her feelings and those of others, which bind them together to form a community of those who recognize the profundity of the performer's music. Second, there is the version of authenticity located 'in the construction of a rhythmic and sexual body' (ibid.: 63), which is often associated with black music. The third form of authenticity celebrates artificiality and 'is built on the explicit recognition of and acknowledgment that the difference that rock constructs (and which in turn is assigned back to rock) is always artificially constructed' (ibid.). Thus style and artifice are valued, but some forms of style and artifice are valued more than others by those who recognize the significance of the construction of style.

Grossberg offers an account of how certain forms of music matter to us – through the production of affect – and how we often try to legitimate such affects through arguments. It may be suggested that the distinctions he draws between pleasure and affect are not as clear-cut as he thinks and that the model of legitimation of fandom might not apply to all fans. However, in the notion of affect he has caught something of the way in which members of an audience respond to a valued performer, which might not always be expressible in words. Thus, young children, for example, seem to be particular fans of certain performers, which may have something to do with current fashion, but which also seems to depend in some part on the ability of the performer to affect, or move, them. Of course, this may apply to adults as well when we are moved by our favourite performers in ways that we find very hard to communicate in language, which never seems adequate to the task; as a result, we justify why someone matters in other terms, using the authenticity sorts of argument identified by Grossberg.

In this section a number of accounts of fans and their different forms of emotional commitment to different pop stars and groups have been considered. The concern has been to examine a variety of the accounts of this process that have been written. To borrow the title of a seminal collection of useful articles on fans, this section has considered the 'adoring audience' (Lewis 1992). This is a clear line of contemporary research on the fans and audiences, which has led to the approach of writers like Grossberg, who focus on affect (see, for example, Hills 2002; Sandvoss 2005). These writers have considered social, cultural and psychological aspects of fandom, drawing on a number of studies of audience processes that have developed in recent years (see further chapter 9). In general, the suggestion is that audiences are active in their relationship to texts. In no sense are they the rather passive creatures implied by the Frankfurt School approach discussed in the Introduction. Other writers have examined this notion of activity in a rather different direction, through consideration of the idea of the productivity of fans.

Pop fans as productive

Fiske (1992) has argued that fans are semiotically, enunciatively and textually productive. By semiotic productivity, he means that activity which is characteristic of popular culture as a whole. It 'consists of the making of meanings of social identity and of social experience from the semiotic resources of the cultural commodity' (1992: 37). When we make commodities mean something for us, we are engaging in semiotic productivity. When such meanings are communicated to others, enunciative productivity takes place. One of the most important vehicles for enunciation is talk. Thus, according to Fiske, the communication of the meanings that we have made for ourselves to others through talk is an important way in which fans can form communities. However, there are other ways, and Fiske draws attention to the wearing of colours by football fans as another example of enunciative productivity (see also Sandvoss 2003). To take another example from Fiske, the Madonna fans who 'claimed that dressing like Madonna made people take more notice of them as they walked down the street were not only constructing for themselves more empowered identities than those normally available to young adolescent girls but were putting those meanings into social circulation' (1992: 38).

The third category, textual productivity, entails the production of texts for circulation within the fan community itself. A lot of the research on fans has drawn attention to the ways in which they produce texts, such as stories, paintings, songs and videos about the characters from their favourite television shows (see, for example, Bacon-Smith 1992; Jenkins 1992). Fans write stories which place the characters from different television shows in a variety of contexts and which allow the development of aspects of the original text that fans felt attracted to. This may involve placing the characters in different universes, or bringing characters from different shows together in one story. Fans also paint pictures of different characters. These activities are discussed at fan conventions and the texts circulate in the fan community.

Music can be very important in fan texts and activities. Fans write and perform songs at gatherings about characters from television shows, not unlike the way that folk songs are sung in folk clubs. This can be seen in the name of this fan form: filk song. According to Jenkins, filk songs take their cue from commercial culture. They are about the characters from commercial television series, but 'Filk turns commercial culture back into folk culture, existing as a mediator between two musical traditions. Its raw materials come from commercial culture; its logic is from folk culture' (1992: 270). The name of the form came from a typographic mistake in a convention programme which misprinted folk music, the term then stuck. The nature of a filksing is described in some detail by Jenkins and an illustrative extract from his account can be found in box 8.2.

Box 8.2 Extract from a case study of a filksing at Philcon, 1989

A closer examination of one specific evening of filksinging (the Friday night session of Philcon 1989) will allow a more concrete discussion of how a conception of cultural inclusion and social integration has been structured into the filking process. Philcon, held in Philadelphia, is fairly typical of the larger East-Coast cons, featuring role-playing games as well as a mix of literary and media-oriented programing. This particular filksing was scheduled to begin at 11 p.m., actually got under way about half an hour later due to straggling and some confusion about room allocations, and continued until 4 a.m. At its peak, this filksing attracted forty participants, though more typically it maintained a steady population of twenty to thirty fans and sometimes dwindled down to six or seven.

The participants were arranged informally either on the floor or in a somewhat lopsided circle hastily formed by rearranging the chairs in the hotel conference room. The filksing preserves no formal separation between performance space and spectator space. Indeed, the organization of the filksing insures that the center of interest circulates fluidly throughout the floor. This filksing was organized according to the principle of 'Midwest chaos', which simply means that whoever wants to play a song starts whenever there is an empty space in the flow of music. Sometimes, there are gaps when no one is ready to perform; more often, several fans want to sing at once and some negotiation occurs. Eventually, anyone who wants to sing gets a chance (though fan humor abounds with jokes about the sufferings of those waiting for their more aggressive friends to yield the floor). Other filksings are organized as what fans called 'bardic circles', a practice which is also called 'pick, pass, or perform'. Here, each person in the room is, in turn, given a chance to perform a song, request a song to be performed, or simply to pass, insuring an even broader range of participation. At still other conventions, special songbooks are distributed to participants and songleaders conduct the sing as a 'choir practice'.

Music is provided in a haphazard fashion with whoever happens to know a particular tune participating and some songs performed a cappella. A number of participants brought guitars and several performed on the harp. Filk's reliance upon tunes 'borrowed' from other well-known or traditional songs ensures that both musicians and singers typically know much of the music that is performed. Filks, like traditional folk music, also often have repeated choruses, which can be easily mastered even by the most 'neo' of filkers and which, thus, encourage all of those in attendance to participate. Those who don't sing hum or whistle, tap their feet, drum on their chairs with pencils. Some particularly complex or moving songs are performed solo, but at this filksing at least, the tendency was for most of the songs to become collective performances, even if only during the chorus.

While some filkers have polished voices and a few earn money by performing professionally, the climate of the filksing is one of comfortable amateurishness. The singing stops periodically as new guitars are tuned or performers struggle to find the right key. Voices crack or wobble far off tune, and, particularly as the evening wears on, songs grind to a halt as the singer struggles to remember the words. Such snafus are accepted with good humor and vocal expressions of support and acceptance. 'If it ain't tuned now, it never will be', one woman jokes and another responds, 'Put it this way, it's close enough for filking.' A harpist, hesitant about the appropriateness of a traditional folk tune for the occasion, was reassured, 'That doesn't matter. Who do you think we steal our tunes from?'

While some filk songs evoke specialized knowledge either about fan culture or popular texts making them cryptic to the uninitiated, the verbal discourse surrounding the filksing provides new fans with the information needed to appreciate the performed material. 'Does anyone need that last verse explained?' one performer asked after a song particularly heavy with fan slang. The nonprofessionalism and the constant verbal reassurances create a highly supportive climate, encouraging contributions even from fans who have previously displayed little or no musical talent.

Some of the songs were original, written by the performer and 'tried out' for the first time at this session; others were older favorites, either part of the singer's personal repertoire or pulled from filk 'hymnal', remembered from other cons, or fondly associated with particular fan musicians. New songs are often greeted with vocal approval, passed around the room and hastily copied by those who wish to add them to their own notebooks. Several fans played half-finished songs, asking other filkers for advice on their completion.

Source: Jenkins 1992: 255–7

A further dimension of fan productivity involves the making of fan music videos by putting together favourite scenes from television shows against a musical background. Jenkins gives an example, explaining:

[One video] adopts 'Leaving the Straight Life Behind' as a playful commentary on the relationship between Starsky and Hutch. The television images (the two men playing chess in their bathrobes, Starsky grabbing his partner and embracing him, the cops dancing together at a disco, even a shot of the two men leaping into bed together) gain new meaning from their insertion within this new context . . . and from their connection to Jimmy Buffet's video. (Ibid.: 225)

The music used in these videos tends to be of the 'soft rock' variety and, according to Jenkins, the videos are strongly narrative, rejecting the postmodernist strategies identified by Kaplan (1987) (see chapter 5). A key way in which the music is used in such videos can be illustrated by the motives imputed to the characters that are the objects of fan affection: 'Fan viewers are often totally disinterested in the identity of the original singer(s) but are prepared to see the musical performance as an expression of the thoughts, feelings, desires and fantasies of the fictional character(s)' (Jenkins 1992: 235).

The literature considered so far has focused directly on fans (however these are defined), but a similar sort of general perspective has been elaborated by writers who have been associated with the sort of writing on youth subculture and music discussed in the previous chapter. This literature moves away from the discussion of fans to look at young people and is the subject of the next section.

Young people and cultural productivity

Willis et al. (1990) argue that as human beings we are symbolically creative, saying that 'we argue for symbolic creativity as an integral ("ordinary") part of the human condition, not as the inanimate peaks (popular or remote) rising above the mists' (Willis et al. 1990: 6). Being symbolically creative involves work of a symbolic kind, which is 'the application of human capacities to and through, on and with symbolic resources and raw materials (collections of signs and symbols – for instance, the language as we inherit it as well as texts, songs, films, images and artefacts of all kinds) to produce meanings' (ibid. 1990: 10). The general structure of this argument can be represented as in figure 8.1. The basic elements of symbolic work include language and the active body, and symbolic creativity involves the 'production of new . . . meanings intrinsically attached to feelings, to energy, to excitement and psychic movement' (ibid.: 11). A number of different products are produced through symbolic work and symbolic creativity. These include our own individual identities, the location of those identities in a wider social context and the notion that we have the capacity to change things in some respect. Thus, in a general sense, Willis argues that:

> In a way the spectacular sub-cultures of the 1950s and '60s prefigured some of the general shifts we are claiming for the contemporary situation. They defined themselves very early and gained their very spectacle from seeking visible identities and styles outside or against work and working respectabilities. Now the idea of a spectacular sub-culture is strictly impossible because all style and taste cultures, to some degree or another, express something of a general trend to find and make identity outside the realm of work. (Ibid.: 16)

Willis's book explores the symbolic creativity of young people across a number of different dimensions, including television, VCR and micro-computer use, relationships to film, advertising, and magazines and engagements with fashion, pub culture, street culture, sport and romance. One of the most important

human capacities	+	symbolic resources raw materials	=	meanings

Figure 8.1 Symbolic productivity

Source: constructed from Willis 1990

arguments of his chapter on pop music is that consumption is creative and productive of meaning. He identifies five different aspects of 'creative consumption' of music:

1   Listening and buying
2   Home taping
3   Interpreting sounds
4   Dance
5   Interpreting songs and symbols

With respect to the first point, it is argued that young people show considerable discrimination in what they buy; they are not simply fed the products of the music industry. This might involve the purchase of old records and the development of extensive knowledge about the history of particular forms of music. Second, it is shown that home taping is extensively used among young people as a means of sharing favourite music. With the widespread availability of twin cassette decks and the high cost of new tapes and albums, this is an extensive practice, which is now being supplanted by similar processes involving CD copying and file-sharing (Laughey 2006; see also Garofalo 1992b).

Third, the argument is made, which should by now be fairly familiar, that it is often the sound itself that is central to the pleasure derived from the music, rather than the actual words. Thus, music can be used, and made, to express feelings, as well as to structure everyday life. An example given of the latter is the use of the personal stereo: 'the ultimate artefact in providing a personal soundscape that can be carried around, quite literally, inside the head, while travelling, walking, waiting or negotiating public spaces' (Willis 1990: 64–5). There is further discussion of this topic in chapter 9.

Dance is the fourth dimension to creative consumption (see also chapter 6). The argument is made that 'Whereas dancing used to be seen as something of a feminine activity by some working-class young men, it has become more acceptable for males to express themselves through body movement. Some of the ties between dance forms and codes of masculinity/femininity have been loosened' (ibid.: 68). Finally, it is suggested that there is often a strong identification with the 'lyrical themes, imagery and symbolism of popular music' (ibid.). These forms of creative consumption can often develop into production. Four different aspects of the development of consumption into production are considered by Willis:

1   sound systems;
2   black music and oral poetry;
3   DIY recording and mixing;
4   music-making and performance.

First, there is the sound system, which, as was noted in chapter 4, has been particularly prominent in black musical traditions. This form has also become prominent in rave culture (McRobbie 1993: 421). The sound system was an institution 'where the activities of consumption merge into and become intertwined with more conventional forms of production' (Willis 1990: 72). Furthermore:

Besides being one of the principal focal points of musical activity within the black community, the sound system also involves a number of primary private production processes, which embrace electronics, sound technology and carpentry. These informal processes are motivated by specifically musical enthusiasms and operate to their own cultural agenda. They often involve the use of independently gained technical knowledge and skills, picked up from electronics magazines. (Ibid.)

Second, connected to the sound system is the form of production engaged in by the DJ, who in black tradition may draw upon forms of oral poetry. Again, the DJ is important within rave culture. Third, there is the increased importance of DIY recording. Especially with the increased availability of cheaper forms of recording equipment and computers (see chapter 2), there have been greater opportunities for the involvement of young people in music-making. 'In this process the hardware and software of consumption have become the instruments and raw materials of a kind of cultural production' (ibid.: 77). Finally, there is the way in which young people develop their interests in music to become involved in the production of music themselves, especially through performance.

This discussion raises a number of issues concerning the nature and relation of production and consumption and how they can be analytically separated. These issues have relevance beyond the cultural activities of young people. The final section of this chapter explores these issues in detail and outlines some possible directions for future analysis. It emphasizes the complexity of contemporary musical production and consumption and the importance of social context.

Production, consumption and music-making

Dave Laing has argued:

> It is a commonplace that production and consumption are interdependent. Without production of material or cultural goods, there can be no consumption. Without a demand for, and consumption of, the use-values embodied in these goods, there is no impetus for continuing production. In certain areas of popular culture, the relation between production and consumption has another aspect. There, the producers of today are frequently the consumers of yesterday. Through the experience of consuming music as a listener, many individuals are drawn into producing music of their own. (1990: 186)

Research has attempted to examine the relationships between production and consumption in more detail. For example, Warde (1992) has argued that discussions of production and consumption are often rather confused, especially between the levels of systems of production and consumption and those of individual production and consumption. Warde argues that it may be possible to show that there are linkages between mass production and the mass consumption of goods in a factory system. For example, the production of a large number of cars entails the consumption of an equally large number if the firms producing the cars are to survive. However, it cannot be argued that the nature of individual consumption is determined by the fact that a good is mass-produced. For example, as shown above, mass-produced Elvis Presley albums or Bay City Rollers pictures and magazines can be consumed in very different ways by particular individuals. This is not to say that there may not be patterns in consumption, but that these are somewhat looser than some theorists have argued. One of the mistakes made by Adorno was to suggest this kind of continuity between the production and consumption of music (see the Introduction).

In an attempt to integrate different current accounts of consumption, Warde develops a conceptual framework which begins with an identification of three different values which guide consumption. These are 'exchange-values, use-values and identity values' (1992: 17). In purchasing a CD, the consumer might be looking to its subsequent value when exchanged. He or she may see it as an investment that may offer a profit at some point in the future. A limited-edition record which is then kept in a plastic bag and never played might be said to have been purchased for its exchange value. A CD might be purchased because of the use to which it may be put; it might relax the consumer, make them happy and so on. Finally, it might be consumed in relation to identity – an idea we have already come across in this chapter – so that the purchase of a particular CD might identify the consumer as a rock fan or someone who can understand and appreciate avant-garde jazz.

Warde further suggests that there are a number of different cycles of production and consumption that occur before a good is finally consumed. He gives the example of food: 'What we eat off our plates typically passes through a number of production processes (the growing, wholesaling, processing, retailing and domestic preparation) and several exchange transactions (some of which are often called consumption) before final enjoyment as a meal' (ibid.: 18). The complex number of processes that could be involved in the overall production and consumption of a record for example or in the production and consumption of a musical performance can immediately be seen. Thus, the work of the sort of 'copy' group described by Bennett (see chapter 2) involves the consumption of an already produced record by a group as the basis on which they produce their own version of the song. This is then consumed by the audience at the gig at which it was played.

All these separable production and consumption episodes will be carried out in different social contexts. Warde identifies four sorts of social relations which govern different episodes of production and consumption: 'market, state, domestic and communal' (ibid.: 19). He exemplifies the differences between these social relations through the example of food, though it is possible to apply the same categories to pop music. Thus, I could pay to see the performance of a pop group, I could play a song myself at home (provided I had the skill), the state may provide performances (as in former communist countries, or a military band playing at a ceremonial occasion) or I can form a band with friends so that we can make music together.

Warde argues that distinct production and consumption 'episodes' should be examined, distinguishing at least four types of phase within an episode: 'the process of production or provision; the conditions of access; the manner of delivery; and the environment or experience of enjoyment' (1992: 20). In the

1   Values which guide consumption:
■   exchange
■   use
■   identity

2   Social relations which govern production and consumption:
■   market
■   state
■   domestic
■   communal

3   Phases in episodes of production/consumption
■   process of provision
■   conditions of access
■   manner of delivery
■   environment or experience of enjoyment

Figure 8.2 Framework for the analysis of production/consumption
Source: adapted from Warde 1992

examination of a musical performance, it would be possible to consider the phases of the episode: was it by a star band contracted to a transnational company or by a copy group? Was the cost of a ticket over £20 or was the group playing for a small fee at a wedding (MacLeod 1993)? Did the band look as if they were drunk, drugged or having an 'off' night, or were they enthusiastic and communicative? Was the experience a pleasant one, or did someone fall on top of, or spill beer over, you?

All these different aspects of the production/consumption episode can be examined separately. Thus, while we might expect a concert costing £50 per ticket to be enjoyable (otherwise it is difficult to understand why we would purchase the ticket), there are no guarantees that this will be the case. Furthermore, we may be pleasantly surprised when we come across a good band playing for nothing in a pub. As Warde maintains 'There is no simple fit between mode of provision and manner of delivery' (1992: 21). This account, which is summarized in figure 8.2, emphasizes the complexity of the social relationships which are involved in production and consumption.

Other accounts of the relationship between production and consumption have emphasized the changing nature of the relationships between producers and consumers. Abercrombie argues that the power of producers has declined relative to that of consumers. He maintains that in some respects this is a loss of authority 'as producer in determining the form and content of production and consumption; it is no longer possible to say with Henry Ford that consumers can have any colour of car so long as it is black' (1991: 173). Furthermore, there has been a decline in 'producer culture', which entails the organization of producers 'around the importance of being a producer making something worthwhile' (ibid.: 175). Such producer cultures have been undermined in the culture industries as the focus has moved away from the product itself to the means of selling it. Furthermore, on this argument there has been 'a shift in authority and power in companies from those directly concerned with production to those who are essentially concerned with other aspects of the company' (ibid.: 177). Thus, in the music industry there has been an increased emphasis on those concerned with the production of image, rather than music per se and by the staff who control the finance, so that it is sometimes contended that these are the people who make the important decisions (see chapters 1 and 2).

This argument suggests that consumers are becoming increasingly powerful. Furthermore, as they become more 'enterprising', they become more involved in 'enthusiasms' (see chapter 9). By enthusiasm, Abercrombie means 'the dedication of leisure time to the intense involvement in some activity, whether it is gardening or fishing, swimming or collecting antiques, model building or body building' (ibid.: 179). Within these enthusiasms, there may be a variety of relationships between production and consumption. One way of considering the complexity of these social relations is to return to the discussions of local music-making summarized earlier in chapter 2.

In *The Hidden Musicians* Finnegan (1989) explores the often drawn distinction between professional and amateur musicians. In common-sense terms, it might be thought that the professional is more of a producer and the amateur more a consumer. This issue is important to Finnegan, as her book is concerned with everyday, local music-making (in Milton Keynes). However, she argues that the distinction between amateur and professional is in practice very difficult to draw:

> The term 'professional' . . . at first appears unambiguous. A 'professional' musician earns his or her living by working full time in some musical role, in contrast to the 'amateur', who does it 'for love' and whose source of livelihood lies elsewhere. But complications arise as soon as one tries to apply this to actual cases on the ground. Some lie in ambiguities in the concept of 'earning one's living', others in differing interpretations about what is meant by working in 'music', and others again – perhaps the most powerful of all – in the emotive overtones of the term 'professional' as used by the participants themselves. (1989: 13)

Therefore, Finnegan argues that the relationship between amateur and professional can best be seen as a continuum, and most of the musicians playing in Milton Keynes can be seen as working at some points in the middle of the continuum. In many respects, the key term used to describe the musicians studied by Finnegan is 'performer'. This catches some important distinctions that can be drawn in the areas of production and consumption and fandom. Thus, Finnegan argues:

> [My research] leads me further to query once again not only the still fashionable view that human beings somehow gain their central social reality from their economic involvement in society (usually based on the 'man as paid worker' model) but even the richer and in my opinion, more realistic 'man as symbolise' approach (current in some social science, specially anthropology) with its overtones of an ideational and ultimately linguistically modelled view of humanity. It is surely equally valid to picture human beings essentially as practitioners and performers: artistic and moral enactors rather than as symbolic perceivers or paid workers. (Ibid.: 341)

It is important to take all these different dimensions into account in considering the activities of fans and the complex sets of relationships between producers and consumers, production and consumption. In accord with the suggestions of Finnegan, these relations should be seen as continuuums. Thus, it is possible to argue that there is a continuum of creativity in musical production. Copying a CD for a friend involves the production of a text in a domestic environment, structured by use value (I hope that my friend will enjoy it) and identity value (it may cement our common identity as jazz fans), but is relatively low in creativity. By contrast, the recording of a piece of music is far more complex and may involve much greater levels of creativity. It may stem from all the forms of value identified by Warde, and aspects (or episodes) of the process are governed by different social relations.

Furthermore, it is possible to trace a process by which someone who begins as a relatively passive consumer of pop music becomes a communal producer. As the music affects them, they become more interested in particular types of music. They may then define themselves (or be defined by others) as a fan, and begin to use arguments about authenticity to defend their tastes in arguments concerning music with other people. They may be enthusiastic enough to form their own band with other like-minded people. This band might rehearse in facilities that are partly sponsored by the local state as part of an attempt to use cultural production to stimulate the local economy (Frith 1993; Street 1993). This might lead to the production of new records, which are then sold locally or on the international market, moving into the commercial sector.

So far, this book has analytically bracketed dimensions of production, textual structure and audience consumption and has shown that such bracketing should not blind the student or the researcher to the complexity of the social relations involved in production and consumption. Likewise, it should be reiterated that general theories which suggest simple relations between the dimensions of production, textual structure and consumption are likely to prove increasingly unhelpful in a future of increased cultural complexity and fragmentation. These issues will be considered further in the next chapter in the context of the development of studies of audience consumption and productivity.

Summary

This chapter has considered:

- ideas of fame and celebrity;
- discussions of fans which argue that they should not be seen in a pejorative light;
- some accounts of fan relationships to different pop stars and groups;
- the general theory of fandom produced by Grossberg;
- accounts and theories of the productive nature of fans;
- studies of the productive consumption of pop music by young people;
- work that has attempted to reformulate the understanding of the relations between production and consumption.

9

Beyond Subcultures and Fans: New Audiences, Scenes and Everyday Life

The last two chapters have examined a number of aspects of the audience processes for popular music. This chapter takes this narrative forward in a number of ways. First, it considers discussions that suggest that, because of the many problems with the theorization of and empirical research on youth subcultures and popular music, a new terminology should be deployed to characterize these links and this field. Second, building on this discussion, some recent studies of young people and popular music are examined to illustrate the way that contemporary research has continued to debate and, indeed, deploy the concept of subculture. Third, specific attention will be paid to the concept of scene that has been used to examine the particular role of music in giving meaning to local (and increasingly translocal) production and consumption of music. Fourth, returning to themes concerning the nature of wider audience processes beyond young people, some recent studies that examine the thesis that middle-class people have become more omnivorous in their musical tastes will be discussed. In the fifth section of the chapter, it will be suggested that another potentially fruitful way of considering audiences and popular music is to consider in some depth how music is a significant part of the processes of everyday life.

Post-subcultures: conceptual innovation

In addressing a number of the issues that have arisen in the theorization and empirical use of the concepts of subculture and the audience that were considered in chapters 7 and 8, a number of writers have argued that the concept of subculture should no longer be used and that the 'space' that it fills in the examination of the culture of young people should be replaced by another concept (see also Hesmondhalgh 2005). The reasons given by these writers vary in their emphases, but key points are that social and cultural life has fragmented so that it is no longer possible to find the clearly isolatable forms of subculture and that, as discussed by writers such as Willis et al. (1990), the spectacular processes deployed by youth subcultures have become more generalized and thus it is no longer possible to locate and identify clear subcultural groupings. Both of these aspects are discussed by Chaney, who suggests that 'The idea of subculture is redundant because the type of investment that the notion of subculture labelled is becoming more general, and therefore the varieties of modes of symbolization and involvement are more common in everyday life' (2004: 37). A clear line of thinking in this respect is represented by the work of Andy Bennett (e.g. 1999), who argues that the idea of subculture is 'deeply problematic in that it imposes rigid lines of division over forms of sociation which may, in effect, be rather more fleeting, and in many cases more arbitrary than the concept of subculture, with its connotations of coherence and solidarity, allows for' (1999: 603).

This line of argument, which emphasiszes fragmentation, fluidity and the increasing lack of distinctiveness of what were often seen as separable subcultural groups, has sometimes been supplemented by another form of argument. This maintains that a key problem of the Birmingham approach to subcultures (see chapter 7) was that it became increasingly concerned with the decoding of the meaning of subcultures as texts and less concerned with the voices and views of those who make them up (see, for example, Widdicombe and Wooffitt 1995; Muggleton 2000). These general concerns have led to a range of arguments and concepts that are able, it is argued, potentially to supersede that of subculture.

In this debate there are three broad positions:

1   That which argues that the concept of subculture is redundant and that it needs to be replaced.
2   That which wishes to retain some aspects of the subculture concept but to consider the way in which subcultures have in some sense been 'postmodernized'.
3   That which suggests that the term 'subculture' can be deployed but only in reference to groups that retain some of the key features of subcultures as examined by writers such as those associated with the Birmingham Centre for Contemporary Cultural Studies.

While these positions often shade into each other, it is possible to see how studies discussed in the subsequent parts of this chapter represent them.

The idea that the concept of subculture needs to be replaced has led to the formulation and deployment of several related concepts (see Hodkinson 2002: 19–24; Bennett and Kahn-Harris 2004: 11–14). The key ideas to have been suggested and deployed here are tribe and neo-tribe, lifestyle (Miles 2000) and scene. The idea of tribe is, in the main, derived from the work of the French sociologist Michel Maffesoli (1996). This emphasizes that in an increasingly consumerist society, groupings are related through consumerist practices. Groups may therefore exist that are more fluid, in the sense that their commitment may shift depending on consumer choices and consumer change. This concept is related to that of lifestyle, which has become popularized into everyday life as depicting in some sense the way in which a series of choices become crystallized into a form of life that has some consistency and which can be related to some social basis (even if it is only those who share a particular postcode). As Hodkinson

MODERN	POSTMODERN
Group identity	Fragmented identity
Stylistic homogeneity	Stylistic heterogeneity
Strong boundary maintenance	Boundary maintenance weak
Subcultural provides main identity	Multiple stylistic identities
High degree of commitment	Low degree of commitment
Membership perceived as permanent	Transient attachment expressed
Low rates of subcultural mobility	High rates of subcultural mobility
Stress on belief and values	Fascination with style and image
Political gesture of resistance	Apolitical sentiments
Anti-media sentiments	Positive attitude towards media
Self-perception as authentic	Celebration of the inauthentic

Figure 9.1 Ideal-typical traits of modern and postmodern subculturalists
Source: Muggleton 2000: 52

(2002) points out, another related term – *Bunde* – was introduced into this conceptual space by Hetherington (1992), which follows many of these emphases, while suggesting that groups may have more solidity and substance. In many ways these concepts recognize the significance of the social changes concerning consumerism, fluidity of commitment and the fragmentation of society into numerous niches that are the hallmarks of the ideas that have been grouped under the heading of postmodernist thinking. A slightly different approach has picked up on the idea of scene as used in everyday speech to examine the production and consumption of music (initially) in a specific locality. This will be further considered in a later section of this chapter.

The second broad trend in contemporary subcultural thinking also picks up on some key aspects of this position, but seeks to retain rather more of the subculture heritage than the writing associated with the first position. Thus, in arguing for a post-subcultural or postmodern subcultural position, Muggleton examines the extent to which 'subculturalists may be expected to display a number of "postmodern" characteristics, some of which have an affinity with certain countercultural sensibilities' (2000: 52). The broad set of 'ideal-typical traits' identified by Muggleton are represented in figure 9.1. In the rest of his book (see next section), Muggleton discusses the extent to which the (post-)subculturalists whom he examines exhibit the features that he has described in these postmodernist ways. In so doing, he perhaps retains more ways of thinking about subcultures than he might have expected and might be represented by the first strand of thinking discussed above.

The third strand of thinking continues to deploy the idea of subculture, while restricting its use to particular subcultures that do (relatively) deploy the forms of coherence that approximate those discussed in the earlier Birmingham literature. Hodkinson's (2002) examination of Goth is a very good example of this.

While, therefore, there are different positions advanced here and, as Muggleton and Weinzierl (2003: 6) point out, 'some of this confusion can . . . be alleviated if we recognize that different concepts can be used to abstract different aspects of social reality', it is important to examine in more detail the findings of different studies which, in various ways, have sought to advance the debate on subculture and music.

Subcultures and music: some key studies

In many ways, the study of subcultures and music was revitalized by the development of dance and rave culture. Key aspects of this have already been examined in chapter 6, where the Bourdieu-influenced work of Thornton (1995) was considered. However, Thornton's book was also important in prompting new thought and work on youth subcultures and music. She makes a number of points, only some key aspects of which will, for the present discussion, be picked up here. First, she points out that the definition of and approach represented by the Birmingham Centre is empirically unworkable. This is important, as it suggests the need for more empirical work on youth and music. As has been suggested above, as it developed, the Birmingham approach was more concerned with the reading of subcultures as texts than with in-depth investigation of the views of the participants themselves. However, it is significant that these views are themselves often relatively neglected in Thornton's study, and it is only in more recent work (e.g. Muggleton 2000, Hodkinson 2002) that they have been represented in more detail.

Second, Thornton points to the role of key divisions within the working of the subculture, rather than focusing on the relationship between the subculture and the dominant culture, or on the youth subculture and the 'parent' culture. This means that she can examine the way in which cultural hierarchies or oppositions work within the subcultural group. These distinctions are complex, but revolve around issues such as the authentic versus the phoney, the hip versus the mainstream and the underground versus the mass media.

Third, and relatedly, Thornton points out that the club culture worked around the possession and deployment of what (following Bourdieu) she terms 'subcultural capital', which is represented through the idea of being 'hip' – that is, culturally aware and on the cutting edge of developments and knowledge that are prized within the subculture – which may be valueless outside it. Different forms of media are critical to the circulation of subcultural capital. These might be flyers for particular events or the fanzines produced by those who are particularly committed to the subculture. In this way, Thornton developed the idea that media are critical to subcultures. Thus, in a world where various forms of media have become increasingly important (Abercrombie and Longhurst 1998), there are still forms of subculture, but they have become increasingly mediatized.

Thornton examined the relationships within the broad area of dance culture and pointed to its media-centred nature, but also to its internal divisions. Different aspects of these developments have been picked up by further studies.

Muggleton (2000) has sought to evaluate the extent to which subcultural adherents had been affected by the development of forms of postmodernist culture, in accordance with the points made in the first section of this chapter. Given the focus of this book on popular music, rather than on subculture per se, the details of Muggleton's findings with respect to this overall thesis can be summarized fairly briefly, in the sense that he finds that the subculturalists had not moved completely to the postmodernized position. As he says:

> We can, I feel, grant a qualified acknowledgement of a postmodern sensibility. Subculturalists are postmodern in that they demonstrate a fragmented, heterogeneous and individualistic stylistic identification. This is a liminal sensibility that manifests itself as an expression of freedom from structure, control and restraint, ensuring that stasis is rejected in favour of movement and fluidity. Yet there is no evidence here of some of the more excessive postmodern claims. Informants did not rapidly discard a whole series of discrete styles. Nor did they regard themselves as an ironic parody, celebrating their own lack of authenticity and the superficiality of an image saturated culture. (2000: 158)

In many ways, Muggleton draws attention to the way in which the subculturalists whom he studied wished to retain (and promote) key aspects of their individuality, partly through music, while also expressing some aspects of commitment to belonging to a recognizable group. However, although it runs through his book in a number of ways, the actual detailed discussion of music in the subcultures is relatively slight and, when it is discussed, some significant themes arise. Thus, when asked about their tastes in music, even those who are committed to a subculture tend to express a preference for a range of different forms of music (see for example, ibid.: 74, 112–13). If this is the case, as Muggleton points out, it raises, at the least, some doubts as to how important the idea of subculture is for the understanding of audience processes for music. This is further discussed below.

In another detailed piece of research, Hodkinson (2002) has examined the Goth subculture in late 1990s Britain. This extended discussion argues for the continuing value of the concept of subculture as applied to those groups that exhibit the relative coherence of features such as those combined in Goth. Thus, although there is significant internal variation in, for example, modes of dress within the subculture (as clearly shown by Hodkinson), there are also clear commonalities and patterns. In reworking the idea of subculture, Hodkinson shows how it can be retained 'to capture the relatively substantive, clearly bounded form taken by certain elective cultural groupings' (2002: 9). He considers the criteria of 'identity, commitment, consistent distinctiveness and autonomy' and argues that 'each of them should be regarded as a contributory feature which, taken cumulatively with the others, increases the appropriateness of the term subculture' (ibid.: 29). Music is a part of this subculture and Hodkinson discusses its importance in a number of places. It remains an important aspect of the subcultural package.

Andy Bennett's (2000) work represents a third study that has considered in some detail a number of groupings and with more focus on music itself. After developing the sort of critique of the Birmingham approach to subculture considered in the opening section of this chapter, Bennett argues that it is important to examine the way in which the experience of popular music is largely local. This can be seen as connected to themes that were considered at the end of chapters 1 and 8 of this book. The local is a space where different forms of culture are brought together and new syntheses created that involve creativity on the ground. This does not mean that the culture (or subculture) is locally bounded, but that it is lived out in localities that are connected to other places and translocal processes (as is also discussed at some length by Hodkinson 2002), which is facilitated by the increasing availability of computers and the Internet.

Bennett includes four case studies in his book that show the significance of the processing of different influences in particular contexts: dance music; Bhangra; hip-hop in Newcastle in the northeast of England and Frankfurt in Germany; and the live music of the Pink Floyd tribute band the Benwell Floyd, again in Newcastle. These studies bring out the further significance of the local interaction of music production and consumption that have been discussed in chapters 2 and 8 of this book. Bennett's conclusion is important in that he argues that: 'Aspects of popular culture, such as music and style, in addition to being understood as global cultural forms, assume particularised "everyday" meanings which respond to the differing local contexts in which they are appropriated and which frame their incorporation into forms of social action' (2000: 197). This is significant in two ways: first, because it suggests the importance of the local consumption of global products and, second, because it links music to other forms of popular culture. Thus, while subculture remains a useful concept in some respects (especially in analyses such as those of Muggleton and Hodkinson), it directs attention to wider production and consumption processes and how they are lived out. An important concept in this respect that has been developed via the study of popular music is 'scene'.

Popular music scenes

In recent years, the concept of scene has been increasingly used to refer to sites of (predominantly) local music production and consumption. In some respects this has built on common-sense understandings of the idea as represented in ideas like the New York scene or the Manchester scene. Furthermore, at times, the term has been used in conjunction with that of subculture, for example in the work on Hodkinson (2002) discussed in the previous section. There is much overlap in the literature in the use of these terms, although there has more often been an attempt to separate them. As discussed in the previous chapter, the work of Finnegan (1989) is an important resource in such rethinking of these relationships in local contexts. A key study that has advanced this research is that of Austin, Texas by Barry Shank (1994). This study builds upon earlier work by Shank and the sort of influential theorization produced by Will Straw, who argues that the musical scene can be defined in the following way:

> That cultural space in which a range of musical practices co-exist, interacting with each other within a variety of processes of differentiation, and according to widely varying trajectories of change and cross-fertilization. The sense of purpose articulated within a musical community normally depends on an affective link between two terms: contemporary musical practices, on the one hand, and the musical heritage which is seen to render this contemporary activity appropriate to a given context, on the other. Within a music scene, that same sense of purpose is articulated

within those forms of communication through which the building of musical alliances and the drawing of musical boundaries take place. The manner in which musical practices within the scene tie themselves to processes of historical change occurring within a larger international musical culture will also be a significant basis of the way in which such forms are positioned within a scene at a local level. (1991: 373)

Shank traces the development of the music scene in Austin, Texas in some detail – filling in the way in which the different influences have come together to produce a changing musical patchwork. In more theoretical terms, Shank argues that the boundaries between producers and consumers break down in the sort of scene that is represented in Austin. As he argues: 'within the fluid stream of potential meanings, the audience and the musicians together participate in a nonverbal dialogue about the significance of music and the construction of their selves' (1994: 125). To develop and summarize this idea, he suggests that '[s]pectators become fans, fans become musicians, musicians are always already fans, all constructing the nonobjects of identification through their performances as subjects of enunciation – becoming and disseminating the subject-in-process of the signifying practice of rock 'n' roll music' (ibid.: 131). This captures the way in which the participants in a scene can take on a number of different roles or can change their roles within it. This sort of change is also captured by Hodkinson (2002) in his study of Goth (as discussed above), where he shows how the Goth subculture can involve the promotion of gigs, tape-swapping, the sale and purchase of clothing, and so on – suggesting the sort of fluidity and complexity of the construction of meaning theorized by Shank. It is illustrative that, in this context, Hodkinson often refers to the Goth scene.

Building on this sort of approach, where the idea of scene 'has increasingly been used as a model for academic research on the production, performance, and reception of popular music' (Peterson and Bennett 2004: 3), Peterson and Bennett argue that three broad types of scene can be identified: local, translocal and virtual.

Local scenes are those based around a particular place; this has been the most common use made of the term. Examples of the studies that represent this usage include the work of Cohen (1991), examined in chapter 2, and that of Shank (1994), considered above. A local scene is:

A focused social activity that takes place in a delimited space and over a specific span of time in which clusters of producers, musicians, and fans realize their common musical taste, collectively distinguishing themselves from others by using music and other cultural signs often appropriated from other places, but recombined and developed in ways that come to represent the local scene. The focused activity we are interested in here, of course, centers on a particular style of music, but such music scenes characteristically involve other diverse lifestyle elements as well. These usually include a distinctive style of dancing, a particular range of psychoactive drugs, style of dress, politics and the like. (Peterson and Bennett 2004: 8)

The translocal scene involves the communication between local scenes and it refers to 'widely scattered local scenes drawn into regular communication around a distinctive form of music and lifestyle' (ibid.: 6). Examples of this include alternative rock in the 1980s, as examined by Kruse (1993), and the way in which hip-hop has diffused across the world, but taken on specific local forms. Another phenomenon discussed under this heading is the so-called 'music carnival' that existed around the American band the Grateful Dead, where 'a band's fans regularly follow their favorite musicians around the country from tour date to tour date and energize local devotees of the music and lifestyle' (Peterson and Bennett 2004: 10).

The virtual scene 'is a newly emergent formation in which people scattered across great physical spaces create the sense of scene via fanzines and, increasingly, through the internet' (ibid.: 6–7). As technologies such as the Internet develop, it can be expected that there might be more virtual scenes developing. In their edited collection, Bennett and Peterson include a range of studies that they locate under these headings of local, translocal and virtual. Local scenes include studies of Chicago blues (Grazian 2004), rave in a city near Detroit (Spring 2004) and Salsa in London (Urquia 2004). Translocal scenes considered include Schilt (2004) on Riot Grrrl, and Hodkinson (2004) on Goth. Examples of virtual scenes include Bennett (2004) on the Canterbury scene and Vroomen (2004) on Kate Bush.

One of the issues raised by this expansion of the conceptualization of the idea of scene to include the translocal and the virtual is that it may reduce the specificity of the concept itself and make it descriptive rather than analytical. Thus, while it may be useful to point out that scenes have translocal and virtual dimensions, it is important to retain the idea that a scene involves some measure of co-present interaction. It seems increasingly likely that those who are enthusiastic about a form of music and a mode of dress will engage, to varying degrees, with others who live locally and who are involved, as well as hoping to meet up with others who are involved but who live elsewhere. Hodkinson's discussion of Goth (2002) illuminates the differential interaction of these processes very well. In addition, Grazian's (2004) study of the blues scene in Chicago discusses the role of tourists in affecting the continuing existence of blues clubs, and so on. There is some danger here of a loss of specificity and purchase once the concept of scene is generalized, unless the particular features to which it draws attention – the aspect of interaction around some degree of performance, the role of place in acting as a node of communication – are recognized. This also takes us back to the idea discussed from Muggleton and Weinzierl (2003) that different concepts may have purchase in different contexts and may refer to different parts of reality. This idea will be further developed in the final part of this chapter, where a particular typology for different audience positions will be considered (see also Abercrombie and Longhurst 1998). However, before this can be discussed, it is important to examine some other related aspects of audience activity.

Omnivorous audiences

As was discussed above with respect to work on subcultures, Muggleton, in his examination of youth subculturalists, found that, in several respects, some of his respondents sought to convey the variety of their musical tastes and that their tastes had changed in quite significant ways over a period of time. Some research has found this to be a very common way of responding when people are asked about their musical taste. In a study of the patterns of middle-class culture in and around Manchester in the northwest of England, Savage et al. point to the way in which, when asked about musical tastes, people usually begin with a statement along the lines of 'I like all sorts of things', or 'I have a wide taste in music' (2005: 168–70; see also Carrabine and Longhurst 1999). And this is despite the fact that when this sort of statement is investigated further or qualified, the range of taste that is being characterized in this way is generally actually relatively narrow. It appears that a socially accepted way of characterizing musical taste is both to admit to liking it, and to suggest that the individual's taste is wide. There is a clear contrast here with the way in which individuals responded in the same study to a similar question about television. In this case, they were usually defensive in the sense that they sought to downplay the amount of television they watch, or to suggest that they only watch particular selected programmes such as news and documentaries (Savage et al. 2005: 157–68). This can be seen as some evidence for the idea that (in particular) the middle classes in societies such as the UK and the USA have become more omnivorous in their musical tastes.

This idea has been developed by (for example) Peterson and Kern (1996), who argue that in the United States there has been a shift in the division between the elite and the mass in culture. In particular, they maintain that middle-class groups have become more omnivorous in taste. This means that they engage with a wider range of cultural forms than was the case in previous historical periods. So, for example, whereas in the past, educated middle-class people might have consumed classical literature and music, they are now likely also to read detective novels, watch soap operas on TV and listen to popular music from around the world. In this sense, they are omnivores, since they consume both high and popular culture. As Peterson and Simkus argue:

> There is mounting evidence that high-status groups not only participate more than do others in high-cultural activities but also tend to participate more often in most kinds of leisure activities. In effect, elite taste is no longer defined as an expressed appreciation of the high art forms (and a moral disdain or bemused tolerance for all other aesthetic expressions). Now it is being redefined as an appreciation of the aesthetics of every distinctive form along with an appreciation of the high arts. Because status is gained by knowing about and participating in (that is to say, by consuming) all forms, the term *omnivore* seems appropriate. (1992: 169)

Further, according to this thesis, those at the bottom of the social scale are univores in that their cultural consumption is more restricted and constrained by material factors (Bryson 1997). Evidence for the omnivore thesis was initially produced with respect to the consumption of music in the US and has now been subject to empirical investigation and theoretical refinement in a number of other countries (see Peterson and Anand 2004). This has suggested that the patterns of omnivorous taste may vary according to the medium being considered.

Although there may be debate about the effects or spread of these forms of taste, it is significant that when younger people discuss their musical tastes, they often do so using omnivorous statements. For example, in research on the musical tastes of young people (17–18 years old) living in a relatively affluent suburb of Greater Manchester in the northwest of England, Carrabine and Longhurst found that 'the most common way of expressing musical taste is *not* to appear to be exclusive. On the contrary, it is important for these young relatively affluent, late teenagers to display a fluid and wide range of musical likes' (1999: 131). While there is some variation in the confidence with which such pluralistic tastes are held and expressed, as Carrabine and Longhurst (ibid.: 131–6), deploying focus group evidence, suggest, it does seem important to recognize that a range of musical taste is common (or the expression that this is the case is) and that this is further evidence for the idea that it is difficult to consistently tie musical preferences to the nature of subcultural taste and practice (see chapter 6, box 6.2). Again, this raises the point that it is important to consider the range of different points or forms of audience experience that exist. It can be suggested that this entails significant attention to the idea of the place of music in everyday life.

Music and everyday life

It is possible to see how significant music can be in everyday life through the following sort of quotation, taken from research based on interviews where respondents were able freely to comment on the meaning of music for them (Crafts et al. 1993: 109):

Q: What does music mean to you?
A: Music is just part of life, like air. You live with it all the time, so it's tough to judge what it means to you. For some people, it's a deep emotional thing, for some people, it's casual. I turn on the radio and it's there in the morning; it's there when I drive; it's there when I go out.
Q: If it isn't there, do you miss it?
A: No.
Q: So you're not really aware that it is there?
A: It's like a companion, or a back-up noise. Just something in the background. A lot of people turn the radio on and they're not listening to it for the most part, but it's there to keep them company, it's background noise. It's like the TV; they leave the TV on all the time, although it never gets watched. But it's background, people use it just to feel comfortable with.

More recent research has continued to explore such themes and ideas in theoretical and empirical terms. A good example of this approach can be found in the work of DeNora (2000). She adopts a stance that has its roots in the premises of interactionist sociology – i.e., she seeks to explore how music is a part of the constitution of the interactions between people and how it plays a role in the constitution of those people themselves. Who we are and how we engage with other people are processes that are brought about significantly by interaction. DeNora points out that some of the subcultural literature explored in chapter 7 went quite a long way towards looking at how music was a part of such interaction processes. In her view, therefore, a strength of this approach was its 'focus not on what can be said about cultural forms, but on what the appropriation of cultural materials achieves in *action*, what culture "does" for its consumers within the contexts of their lives' (2000: 6). In seeking to add some theoretical context to the relatively descriptive approach adopted by authors such as Crafts et al., DeNora explores three main dimensions of music's place in everyday life: its place in the constitution of our senses of self, or what might also be termed identity; its role in the construction of the body and the physical self (see also chapter 6); and its role in the 'ordering' of social relationships.

With respect to the former, DeNora shows, through a number of examples, how music is involved in the construction of feelings, as well as preventing the onset of moods and feelings that are not wished for. Thus, for DeNora, 'Music is not simply used to express some internal emotional state. Indeed, that music is part of the reflexive constitution of that state; it is a resource for the identification work of "knowing how one feels" – a building material of "subjectivity"' (ibid.: 37). DeNora discusses a number of examples of this process and argues that:

> In none of these examples . . . does music simply *act upon* individuals, like a stimulus. Rather, music's 'effects' come from the ways in which individuals orient to it, how they interpret it and how they place it within their personal musical maps, within the semiotic web of music and extra-musical associations. (Ibid.: 61)

The interaction between music and the body has already been considered in chapter 6. DeNora shows in some detail how some of the themes explored in that discussion play out in practice. A good example of this is her discussion of the role of music in an aerobics class. On one level, music 'defines the components of a session through its tempo changes (for example, music for warm up, core and cool down) and it also profiles the bodily movements associated with each of these components' (ibid.: 92). However, on another level, the music is also part of structuring how the body is to be deployed in the course of the particular movements of aerobics. Music is not just the background for those movements; it is a part of how those movements are defined. As DeNora puts it: 'Following aerobics' musical changes and the ways in which real bodies interact with prescribed musical bodily changes, bodily changes allow us to examine the body, moment by moment, as it interacts with, and is configured in relation to, music' (ibid.: 93). The aerobic body is (partly) constituted through the interaction with music, which is just a specific example of how '[m]usic is, or rather can serve as, a constitutive property of bodily being' (ibid.: 99).

In a third broad theme, DeNora considers the way in which music is involved in the production and reproduction of ordered social life. Such social order is not simply imposed; rather, it is itself produced through a process of 'ordering'. As the extract in box 9.1 shows, music can be part of the ordering and re-ordering of close relationships.

To take another example, music is also used in the ordering of the consumption practices involved in shopping and this is discussed in empirical research by DeNora and Belcher (2000). Another important study that addresses the role of music in everyday life in a different way was written by Bull (2000), who deploys a

Box 9.1 Music and the ordering of relationships

[Let us] consider how music is used not only to reinforce but also to undermine particular relations between friends and intimates. Here, for example, Lesley describes how a shift in music listening habits and tastes at home was associated with the deterioration of her relationship with her partner.

> Lesley: In the '80s I sort of got distanced from music. My [children] were little and my husband didn't really like a lot of the music going on – he wasn't particularly keen on the radio being on all the time, probably – I suppose the bands I didn't identify with at the time were Dire Straits – those sort of bands. I liked some of the things they did but I think it was more excitable and so my ex-husband liked them and didn't mind them being put on, whereas some of the other music I'd put on he thought would upset the [children] and of course then they got to identify with some of the things I liked with being morose, like the Leonard Cohen. So it tended to be more popular jiggly music. . . . Normally if I listened to Leonard Cohen I wanted to be in my own space listening and of course so normally I would have been in a bit of a strange mood in comparison to how I would be, and I suppose he picked up on that and maybe the [children] did as well. . . . When we first got married we used to listen to the radio a lot, and within nine months I was listening to Radio 4 rather than Radio 1 because he didn't like Radio 1 at all. When the boys were young, babies, occasionally I'd put something on raucous or heavy metal or something and his attitude was that he definitely didn't want it on because it was too noisy. But I think the [children] picked up on that as well because if I put anything on that was a bit loud – [here she gestures that they would act up] . . . during the '80s I didn't really bother with music because I thought it would cause friction – be upsetting or whatever – so I stopped. . .The late '80s I started listening to Beehive and the Thompson Twins, which of course my husband didn't identify with at all . . .

Lesley describes how she began to make a deliberate musical move away from her relationship, replacing the 'popular jiggly' music that she perceived as within the bounds of the relationship – for example, Dire Straits – and also the more, as she perceived it, 'intellectual' mode of Radio 4, with music that her husband disliked and viewed with disapproval. Lesley goes on to describe how, near the end of her relationship with her ex-husband, she would sometimes, when she was angry, play a Soft Cell song entitled, 'Say hello, wave goodbye' (from an album called *Erotic Cabaret*). She would play the track at high volume so that it would be audible from any room in the house. As she puts it, 'It was a hint really', but admits she is not sure her husband understood ('He didn't say anything').

> Lesley used music to convey a message (perhaps about her evolving aesthetic and stylistic stance) that she had not yet formulated in words – she was formulating a sense of how she was 'different' from her partner, thinking through musical practice about leaving that partner. Via music, Lesley may also have been undermining the aesthetic basis of their relationship, preparing the aesthetic ground for her departure, creating an aesthetic trajectory for the agency of her departure.
>
> Source: DeNora 2000: 126–7

detailed consideration of the role of personal stereos in the everyday lives of listeners, with a conceptualization of everyday life that draws on aspects of the work of the Frankfurt School (see the Introduction).

Bull explores a number of different aspects of personal stereo use, only the most significant of which can be considered here. First, he points out how users deploy the music that they listen to in order to give pleasure to an otherwise dull routine. Second, personal stereos are used in a related way to 'escape' from aspects of everyday life, but in addition to go into 'dream worlds', which Bull compares to films that the users construct, drawing on bodily and visual experiences. In a sense the personal stereo provides a sound-track to the filmic transformation of everyday life on the part of the user. Bull uses these insights to argue that music should be seen as a more important part of everyday life, which has not often been the case in the past, when the emphasis was more on the visual.

However, there are important connections between the visual and the musical, as has already been considered in this book (see chapter 6). One speculative way of thinking about this relationship is via the convergence of technological consumption and the way that audience processes are changing. Bull's study was carried out when tape-based personal stereos were common. Since then, CD players have come and are already going as MP3 players such as iPods have gained ground. In the view of Kusek and Leonhard:

> Along with the utterly astounding growth of the Internet has come a new, networked mobility exemplified by the explosion of the digital music player and cell phone usage, particularly in Europe and Asia. Today's kids are 'always on', natural digeratis, constantly networking, plugged-in and communicating with each other in many unprecedented ways. They are the *screenagers* – and are rapidly changing the way that music is discovered and that business is conducted. (2005: 99)

As was discussed in chapter 1, the suggestion here is that the music business will have to change to take account of the desires of this group or 'generation'. The digital kids may therefore be leading shifts in the place of media, including popular music (which increasingly is linked to other forms such as phone ring-tones and mobile TV) in the place of everyday life. While detailed studies of these practices are in their infancy, it has been argued that, with respect to younger people in societies like the UK and the USA:

Their way of communicating with their friends is profoundly different than that of previous generations. Instant messaging and e-mail have eclipsed many prior means of socializing; for some, online networking has become as popular as actual dating. This generation is far more into interactivity than into passive consumption – couch potatoes have become cyber-networkers. (Ibid.: 99)

While this may be over-hyped, it is important to recognize that these potential shifts are occurring in the context of wider audience changes. Thus, in broad terms the attention to the role of music in everyday life paid by DeNora and Bull, and the speculation of Kusek and Leonhard need to be seen as part of a more general understanding of audience processes in everyday life.

In *Audiences*, Abercrombie and Longhurst (1998) argue that while the move towards greater research attention to everyday audiences is important, future work will be weakened unless it takes account of the changing nature of audience processes and the way in which such processes are conceptualized. They argue that the two most significant ways of conceptualizing the audience, which they term the behavioural paradigm and the incorporation/resistance paradigm, are deficient in crucial respects. The behavioural paradigm tends to consider the audience as individuals in two ways. On the one hand, individuals in social contexts are affected by the media (often in a pernicious way), for example by some forms of pop music, as discussed in the first section of chapter 7. On the other hand, as also considered in chapter 7, individuals are seen to use the media to satisfy certain wants and needs (in the so-called 'uses and gratifications' approach). There are significant difficulties with this approach, such as its relatively restricted understanding of social life, its inattention to power relations and its lack of attention to the textual nature of media products. Furthermore, as was also considered in chapter 7, it was severely criticized by what has been called a critical approach to the study of the media (Hall 1980), or what Abercrombie and Longhurst called the incorporation/resistance paradigm (see figure 9.2).

The incorporation/resistance paradigm, reflecting its Marxist origins, takes the operation of power in society seriously. It pays particular attention to the way in which society is structured, especially in the earlier work done within its parameters in terms of class, but, subsequently, with respect to gender, race and age. Its key research problem concerns the extent to which such social structuring and social location influence particular modes of decoding of media texts (rather than media messages or stimuli in the behavioural approach) in ideological terms. As considered in chapter 7, this approach considers the extent to which audiences resist or are incorporated by media texts (see, for example, Morley 1980). The classic studies showed that resistance, while hugely significant, needed to be considered in the context of ideological incorporation into the dominant structures of society. Thus much of the work with respect to youth subcultures examined in chapter 7 and in the earlier parts of this chapter is at least partly concerned with how such groups resist, to some extent, the dominant order. However, this approach tended to overemphasize the coherence of the response to different texts, often in line with one of the social bases identified above, or to conflate an active response to media with a critical one. In this context, Abercrombie and Longhurst

	1 Behavioural	2 Incorporation/Resistance	3 Spectacle/Performance
Audience	Individuals (in social context)	Socially structured (e.g. by class, gender, race)	Socially constructed and reconstructed especially by spectacle and narcissism
Medium	Stimulus (message)	Text	Mediascape(s)
Social consequence(s)	Functions/ dysfunctions, propaganda, influence, use, effects	Ideological incorporation and resistance	Identity formation and reformation in everyday life
Representative studies and approaches	'Effects' literature, uses and gratifications	Encoding and decoding, Morley (1980), Radway (1987), fan studies	Silverstone (1994), Hermes (1995), Gillespie (1995)

Figure 9.2 The three paradigms

Source: Abercrombie and Longhurst 1998: 37

speculated that such problems could only be rectified through the formulation of a new paradigm for audience research.

The argument for the spectacle/performance paradigm (SPP) rests on the recognition that both audiences and conceptualizations of the audience were changing. Abercrombie and Longhurst propose that three different types of audience currently co-exist: simple, mass and diffused (see figure 9.3). The simple audience, as represented, for example, by an audience at a pop music concert, involves relatively direct communication from performers to audience; the performance takes place in a confined locale, tends to be highly ceremonial in the sense that it is a special event and the space of performance is ritualistic, and the site has a high level of meaning for participants. The performance and the audience response take place in public and the performers are separated from the audience by clear boundaries. The attention level of the audience with respect to the performance is high.

The development of mass audiences reflects the growth of more mediated forms of communication. An example of this would be listening to a CD at home. Here, communication is highly mediated in that performance takes place a long way from the audience spatially and is normally recorded at an earlier time and place. The relatively direct connection between 'live' performance and audience is broken. As has been discussed at several points in this book, the texts of the music industry are globally available and are not restricted to a one-off performance in time and space. The ritual aspects of the simple audience decline as the mass audience becomes used to texts and media being part of everyday life. Much CD listening is done while other things are going on. The mass audience tends to exist in private rather than public spaces. CD listening takes place in the home or

	Simple	Mass	Diffused
Communication	Direct	Mediated	Fused
Local/Global	Local	Global	Universal
Ceremony	High	Medium	Low
Public/Private	Public	Private	Public and Private
Distance	High	Very high	Low
Attention	High	Variable	Civil inattention

Figure 9.3 Modes of audience experience

Source: Abercrombie and Longhurst 1998: 44

in the car. Likewise, the attention of the audience can vary from highly engaged, focused viewing to complete distraction. Finally, the distance in spatial and time dimensions of the audience from the performance is high.

Key to the Abercrombie and Longhurst argument is the development of what is termed the diffused audience:

> The essential feature of this audience-experience is that, in contemporary society, everyone becomes an audience all the times. Being a member of an audience is no longer an exceptional event, nor even an everyday event. Rather it is constitutive of everyday life. This is not a claim that simple audiences or mass audiences no longer exist, quite the contrary. These experiences are as common as ever, but they take place against the background of the diffused audience. (1998: 68–9)

Several social processes are related to the development of the diffused audience. First, people spend increasing amounts of time in media consumption. Second, such consumption is increasingly woven into the fabric of everyday life, as explored by writers like DeNora (2000). Third, Western societies have become more performative in the broadest sense (see chapter 6).

Abercrombie and Longhurst argue that in studying audience processes, it is crucially important to consider the interaction between simple, mass and diffused audiences. For example, the relationship between the seemingly increasing importance of attending live performances and festivals (Kusek and Leonhard 2005: 114), which are on one level simple audience experiences. However, these can also be relayed via the mass media, as at Glastonbury, and therefore become mass televisual experiences, and diffused as aspects of identity work in everyday life. The previous two paradigms identified by Abercrombie and Longhurst were not up to studying these relationships. They proposed that the spectacle/performance paradigm provided the more adequate account of audience processes. This approach pays greater attention to how the audience is socially constructed and reconstructed (rather than being determined or structured). Attention would focus on the way in which media interact to form a mediascape (Appadurai 1990), rather than media messages or texts per se. Rather than

> Consumer—Fan—Cultist—Enthusiast—Petty Producer

Figure 9.4 The audience continuum
Source: Abercrombie and Longhurst 1998: 141

considering the effects, functions or ideological operations of the media, the SPP focuses on the interaction between everyday life, audience processes and identity formation and reformation.

In elaborating the SPP, Abercrombie and Longhurst argued that there were a number of potential positions that audience members could occupy (see figure 9.4; for further elaboration and critique, see Hills 2002 and Crawford 2003). At one end of this audience continuum was the consumer, who interacted with the media in a relatively generalized and unfocused fashion. It is important to stress that the term 'consumer' is not intended to have pejorative connotations in this respect. The next step along the continuum is that of the fan (again without any intended pejorative connotations), who becomes particularly attached to certain programmes or stars within the context of relatively high media usage. At the next point are the cultists, who build on such attachments to focus their media and audience activities around certain key programmes. Cultists also tend to interact more directly with those who have similar tastes. Enthusiasts tend to be more involved in actual production of artefacts connected to their fan and cultic activities. Classic studies, such as those of Star Trek fandom, point to the writing of stories and the making of videos and paintings (see, for example, Bacon-Smith 1992; Jenkins 1992; Penley 1992). The final point on the continuum is that of the petty-producer who is reaching the point where enthusiasm is becoming professionalized into a full-time activity (see Moorhouse 1991). The identification of this continuum allows further differentiation in contemporary audience positions than had hitherto been the case (see also chapter 8). These positions can be considered in the context of popular music.

In his discussion of Goth, Hodkinson (2002) shows how this 'subculture' contains several of the positions identified by Abercrombie and Longhurst. Some of the engagers with Goth may be fanlike in that they are particularly attached to Goth bands, but they may be relatively unengaged with other forms of the culture; cultists become more engaged and may dress in a Goth way; others may move more into the enthusiast position if, for example, they become an author of a fanzine. Those who run record or clothes shops specializing in Goth artefacts as a full-time occupation have moved into the final category. These positions would contrast with someone who might be said to be a consumer of Goth or Goth-related music – someone who owned one of the records that have been defined as part of Goth.

This approach can also be used to capture the fluidity of the way in which people relate to music (Williams 2001). For example, in a study of young people and music, Laughey (2006) demonstrates the way in which ideas of different audience positions and of everyday life can be combined to excellent effect. He demonstrates how fluidity of commitment to different forms of music is played out in personal terms as well as a range of public performances. This surely captures the way in which music flows through contemporary life in a range of interacting ways.

Summary

This chapter has considered:

- current debates on the idea of youth subcultures and music;
- recent work that has continued to deploy the idea of subculture;
- the idea of scene;
- the theory of the omnivore with respect to music;
- the place of music in everyday life, including the implications of digitization;
- recent theories of audiences and performance.

Conclusion

Chapters 8 and 9 of this book suggested that the relationships between the production and consumption of contemporary popular music are very complex. Consequently, it is worth stressing again that the division of this book into discussions of production, text and audience, as well as reflecting how the field of popular music studies has developed, is meant to facilitate the presentation and understanding of different aspects of popular music and society. These aspects are not completely separate nor can they be related in a simple fashion. This, in lots of ways, is the major problem with the sort of account offered by Adorno and the rationalization approach outlined in the Introduction. Here, clear linkages are hypothesized between the nature of production, the form and content of texts and their understanding by audiences. However, as was suggested in the critiques of these approaches, such accounts are deficient in not realizing the complexity of the different dimensions of production, text and audience and the complicated relationships between them. The claim of this book is that an analytic separation of production, text and audience facilitates more detailed examination of the nature of these different aspects and the relations between them.

This approach is similar to that outlined by Richard Johnson (1986), who maintains that cultural studies need to consider the production of texts, the nature of texts themselves, the 'readings' that have and can be made of such texts and the way in which such readings take place in the context of the 'lived cultures' of everyday social relations.

This book has followed through the five sets of issues or questions outlined towards the end of the Introduction. These were:

1   What is meant by production and producers?
2   How does production take place?
3   How are texts structured and what meanings do they contain?
4   What is an audience?
5   How are texts consumed by an audience?

A full understanding of popular music requires consideration of all these dimensions. Thus, for example, Frith (1990) in his criticism of his earlier work with McRobbie noted how they had tended to overvalue production and downplay the importance of consumption in the creation of musical meaning. To take another example, the full understanding of the advent of rock and roll would need to combine the emphasis laid on production by Peterson with the attention to textual nuance and meaning given by writers like Middleton or Brackett and the reconstruction of the meaning of this form for its audience in a way similar to the discussion of the Beatles in chapter 8.

The complexity of some of these issues can be shown through the example of the fan music video texts, also considered in chapter 8. These are texts whose source material was originally produced within large companies for transmission on broadcast television and for mass circulation as music. The television texts and music were structured as realist narratives, with the aim of appealing to mass audiences. However, such television programmes became exceptionally popular with groups of fans who formed subcultures that met at conventions and located different meanings in the texts from those perhaps intended by the producers. One of the things these audience members then did was to make videos, using music to foreground their own favourite meanings. The texts produced by multinational corporations in the pursuit of profit were understood and used by distinct groups for their own ends and new meanings and texts were created. One way of understanding this is to say that these fans were actually producing new texts and new meanings and that they had therefore moved away from being consumers of these texts. Contemporary rap and hip-hop music involve similar processes of transformation and relocation of meaning. What remains to be further investigated is the extent to which such active understandings and relocations of texts are going on in other sectors of the population, as well as the specific transformations that are occurring as a consequence. Despite the many advances made in the study of fans and audiences (see for example, Hills 2002; Sandvoss 2005; Staiger 2005), there remains much to be done. An exemplar with respect to young people and popular music can be found in the work of Laughey (2006).

The analyst should be wary of making judgements of political worth and aesthetic value simply on the creativity involved in the sorts of transformation carried out in the production of fan music video and rap music. My suggestion is that cultural forms should be evaluated in social context and that even once this has been done it may be possible to say that some aspects of music are progressive, while others are less so. For example, consider again the Madonna phenomenon. Madonna may be an empowering figure for some young – and older – women, but she may also be used as a pin-up for young men, replacing pornographic images. This could also be the case with many other female pop stars.

In general, my view is that even what seem to be the most commodified products of the culture industry need to be examined in their social contexts of production and consumption before any judgements of value can begin to be made. I am suspicious of accounts that 'write off' whole forms of music because they do not seem to conform to traditional standards of high art. If this sounds like a call for appreciation of the relativity of worth and the suspension of critical judgement in the interest of sustained empirical enquiry informed by theoretical innovation, then so much the better.

A key strength of a framework that considers production, text and audience and which resists premature critical or celebratory judgements is that it provides a solid base on which to consider not only what has been achieved in the study of popular music, but also how it can respond to changes in technology, society and culture. It seems clear that technological shifts around digitization and convergence of technologies have the possibility to change the production, textual nature and consumption of popular music greatly. While the prevalence of downloading and file-sharing can be over-estimated, there is no doubt that there are some potential major changes in play. The detailed research evidence on the social and cultural aspects of these shifts is only just beginning to appear. But it is likely to show some significant changes in consumption practices. Being able to carry a large collection of music (and images) in tiny devices must have some implications. However, it is important to recognize that there are some ongoing issues that continue to be significant even in the context of major technological change. Thus, digitization raises important issues about the ownership of rights and brings these even more to the fore in debate. However, as a topic, this in itself is not new, as the research considered in this book demonstrates. The future of music production and consumption will therefore take important and in many ways unanticipated turns, but they can be studied on the basis of what has been found out already. Many other shifts can be thought about in the same way. The studies that have been accumulated during the progress of the development of popular music, media and cultural studies (even if, on the face of it, they may seem dated) therefore have much to offer in helping the thinking through of new directions and practices. It is easy to think that we stand on the verge of major shifts. Indeed, while I share the view that greater mobility of music and other media is a pretty fundamental change, we must not forget that other changes have been thought of in similar terms in the past. Thus, the introduction of portable transistor radios was much debated in technological social and cultural terms in Britain in the 1960s, as were 'ghetto blasters' in the 1980s. This is not in any way to downplay current shifts, which are, I suggest, major. It does mean taking a considered approach to them on the basis of evidence (of the sort of different kinds considered here) and the theoretical frameworks that I have introduced in this book. For example, to what extent will large companies succeed in protecting their positions? What will happen to the way in which musicians work? What do we mean by a musician? Will there be new rights regimes? Will new texts develop? What will be their implications for politics, globalization and sexuality? By whom will the texts be consumed? What technologies are likely to be popular with consumers? These are all questions that the research examined in this book can begin to allow us to address.

It is clear that work on popular music (and in cultural and media studies in general) has advanced significantly in the period since the first edition of this book was written. One of the pleasures of doing a second edition has been to reflect as much of this as space allows, but this has still meant leaving much out. This is especially the case with the research papers published in journals such as *Popular Music* and *Popular Music and Society*. Some of this research has been addressed in this book, but there is still much more out there for the student, researcher and fan to explore. This is a very positive development and I hope that it continues, so that the field can continue to expand and further take account of contemporary changes.

Further Reading

A number of the most important books and articles on pop music are discussed in the individual chapters of this book. The reference list that follows provides full references for these and other cited texts. In this section, I briefly comment on the key books in this field, primarily as an initial further guide for students to move beyond this text. This is not meant to be exhaustive. Publication details can be found in the references.

The best places to start in the sociological study of popular music are with Frith and Goodwin's excellent edited collection *On Record* (1990) and *The Popular Music Studies Reader* (2006), edited by Bennett, Shank and Toynbee. These are very impressive and useful books, which stand comparison with the best of readers. I think that both can be consulted profitably by a student, as the former provides a base that the latter updates and develops in a number of ways. Another, shorter useful reader is *Popular Music Studies* edited by Hesmondhalgh and Negus (2002). Other introductory books that can be consulted with profit are Negus (1996), Shuker (2001) and Bennett (2001). Also helpful as a companion is Shuker (2002).

The pre-eminent sociologist of pop is Simon Frith and any of his work is worth study. His most well-known book is *Sound Effects* (1983), which is a revision of his earlier *Sociology of Rock* (Constable, 1978). *Sound Effects* is still worth reading, though it is obviously now rather dated in some respects. *Music for Pleasure* (1988) is a good collection of Frith's essays and journalism. Frith is one of the editors (along with Bennett, Grossberg, Shepherd and Turner) of *Rock and Popular Music: Politics, Policies, Institutions* (1993), which is another useful collection, and he is a co-editor (with Straw and Street) of another useful edited collection in *The Cambridge Companion to Pop and Rock* (2001). His *Performing Rights* (1996) is excellent. This is only a selection of Frith's work. Yet another useful collection is the *Continuum Encyclopaedia of Popular Music of the World: Vol 1, Media, Industry and Society* (Shepherd et al. 2003).

Middleton's *Studying Popular Music* (1990) is a thought-provoking, musicologically based discussion of a number of issues arising in the study of popular music. It can be hard-going in places, but the considerations of Adorno, folk culture and subculture are particularly rewarding. Relatively little attention has been given in the current book to the more philosophically based studies of the role of music in society, and the ways in which society is structured through music. The work of John Shepherd – see his collection *Music as Social Text* (1991) – is central here. Peter Martin's *Sounds and Society* (1995) is also useful.

Good introductions to the music industry can be found in Negus's *Producing Pop* (1992) and Burnett's *The Global Jukebox* (1996). More generally Hesmondhalgh's *The Cultural Industries* (2002) is very useful in locating the music industry in connection to wider developments. The detail of who owns what changes, so such books can always be supplemented for these matters by the quality daily press and current affairs magazines, as well as their websites. The work of Marshall (2005) is excellent on copyright. Musicians and local music-making can be examined through the work of Bennett in *On Becoming a Rock Musician* (1980), which is dated but clear and to the point. Cohen's *Rock Culture in Liverpool* (1991) is particularly good on masculinity and gender and only small parts of Finnegan's admirable *The Hidden Musicians* (1989) have been reported on here. Bayton's *Frock Rock* (1998) is very readable and addresses a number of issues concerning gender. Toynbee's excellent *Making Popular Music* (2000) covers a wide range of issues, including musicians and creativity. As with the work of Finnegan, only limited aspects of his work have been considered in this book.

Histories of pop abound, as do its different genres. Gillett's *The Sound of the City* (1983) is the classic source on the origins of rock. Bradley's *Understanding Rock 'n' Roll* (1992) is useful, as is Chambers's *Urban Rhythms* (1985). An extended examination of the politics of pop can be found in Street's *Rebel Rock* (1986). His articles can also be consulted with profit. A useful collection of articles on different aspects of the interconnections of pop and cultural politics can be found in Garofalo's *Rockin' the Boat* (1992). A particular slant on this issue can be found in Grossberg's *We Gotta Get Out of this Place* (1992). Like the work of Frith, Grossberg's publications are always worth reading, but can be difficult. Book-length examinations of punk include Laing's *One Chord Wonders* (1985), Savage's *England's Dreaming* (1991), which focuses on McLaren and the Sex Pistols, and Heylin's *From the Velvets to the Voidoids* (1993), which concentrates on the USA.

Despite its age, a good introduction to a variety of issues concerning gender can be found in Steward and Garratt's excellent *Signed, Sealed and Delivered* (1984). Sheila Whiteley's edited collection *Sexing the Groove* (1997) is also useful. A good, if more journalistic, read is Reynolds and Press (1995). The best collection on the over-examined Madonna phenomenon is *The Madonna Connection* (1993), edited by Schwichtenberg.

Oliver's edited collection, *Black Music in Britain* (1990), is a useful overview of a number of different dimensions of this topic. Hatch and Millward's *From Blues to Rock* (1987) is informative and relatively neglected. Gilroy argues for a political definition of black music in *There Ain't No Black in the Union Jack* (1987) and again in his *The Black Atlantic* (1993). His work is of ongoing importance. Some of the debates around black music have been brought into sharp focus by the popularity of rap. A key text is Rose's *Black Noise* (1994), and the reader edited by Forman and Neal, *That's the Joint!* (2004), is comprehensive. On the development of this, see Toop's *The Rap Attack* (1984) and Cross's *It's Not About a Salary . . .* (1993). Good discussions of reggae can be found in Clarke's *Jah Music* (1980) and Hebdige's *Cut 'N' Mix* (1987). However, all these genres are now well served by an extensive critical literature.

A useful discussion of musical meaning is contained in Moore's *Rock: The Primary Text* (1993). Also excellent is Brackett's *Interpreting Popular Music* (1995). A good collection of popular musicology can be found in Middleton's edited *Reading Pop* (2000). Much of the discussion of this topic is best found in studies of specific musical forms. Walser's examination of heavy metal in *Running with the Devil* (1993) is most interesting and Whiteley has discussed progressive rock in *The Space Between the Notes* (1992). Her subsequent books contain analyses of the work of a number of different musicians in the context of cultural theory: see her *Women and Popular Music* (2000) and *Too Much Too Young* (2005). The most important and complete discussion of music video can be found in Goodwin's *Dancing in the Distraction Factory* (1993). Many of Goodwin's other writings can also be consulted with profit. An earlier, and much more text-based, discussion of music video is contained in Kaplan's *Rocking Around the Clock* (1987). A collection of articles on music video can be found in the edited collection by Frith, Goodwin and Grossberg: *Sound and Vision: The Music Video Reader* (1993). An overview of music and the visual can be found in Mundy (1999).

Salih's (2002) excellent commentary is a good way into the work of Judith Butler. Helen Thomas has written much on dance and the body, which has only been touched on in this book, in her *The Body, Dance and Cultural Theory* (2003). The main texts on dance culture are discussed above in chapters 7 and 9. Thornton's *Club Cultures* (1995) has been much discussed and set new terms for discussion for subcultural theory. As with other genres, there is a large literature on dance culture.

Much recent work on audiences has been based around television. Clear summaries of this can be found in Lewis's *The Ideological Octopus* (1991) and Moores's *Interpreting Audiences* (1993). In addition to arguing for a new approach to the study of audiences, Abercrombie and Longhurst also summarize the literature in *Audiences* (1998); see also Staiger's *Media Reception Studies* (2005). The most well-known discussion of subculture and music is Hebdige's influential *Subculture* (1979). The best place to start for an overview of the literature is Gelder and Thornton's *The Subcultures Reader* (1997). Other case studies are present in Hall and Jefferson's seminal edited collection, *Resistance Through Rituals* (1976). Willis's *Profane Culture* (1978) still repays reading and Jones' *Black Culture, White Youth* (1988) contains an interesting ethnography. The feminist critique of work from the Birmingham Centre for Contemporary Cultural Studies is collected in McRobbie's *Feminism and Youth Culture* (1991). Recent edited collections on subcultures and subcultural debate include Muggleton and Weinzierel's *The Post-Subcultures Reader* (2003) and Bennett and Kahn-Harris's *After Subculture* (2004). Useful additions to the subcultural literature can be found in Bennett's *Popular Music and Youth Culture* (2000), Muggleton's *Inside Subculture* (2000) and Hodkinson's *Goth* (2002).

The best edited collection on fans is Lewis's *The Adoring Audience* (1992), which contains interesting theoretical and substantive material. Everyday creativity is stressed by Willis et al. in *Common Culture* (1990). Again, much of the most interesting work on fans has been concerned with television, for example by Jenkins in *Textual Poachers* (1992) and Bacon-Smith in *Enterprising Women* (1992), though music does figure in these accounts in several places. The literature on fans has grown significantly in recent years. Useful discussions of this can be found in Hills's *Fan Cultures* (2002) and Sandvoss's *Fans: The Mirror of Consumption* (2005). Music and everyday life is explored to excellent effect in DeNora's *Music in Everyday Life* (2000) and Laughey's *Music and Youth Culture* (2006) points the way forward on youth, music and everyday life. A useful edited collection on scenes can be found in Bennett and Peterson's *Music Scenes* (2004) and Shank's ground-breaking examination of the Austin, Texas scene, *Dissonant Identities* (1994), is worth close study.

The leading academic journals on popular music are *Popular Music* and *Popular Music and Society*. They are both interdisciplinary and contain many useful articles.

In my view, the tip of the icebergs of rock journalism and history can be found in the works of both Marcus and Guralnick. All their books are worth reading. Heylin's *The Penguin Book of Rock & Roll Writing* (Penguin, 1993) also contains much of the best of the rock era's journalism. Simon Reynolds' work is always thought-provoking, as is that of John Harris. For factual information about rock, see the wonderful efforts of Strong in the seventh edition of *The Great Rock Discography* (2004) and for a guide to jazz, see the sixth edition of Cook and Morton's *Penguin Guide to Jazz on CD* (2002). The *Rough Guide* series of books and CDs are also very informative on almost any genre that could be explored.

References

Abercrombie, N. 1990: Popular culture and ideological effects. In N. Abercrombie, S. Hill and B. Turner (eds), *Dominant Ideologies*, London: Unwin Hyman, pp. 199–228.

Abercrombie, N. 1991: The privilege of the producer. In R. Keat and N. Abercrombie (eds), *Enterprise Culture*, London: Routledge, pp. 171–85.

Abercrombie, N. and Longhurst, B. 1998: *Audiences: A Sociological Theory of Performance and Imagination*, London: Sage.

Abercrombie, N., Lash, S. and Longhurst, B. 1992: Popular representation: recasting realism. In S. Lash and J. Friedman (eds), *Modernity and Identity*, Oxford: Blackwell, pp. 115–40.

Adorno, T. 1990: On popular music. In S. Frith and A. Goodwin (eds), *On Record: Rock, Pop, and the Written Word*, London: Routledge, pp. 301–14.

Adorno, T. and Horkheimer, M. 1977: The culture industry: enlightenment as mass deception. In J. Curran, M. Gurevitch and J. Woollacott (eds), *Mass Communication and Society*, London: Edward Arnold, in association with The Open University Press, pp. 349–83.

Alfino, M., Caputo, J. S. and Wynyard, R. (eds) 1998: *McDonaldization Revisited: Critical Essays on Consumer Culture*, Westport, CT: Praeger.

Anderson, B. 1983: *Imagined Communities*, London: Verso.

Ang, I. 1986: *Watching 'Dallas': Soap Opera and the Melodramatic Imagination*, London: Methuen.

Ang, I. 1991: *Desperately Seeking the Audience*, London: Routledge.

Angelou, M. 1985: *Singin' and Swingin' and Gettin' Merry Like Christmas*, London: Virago.

Appadurai, A. 1990: Disjuncture and difference in the global cultural economy. *Theory, Culture and Society*, 7: 295–310.

Appadurai, A. 1996: *Modernity at Large*, Minneapolis and London: University of Minnesota Press.

Bacon-Smith, C. 1992: *Enterprising Women: Television Fandom and the Creation of Popular Myth*, Philadelphia: University of Pennsylvania Press.

Bagguley, P. 1991: Post-Fordism and enterprise culture: flexibility, autonomy and changes in economic organization. In R. Keat and N. Abercrombie (eds), *Enterprise Culture*, London: Routledge, pp. 151–68.

Baldwin, E., Longhurst, B., McCracken, S., Ogborn, M. and Smith, G. 2004: *Introducing Cultural Studies* (rev. 1st edn), Harlow: Pearson.

Ball, M. S. and Smith, G. W. H. 1992: *Analyzing Visual Data*, London: Sage.

Banerji, S. and Baumann, G. 1990: Bhangra 1984–8: fusion and professionalization in a genre of South Asian dance music. In P. Oliver (ed.), *Black Music in Britain:*

Essays on the Afro-Asian Contribution to Popular Music, Milton Keynes: Open University Press, pp. 137–52.

Barber-Kersovan, A. 2003: German Nazi bands: between provocation and repression. In M. Cloonan and R. Garofalo (eds), *Policing Pop*, Philadelphia: Temple University Press, pp. 186–204.

Barnard, S. 1989: *On The Radio: Music Radio in Britain*, Milton Keynes: Open University Press.

Barnes, K. 1990: Top 40 radio: a fragment of the imagination. In S. Frith (ed.), *Facing the Music: Essays on Pop, Rock and Culture*, London: Mandarin, pp. 8–50.

Barthes, R. 1976: *Mythologies*, St Albans: Granada.

Barthes, R. 1990: The grain of the voice. In S. Frith and A. Goodwin (eds), *On Record: Rock, Pop, and the Written Word*, London: Routledge, pp. 293–300.

Bayton, M. 1990: How women become musicians. In S. Frith and A. Goodwin (eds), *On Record: Rock, Pop, and the Written Word*, London: Routledge, pp. 238–57.

Bayton, M. 1992: Out on the margins: feminism and the study of popular music. *Women: A Cultural Review*, 3: 51–9.

Bayton, M. 1993: Feminist musical practice: problems and contradictions. In T. Bennett, S. Frith, L. Grossberg, J. Shepherd, and G. Turner (eds), *Rock and Popular Music: Politics, Policies, Institutions*, London: Routledge, pp. 177–92.

Bayton, M. 1998: *Frock Rock: Women Performing Popular Music*, Oxford: Oxford University Press.

Beadle, J. J. 1993: *Will Pop Eat Itself? Pop Music in the Soundbite Era*, London: Faber and Faber.

Becker, H. 1963: *Outsiders: Studies in the Sociology of Deviance*, New York: The Free Press.

Belk, R. 1995: *Collecting in a Consumer Society*, London: Routledge.

Bell, V. 1999a: Historical memory, global movements and violence: Paul Gilroy and Arjun Appadurai in conversation. In V. Bell (ed.), *Performativity and Belonging*, London: Sage, pp. 21–40.

Bell, V. 1999b: Performativity and belonging: an introduction. In V. Bell (ed.), *Performativity and Belonging*, London: Sage, pp. 1–10.

Bennett, A. 1999: Subcultures or neo-tribes? Rethinking the relationship between youth, style and musical taste. *Sociology*, 33: 599–617.

Bennett, A. 2000: *Popular Music and Youth Culture: Music, Identity and Place*, Basingstoke: Macmillan.

Bennett, A. 2001: *Cultures of Popular Music*, Milton Keynes: Open University Press.

Bennett, A. 2004: New tales from Canterbury: the making of a virtual scene. In A. Bennett and R. A. Peterson (eds), *Music Scenes: Local, Translocal, and Virtual*, Nashville: Vanderbilt University Press, pp. 205–20.

Bennett, A. and Kahn-Harris, K. 2004: Introduction. In A. Bennett and K. Kahn-Harris (eds), *After Subculture: Critical Studies in Contemporary Youth Culture*, Basingstoke: Palgrave Macmillan, pp. 1–18.

Bennett, A. and Peterson, R. A. (eds) 2004: *Music Scenes: Local, Translocal, and Virtual*, Nashville: Vanderbilt University Press.

Bennett, A., Shank, B. and Toynbee, J. 2006: *The Popular Music Studies Reader*, London: Routledge.

Bennett, H. S. 1980: *On Becoming a Rock Musician*, Amherst: University of Massachusetts Press.

Bennett, T., Frith, S. Grossberg, L., Shepherd, J. and Turner, G. (eds) 1993: *Rock and Popular Music: Politics, Policies, Institutions*, London: Routledge.

Bishop, J. 2005: Building international empires of sound: concentrations of power and property in the 'global' music market. *Popular Music and Society*, 28: 443–71.

Björnberg, A. 2000: Structural relationships of music and images in music video. In R. Middleton (ed.), *Reading Pop: Approaches to Textual Analysis in Popular Music*, Oxford: Oxford University Press, pp. 347–78.

Blair, M. E. 2004: Commercialization of the rap music youth subculture. In M. Forman and M. A. Neal (eds), *That's the Joint! The Hip-Hop Studies Reader*, London: Routledge, pp. 497–504.

Bourdieu, P. 1984: *Distinction: A Social Critique of the Judgement of Taste*, London: Routledge and Kegan Paul.

Brackett, D. 1995: *Interpreting Popular Music*, Berkeley: University of California Press.

Bradby, B. 1990: Do-talk and don't talk: the division of the subject in girl-group music. In S. Frith and A. Goodwin (eds), *On Record: Rock, Pop, and the Written Word*, London: Routledge, pp. 341–68.

Bradby, B. 1992: Like a virgin-mother? Materialism and maternalism in the songs of Madonna. *Cultural Studies*, 6: 73–96.

Bradby, B. and Torode, B. 2000: Pity Peggy Sue. In R. Middleton (ed.), *Reading Pop: Approaches to Textual Analysis in Popular Music*, Oxford: Oxford University Press, pp. 203–27.

Bradley, D. 1992: *Understanding Rock 'n' Roll: Popular Music in Britain 1955–1964*, Buckingham: Open University Press.

Braudy, L. 1997: *The Frenzy of Renown: Fame and its History*, New York: Vintage Books.

Brett, P., Wood, E. and Thomas, G. C. (eds) 1994: *Queering the Pitch: The New Gay and Lesbian Musicology*, London: Routledge.

British Phonographic Industry (BPI) 2005: *Statistical Handbook 2005*, London: British Phonographic Industry.

Browne, M. E. and Fiske, J. 1987: Romancing the rock: romance and representation in popular music videos. *OneTwoThreeFour*, 5.

Brunsdon, C. and Morley, D. 1978: *Everyday Television: 'Nationwide'*, London: British Film Institute.

Bryson, B. 1997: What about the univores? Musical dislikes and group-based identity construction among Americans with low levels of education. *Poetics*, 25: 141–56.

Bull, M. 2000: *Sounding Out the City: Personal Stereos and the Management of Everyday Life*, Oxford: Berg.

Burchill, J. and Parsons, T. 1978: *'The Boy Looked at Johnny': The Obituary of Rock and Roll*, London: Pluto.

Burkart, P. 2005: Loose integration in the music industry. *Popular Music and Society*, 28: 489–500.

Burnett, R. 1996: *The Global Jukebox: The International Music Industry*, London: Routledge.

Butler, J. 1990: *Gender Trouble: Feminism and the Subversion of Identity*, London: Routledge.

Butler, J. 1993: *Bodies that Matter: On the Discursive Limits of Sex*, London: Routledge.

Butler, J. 1997: *Excitable Speech: A Politics of the Performative*, London: Routledge.

Butler, J. 1999: *Gender Trouble: Feminism and the Subversion of Identity* (10th anniversary edn), London: Routledge.

Carr, I. 1999: *Miles Davis: The Definitive Biography*, London: HarperCollins.

Carrabine, E. and Longhurst, B. 1997/8: What difference does a course make? Music, education and everyday life. *The Journal of Popular Music Studies*, 9–10: 79–91 (published 2000).

Carrabine, E. and Longhurst, B. 1999: Mosaics of omnivorousness: middle-class youth and popular culture. *New Formations*, 38: 125–40.

Chambers, I. 1985: *Urban Rhythms: Pop Music and Popular Culture*, Basingstoke: Macmillan.

Chaney, D. 2004: Fragmented culture and subcultures. In A. Bennett and K. Kahn-Harris (eds), *After Subculture: Critical Studies in Contemporary Youth Culture*, Basingstoke: Palgrave Macmillan, pp. 36–48.

Chapman, R. 1992: *Selling the Sixties: The Pirates and Pop Music Radio*, London: Routledge.

Chester, A. 1990: Second thoughts on a rock aesthetic: The Band. In S. Frith and A. Goodwin (eds), *On Record: Rock, Pop and the Written Word*, London: Routledge, pp. 315–19.

Christian, H. 1987: Convention and constraint among British semi-professional jazz musicians. In A. L. White (ed.), *Lost in Music: Culture, Style and the Musical Event*, London: Routledge and Kegan Paul (Sociological Review Monograph 34), pp. 220–40.

Clarke, G. 1990: Defending ski-jumpers: a critique of theories of youth subcultures. In S. Frith and A. Goodwin (eds), *On Record: Rock, Pop, and the Written Word*, London: Routledge, pp. 81–96.

Clarke, J., Hall, S., Jefferson, T. and Roberts, B. 1976: Subcultures, cultures and class: a theoretical overview. In S. Hall and T. Jefferson (eds), *Resistance Through Rituals: Youth Subcultures in Post-war Britain*, London: Hutchinson, pp. 9–79.

Clarke, M. 1982: *The Politics of Pop Festivals*, London: Junction.

Clarke, S. 1980: *Jah Music: The Evolution of the Popular Jamaican Song*, London: Heinemann.

Cline, C. 1992: Essays from Bitch: the women's newsletter with bite. In L. Lewis (ed.), *The Adoring Audience: Fan Culture and Popular Media*, London: Routledge, pp. 69–83.

Cloonan, M. and Garofalo, R. 2003. Introduction. In M. Cloonan and R. Garofalo (eds), *Policing Pop*, Philadelphia: Temple University Press, pp. 1–9.

Cohen, P. 1980: Subcultural conflict and working-class community. In S. Hall et al. (eds), *Culture, Media, Language: Working Papers in Cultural Studies, 1972–79*, London: Hutchinson, pp. 78–87.

Cohen, S. 1991: *Rock Culture in Liverpool: Popular Music in the Making*, Oxford: Clarendon.

Cohodas, N. 2000: *Spinning Blues into Gold: Chess Records, The Label that Launched the Blues*, London: Aurum.

Cole, B. 2001: *John Coltrane*, Da Capo Press.

Collins, Jim 1989: *Uncommon Cultures: Popular Culture and Post-Modernism*, London: Routledge.

Collins, John 1992: Some anti-hegemonic aspects of African popular music. In R. Garofalo (ed.), *Rockin' the Boat: Mass Music and Mass Movements*, Boston: South End Press, pp. 185–94.

Cook, R. and Morton, B. 2002: *The Penguin Guide to Jazz on CD* (6th edn), London: Penguin.

Coupland, D. 1992: *Generation X*, London: Abacus.

Coward, R. 1984: *Female Desire: Women's Sexuality Today*, London: Paladin.

Cowie, C. and Lees, S. 1981: Slags or drags. *Feminist Review*, 9: 17–31.

Crafts. S. D., Cavicchi, D. and Keil, C. 1993: *My Music*. Hanover and London: Wesleyan University Press, University Press of New England.

Crawford, G. 2003: The career of the sport supporter: the case of the Manchester Storm. *Sociology*, 37: 219–37.

Crisell, A. 1994: *Understanding Radio*, London: Routledge.

Cross, B. 1993: *It's Not About a Salary ... Rap, Race and Resistance in Los Angeles*, London: Verso.

Cubitt, S. 2000: 'Maybellene': meaning and the listening subject. In R. Middleton (ed.), *Reading Pop: Approaches to Textual Analysis in Popular Music*, Oxford: Oxford University Press, pp. 141–59.

Cultural Trends, 1990: 7, London: Policy Studies Institute.

Cultural Trends, 1991: 12, London: Policy Studies Institute.

Cultural Trends, 1993: 19, London: Policy Studies Institute.

Davis, M. with Troupe, Q. 1990: *Miles: The Autobiography*, London: Picador.

Davis, S. 1984: *Bob Marley: The Biography*, London: Panther.

De Kloet, J. 2003: Confusing Confucious: rock in contemporary China. In M. Cloonan and R. Garafalo (eds), *Policing Pop*, Philadelphia: Temple University Press, pp. 166–85.

DeNora, T. 2000: *Music in Everyday Life*, Cambridge: Cambridge University Press.

DeNora, T. and Belcher, S. 2000: 'When you're trying something on you picture yourself in a place where they are playing this kind of music': musically sponsored agency in the British clothing retail sector. *Sociological Review*, 48: 80–101.

Dery, M. 2004: Public Enemy confrontation. In M. Forman and M. A. Neal (eds), *That's the Joint! The Hip-Hop Studies Reader*, London: Routledge, pp. 407–20.

DeVeaux, S. 1997: *The Birth of Bebop: A Social and Musical History*. Berkeley: University of California Press.

Drewett, M. 2003: Music in the struggle to end Apartheid: South Africa. In M. Cloonan and R. Garofalo (eds), *Policing Pop*, Philadelphia: Temple University Press, pp. 153–65.

Dyer, R. 1979: *Stars*, London: British Film Institute.

Dyer, R. 1987: *Heavenly Bodies: Film Stars and Society*, Basingstoke: Macmillan.

Ehrenreich, B., Hess, E. and Jacobs, G. 1992: Beatlemania: girls just want to have fun. In L. Lewis (ed.), *The Adoring Audience: Fan Culture and Popular Media*, London: Routledge, pp. 84–106.

Elliott, A. 1999: *The Mourning of John Lennon*, Berkeley: University of California Press.

Featherstone, M. 1988: In pursuit of the postmodern: an introduction. *Theory, Culture and Society*, 5: 195–215.

Finnegan, R. 1989: *The Hidden Musicians: Music-making in an English Town*, Cambridge: Cambridge University Press.

Fischer, P. D. 2003: Challenging music as expression in the United States. In M. Cloonan and R. Garofalo (eds), *Policing Pop*, Philadelphia: Temple University Press, pp. 221–37.

Fiske, J. 1987: *Television Culture*, London: Methuen.

Fiske, J. 1992: The cultural economy of fandom. In L. Lewis (ed.), *The Adoring Audience: Fan Culture and Popular Media*, London: Routledge, pp. 30–49.

Fiske, J. and Hartley, J. 1978: *Reading Television*, London: Methuen.

Forman, M. 2002: *The Hood Comes First: Race, Space and Place in Rap and Hip-Hop*, Middletown, CT: Wesleyan University Press.

Forman, M. 2004: Ain't no love in the heart of the city: hip-hop, space and place. In M. Forman and M. A. Neal (eds), *That's the Joint! The Hip-Hop Studies Reader*, London: Routledge, pp. 155–7.

Forman, M. and Neal. M. A. (eds) 2004: *That's the Joint! The Hip-Hop Studies Reader*, London: Routledge.

Fornäs, J., Lindberg, U. and Sernhede, O. 1995: *In Garageland: Rock, Youth and Modernity*, London: Routledge.

Fowler, B. 2000: Introduction. In B. Fowler (ed.), *Reading Bourdieu on Society and Culture*, Oxford: Blackwell/Sociological Review, pp. 1–21.

Freeman, P. 2005: *Running the Voodoo Down: The Electric Music of Miles Davis*, San Francisco: Backbeat.

Frith, S. 1983: *Sound Effects: Youth, Leisure, and the Politics of Rock*, London: Constable.

Frith, S. 1987: Copyright and the music business. *Popular Music*, 7: 57–75.

Frith, S. 1988a: Afterword: making sense of video: pop into the nineties. In S. Frith, *Music for Pleasure: Essays in the Sociology of Pop*, Cambridge: Polity, pp. 205–25.

Frith, S. 1988b: Why do songs have words? In S. Frith, *Music for Pleasure: Essays in the Sociology of Pop*, Cambridge: Polity, pp. 105–28.

Frith, S. 1990: Afterthoughts. In S. Frith and A. Goodwin (eds), *On Record: Rock, Pop, and the Written Word*, London: Routledge, pp. 419–24.

Frith, S. 1992: The industrialization of popular music. In J. Lull (ed.), *Popular Music and Communication* (2nd edn), Newbury Park: Sage, pp. 49–74.

Frith, S. 1993: Popular music and the local state. In T. Bennett, S. Frith, L. Grossberg, J. Shepherd and G. Turner (eds), *Rock and Popular Music: Politics, Policies, Institutions*, London: Routledge, pp. 14–24.

Frith, S. 1996: *Performing Rites: Evaluating Popular Music*, Oxford: Oxford University Press.

Frith, S. and Goodwin, A. (eds) 1990: *On Record: Rock, Pop, and the Written Word*, London: Routledge.

Frith, S. and Horne, H. 1987: *Art into Pop*, London: Routledge.

Frith, S. and McRobbie, A. 1990: Rock and sexuality. In S. Frith and A. Goodwin (eds.), *On Record: Rock, Pop, and the Written Word*, London: Routledge, pp. 371–89.

Frith, S. and Street, J. 1992: Rock Against Racism and Red Wedge: from music to politics, from politics to music. In R. Garofalo (ed.), *Rockin' the Boat: Mass Music and Mass Movements*, Boston: South End Press, pp. 67–80.

Frith, S., Goodwin, A. and Grossberg, L. (eds) 1993: *Sound and Vision: The Music Video Reader*, London: Routledge.

Frith, S., Straw, W. and Street, J. (eds) 2001: *The Cambridge Companion to Pop and Rock*, Cambridge: Cambridge University Press.

Garofalo, R. 1992a: Introduction. In R. Garofalo (ed.), *Rockin' the Boat: Mass Music and Mass Movements*, Boston: South End Press, pp. 1–13.

Garofalo, R. (ed.) 1992b: *Rockin' the Boat: Mass Music and Mass Movements*, Boston: South End Press.

Garofalo, R. 1992c: Understanding mega-events: if we are the world, then how do we change it? In R. Garofalo (ed.), *Rockin' the Boat: Mass Music and Mass Movements*, Boston: South End Press, pp. 15–35.

Garratt, S. 1984: All of us love all of you. In S. Steward and S. Garratt, *Signed, Sealed and Delivered: True Life Stories of Women in Pop*, London: Pluto, pp. 138–51.

Gelder, K. and Thornton, S. (eds) 1997: *The Subcultures Reader*, London: Routledge.

Gendron, B. 1986: Theodor Adorno meets the Cadillacs. In T. Modleski (ed.), *Studies in Entertainment: Critical Approaches to Mass Culture*, Bloomington: Indiana University Press, pp. 272–308.

Gilbert, J. and Pearson, E. 1999: *Discographies: Dance Music, Culture and the Politics of Sound*, London: Routledge.

Gillett, C. 1983: *The Sound of the City: The Rise of Rock and Roll*, London: Souvenir.

Gillett, C. 1988: *Making Tracks: The Story of Atlantic Records*, London: Souvenir.

Gilroy, P. 1987: *'There Ain't No Black in the Union Jack': The Cultural Politics of Race and Nation*, London: Hutchinson.

Gilroy, P. 1993: *The Black Atlantic: Modernity and Double Consciousness*, London: Verso.

Gledhill, C. 1991: Introduction. In C. Gledhill (ed.), *Stardom: Industry of Desire*, London: Routledge.

Goodwin, A. 1991: Popular music and postmodern theory. *Cultural Studies*, 5: 174–90.

Goodwin, A. 1992: Rationalization and democratization in the new technologies of popular music. In J. Lull (ed.), *Popular Music and Communication* (2nd edn), Newbury Park: Sage, pp. 75–100.

Goodwin, A. 1993: *Dancing in the Distraction Factory: Music, Television and Popular Culture*, London: Routledge.

Gordon, R. 1995: *It Came From Memphis*, London: Secker and Warburg.

Grazian, D. 2004: The symbolic economy of authenticity in the Chicago blues scene. In A. Bennett and R. A. Peterson (eds), *Music Scenes: Local, Translocal, and Virtual*, Nashville: Vanderbilt University Press, pp. 31–47.

Griffiths, D. 1999: The high analysis of low music. *Music Analysis*, 18: 389–435.

Griffiths, D. 2000: Three tributaries of 'The River'. In R. Middleton (ed.), *Reading Pop: Approaches to Textual Analysis in Popular Music*, Oxford: Oxford University Press, pp. 192–202.

Grossberg, L. 1983: The politics of youth culture: some observations on rock and roll in American culture. *Social Text*, 8: 104–26.

Grossberg, L. 1992a: Is there a fan in the house? The affective sensibility of fandom. In L. Lewis (ed.), *The Adoring Audience: Fan Culture and Popular Media*, London: Routledge, pp. 50–65.

Grossberg, L. 1992b: *We Gotta Get Out of this Place*, London: Routledge.

Guralnick, P. 1991: *Sweet Soul Music: Rhythm and Blues and the Southern Dream of Freedom*, London: Penguin.

Guralnick, P. 1992: *Feel Like Going Home: Portraits in Blues and Rock 'n' Roll*, London: Penguin.

Guralnick, P. 1995: *Last Train to Memphis: The Rise of Elvis Presley*, London: Abacus.

Hall, S. 1980: Encoding/decoding. In S. Hall et al. (eds), *Culture, Media, Language: Working Papers in Cultural Studies, 1972–79*, London: Hutchinson, pp. 128–38.

Hall, S. 1992: The question of cultural identity. In S. Hall, D. Held and T. McGrew (eds), *Modernity and its Futures*, Cambridge: Polity, in association with The Open University, pp. 273–325.

Hall, S. and Jefferson, T. (eds) 1976: *Resistance Through Rituals: Youth Subcultures in Post-war Britain*, London: Hutchinson.

Harker, D. 1980: *One for the Money: Politics and Popular Song*, London: Hutchinson.

Harris, J. 2003: *The Last Party: Britpop, Blair and the Demise of English Rock*, London: Harper Perennial.

Hatch, D. and Millward, S. 1987: *From Blues to Rock: An Analytical History of Pop Music*, Manchester: Manchester University Press.

Hawkins, S. 2000: Prince: harmonic analysis of 'Anna Stesia'. In R. Middleton (ed.), *Reading Pop: Approaches to Textual Analysis in Popular Music*, Oxford: Oxford University Press, pp. 58–70.

Hebdige, D. 1979: *Subculture: The Meaning of Style*, London: Methuen.

Hebdige, D. 1987: *Cut 'N' Mix: Culture, Identity and Caribbean Music*, London: Methuen.

Hebdige, D. 1988: *Hiding in the Light*, London: Comedia.

Heble, A. 2000: *Landing on the Wrong Note: Jazz, Dissonance and Critical Practice*, London: Routledge.

Held, D. 1980: *Introduction to Critical Theory: Horkheimer to Habermas*, London: Hutchinson.

Hesmondhalgh, D. 1997: Post-punk's attempt to democratise the music industry; the success and failure of Rough Trade. *Popular Music*, 16: 255–74.

Hesmondhalgh, D. 1998: The British dance music industry: a case study in independent cultural production. *British Journal of Sociology*, 49: 234–51.

Hesmondhalgh, D. 2002a: *The Cultural Industries*, London: Sage.

Hesmondhalgh, D. 2002b: Popular music audiences and everyday life. In D. Hesmondhalgh and K. Negus (eds), *Popular Music Studies*, London: Arnold, pp. 119–30.

Hesmondhalgh, D. 2005: Subcultures, scenes or tribes? None of the above. *Journal of Youth Studies*, 8: 21–40.

Hesmondhalgh, D. and Negus, K. (eds) 2002: *Popular Music Studies*, London: Arnold.

Hetherington, K. 1992: Stonehenge and its festival: spaces of consumption. In R. Shields (ed.), *Lifestyle Shopping: The Subject of Consumption*, London: Routledge.

Heylin, C. 1993: *From the Velvets to the Voidoids: A Pre-Punk History for a Post-Punk World*, London: Penguin.

Hills, M. 2002: *Fan Cultures*, London: Routledge

Ho, W.-C. 2003: Between globalisation and localisation: a case study of Hong Kong popular music. *Popular Music*, 22: 143–57.

Hobson, D. 1980: Housewives and the mass media. In S. Hall et al. (eds), *Culture, Media, Language: Working Papers in Cultural Studies, 1972–1979*, London: Hutchinson, pp. 105–14.

Hodkinson, P. 2002: *Goth: Identity, Style and Subculture*, Oxford: Berg.

Hodkinson, P. 2004: Translocal connections in the Goth scene. In A. Bennett and R. A. Peterson (eds), *Music Scenes: Local, Translocal, and Virtual*, Nashville: Vanderbilt University Press, pp. 131–48.

Hoggart, R. 1958: *The Uses of Literacy*, Harmondsworth: Penguin.

Hosokawa, S. 1998: Singing in a cultural enclave: karaoke in a Japanese-Brazilian community. In T. Mitsui and S. Hosokawa (eds), *Karaoke Around the World*, London: Routledge, pp. 139–65.

Hung, M. and Morencos, E. G. 1990: *World Record Sales: 1969–1990*, London: The International Federation of the Phonographic Industry.

International Federation of the Phonographic Industry 1990: *World Sales 1989*, London: International Federation of the Phonographic Industry.

International Federation of the Phonographic Industry 1992: *1992 World Music Sales and 1991 World Music Sales*, London: International Federation of the Phonographic Industry.

Irving, K. 1993: 'I want your hands on me': building equivalences through rap music. *Popular Music*, 12: 105–21.

Jackson, P. 2004: *Inside Clubbing: Sensual Experiments in the Art of Being Human*, Oxford: Berg.

Jameson, F. 1991: *Postmodernism, or, The Cultural Logic of Late Capitalism*, London: Verso.

Jay, M. 1973: *The Dialectical Imagination: A History of the Frankfurt School and the Institute of Social Research 1923–1950*, London: Heinemann.

Jenkins, H. 1992: *Textual Poachers: Television Fans and Participatory Culture*, London: Routledge.

Jenson, J. 1992: Fandom as pathology: the consequences of characterization. In L. Lewis (ed.), *The Adoring Audience: Fan Culture and Popular Media*, London: Routledge, pp. 9–29.

Johnson, R. 1986: What is cultural studies anyway? *Social Text*, 6: 38–80.

Jones, Simon. 1988: *Black Culture, White Youth: The Reggae Tradition from JA to UK*, Basingstoke: Macmillan.

Jones, Steve. 1992: *Rock Formation: Music, Technology and Mass Communication*, Newbury Park: Sage.

Kahn-Harris, K. 2003: Death metal and the limits of musical expression. In M. Cloonan and R. Garofalo (eds), *Policing Pop*, Philadelphia: Temple University Press, pp. 81–99.

Kaplan, E. A. 1987: *Rocking Around the Clock: Music Television, Postmodernism, and Consumer Culture*, London: Routledge.

Kealy, E. 1990: From craft to art: the case of sound mixers and popular music. In S. Frith and A. Goodwin (eds), *On Record: Rock, Pop, and the Written Word*, London: Routledge, pp. 207–20.

Keat, R. and Urry, J. 1975: *Social Theory as Science*, London: Routledge and Kegan Paul.

Kitwana, B. 2004: The challenge of rap music from cultural movement to political power. In M. Forman and M. A. Neal (eds), *That's the Joint! The Hip-Hop Studies Reader*, London: Routledge, pp. 341–62.

Kruse, H. 1993: Subcultural identity in alternative music. *Popular Music*, 12: 33–41.

Kusek, D. and Leonhard, G. 2005: *The Future of Music: Manifesto for the Digital Music Revolution*, Boston, MA: Berklee.

Laing, D. 1985: *One Chord Wonders: Power and Meaning in Punk Rock*, Milton Keynes: Open University Press.

Laing, D. 1990: Making popular music: The consumer as producer. In A. Tomlinson (ed.), *Consumption, Identity and Style: Marketing, Meanings, and the Packaging of Pleasure*, London: Routledge.

Laing, D. 2004: World record sales 1992–2002. *Popular Music*, 23: 88–9.

Laughey, D. 2006: *Music and Youth Culture*. Edinburgh: Edinburgh University Press.

Lee, S. 1995: Re-examining the concept of the 'independent' record company: the case of Wax Trax! Records. *Popular Music*, 14: 13–31.

Lewis, J. 1991: *The Ideological Octopus: An Exploration of Television and its Audience*, London: Routledge.

Lewis, L. (ed.) 1992: *The Adoring Audience: Fan Culture and Popular Media*, London: Routledge.

Lewis, L. 1993: Being discovered: the emergence of female address on MTV. In S. Frith, A. Goodwin and L. Grossberg (eds), *Sound and Vision: The Music Video Reader*, London: Routledge, pp. 129–51.

Lin, N. 2001: *Social Capital: A Theory of Social Structure and Action*, Cambridge: Cambridge University Press.

Lipsitz, G. 1994: *Dangerous Crossroads: Popular Music, Postmodernsim and the Poetics of Place*, London: Verso.

Longhurst, B. and Savage, M. 1996: Social class, consumption and the influence of Bourdieu: some critical issues. In S. Edgell, K. Hetherington and A. Warde (eds), *Consumption Matters: The Production and Experience of Consumption*, Oxford: Blackwell (The Sociological Review), pp. 274–301.

Longhurst, B., Bagnall, G. and Savage, M. 2001: Ordinary consumption and personal identity: radio and the middle classes in the north west of England. In J. Gronow and A. Warde (eds), *Ordinary Consumption*, London: Routledge, pp. 125–41.

Lum, C. M. N. 1998: The karaoke dilemma: on the interaction between collectivism and individualism in the karaoke space. In T. Mitsui and S. Hosokawa (eds), *Karaoke Around the World*, London: Routledge, pp. 166–77.

Lury, C. 1993: *Cultural Rights: Technology, Legality and Personality*, London: Routledge.

McClary, S. and Walser, R. 1990: Start making sense: musicology wrestles with rock. In S. Frith and A Goodwin (eds), *On Record: Rock, Pop, and the Written Word*, London: Routledge, pp. 277–92.

McGuigan, J. 1992: *Cultural Populism*, London: Routledge.

McKay, G. 1996: *Senseless Acts of Beauty: Cultures of Resistance since the Sixties*, London: Verso.

MacKenzie, D. and Wajcman, J. 1985: Introduction. In D. MacKenzie and J. Wajcman (eds), *The Social Shaping of Technology: How the Refrigerator Got its Hum*, Milton Keynes: Open University Press.

MacLeod, B. 1993: *Club Date Musicians: Playing the New York Party Circuit*, Urbana and Chicago: University of Illinois Press.

McLeod, K. 2005: MP3s are killing home taping: the rise of Internet distribution and its challenge to the major label music monopoly. *Popular Music and Society*, 28: 521–31.

McRobbie, A. 1978: Working class girls and the culture of femininity. In Women's Studies Group, Centre for Contemporary Cultural Studies, University of Birmingham, *Women Take Issue: Aspects of Women's Subordination*, London: Hutchinson, pp. 96–108.

McRobbie, A. 1980: Settling accounts with subcultures: a feminist critique. *Screen Education*, 34: 37–49.

McRobbie, A. 1984: Dance and social fantasy. In A. McRobbie and M. Nava (eds), *Gender and Generation*, Basingstoke: Macmillan, pp. 130–61.

McRobbie, A. 1991: Jackie and Just Seventeen: girls' comics and magazines in the 1980s. In A. McRobbie, *Feminism and Youth Culture: From 'Jackie' to 'Just Seventeen'*, Basingstoke: Macmillan, pp. 135–88.

McRobbie, A. 1993: Shut up and dance: youth culture and changing modes of femininity. *Cultural Studies*, 7: 406–26.

McRobbie, A. and Garber, J. 1976: Girls and subcultures: an exploration. In S. Hall and T. Jefferson (eds), *Resistance through Rituals: Youth Subcultures in Post-war Britain*, London: Hutchinson, pp. 209–22.

Maffesoli, M. 1996: *The Time of the Tribes: The Decline of Individualism in Mass Society*, London: Sage.

Malbon, B. 1999: *Clubbing: Dancing, Ecstasy and Vitality*, London: Routledge.

Marcus, G. 1991: *Mystery Train: Images of America in Rock 'n' Roll Music* (1st edn, USA 1975) London: Penguin.

Marcus, G. 1992: *Dead Elvis: A Chronicle of a Cultural Obsession*, London: Penguin.

Marcus, G. 1993: *Lipstick Traces: A Secret History of the Twentieth Century*, London: Penguin.

Marshall, G. 1990: *The Two Tone Story*, Dunoon, Argyll: S. T. Publishing.

Marshall, L. 2005: *Bootlegging: Romanticism and Copyright in the Music Industry*, London: Sage.

Martin, P. J. 1995: *Sounds and Society: Themes in the Sociology of Music*, Manchester: Manchester University Press.

Martindale, D. and Reidel, J. 1958: Introduction: Max Weber's sociology of music. In M. Weber, *The Rational and Social Foundations of Music*, Illinois: Southern Illinois University Press.

Middleton, R. 1990: *Studying Popular Music*, Milton Keynes: Open University Press.

Middleton, R. 1993: Popular music analysis and musicology: bridging the gap. *Popular Music*, 12: 177–90.

Middleton, R. 2000: Introduction: locating the popular music text. In R. Middleton (ed.), *Reading Pop: Approaches to Textual Analysis in Popular Music*, Oxford: Oxford University Press, pp. 1–19.

Middleton, R. and Muncie, J. 1981: Pop culture, pop music and post-war youth: countercultures. Unit 20, *Popular Culture*, Milton Keynes: Open University.

Miles, S. 2000: *Youth Lifestyles in a Changing World*, Buckingham: Open University.

Mitsui, T. 1998: The genesis of karaoke: how the combination of technology and music evolved. In T. Mitsui and S. Hosokawa (eds), *Karaoke Around the World*, London: Routledge, pp. 31–44.

Mitsui, T. and Hosokawa, S. 1998a: Introduction. In T. Mitsui and S. Hosokawa (eds), *Karaoke Around the World*, London: Routledge, pp. 1–27.

Mitsui, T. and Hosokawa, S. (eds) 1998b: *Karaoke Around the World*, London: Routledge.

Moore, A. F. 1993: *Rock: The Primary Text*, Buckingham: Open University Press.

Moore, J. 2000: 'The hieroglyphics of love': The Torch Singers and interpretation. In R. Middleton (ed.), *Reading Pop: Approaches to Textual Analysis in Popular Music*, Oxford: Oxford University Press, pp. 262–96.

Moores, S. 1993: *Interpreting Audiences*, London: Sage.

Moorhouse, H. F. 1991: *Driving Ambitions: An Analysis of the American Hot Rod Enthusiasm*, Manchester: Manchester University Press.

Morley, D. 1980: *The 'Nationwide' Audience*, London: British Film Institute.

Morley, D. 1986: *Family Television: Cultural Power and Domestic Leisure*, London: Comedia.

Morley, D. 1992: *Television Audiences and Cultural Studies*, London: Routledge.

Muggleton, D. 2000: *Inside Subculture: The Postmodern Meaning of Style*, Oxford: Berg.

Muggleton, D. and Weinzierel, R. (eds) 2003: *The Post-Subcultures Reader*, Oxford: Berg.

Mundy, J. 1999: *Popular Music on Screen: From Hollywood Musical to Music Video*, Manchester: Manchester University Press.

Murdock, G. and Golding, P. 1977: Capitalism, communications and class relations. In J. Curran, M. Gurevitch and J. Woollacott (eds), *Mass Communication and Society*, London: Edward Arnold, in association with the Open University Press, pp. 12–43.

Neal, M. A. 1999: *What the Music Said: Black Popular Music and Black Public Culture*, London: Routledge.

Neal, M. A. 2004: I used to love H.E.R.: hip-hop in/and the culture industries. In M. Forman and M. A. Neal (eds), *That's the Joint! The Hip-Hop Studies Reader*, London: Routledge, pp. 493–95.

Negus, K. 1992: *Producing Pop: Culture and Conflict in the Popular Music Industry*, London: Edward Arnold.

Negus, K. 1996: *Popular Music in Theory*, Cambridge: Polity.

Negus, K. 1999: *Music Genres and Corporate Cultures*, London: Routledge.

Oliver, P. (ed.) 1990: *Black Music in Britain: Essays on the Afro-Asian Contribution to Popular Music*, Milton Keynes: Open University Press.

Owens, J. 1979: *Dread: The Rastafarians of Jamaica*, London: Heinemann.

Palmer, R. 1981: *Deep Blues*, London: Macmillan.

Pearce, S. 1995: *On Collecting: An Investigation into Collecting in the European Tradition*, London: Routledge.

Pekacz, J. A. 1994: Did rock smash the wall? The role of rock in political transition. *Popular Music*, 13: 41–9.

Penley, C. 1992: Feminism, psychoanalysis and the study of popular culture. In L. Grossberg, C. Nelson and P. Treichler (eds), *Cultural Studies*, London: Routledge.

Peterson, R. A. 1972: A process model of the folk, pop and fine art phases of jazz. In C. Nanry (ed.), *American Music: From Storyville to Woodstock*, New Brunswick, NJ: Transaction, pp. 135–50

Peterson, R. A. 1990: Why 1955? Explaining the advent of rock music. *Popular Music*,
    9: 97–116.

Peterson, R. A. and Anand, N. 2004: The production of culture perspective. *Annual
    Review of Sociology*, 30: 311–34.

Peterson, R. A. and Bennett, A. 2004: Introducing music scenes. In A. Bennett and
    R. A. Peterson (eds), *Music Scenes: Local, Translocal and Virtual*, Nashville:
    Vanderbilt University Press, pp. 1–15.

Peterson, R. A. and Berger, D. G. 1990: Cycles in symbol production: the case of
    popular music. In S. Frith and A. Goodwin (eds), *On Record: Rock, Pop, and the
    Written Word*, London: Routledge, pp. 140–59.

Peterson, R. A. and Kern, R. M. 1996: Changing highbrow taste: from snob to
    omnivore. *American Sociological Review*, 61: 900–7.

Peterson, R. A. and Simkus, A. 1992: How musical taste groups mark occupational
    status groups. In M. Lamont and M. Fournier (eds), *Cultivating Differences:
    Symbolic Boundaries and the Making of Inequality*, Chicago: University of Chicago
    Press.

Pini, M. 2001: *Club Cultures and Female Subjectivity: The Move from Home to House*,
    Basingstoke: Palgrave Macmillan.

Plotkin, F. 2003: *Classical Music Unbuttoned: A Complete Guide to Learning and Loving
    Classical Music*, London: Aurum.

Popular Music 2002: Music and Television, 21.

Prinsky, L. E. and Rosenbaum, J. L. 1987: 'Leer-ics' or lyrics: teenage impressions of
    rock 'n' roll. *Youth and Society*, 18: 384–97.

Redhead, S. 1990: *The End-of-the-Century Party: Youth and Pop Towards 2000*,
    Manchester: Manchester University Press.

Redhead, S. (ed.) 1993: *Rave Off: Politics and Deviance in Contemporary Youth Culture*,
    Aldershot: Avebury.

Reynolds, S. 1998: *Energy Flash: A Journey through Rave Music and Dance Culture*,
    London: Picador.

Reynolds, S. 2005: *Rip it Up and Start Again: Postpunk 1978–1984*, London: Faber and
    Faber.

Reynolds, S. and Press, J. 1995: *The Sex Revolts: Gender, Rebellion and Rock 'n' Roll*,
    London: Serpent's Tail.

Rietveld, H. 1993: Living the dream. In S. Redhead (ed.), *Rave Off: Politics and
    Deviance in Contemporary Youth Culture*, Aldershot: Avebury.

Rietveld, H. 1998: *This is Our House: House Music, Cultural Spaces and Technologies*,
    Aldershot: Ashgate.

Ritzer, G. 1993: *The McDonaldization of Society: An Investigation Into the Changing
    Character of Contemporary Social Life*, Thousand Oaks: Pine Forge Press.

Ritzer, G. (ed.) 2002a: *McDonaldization: The Reader*, Thousand Oaks: Pine Forge
    Press.

Ritzer, G. 2002b: Some thoughts on the future of McDonaldization. In G. Ritzer
    (ed.), *McDonaldization: The Reader*, Thousand Oaks: Pine Forge Press,
    pp. 255–66.

Ritzer, G. 2004: *The McDonaldization of Society: An Investigation Into the Changing
    Character of American Life* (Revised New Century Edition), Thousand Oaks: Pine
    Forge Press.

Robertson, R. 1995: Glocalisation: time–space and homogeneity–heterogeneity. In M. Featherstone, S. Lash and R. Robertson (eds), *Global Modernities*, London: Sage.

Robertson, R. and White, K. E. 2005: Globalization: sociology and cross-disciplinarity. In C. Calhoun, C. Rojek and B. Turner (eds), *The Sage Handbook of Sociology*, London: Sage, pp. 345–66.

Robins, P. and Cohen, P. 1978: *Knuckle Sandwich: Growing up in the Working Class City*, Harmondsworth: Penguin.

Robinson, J. Bradford 1994: The jazz essays of Theodor Adorno: some thoughts on jazz reception in Weimar Germany. *Popular Music*, 13: 1–25.

Rodman, G. B. 1996: *Elvis after Elvis: The Posthumous Career of a Living Legend*, London: Routledge.

Rogan, J. 1993: *Morrissey & Marr: The Severed Alliance*, London: Omnibus.

Rojek, C. 2001: *Celebrity*, London: Reaktion.

Rose, T. 1994: *Black Noise: Rap Music and Black Culture in Contemporary America*, Hanover and London: Wesleyan University Press, University Press of New England.

Ross, P. G. 2005: Cycles in symbol production research: foundations, applications, and future directions. *Popular Music and Society*, 28: 473–87.

Salih, S. 2002: *Judith Butler*, London: Routledge.

Sandvoss, C, 2003: *A Game of Two Halves: Football, Television and Globalization*, London: Comedia.

Sandvoss, C. 2005: *Fans: The Mirror of Consumption*, Cambridge: Polity.

Savage, J. 1991: *England's Dreaming: Sex Pistols and Punk Rock*, London: Faber and Faber.

Savage, M., Bagnall, G. and Longhurst, B. 2005: *Globalization and Belonging*, London: Sage.

Schilt, K. 2004: 'Riot Grrrl is . . .': contestation over meaning in a music scene. In A. Bennett and R. A. Peterson (eds), *Music Scenes: Local, Translocal, and Virtual*, Nashville: Vanderbilt University Press, pp. 115–30.

Schloss, J. G. 2004: *Making Beats: The Art of Sample-Based Hip-Hop*. Middletown, CT: Wesleyan University Press.

Schulze, L., Barton White, A. and Brown, J. D. 1993: 'A sacred monster in her prime': audience construction of Madonna as low-other. In C. Schwichtenberg (ed.), *The Madonna Connection: Representational Politics, Subcultural Identities, and Cultural Theory*, Oxford: Westview Press, pp. 15–37.

Schwichtenberg, C. (ed.) 1993: *The Madonna Connection: Representational Politics, Subcultural Identities and Cultural Theory*, Oxford: Westview Press.

Shank, B. 1994: *Dissonant Identities: The Rock 'n' Roll Scene in Austin, Texas*, Hanover, NH: Wesleyan University Press, University Press of New England.

Sharma, S., Hutnyk, J. and Sharma, A. (eds) 1996: *Dis-orienting Rhythms: The Politics of the New Asian Dance Music*, London: Zed Books.

Shepherd, J. 1991: *Music as Social Text*, Cambridge: Polity.

Shepherd, J., Horn, D., Laing, D. Oliver, P. and Wicke, P. (eds) 2003: *Continuum Encyclopaedia of Popular Music of the World: Volume 1, Media, Industry and Society*, London: Continuum.

Shuker, R. 2001: *Understanding Popular Music*, London: Routledge.

Shuker, R. 2002: *Popular Music: The Key Concepts*, London: Routledge.

Skeggs, B. 2001: The toilet paper: femininity, class and mis-recognition. *Women's Studies International Forum*, 24: 295–307.

Smith, L. S. 1978: Sexist assumptions and female delinquency: an empirical investigation. In C. Smart and B. Smart (eds), *Women, Sexuality and Social Control*, London: Routledge and Kegan Paul, pp. 74–88.

Spring, K. 2004: Behind the rave: structure and agency in a rave scene. In A. Bennett and R. A. Peterson (eds) 2004: *Music Scenes: Local, Translocal, and Virtual*, Nashville: Vanderbilt University Press, pp. 48–63.

Staiger, J. 2005: *Media Reception Studies*, New York: New York University Press.

Stephens, G. 1992: Interracial dialogue in rap music: call-and-response in a multicultural style. *New Formations*, 16: 62–79.

Steward, S. and Garratt, S. 1984: *Signed, Sealed and Delivered: True Life Stories of Women in Pop*, London: Pluto.

Stratton, J. 1989: Beyond art: postmodernism and the case of popular music. *Theory, Culture and Society*, 6: 31–57.

Straw, W. 1991: Systems of articulation, logics of change: communities and scenes in popular music. *Cultural Studies*, 15: 368–88.

Straw, W. 1997: Sizing up record collections: gender and connoisseurship in rock music culture. In S. Whiteley (ed.), *Sexing the Groove: Popular Music and Gender*, London: Routledge, pp. 3–16.

Street, J. 1986: *Rebel Rock: The Politics of Popular Music*, Oxford: Basil Blackwell.

Street, J. 1993: Local differences? Popular music and the local state. *Popular Music*, 12: 43–55.

Street, J. 2001: Rock, pop and politics. In S. Frith, W. Straw and J. Street (eds.), *The Cambridge Companion to Pop and Rock*, Cambridge: Cambridge University Press, pp. 243–55.

Strinati, D. 1992: Postmodernism and popular culture. *Sociology Review*, 1: 2–7.

Strong, M. C. 2004: *The Great Rock Discography* (7th edn), Edinburgh: Canongate.

Struthers, S. 1987: Technology in the art of recording. In A. L. White (ed.), *Lost in Music: Culture, Style and the Musical Event*, London: Routledge and Kegan Paul (Sociological Review Monograph 34), pp. 241–58.

Swendenberg, T. 1992: Homies in the hood: rap's commodification of insubordination. *New Formations*, 18: 53–66.

Tagg, P. 1989: Open letter: 'black music', 'Afro-American music' and 'European music'. *Popular Music*, 8: 285–98.

Tagg, P. 2000: Analysing popular music: theory, method, and practice. In R. Middleton (ed.), *Reading Pop: Approaches to Textual Analysis in Popular Music*, Oxford: Oxford University Press, pp. 71–103.

Taylor, T. 1997: *Global Pop: World Music, World Markets*, London: Routledge.

Taylor, T. 2000: His name was in lights: Chuck Berry's 'Johnny B. Goode'. In R. Middleton (ed.), *Reading Pop: Approaches to Textual Analysis in Popular Music*, Oxford: Oxford University Press, pp. 165–82.

Théberge, P. 1989: The 'sound' of music: technological rationalization and the production of popular music. *New Formations*, 8: 99–111.

Théberge, P. 1997: *Any Sound You Can Imagine: Making Music/Consuming Technology*, Hanover and London: Wesleyan University Press, University Press of New England.

Thomas, H. 2003: *The Body, Dance and Cultural Theory*, Basingstoke: Palgrave Macmillan.

Thompson, J. 1995: *The Media and Modernity: A Social Theory of the Media*, Cambridge: Polity.

Thornton, S. 1995: *Club Cultures: Music, Media and Subcultural Capital*, Cambridge: Polity.

Tingen, P. 2001: *Miles Beyond: The Electric Explorations of Miles Davis, 1967–1991*, New York: Billboard.

Tomlinson, J. 1999: *Globalization and Culture*, Cambridge: Polity.

Toop, D. 1984: *The Rap Attack: African Jive to New York Hip Hop*, London: Pluto.

Toynbee, J. 2000: *Making Popular Music: Musicians, Creativity and Institutions*, London: Arnold.

Turner, G. 1990: *British Cultural Studies*, London: Unwin Hyman.

Urquia, N. 2004: 'Doin' it right': contested authenticity in London's salsa scene. In A. Bennett and R. A. Peterson (eds), *Music Scenes: Local, Translocal, and Virtual*, Nashville: Vanderbilt University Press, pp. 96–112.

Vroomen, L. 2004: Kate Bush: teen pop and older female fans. In A. Bennett and R. A. Peterson (eds.), *Music Scenes: Local, Translocal, and Virtual*, Nashville: Vanderbilt University Press, pp. 238–253.

Wallis, R. and Malm, K. 1984: *Big Music From Small Peoples*, London: Constable, 1984.

Wallis, R. and Malm, K. 1990: Patterns of change. In S. Frith and A. Goodwin (eds), *On Record: Rock, Pop, and the Written Word*, London: Routledge, pp. 160–80.

Walser, R. 1993: *Running with the Devil: Power, Gender, and Madness in Heavy Metal Music*, Hanover: Wesleyan University Press/University Press of New England.

Warde, A. 1992: Notes on the relationship between production and consumption. In R. Burrows and C. Marsh (eds), *Consumption and Class: Divisions and Change*, Basingstoke: Macmillan, pp. 15–31.

Weber, M. 1958: *The Rational and Social Foundations of Music*, Illinois: Southern Illinois University Press.

Weinstein, D. 1991: *Heavy Metal: A Cultural Sociology*, New York: Lexington Books.

Weinzierl, R. and Muggleton, D. 2003: What is 'Post-subcultural studies' anyway? In D. Muggleton and R. Weinzierl (eds), *The Post-Subcultures Reader*, Oxford: Berg, pp. 3–23.

Wernick, A. 1991: *Promotional Culture: Advertising, Ideology and Symbolic Expression*, London: Sage.

White, A. L. 1987: A professional jazz group. In A. L. White (ed.), *Lost in Music: Culture, Style and the Musical Event*, London: Routledge and Kegan Paul (Sociological Review Monograph 34), pp. 191–219.

White, T. 1984: *Catch a Fire: The Life of Bob Marley*, London: Corgi.

Whiteley, S. 1992: *The Space Between the Notes: Rock and the Counter-Culture*, London: Routledge.

Whiteley, S. (ed.) 1997, *Sexing the Groove: Popular Music and Gender*, London: Routledge.

Whiteley, S. 2000a: Progressive rock and psychedelic coding in the work of Jimi Hendrix. In R. Middleton (ed.), *Reading Pop: Approaches to Textual Analysis in Popular Music*, Oxford: Oxford University Press, pp. 235–61.

Whiteley, S. 2000b: *Women and Popular Music: Sexuality, Identity and Subjectivity*, London: Routledge.

Whiteley, S. 2005: *Too Much Too Young: Popular Music, Age and Gender*, London: Routledge.

Wicke, P. 1992a: The role of rock music in the political disintegration of East Germany. In J. Lull (ed.), *Popular Music and Communication* (2nd edn), Newbury Park: Sage, pp. 196–206.

Wicke, P. 1992b: The times they are a-changin': rock music and political change in East Germany. In R. Garofalo (ed.), *Rockin' the Boat: Mass Music and Mass Movements*, Boston: South End Press, pp. 81–92.

Wicke, P. and Shepherd, J. 1993: 'The cabaret is dead': rock culture as state enterprise – the political organization of rock in East Germany. In T. Bennett, S. Frith, L. Grossberg, J. Shepherd and G. Turner (eds), *Rock and Popular Music: Politics, Policies, Institutions*, London: Routledge, pp. 25–36.

Widdicombe, S. and Wooffitt, R. 1995: *The Language of Youth Subcultures*. Hemel Hempstead: Harvester Wheatsheaf.

Widgery, D. 1986: *Beating Time*, London: Chatto & Windus.

Williams, C. 2001: Does it really matter? Young people and popular music. *Popular Music*, 20: 223–42.

Williams, R. 1973: Base and superstructure in Marxist cultural theory. *New Left Review*, 82: 3–16. Reprinted with alterations in Williams, *Problems in Materialism and Culture*, London: Verso, 1980, pp. 31–49.

Williams, R. 1983: *Towards 2000*, London: Chatto & Windus.

Williams, R. 1989: *The Politics of Modernism: Against the New Conformists*, London: Verso.

Willis, P. 1977: *Learning to Labour: How Working Class Kids Get Working Class Jobs*, Farnborough: Saxon House.

Willis, P. 1978: *Profane Culture*, London: Routledge & Kegan Paul.

Willis, P. with Jones, S., Canaan, J. and Hurd, G. 1990: *Common Culture: Symbolic Work at Play in the Everyday Cultures of the Young*, Milton Keynes: Open University Press.

Winkler, P. 2000: Randy Newman's Americana. In R. Middleton (ed.), *Reading Pop: Approaches to Textual Analysis in Popular Music*, Oxford: Oxford University Press, pp. 27–57.

Wise, S. 1990: Sexing Elvis. In S. Frith and A. Goodwin (eds), *On Record: Rock, Pop, and the Written Word*, London: Routledge, pp. 390–8.

<www.mcps-prs-alliance.co.uk>

<www.ppluk.com>

Index

Note: Page references in *italics* indicate tables and diagrams, while those in **bold** type indicate boxes in the text.